Foul or Fair?

Foul or Fair?

Ethical and Social Issues in Sports

Larry Atkins

McFarland & Company, Inc., Publishers
Jefferson, North Carolina

This book has undergone peer review.

ISBN (print) 978-1-4766-8621-9
ISBN (ebook) 978-1-4766-5099-9

LIBRARY OF CONGRESS AND BRITISH LIBRARY
CATALOGUING DATA ARE AVAILABLE

Library of Congress Control Number 2024002133

© 2024 Larry Atkins. All rights reserved

No part of this book may be reproduced or transmitted in any form or by any means, electronic or mechanical, including photocopying or recording, or by any information storage and retrieval system, without permission in writing from the publisher.

Front cover image: © Dmytro Aksonov/iStock

Printed in the United States of America

*McFarland & Company, Inc., Publishers
Box 611, Jefferson, North Carolina 28640
www.mcfarlandpub.com*

This book is dedicated to my beloved mother, Phyllis,
and my family, friends, and professional colleagues.
Thank you to my agent, Maryann Karinch,
and to McFarland.

Table of Contents

Preface	1
Introduction	3
CHAPTER 1. What Is a Sport?	7
CHAPTER 2. Values of Sports and Sportsmanship	21
CHAPTER 3. Gambling	42
CHAPTER 4. Media Coverage	53
CHAPTER 5. Athletes as Social Advocates	70
CHAPTER 6. Fan Obsession	85
CHAPTER 7. Medical and Psychological Issues	101
CHAPTER 8. Legal Issues	127
CHAPTER 9. Youth Sports	147
CHAPTER 10. College Sports	163
CHAPTER 11. Professional Sports	181
CHAPTER 12. Olympic Sports	203
Conclusion	216
Chapter Notes	221
Bibliography	267
Index	269

Preface

SPORTS HAVE ALWAYS BEEN AN ESSENTIAL PART OF MY LIFE. As a participant, I played Little League baseball, pickup games, junior high school wrestling and tennis, high school varsity soccer, and college varsity tennis. I've participated in college intramurals, various softball leagues, and many over-age-40 and -50 basketball leagues at the local gym, among others. As a fan, I've dedicated many days and hours to watching and rooting for Philadelphia pro sports teams, as well as Temple University football and basketball and La Salle University basketball. I went to the two Flyers championship parades in the 1970s, the Eagles Super Bowl parade in 2018, and the two Phillies World Series victory parades in 1980 and 2008. I also attended the Atlanta Olympics in 1996 and several World Cup games in 1994. I was at the Forum in Los Angeles in 1983 when the 76ers beat the Lakers in Game 4 to win the NBA Championship.

Growing up, I idolized star athletes like Mike Schmidt, Julius Erving, and Bernie Parent, but I also idolized sports broadcasters and thought at an early age that I would want to go into sports journalism. My favorite announcer was Howard Cosell, due to his unusual staccato voice. In elementary school, I would go around interviewing my classmates, using a stick as a pretend microphone. I also imitated Cosell at numerous talent shows.

I have taught college courses at Temple University, Arcadia University, and Montgomery County Community College as an adjunct professor since 2004. Most of my courses were journalism related. However, in 2007, Arcadia started a new series of courses called university seminars, where professors could choose to teach a topic that they have always had a passion for. The first thing that popped into my mind was a sports-related course. For 15 years, I have taught a university seminar called Social and Ethical Issues in Sports. The course became very popular, and I was asked to also teach a separate course at Arcadia on sports law and ethics. I love teaching these courses, and over the years I realized that I wanted to write a book to share my passion for and knowledge of the topic. Every semester, I learn something new about the topic, both through my own research and from my students' insights.

While I've always loved watching the games, my love of sports goes beyond the games themselves. I've always had an interest in the social and ethical issues that pertain to sports at all levels, whether it be youth sports, college sports, pro sports, or the Olympics. Growing up, I liked reading about these issues in *Sports Illustrated*. As an adult, I liked the various ESPN series and programs that focused on social issues in sports, as well as HBO's *Real Sports*.

The process of researching my book involved both internet research and contacting sources to interview and quote. Persistence was key when it came to reaching out to dozens of sources that I didn't know personally. In some cases, I needed to badger them with weekly requests to get back to me for an interview. Although not everyone responded, I was able to get terrific insight and quotes from many outstanding experts in their fields, and I'm very grateful for their participation.

Since I teach three to five college courses per semester, it was a challenge to find the time to work on my book during the school year. It took about three years to research and write this book, but I've been thinking about these issues on a regular basis my entire life. I hope that my book will lead readers to think about them as well.

Photos by SportsAngle.com, Lorie Shaull, samuelnabi, missycaulk, and Nick J. Webb are from Flickr and licensed under Creative Commons 2.0: CC BY-SA 2.0, https://creativecommons.org/licenses/by-sa/2.0/?ref=openverse.

The photo by Lafayette College is from Flickr and licensed under Creative Commons Public Domain Mark 1.0: https://creativecommons.org/publicdomain/mark/1.0/?ref=openverse.

The photo by Thomson200 is from Wikimedia Commons and licensed under Creative Commons CC0 1.0. https://creativecommons.org/publicdomain/zero/1.0/deed.en?ref=openverse.

Introduction

THERE'S MUCH MORE TO SPORTS than what occurs on the court or on the field during games. Just check your social media feed, listen to sports talk radio, read the sports page, or watch ESPN on any particular day—there are stories of social and ethical issues in sports regarding concussions; playing hurt; gambling; the Olympics and politics; athletes as social activists; steroid abuse; recruiting violations; academic eligibility; paying college athletes and allowing them to profit from their name, image, or likeness; graduation rates of student-athletes; youth sports; diversity and gender issues; violence; hazing; mental health of athletes; rights of disabled athletes; moral and sportsmanship issues; and media coverage of sports.

How and why do these issues affect us as athletes, sports fans, and society as a whole?

This book will give a comprehensive analysis of these social issues in sports in a journalistic, nonacademic, and entertaining manner. The book will contain information; extensive research; anecdotes; and quotes from various media professionals, columnists, sports talk radio hosts, media personalities, athletes, coaches, athletic directors, and university professors. It will also include my opinions and personal observations on various social issues in sports that affect large portions of society as a whole. The book will appeal to both hard-core and casual sports fans. It will show the pros and cons of how sports affect our daily lives and society as a whole. While sports can inspire and excite all of us and lead to social change such as the civil rights movement, Title IX, and recognition of the rights of disabled people, controversies surrounding sports such as violence, steroid abuse, concussions, tanking, running up the score, and rule breaking are thought-provoking and can't be ignored. Sports can be a uniting factor in society, but they can also be divisive. The social issues in sports discussed in this book will frequently be in the news on a regular basis.

Whether someone is rich or poor, urban or rural, Democrat or Republican, most people love sports. For many people, following sports consumes a huge part of our lives. Most sports fans don't care just about the games themselves; they care passionately about off-the-field social issues that affect their favorite sport, team, or athlete.

Most sports fans' time investment isn't limited to just watching games in person or on television. There is no offseason for sports fans who want information about their favorite teams and sports throughout the year. Sports fans constantly want to be informed about on-the-field and off-the-field issues that have an impact on their favorite sports. The social issues discussed in this book will help to educate readers about the successes, problems, and concerns of those sports. For instance, fans of a powerful college program are affected when their team is embroiled in a controversy regarding recruiting violations, academic scandals, point shaving, criminal conduct by their players, or hazing. Reading about social issues in sports can enlighten both casual and hard-core fans, heighten their knowledge and understanding about the sports that they love, give readers the big picture of off-the-field issues, and influence the way that they view sports in general.

The United States is addicted to sports and the social issues surrounding them. Sports talk radio is popular, and there are numerous sports networks on television, including several ESPN platforms, CBS Sports Network, NBC Sports Network, and the Big Ten Network. There have been many successful longtime television programs and series related to social issues in sports, including ESPN's *Outside the Lines*, HBO's *Real Sports*, and ESPN's *30 for 30* series, all of which investigate off-the-field sports social issues and controversies. Popular sports-related publications such as *Sports Illustrated* and *Sports Business Journal* cover social issues in sports on a regular basis. Millions of people nationwide play and watch sports and can relate to the topics discussed in this book. People are passionate about sports and love to discuss and argue various sports social issues with friends and family.

From a personal standpoint, sports has meant a lot to me during my entire life. I had a distant relationship with my father, and my parents divorced when I was 13. However, sports was the one way in which my father and I connected. We would play doubles tennis against other people, and he took me to tennis clinics to learn the game when I was young. He was one of my Little League coaches. He also took me to many sporting events, including 76ers playoff games; Phillies, Eagles, and Flyers games; college basketball games at the Palestra; and Temple football games at Franklin Field. My mom was not a big sports fan, but she always supported my playing sports and being on various teams as I was growing up.

Playing sports helped me a great deal. When I moved to a new neighborhood and a new school in ninth grade, being on the wrestling and tennis teams at Elkins Park Junior High School helped my self-esteem and I established new friendships. It also established the concepts of work ethic and being a good teammate. My brief soccer career was a great lesson in perseverance. When I started playing soccer for the first time in 10th grade, I had no idea what I was doing in this new sport and I was at a disadvantage in that I had very poor eyesight and couldn't wear glasses or contacts while playing. Eventually, I worked hard to improve, and I made the varsity soccer team as a senior at Cheltenham High School in suburban Philadelphia. Tennis, however, was my best sport, and I ended up playing Division I varsity tennis at La Salle University for two seasons. Again, being on that team was a great confidence booster and led to many good experiences. However, a bad experience on that team taught me a valuable life lesson about maturity and being a team player. I frequently complained to my coach that I thought I should be playing in more matches because there were times when I had beaten some of the players on our team in practice who were getting to play. My constant complaining was the main reason why the coach cut me from the team before my junior year season. It was a crushing blow to me, and for years I resented the coach. However, years later, I came to realize that I was completely wrong for constantly complaining and speaking out.

Perhaps no event in modern history showed how important sports are to people as the worldwide coronavirus pandemic of 2020 and 2021. Youth, high school, college, and pro seasons ended abruptly in March 2020. For many people, it wasn't until the NBA shut down its season that people realized how serious the coronavirus was. Winter sport athletes didn't get a chance to compete in state high school championship competitions, and college athletes didn't get to compete for national championships. Most spring sport athletes didn't even get a chance to take the field. This was especially crushing for seniors who were deprived of their last chance to compete at the high school level. For pro athletes, the virus disrupted their lives and careers. Fans of college and pro sports were deprived of an important part of their lives. For several months, there were no live sporting events taking place at any level, anywhere in the world. Slowly, during the summer of 2020, sports returned. Even though no fans were in the stands at first, it was a welcome sight to see sports come back. It was odd hearing taped fan noise being played during the games. By spring 2021, the rate of vaccinations improved enough to the point where stadiums could be filled with people again. It was a sign that life was becoming normal again.

Chapter 1

What Is a Sport?

Is cheerleading a sport? What about golf? Debating whether a certain activity is a sport or a skill is not just an academic debate. This determination could make the difference as to whether a certain activity can be sanctioned by the International Olympic Committee or the NCAA as a sport. For instance, in a lawsuit involving Quinnipiac University, a judge determined that competitive cheerleading could not be considered a sport for Title IX purposes because it was not sufficiently organized. There are legitimate debates as to whether other activities are sports or games, such as auto racing, Quidditch (Quadball), pole dancing, esports, poker, golf, darts, and bowling. Some activities have evolved and developed as recognized sports, such as skateboarding and snowboarding. While most experts agree that sports require physical activity, such as running and jumping, that alone does not make an activity a sport. This chapter explores what constitutes a sport and whether certain activities should qualify.

There is no magic formula as to what constitutes a sport, a game, or a skill. Many experts have attempted to provide some guidelines and parameters. Most experts believe that there needs to be a physical element involved to constitute a sport.

In his chapter in the book *Ethics in Sport,* Bernard Suits wrote, "I would like to submit for consideration four requirements which, if they are met by any given game, are sufficient to denominate that game a sport. They are: (1) that the game be a game of skill, (2) that the skill be physical, (3) that the game have a wide following, and (4) that the following achieve a certain level of stability."[1]

Author Ronald B. Woods illustrates the definition of sports through a pyramid that displays four items: Play, Games, Sport, and Work. At the bottom of the pyramid is Play, which Woods describes as "a free activity that involves exploration, self-expression, dreaming, and pretending," in which the outcome is unimportant and follows no firm rules. On the next level of the pyramid are Games, which have greater structure than play, are competitive, and have rules. Woods lists Monopoly and card games as examples. At the next level is Sport, which involves some sort of physical component; is competitive and has an important outcome; is institutionalized; has a certain set of rules; is governed by an outside group or institution, such as the NCAA, that enforces those rules and oversees conduct and results; and has specialized facilities and equipment, such as fields with set boundaries and the precise quality of a baseball bat. At the highest level of the pyramid is Work, in which professional athletes are paid to compete at the highest level of competition. As Woods notes, these classifications are not set in stone, as certain games have become more organized and structured and are now considered sports, such as skateboarding and snowboarding.[2]

As crazy as it sounds, I suppose that in the future, theoretically, the annoying kids' pool tag game of Marco Polo could be structured, formalized, and timed so that there could be a professional Marco Polo league.

In his journal article in *Sport, Ethics, and Philosophy*, Felix Lebed offered a dissenting view regarding the requirement regarding physicality in assessing whether an activity is a sport, arguing that physicality is not required in such an assessment. He claimed, "I attempt in this article to transfer the centre of gravity in reasoning from physical activity (a concept that I try to consider more accurately) to three other properties that are necessary and which taken together are sufficient for understanding sport as a category. These are: unproductiveness (as opposed to playing performances in arts), attachment to competitive game as a special form of human play, and the public and widely accepted official status and functioning of such game."

Lebed added, "I define sport as: an unproductive and officially regulated game that is played by using, as well as possible, one's special skills and mind-body abilities directed toward winning in purposive contests as well as to be the best in measured athletic or refereed aesthetic performances."[3]

There is an ongoing debate as to which activities should be classified as games or as sports. It can be an important distinction, because classification as a sport can have many benefits, such as inclusion in the Olympics or validation by the NCAA, which can have ramifications as to scholarships and Title IX compliance. One of the most highly debated sports is competitive cheerleading. As of September 2022, the NCAA does not recognize competitive cheer as a sanctioned sport. Instead, at the college level, there is an annual National Cheerleaders Association (NCA) Championship competition.[4]

For many decades, cheerleading was solely intended to support other sports on the sideline. However, cheerleading is no longer just people standing on the sideline waving pompoms and cheering for the home team and individual players. In recent years, competitive cheerleading has become extremely popular. The question of whether cheerleading is a competitive sport is not just a philosophical exercise. There are serious ramifications as to its classification.

Competitive cheerleading involves athleticism, including elements of dance, strength, choreography, stunts, tumbling, tossing, extensive practice, and forming pyramids. It's a dangerous activity that results in frequent injuries.

In 2011, USA Cheer created the competitive cheerleading sport of STUNT. In 2016, the International Olympic Committee (IOC) gave provisional recognition to the International Cheer Union (ICU) as the sport's governing body. As of 2016, the

ICU had 110 federations around the world and 70 countries were represented in the World Cheerleading Championships.[5] As of 2021, over 250 colleges had cheerleading programs, and in July 2021, the IOC granted full recognition to the ICU and cheerleading, which meant that the sport of cheerleading could apply for inclusion as an Olympic sport.[6]

Every year, ESPN televises the National High School Cheerleading Championship. Over 1,000 teams competed in the 2017 NCA's All Star National Championship, according to *The Atlantic*.[7]

In 2003, the University of Maryland became the first Division 1 school to recognize competitive cheerleading as a varsity sport and count it as part of its Title IX requirements.[8] The 2018 Intermediate Division 1 level NCA competitive cheer championship had a field of 13 schools, including DePaul; American; Holy Cross; Maine; and Kennesaw State, the national champion.[9] Texas A&M topped 13 cheerleading teams at the 2018 National Cheerleaders Association championships.[10]

The Universal Cheerleaders Association (UCA) hosts the National High School Cheerleading Championship (NHSCC) and the UCA College Cheerleading National Championship every year in Orlando, Florida, both of which are televised on ESPN.[11]

In 2014, the American Medical Association urged that cheerleading should be considered as a sport due to its rigors and risks, and therefore participants should receive more training and safety measures.[12] Mollie Vehling, UCLA's spirit squad adviser, told Wayne Drehs of ESPN that people shouldn't question whether competitive cheerleaders are athletes. "Try it for one day. Honestly. There's no way. That shocks me. You can't just go out there and act stupid. It's a dangerous activity. And there's absolutely no way that if you did it for one day you wouldn't come back saying it's a sport."[13]

Two recent studies in *The Sport Journal* and *Pediatrics* argued that cheerleading should be considered a sport due to the high rates of concussions, and that classifying cheerleading as a sport would help cheerleading receive better concussion management and education protocols.[14]

Naturally, considering cheerleading as a sport has its skeptics. ESPN's Alyssa Roenigk, a former college cheerleader, wrote that although cheerleaders are athletic, cheerleading is not a sport because the main focus of cheerleading in schools is to promote school spirit and support other teams as they compete. She wrote, "Because of the highly athletic nature of modern cheerleading, annual competitions were created to showcase these athletes on their own and away from the sidelines, and the sport-or-not debate began." She noted that the high school and collegiate national cheer championships occurred only once a year, which wasn't frequent enough to satisfy sport requirements of the NCAA, the National Federation of State High School Associations (NFHS), or Title IX. "If cheerleading squads began practicing and competing enough to satisfy those requirements, they would be forced to drastically scale back the number of games at which they cheer. Or stop cheering at games entirely. The minute that happens, rest in peace, cheerleading."[15]

A federal judge in Connecticut ruled in 2010 that Quinnipiac University could not use competitive cheerleading as an official sport to meet Title IX requirements. US District Court judge Stefan Underhill concluded that the school improperly pulled funding from its women's volleyball team to support and fund a competitive cheerleading team. He determined that cheerleading did not meet the criteria to be defined as a sport under Title IX because it was underdeveloped and disorganized. There was no structure for competition, inconsistent competitive divisions, and minimum financial support. Therefore, the 30 roster spots for Quinnipiac's competitive cheer team could not be counted for Title IX purposes. However, the judge did indicate that competitive cheer could possibly qualify as a sport under Title IX in the future if it became more organized.

In 2012, the Second Circuit federal appeals court affirmed that decision, stating, "Like the district court, we acknowledge record evidence showing that competitive cheerleading can be physically challenging, requiring competitors to possess 'strength, agility, and grace.' Similarly, we do not foreclose the possibility that the activity, with better organization and defined rules, might someday warrant recognition as a varsity sport. But, like the district court, we conclude that the record evidence shows that that time has not yet arrived."[16]

In order to be a sport, it must be a competitive endeavor. Therefore, even though professional wrestlers are terrific athletes, suffer injuries, and engage in spectacular athletic and strength moves, it is not a sport because the results are predetermined and scripted (sorry to break the news to some of you about that). For decades, pro wrestling dodged the question of whether it was real or staged, but it eventually came clean. Despite that admission, it remains very popular as entertainment.

Many sports are clearly sports because of the athleticism and physical skill involved, such as baseball, football, basketball, soccer, track and field, hockey, ice skating, gymnastics, and volleyball.

For some sports, there can be a debate as to whether it should be considered a sport, a skill, or a game, especially those that do not involve running and jumping or other physical exertion.

Just because ESPN televises cornhole leagues, poker, and competitive eating doesn't necessarily mean that they are sports. Joey Chestnut's eating of 76 hot dogs in the 2021 Nathan's Famous International Hot Dog Eating Contest was amazing, but it doesn't mean that he is an athlete.

However, competitive eaters have staked a claim that their endeavors are a sport. The organization Major League Eating, which includes the sport's governing body, the International Federation of Competitive Eating, oversees all professional eating contests. Major League Eating has an Eaters Hall of Fame.

In 2003, Richard Shea, president of the International Federation of Competitive Eaters, told the *New York Times*, "Our sport faces a parochial attitude and a lot of misconceptions that are diminished when people attend our events. Eating is as inherent to man and as athletically demanding as running and jumping."[17]

In acknowledging the argument of those who believe that competitive eating is a sport, Gabriel Muller of *the Atlantic* wrote in 2014, "With this kind of focus from participants, it might seem reasonable to place competitive eating among the ranks of other legitimate sports; a strong audience base, highly organized league structure, and meticulous training regimen add an element of validity, and Major League Eating considers competitive eating a demanding athletic undertaking."[18]

For 26 years, the annual Wing Bowl in Philadelphia, organized by sports talk radio station WIP, drew over 20,000 spectators who lined up at 5 a.m. to get into the Wells Fargo Center to see dozens of competitors eat over 100 wings each in one timed sitting.[19]

In a book chapter, university professor K. Jeanine Congalton asserted that the structure and organization of competitive eating contests lends credence to the perception that competitive eating is a sport. She wrote, "The IFOCE serves as the governing body of several major competitive eating contests and as the overseer of a number of competitive eaters. The IFOCE's taking of the form and structure of other professional sports associations enables its resemblance to other legitimate sports. The mimicking of and identification with other professional sports structures creates the perception of competitive eating as legitimate sport." Congalton also cites rules, the keeping of official records, ranking systems, dramatic storylines, rivalries, and the adoption of language of traditional, established sports as reasons why competitive eating continues its performance as a sport.[20]

However, competitive eating has its detractors who do not relish it as a sport. Robert Kushner, a professor of medicine at Northwestern University, told Jon Yates of the *Chicago Tribune* in 2004, "I don't think we need to reward competitive eating when obesity is such a serious health problem in our country. It leads to health problems; it shouldn't be leading to medals."[21]

In light of this, the University of Iowa canceled its annual corn-eating contest due to health concerns. The following year, it brought back the competition, but modified it to emphasize the speed of eating one ear of corn instead of the quantity eaten. Mike Downey of the *Chicago Tribune* opined that competitive eating was not a sport, and he expressed his distaste for competitive eating by writing, "We need to stop treating this carnival of sideshow weirdos as if it is cute.... If I wanted to watch uncivilized creatures eat, I would go to a zoo."[22]

I make it a point to watch the annual July Fourth Nathan's Hot Dog Eating Contest on ESPN for the entertainment and colorful broadcasting (the introductions of the competitors are great), but I don't consider it to be a sport. It's remarkable that the competitors can go on a roll and eat dozens of hot dogs at a time, but that doesn't make them athletes. When announcers and social media commentators compare Joey Chestnut to Michael Jordan and Tom Brady as far as being a dominant athlete, that's hard to digest. No matter how many Mustard Belts Chestnut wins, he'll never catch up to Jordan and Brady.

Another purported rising sport that does not involve extensive physical activity is esports. An interesting recent trend is the rise in popularity of esports, short for electronic sports, in which teams of video gamers compete against each other in games such as *League of Legends*. A few years ago, it surprised me when one of my university students indicated that while his friends had favorite pro athletes in various sports, his favorite athlete was "Happy" from esports Team LDLC. The legion of esports fans and viewers continues to grow exponentially. A 2021 Business Insider article estimated that there would be 26.6 million monthly esports viewers in 2021, an increase of 11.4 percent from 2020. The Business Insider article cited projections from market researcher Newzoo that esports would earn $1.8 billion in revenue by 2022.[23] Many millennials have just as strong identification with esports athletes as they do traditional athletes. Many major television networks, including ESPN, ABC, Disney, and Turner, feature esports competitions, including the Overwatch League. Many esports-specific venues have been built in the United States and around the world. Many states and foreign countries are now allowing people to place legal bets on esports competitions, such as *Counter-Strike, Call of Duty*, and *FIFA*.[24]

However, does the popularity of esports make it a sport?

In 2014, Robert Morris University Illinois became the first university to recognize esports as a varsity sport and offered scholarships to esports athletes. According to *USA Today* in 2018, 63 universities have varsity esports teams.[25] The *Wall Street Journal* reported that over 475 colleges and universities had esports at the club level.[26] As of 2021, the National Association of Collegiate Esports' (NACE) website indicated that there were over 170 member schools with over 5,000 student-athletes, and that over $16 million in scholarships and aid had been awarded to esports college athletes.[27]

Several countries, such as South Korea, China, Russia, Italy, South Africa, and Germany, agreed to recognize esports as an official sport.[28] There is a movement to include esports as an Olympic sport, and the 2022 Asian Games added esports as a competition. There is also a possibility that esports could be a demonstration sport at the 2024 Olympic Games.[29] Some people have expressed concern about the violence in video games as an excuse to exclude esports in the Olympics. Others believe that the absence of a physical element prevents esports from being considered a real sport.

US Olympic gold medal skier Ted Ligety told Reuters that although he acknowledged that esports were popular and here to stay, "Physical sports belong in the Olympics. I don't think esports belong in the Olympics.... The mental side of esports can be tough I'm guessing for those guys, but the Olympics is where you have to do some sort of a physical exertion."[30]

However, some esports stars have trainers, psychologists, and nutritionists and train many hours per day. Arguably, endurance, physical dexterity with hands and fingers, concentration, and mental focus help their argument.

In arguing that esports constituted a sport, Vlad Savov wrote (in a debate with Sam Byford) in *The Verge* that esports are popular due to the conflict involved, and that athleticism is a secondary aspect of esports. Savov said, "That's why gymnastics and weightlifting, some of the most physically intensive competitions you can engage in, are nowhere near as popular as games like baseball where the batter and pitcher can stare each other down. If sports are a metaphor for war, then e-sports are an even more suitable medium given that most of them are literally about killing the enemy."[31]

In addressing the physical nature of video games, Bowman and Cranmer distinguish esports from a game such as chess where the players have to physically move the pieces on a board but the game itself is not impacted by the way the player accomplishes moves, such as how hard or quickly they do so. They state, "[We] assert that effective video game play does require a clear physical component beyond simply providing system input, and that the player's careful and skillful execution of this physical component directly impacts on-screen performance." They state that even though video games are not as physically strenuous as sports like football or boxing, the physical exertion in video games does directly influence the outcome.[32]

Can a fictional, made-up sport become a sport? The hugely popular *Harry Potter* book series and movies featured a sport called Quidditch, in which wizards on broomsticks play a game somewhat similar to a mix of team handball, rugby, tag, and dodgeball. Quidditch has spread to the Muggle world, as people are playing Quidditch by holding a broomstick between their legs while they run. The first Muggle Quidditch matches took place in 2005 at Middlebury College in Vermont involving seven players, three different balls, and broomsticks between the legs. It has seekers, chasers, rings, and a snitch. It's a physical sport that involves tackling and stiff arms, has a penalty box, and can result in concussions.

In 2022, Quidditch governing bodies in the United States and elsewhere changed the sport's name to Quadball due to trademark concerns as well as an attempt to distance itself from allegedly controversial remarks on gender identity made by J.K. Rowling, the author of the *Harry Potter* books.[33]

US Quidditch, the national governing body for the sport that organizes events and programs, was founded in 2010. As of 2021, its website stated that there were over 3,500 athletes on over 150 Quidditch teams nationwide. Major League Quidditch (now Quadball) is composed of 16 teams in the United States and Canada. Many American universities have Quidditch (now Quadball) teams, including Emerson College, UCLA, University of Texas, University of Maryland, and Michigan State. There is an International Quidditch (now Quadball) Association.[34] According to the BBC, there were 700 Quidditch teams spread across 25 countries, as of 2012.[35] In 2016, Australia won the Quidditch World Cup held in Germany, topping the United States 150–130.[36]

Just like other sports, there is a movement to make Quidditch an Olympic sport. An ESPN poll taken in 2016 found that 5 percent of the respondents felt that Quidditch should be added to the Olympic roster, falling behind only softball and surfing and tied with skateboarding.[37]

Alex Benepe of the International Quidditch Association told *The Telegraph*, "There are a lot more ridiculous sports in the Olympics right now if you ask me, so I think anyone who doubts it should come out and see Quidditch and see how intense it is, it's a rough sport it's an exciting and dynamic sport and I would encourage anyone who has their doubts to come out and try it for themselves."[38]

Filmmaker Farzad Sangari, who did a documentary on Quidditch, told CNN in 2014, "If anybody actually watched it or played it, they would realize the amount of athleticism and mental dexterity it takes to play this sport."[39]

Naturally, there are skeptics. Emma Bound, a spectator at a Quidditch match in England, told Reuters in 2012, "I don't think it's for the Olympics. It's probably better when the broomsticks actually fly."[40]

Mary Kimball, executive director of US Quidditch, told me in an email interview in 2020 about the rise in popularity of Quidditch as a participatory sport.[41] "Quidditch was started in October 2005 by two college students at Middlebury College in Vermont. The sport really began to take off in 2008, when World Cup II happened with 12 teams from across the country. Many of those teams who attended that tournament are still active today, like Boston University, LSU, and of course, Middlebury. After that point, quidditch exploded in popularity. World Cup V, hosted in New York City in fall 2011, had over 90 teams attend. That was around the time that more countries started their own leagues. Today, quidditch is played by over 8,000 people in nearly 40 countries."

She added, "Initially, people were mostly interested in the sport because of its literary roots. Over the years, the quidditch community has moved away from that, developing unique rules and policies that set it apart not only from its origins but also from other sports. In quidditch, all genders have the opportunity to compete together. There are no single gender quidditch leagues. As a community, we also affirm the idea that the gender a player identifies with is their gender. We're changing the world of sports, one broom at a time."

As to why Quidditch should be considered a "real" sport, Kimball said, "Because it's an activity with rules that allow people to form teams and compete against other teams. We have tournaments, stats, gameplay policies, 14 editions of the rulebook, etc."

Kimball rebuts the skeptics who say that it can't be a sport because it was created from a book and/or players have brooms between their legs. "We shouldn't discount a new idea just because it comes from a book. Also, the sport of quidditch has made so many rule changes over the years. It's completely different from the source material now."

She added, "Many sports introduce limitations to make their games more interesting. In rugby, for example, you can only pass backwards. In basketball, you have to dribble the ball. In quidditch, players must keep a broom between their legs at all times. It's the exact same concept as what's commonly accepted in every other sport out there, just with different equipment and modifications."

Regarding advancement in trying to get Quidditch recognized as an Olympic sport or an NCAA-recognized sport, Kimball said, "It would be great to get more official recognition for what we're doing, but also, we don't want to compromise on our values in order to get there. So while, yes, we're doing what we can to be set up for acceptance by the Olympic movement, it's not our sole focus right now. Moreover, quidditch, and by extension USQ, is challenging the notion of what a sport can be. We don't want to go down a certain path just because that's what everyone else is doing. We want to do what's right for our community, first and foremost. What's more important right now than official recognition is getting quidditch offered in elementary, middle, and high schools. We're developing a PE curriculum that will help with just that, and already have a special youth rulebook available for educators."

I would say in defense of Quidditch/Quadball that it is an athletic endeavor that involves running and physical contact. Also, most sports were made up or created by someone, such as basketball, baseball, and volleyball. However, Quidditch/Quadball will always have its detractors due to the use of broomsticks between the legs and the fact that it came from a kids' book.

Another purported sport that will always have detractors due to its origins is pole dancing. This is an activity commonly performed by scantily clad performers at strip clubs and involves a combination of dance and aerobics. However, the activity has become much more mainstream in recent years, as aerobic pole dancing is a common activity at gyms and fitness centers across the country.

Should pole dancing be considered an actual sport? It is physical and requires agility, flexibility, and athleticism. In 2017, the Global Association of International Sports Federation granted the activity's international governing federation "observer status," which could pave the way for it to be admitted as an Olympic sport. There is an annual World Pole Sports Championship. Wendy Traskos, the owner of NY Pole Dancing Studio, told the *New York Daily News* that pole dancing should qualify technically as an Olympic sport. "It requires strength, timing, coordination, flexibility and an extreme amount of dedication for it to be safe and to excel in the sport." However, Traskos personally didn't want pole dancing in the Olympics, telling the *New York Daily News*, "I don't need to see pole dancing in the Olympics. I don't think this is necessarily the path that we need to take, as a sport."[42]

Granted, pole dancing is athletic. However, the alleged stigma of its origins could be hard to overcome for a long time.

Caitlin Roper, spokesperson for Collective Shout, a women's rights initiative dedicated to ending the objectification of women and sexualization of girls, told Rachel Moss of the *Huffington Post UK*, "Proponents of pole-dancing argue it promotes sexual expression and empowerment, but sexualizing women and girls does not advance the status of women, nor is it the means to any meaningful power. If pole dancing was truly empowering, we would see men lining up to have a go."[43]

Some sports were treated with skepticism and ridicule at first but then became mainstream, respected, and popular with participants and fans. Some of the extreme sports featured at the X Games and Winter X Games eventually were adopted by the Olympics, such as freestyle skiing aerials, short track speed skating, snowboarding, halfpipe, and slopestyle. Surfing, skateboarding, BMX bike freestyle, and rock climbing became Olympic sports in the 2021 Tokyo Olympics.[44]

Some sports are traditionally accepted as sports, but should they be? One example would be auto racing. NASCAR and Formula 1 racing is hugely popular and gets extensive media coverage. Some major race competitions, such as the Indianapolis 500, draw hundreds of thousands of spectators. This activity needs good vision, stamina, attention, and reflexes, but there is no physical activity by the driver. He or she is just sitting in a car. The only substantial physical activity is done by the pit crew, which changes tires and refuels the car at lightning speed.

In 2013, former pro quarterback Donovan McNabb said that Sprint Cup champion Jimmie Johnson was not an athlete, stating on *Fox Sports Live*, "No, he sits in a car and drives."[45]

In questioning the concept of auto racing as a sport, Joshua David Stein wrote in the *Daily Beast*, "Perhaps the real athletic feat isn't at the race track at all but is, rather, in the sterile and analytic engineering laboratories in Bologna, Modena, Stuttgart, and Detroit? Instead of bodies breathing, motorsports are about engines aspirating. Muscles are carefully angled cylinders and fuel comes in gallons not carbohydrates."[46]

Defenders of considering auto racing to be a sport would point to traits such as endurance and quick reflexes. Noting that auto racing involves conditions such as dangerous body heat and G loads, Dr. Lara Carlson's research "determined that in order to withstand those conditions in modern racing, drivers must put themselves through intense physical training, much like what their counterparts in more widely accepted sports do," according to Seth Koenig's 2016 article on the Motorsport Safety Foundation's website, motorsport-safety.org.[47]

Another traditionally accepted sport that could be questioned is golf. Mark Twain referred to it as a good walk spoiled. Some people have questioned the athleticism involved in golf as well as its inclusion in the Olympics. Golf does involve hand-eye coordination, mental pressure, and walking, but doesn't include running or jumping.

Golf is very difficult to master, but that and the fact it involves a substantial amount of walking doesn't necessarily make it a sport. In support of Casey Martin's quest to use a golf cart on the PGA tour due to his physical disability, I argued in my op-ed in the *Chicago Tribune* that golf was more of a skill like bowling, billiards, or darts and therefore did not qualify as a sport. I wrote that golf is "an activity that older people take up when their knees go bad and they can't play real sports like basketball, baseball and football anymore. Sorry, but real sports involve running and jumping."[48]

ESPN's Peter McCleery wrote that a 2004 study conducted for ESPN.com by a panel of experts including sports scientists, academics, and sports journalists ranked golf 51st out of 60 sports as far as being the most athletically demanding, finishing just behind table tennis. Former Olympic speed skating gold medal winner Dan Jansen told McCleery that golf wasn't on the same level as other sports. "I don't know that it is a sport. The difference is, you can smoke a cigarette while doing it. But it is a game, and it's the hardest game I've ever played."[49]

Obviously, golf has numerous defenders who would suggest that it's one of the hardest sports to master and that it involves physical strength and dexterity.

Former NHL superstar and scratch golfer Brett Hull told ESPN's McCleery that golf was a sport. "People don't understand what it takes to be an elite athlete in any sport. To me the mental preparation and toughness in golf blows away what it takes in any sport. Just because golfers don't wear running shoes and don't run down the fairway doesn't mean they aren't athletes."[50]

This might tee off some people, but in my view, there's no way that golf should be an Olympic sport.

Should poker be considered a real sport? There's no running, jumping, or physical exertion involved aside from lifting up the cards. Its stereotype is basically a bunch of overweight guys in Hawaiian shirts and backward baseball caps sitting around a table smoking cigarettes and drinking beer. However, in recent years, many major television networks, including ESPN, CBS Sports Network, and FOX Sports, have placed their bets on poker and treated it like a sport and given it extensive publicity and coverage. There is strategy, mental toughness, psychology, and pressure involved. There is an annual World Series of Poker held in Las Vegas.

As reported by the *New York Times*, in 2012, a federal district court judge in New York ruled that poker was more of a game of skill than a game of chance and that therefore the game operators could not be prosecuted under federal law for running an illegal gambling business.[51]

In 2017, the Global Association of International Sports Federations granted observer status to the International Federation of (Match) Poker, which could pave the way toward poker becoming an Olympic sport.[52]

Gary Wise of ESPN opposed the concept of poker as an Olympic sport, writing in 2010, "While there's something to the argument that playing the WSOP main event 12 hours a day for a week takes some stamina and fortitude, poker isn't physical in the way Olympic sports are and as such, the Olympics wouldn't be the right venue for it unless the dynamic were to drastically shift."[53]

Personally, due to the absence of a physical aspect, I think that those who suggest that poker is a sport aren't playing with a full deck.

Should competitive dancing be considered to be a real sport? A new Olympic sport that will debut in the Paris 2024 Summer Olympics will be competitive breakdancing, which was added to bring in a younger audience.[54] The IOC stated that adding breakdancing would help make the Olympics "gender-balanced, more youth-focused and more urban." Breakdancing was an event at the 2018 Youth

Golf is difficult to master but is it a sport? Many talented golf legends, like Byron Nelson, shown here at right in 1939, have had incredible skill and talent. But does the absence of physical qualities like running and jumping mean that golf should not be considered a sport? (photo courtesy Temple University Libraries, Special Collections Research Center, George D. McDowell *Philadelphia Evening Bulletin* Collection).

Olympic Games in Buenos Aires, with boys, girls, and mixed teams. Breakdancing will become the first dance discipline to have Summer Olympic status.[55] Professional hip-hop dancer and breaker and professor of hip-hop dance history at Princeton Raphael Xavier told Lulu Garcia-Navarro of NPR, "[I]t's a great opportunity for the younger generation to have something to look forward to, as with any, you know, athletic sport, the older guys—you know, you didn't have that. It was just battling. But I think now that the Olympics are, you know, on the table, this younger generation has something else to look forward to."[56]

There has been an ongoing effort to try to add ballroom dancing (dancesport) to the Olympics. The IOC officially recognized the International DanceSport Federation (IDSF) as the sport's official representative body in 1997, but it rejected attempts to add ballroom dancing to the roster of sports at the 2008 Beijing Olympics and the 2012 London Olympics. People point to the success of the television program *Dancing with the Stars* as evidence of the sport's popularity. Ice dancing made its debut as an Olympic sport at the 1976 Winter Olympics in Austria. While some traditionalists might argue against recognizing dancing as a sport, arguing that it's more of an

Horse racing, as shown here at Liberty Bell Park in 1974, has been a popular spectator sport for centuries. But are jockeys athletes or are they just along for the ride? Shown here is Level, second from right, with jockey Weston Soirez (photo courtesy Temple University Libraries, Special Collections Research Center, George D. McDowell *Philadelphia Evening Bulletin* Collection).

art, it does meet the criteria of involving physical activity, stamina, flexibility, coordination, and athleticism. The Tokyo Summer Olympics of 2021 added skateboarding, sport climbing, and surfing as medal sports. Other suggested Olympic sports have included squash, yoga, and sheep shearing.[57] I'm not sure how the sheep feel about being counted in this list.

Can a sport be considered a sport if its main participants aren't human? Horse racing has been popular for centuries and was nicknamed "the sport of kings." In 1999, ESPN named 1973 Triple Crown winner Secretariat as the 35th greatest North American athlete of the 20th century. Two other horses, Man O' War and Citation, also finished in the top 100.[58] Although *Sports Illustrated* named race car driver Jackie Stewart the 1973 Sportsman of the Year, it indicated that the other two finalists were Secretariat and O.J. Simpson.[59] Equestrian is an Olympic sport.

But are jockeys athletes or are they just along for the ride? Isn't it the horses, not the jockeys, who are the athletes? If you take away the horses, there is no event. Yet, in the Olympics, the riders, not the horses, get the gold medals. Winning horses get only ribbons (and maybe some extra carrots, if they're lucky).

Many believe that jockeys are athletes. In defending jockeys as athletes, ESPN's Tim Keown wrote in 2010, "Jockeys are the toughest athletes in the world. Pound for pound, it's not even close. You think a 330-pound offensive lineman is tough? I'll stack a 110-pound jockey up against those big guys any day when it comes to playing through pain. A broken rib is two months off for a football player; it's a couple of strips of tape and a deep breath for a jockey." He added, "What he does is harder than driving a race car, more physically demanding than golf, more dangerous than just about anything."[60]

Other nonhuman sports include greyhound racing, bullfighting, rodeo, cockfighting, dogfighting, fox hunting, and polo. But are sports involving animals cruel and should they be banned? PETA argues, "There is nothing remotely 'sporting' about sports that involve unwilling animal participants."[61] In many countries, bulls are killed in the bullfighting ring. I remember the first and only time that I saw bullfighting. I went to Cancun, Mexico, in 1993 and decided to go to a bullfight downtown. At first it was colorful and entertaining when the crowd yelled "Olé," but after the match several employees proceeded to throw spears into the bull until it was killed. I was shocked. I was unaware that this took place. I think that other Americans in the stands were also disappointed. Some started to root for the bull and chant "Go Toro" during the subsequent matches. In Portugal, the bulls are killed out of sight after the matches. In 2018, Portugal's parliament voted overwhelmingly to reject a proposal to ban bullfighting.[62] According to the Humane Society International, bullfighting has been banned by several countries, including Argentina, Canada, Cuba, Denmark, Italy, and the United Kingdom.[63] Even though there is athleticism and skill exhibited by toreadors in evading a charging bull, the brutality of the killing of the bulls should disqualify it as a legitimate sport. Similarly, cockfighting and dogfighting have been appropriately deemed as inhumane and banned by most states.

I enjoy debating with friends and students whether certain activities constitute sports, games, or skills. It's not an abstract argument like debating how many angels can dance on the head of a pin. It's an interesting topic that often has impactful determinations as to whether a sport can be recognized by the NCAA or the IOC. Oftentimes, there are no clear-cut answers. While I, along with many others, might have initial skepticism about certain activities being considered sports, it's important to have an open mind (most of the time) and be willing to evolve in your viewpoints.

Chapter 2

Values of Sports and Sportsmanship

There are many societal norms associated with playing sports that reflect morality and cultural values. Sports have psychological and socializing benefits, but there is frequent disillusionment and criticism of sports by many. Playing and watching sports is an important diversion in society. Competition and victory are important, but some athletes break rules in order to achieve victory. There is a balance and conflict between sportsmanship and winning at all costs. Among the issues related to sportsmanship and the values of sports are following the rules of the game, fair play, respect for the game, running up the score, teamwork, sitting out players before the playoffs, tanking in order to get high draft picks, intentionally losing games to get a better playoff seeding or to rest players, and winning at all costs. Among the high-profile incidents of cheating or questionable conduct were the Deflategate and Spygate scandals involving the New England Patriots; bounties for targeting football players; use of spitballs, corked bats, pine tar, and other foreign substances in baseball; and flopping, intentional fouls, and taking dives in soccer and basketball. This chapter will examine the values of sports and fair competition.

Sports and competition have been long-standing activities for human beings. Presumably, cavemen had competitions in running, fighting, and hunting. The first concept of formal organized sports competition took place in ancient Greece. The first Olympics were held in 776 BC and featured events such as running, chariot races, wrestling, and jumping.[1]

As formal sports evolved, so did the norms and rules that governed those sports. Part of the allure of sports is that it is a fair competition governed by the relevant rules and guidelines. If people break the rules or cheat, what is the point of having the competition? For instance, boxing established the Marquess of Queensberry rules in 1867 to set a general code of ethics in the sport. Those rules included a standard ring size and three-minute rounds.[2]

Without boundaries and rules, there would be repeated low blows in boxing, tackling and hip checks in golf, biting off ears in boxing and soccer, and pulling of ponytails in women's soccer.

One of the main values of sports is honesty. Athletes need to abide by the rules and boundaries of their sport in order to ensure a fair competition.

There are many benefits of playing and watching sports. There is a physical benefit to playing sports and keeping in good physical shape and conditioning. It can have a positive effect in terms of weight loss, body mass index, cholesterol, increased physical strength and flexibility, lower blood pressure, stronger bones and muscles, improved psychological health, and preventing heart disease. Being physically fit is a trait that can help us throughout our lives, ranging from Little League to playing in an over-age-60 basketball league or participating in the Senior Olympics. It's important that kids learn about the physical benefits of playing sports at an early age.

Young people learn discipline; self-esteem; respect for opponents, teammates, umpires, and coaches; dedication; hard work; patience; persistence; sportsmanship; and teamwork by playing on sports teams at a young age. Playing an organized sport is not easy. As a player, you are expected to show up for practice, come to games on time, study and learn a playbook, and learn how to be a team player. You learn at an early age that there's no "I" in team. Many coaches preach that by being part of a team, you're becoming part of a family, whether you're a star player or a deep sub. You're expected to follow the instructions and advice from your coaches and to respect the calls made by officials and umpires even if you disagree with them.

The lessons learned from sports can translate to aspects of the rest of your life, including work and family. Playing sports builds character. You learn that sometimes you win and sometimes you lose. Losing can be a lesson that you or your team need to work harder to improve your skills or mental toughness. Overcoming adversity, whether it be healing from an injury, getting blown out by another team, losing a championship game in a heartbreaking ending, or losing your starting position to another player is something that you can learn from. When you're in a slump and not playing well, you need perseverance to fight through it. Committing to play on a sports team for your school means that you have to learn how to budget your time and focus on homework after games or practices.

For many young athletes, one of the skills that they learn and develop is leadership. Being one of a team's better or more experienced players leads to the responsibility of leading and teaching the younger, more inexperienced players how to act and compete. The veteran players can serve as role models to the younger players. In many cases, sports can expose you to a diverse range of people that are different from you, including in terms of race, ethnicity, religion, socioeconomics, social and political values, gender, geography, culture, and sexual orientation. Communication skills can also be learned through sports, as they can help introverted and shy kids break out of their shell, make new friends, and learn how to relate to their peers.

Sports can teach you how to set goals, whether that means making your high school's varsity team, becoming a starter on a team, being named an all-star or all-league in your sport, winning a team or individual championship, or setting a personal record in a track meet or swimming competition. In order to reach those goals, it means that you have to work hard, dedicate yourself to that sport, improve your

Chapter 2. Values of Sports and Sportsmanship

Winning is important but so is sportsmanship. The handshake line, shown here in a baseball game between Georgia Tech and the University of Georgia in May 2017, is one way for players of opposing teams to show sportsmanship and respect for opponents (photo from Creative Commons. "File: May 2017 GT vs. UGA baseball—Handshake line.jpg" by Thomson200 is marked with CC0 1.0).

skills, be receptive to coaching and advice, and practice on a regular and frequent basis.

An overlooked value of sports is that they should be fun, especially at the youth level. If kids view playing their sport as a chore or a burden or do it because their parents made them join a team, it can lead to burnout and kids dropping out from playing youth sports. As noted in a later chapter, this increased dropout rate is an unfortunate trend in youth sports. Being on a sports team will likely lead to friendships that can last a lifetime. You spend days, weeks, months, and years sharing a common experience with teammates on Little League teams, youth travel teams, AAU teams, junior high school teams, and high school teams. Oftentimes, one of the main reasons that kids join a team is to be with their friends or to make new friends. It can be a great way to break in if you're new to a neighborhood or a school. Instead of sitting on the couch watching television, playing video games, or tethered to your cell phone, you're engaged in a positive, healthy shared experience with other people.

As Joseph Doty stated in the *Journal of College and Character,* "Does an individual's sport experience make up the totality of his character development? Obviously not! As many scholars and researchers on moral/character development have shown, character development is a lifelong, holistic process that is primarily influenced by contextual variables throughout a person's life. But if sport is part of a young person's life, then the sport experience will influence his or her character development—and hopefully in a positive way."[3]

One of the most important parts of playing sports is learning sportsmanship. Attempting to define sportsmanship, Jay D. Goldstein and Seppo E. Iso-Ahola indicated in their article in the *Journal of Physical Education, Recreation & Dance* that sportsmanship is hard to clearly define for many people. They wrote, "Unfortunately, to some youth sport participants, coaches, and parents, the practical application of the concept has been reduced to little more than the mandatory shaking of hands at the end of a game. The National Collegiate Athletic Association (NCAA, 2003) defined the concept as the set of behaviors to be exhibited by athletes, coaches, officials, administrators and fans (parents) in athletic competition. These behaviors are based on such fundamental values as respect, fairness, civility, honesty, and responsibility (p. 15). Taking the concept a step further, the NCAA's bylaws state that those associated with intercollegiate athletics must also abide by a code of ethical conduct that is defined as the set of guiding principles with which each person follows the letter and spirit of the rules."[4]

Throughout the years, there have been many highly publicized incidents of positive sportsmanship. Some were done by famous athletes, while others were done by athletes not in the public eye.

In 2014, during a high school cross-country meet in North Dakota, one of the runners, Danielle LeNoue, injured her tendons two miles into the race in a secluded area of the course. One of the other runners, Melanie Bailey, carried LeNoue by piggyback for a quarter mile to medical staff. Bailey finished the race 178th out of 180th, but her actions were later hailed by many as heroic and a great example of sportsmanship, as other runners had run past LeNoue without offering to help her. LeNoue and Bailey appeared as guests on Ellen DeGeneres's television show and received a one-week vacation to the Bahamas.[5] I discuss this incident every semester with my sports ethics class. Most of the students admire what Bailey did, but they say that if they were in contention in the race, they would likely keep running and not help the injured runner since getting disqualified from the race could affect their team's score. My students said that they would alert nearby medical staff when they saw them on the course.

During the 1936 Berlin Olympics, German athlete Luz Long famously gave advice to Jesse Owens, an American, during the long jump competition after Owens had fouled twice during the qualifying rounds. He told Owens to adjust his takeoff point to several inches before the takeoff line to ensure that he wouldn't foul again. Owens proceeded to win the gold medal in the event.[6]

During the 1956 Australian national championship mile race, one of the runners, Ron Clarke, tripped and fell on the track. Another runner, John Landy, leaped over Clarke and accidentally scraped him with his spikes. Landy momentarily stopped running to make sure that Clarke was all right before starting to run again. Landy was able to catch up to the field and won the race. A bronze statue was later erected in Melbourne dedicated to Landy's act, titled *Sportsmanship*. During the 1969 Ryder Cup, Jack Nicklaus made his four-foot par putt and then picked up the ball marker of his British opponent, Tony Jacklin, and conceded the putt so that Jacklin would not have to make his two-foot putt. Nicklaus's gesture resulted in a tie in the competition.[7]

In general, golf is a sport that emphasizes sportsmanship and strict ethics rules. Golf has been called "the gentleman's game," based on its etiquette. According to *Golf Digest*, among the USGA's rules are limits on the number of clubs golfers can have in their bag, preventing golfers from giving competitors advice, how to handle balls in water hazards and bunkers, time limits to find lost balls, and order of play.[8] In 2015, Phil Mickelson was penalized for having two different models of balls in his bag during a tournament.[9] According to *Golf Week*, among the ways golfers can be disqualified from a tournament are misrepresenting their handicap, missing their starting time, starting their round too early, turning in an incorrect or unsigned scorecard, and using nonconforming equipment or foreign substances on clubs. In 2011, the USGA and the Royal & Ancient enacted a new policy that gave tournaments the option of waiving disqualification in some instances.[10]

During the 2014 Winter Olympics in Russia, a Canadian cross-country ski coach, Justin Wadsworth, helped a Russian skier, Anton Gaforov, who had crashed during the semifinal of the men's freestyle sprint race. The coach gave the Russian a new ski, allowing him to finish the race in front of his home country's fans.[11]

In soccer, it is standard practice that when a player is seriously injured, a player on either team will kick the ball out of bounds, and then when play resumes, the thrower will throw the ball to the team that had possession and kicked the ball out of bounds.

Unfortunately, while there are many examples of good sportsmanship, there are also many examples of poor sportsmanship.

Is winning the only thing that matters in a sport? Legendary Green Bay Packers coach Vince Lombardi is associated with the famous quote, "Winning isn't everything. It's the only thing." However, that sentiment does not mean that athletes should cheat and break the rules in order to win. Lombardi later said about his famous quote, "I wished I'd never said the thing.... I meant the effort. I meant having a goal. I sure didn't mean for people to crush human values and morality."[12]

Regarding the balance and conflict between sportsmanship and winning at all costs, Brian Schiff, longtime head coach for eight gold medal United States Maccabiah 16 & Under Boys basketball teams, former assistant coach at Abington Friends School, middle school head coach at AFS, and a member of the Philadelphia Jewish Sports Hall of Fame, said in an email interview, "Sports are a competitive endeavor and there does need to be some semblance of wanting to win. What we try and preach is to be better and winning more comes from being committed to the craft and working hard toward that every time you are in a gym, on a court or in a field. Another line I use I call, 'KAWC' (pronounced Caulk). Stands for 'Kick Ass with Class.'"[13]

There is a balance and conflict between sportsmanship and winning at all costs. Athletes, coaches, and teams at all levels need to follow the rules of the game, engage in fair play, and have respect for the game. Some acts are clearly unsportsmanlike, such as a low blow in boxing or biting another soccer or basketball player. Professional teams were rightly criticized for incidents such as "Deflategate" and "Spygate" by the New England Patriots, the signal stealing of the Houston Astros, the imposition of bounties by the New Orleans Saints, and the use of illegal substances in baseball such as corked bats, spitballs, and pine tar. However, there are many gray areas as to what constitutes sportsmanship or unsportsmanlike behavior. Among the topics that are frequently debated as gray areas regarding the ethics of competition include running up the score, flopping and diving in soccer, intentional fouls in basketball, sitting out players before the playoffs, refusing to shake hands after games, intentionally losing games to get a better draft slot or to rest players, and winning at all costs.

In many situations, reasonable people can differ as to what sportsmanship should entail. Every semester, I show the students in my sports ethics class a video from the Foundation for a Better Life's website, Passiton.com, in which a high school basketball player tells his coach during a championship game that he touched the ball last before the ball went out of bounds and that he wants to admit it to the referee to have the call changed. His teammates are upset, but the coach tells him "good call," and the player goes ahead and tells the referee. The video's message is that this is what constitutes good sportsmanship.[14] However, in my 10 or so years of showing this video to my class, very few of my students agreed with the video's message that the player should have told the ref about the mistake. They said that it's up to the referee to make the call and that if he or she misses it, so be it. In the long run, good calls and bad calls will even out over the game and the entire season. While I admire the thought and positive message of the video, I agree with my students that it isn't a realistic scenario in the real world with competitive athletes trying to win. In fact, most of the time, players and coaches will try to work the refs to try to get a call in their favor.

Generally, most of us have been taught as kids not to lie or deceive others. However, in some cases, certain types of deception, behaviors, and trickery are considered to be a normal and accepted part of the sport, such as a pump fake in basketball, a flea flicker or "fumblerooski" play in football, shrieking or grunting in tennis, using a fake bunt, raising your glove to convince the umpire that you made a catch even though you trapped the ball, or stepping out of the batter's box in baseball to annoy the pitcher. In the NFL, it has become a common technique for a defensive player to pretend to be injured in order to break the momentum of a hurry-up offense.

Some techniques and behaviors in sports clearly go beyond the pale, such as Mike Tyson biting Evander Holyfield's ear during a fight, Luis Suarez biting other players during a soccer match, or Zinedine Zidane's head butt of another player during the World Cup final in 2006. Diego Maradona's "hand of God" goal in the World Cup quarterfinals in 1986 took place when Maradona punched the ball past the goalkeeper, making him a hero in Argentina but a goat in the rest of the soccer world.[15]

However, what about flopping in soccer in order to try to get a direct kick or penalty kick, or to get a yellow card or red card administered to an opposing player? Is that a strategic part of the game or a sign of poor sportsmanship? That's where the debatable, gray areas of sportsmanship kick in.

Let's look in detail at some of the most debated gray areas of sports ethics, where people can reasonably differ as to what is appropriate and sportsmanlike.

Running Up the Score

One of the most debated ethical issues in sports is whether it is appropriate for a team to run up the score against an opponent. This takes place when a team continues to play all out even when they have a commanding and seemingly insurmountable lead. This might consist of a football team with a 50-point lead continuing to use a hurry-up offense and throwing 60-yard bombs, instead of using running plays. Running up the score or blowout wins date back over a century, as evidenced by Georgia Tech's 222–0 thumping of Cumberland College in 1916. A recent example of an overwhelming blowout took place in 2015, when a high school girls basketball team in California beat an opponent 161–2.[16] Almost every year there are outrageous lopsided scores in sports that get national attention.

Is running up the score an appropriate technique? On one hand, assuming that the coach clears the bench to let his or her substitutes play, it's unfair to those subs to tell them to take it easy and not to play hard. These subs spend hours per week at practice and want a chance to play to show what they can do. A huge blowout game might be one of the few chances during the season when the deep subs get to play. In addition, it would be offensive to the other team to stall and stop playing by just passing the ball to each other without trying to score in a basketball or soccer game. Furthermore, losing by a large margin arguably can be a lesson that the team or individual athlete needs to work harder and get better.

Nicholas Dixon argued in his article in the *Journal of the Philosophy of Sport* that running up the score and blowout wins can be appropriate: "[M]y main thesis in this paper is that there is absolutely nothing intrinsically wrong with pressing for a lopsided victory in a competitive game, whether it be football, basketball, soccer, or any other sport.... Winning is not the only thing that matters. Players who win blowouts can be justly proud of their display of athletic excellence, the personal and team records they have set, and the excitement provided for fans."

Dixon rejected what he called the Anti-Blowout thesis, stating, "I wish to argue against a widely-held view concerning sportsmanship. I call this view the

Anti-Blowout thesis (AB): AB: it is intrinsically unsporting for players or teams to maximize the margin of victory after they have secured victory in a one-sided contest."[17]

Rejecting Dixon's claims and supporting the anti-blowout thesis, Hardman et al. argued in their article in the *Journal of the Philosophy of Sport*, "We believe, in conclusion, that at least three good reasons can be given for supporting the AB thesis. First, strong humiliation, on Dixon's own terms, appears to be both a logical possibility and an empirical likelihood in extremely one-side games. In addition, Dixon's lack of concern for comparative results and his interest in the pursuit of excellence seem to be warranted (if at all) only in one species of sport—the kind that involves parallel rather than interactive testing. Finally, it is difficult to accept Dixon's cavalier dismissal of concrete harm experienced by victims of severely lopsided contests, even if this harm is not logically required."[18]

Some people would prefer that their opponent not let up on them, even though they might get crushed. Noting that he was offended when his opponent in a tennis tournament gave him a game by purposefully missing shots so as not to beat him 6–0, 6–0, ESPN's LZ Granderson said that he didn't want pity points. "In some circles it might be in poor taste to run up the score, but where I'm from, point shaving to spare feelings is far more disrespectful to the losing party. If you step out there, you should be prepared to be stepped on. Real competitors understand this. That's why we don't ask our opponents for mercy, we ask them for a rematch. And we ask the gods for revenge."[19]

For some sports, running up the score is a necessary evil. In college football, point spreads are an important factor in rankings as well as determining who gets selected for the College Football Playoff. For instance, Ohio State's 59–0 blowout win over Wisconsin in the Big Ten Championship football game in 2014 helped the Buckeyes get selected for the College Football Playoff. If a top 10 team favored by 30 points wins by only a field goal, it could hurt them in the rankings. In basketball, victory margins can help a team's NET ranking, RPI, and BPI, which are factors in NCAA Tournament selection. In World Cup soccer, goal differential is a tiebreaker when it comes to advancing to the second round of the tournament.

In college football, there can be a temptation and desire from players, coaches, and fan bases for their teams to run up the score, especially for those in the Group of Five conferences that had unfairly been excluded from the College Football Playoff even though several of their teams had undefeated seasons. Cincinnati finally broke that glass ceiling in 2022 when it became the first Group of Five team selected for the College Football Playoff. Many people criticized undefeated Cincinnati for running a fake punt against East Carolina in 2020 while having a 42–10 lead in the fourth quarter. The Bearcats ended up winning 55–17, and their coach, Luke Fickell, apologized for the play after the game, saying it was not called from the sidelines.[20]

In some cases, running up the score can be appropriate because sometimes you never know when a lead will be safe. Cincinnati blew a 22-point lead over Nevada midway through the second half in the second round of the 2018 NCAA men's basketball tournament. Also in 2018, the Drexel Dragons came back from a 34-point deficit to beat Delaware, which was the largest comeback win in the history of Division I basketball. In the second round of the 2016 NCAA Tournament, Texas A&M stormed back from a 12-point deficit with 35 seconds to go in the game against Northern Iowa to force the game into overtime, where the Aggies eventually won by four points. In college football, in 2019, UCLA overcame a 32-point deficit halfway through the third quarter to beat Washington State 67–63. In the 1979 Cotton Bowl, Joe Montana led Notre Dame to a miraculous 35–34 comeback win against Houston, which led 34–12 with 7:37 left to go.[21] Incidents like this are a reminder to coaches that your team shouldn't let up until the last minute or two just to be safe.

As to handling a big lead, Coach Brian Schiff said in an email interview, "As a coach you have to have a feel for the game. In most contests you should be able to tell early if the game will be close and the teams are evenly matched or if one squad has a decided advantage. You go from there. If I had a team that was way better, I did not play my best players until we had a huge lead and then play my subs (which most seem to do), but just start subbing early and often and let everyone play throughout the contest. That way if you have a big lead and the other team makes some sort of run, it doesn't look like you are panicking by putting your better players back in the game."[22]

Coaches have great influence on whether running up the score is a problem. Evan Barnes wrote in the *Los Angeles Daily News* that a coach runs up the score if he keeps his best players in the game and runs plays to score on offense, but that it's not running up the score if the coach is playing his subs. Barnes wrote, "If a coach has backups in play and those backups happen to catch fire, then you can't blame the coach for how his second/third string players perform."[23]

Noting an increase in blowout scores in high school football games in Pennsylvania, Mike White of the *Pittsburgh Post-Gazette* wrote in 2017, "It makes one wonder what these coaches are thinking. And what in the name of sportsmanship are they trying to prove? Maybe it's time some of these coaches get called out."[24]

In 2009, Micah Grimes, the coach of the Covenant School in Texas, was fired in the aftermath of his team clobbering an opponent 100–0 and his sending a letter to a newspaper defending his team right after the school had issued an apology on its website for the blowout. Grimes told ESPN that he did not run up the score and that he didn't have anything to apologize for, noting that he stopped pressing midway through the first quarter, when his team led 27–0.[25]

Huge blowout scores like that are less common at the college level, but occasionally it happens. For instance, the UConn women's basketball team routed St. Francis 140–52 in a first-round NCAA Tournament game in 2018. However, blowouts at the college level aren't likely as psychologically harmful as blowouts at the high school or youth sports level.

Running up the score, especially at the youth and high school level, can embarrass the losing team. For young athletes it could be a turnoff and lead to their quitting the sport. There are times when it's apparent that a team is overmatched and there's no point to keep pouring it on. It's even worse when the winning team gloats or taunts the losing team and rubs it in.

One popular measure that has been instituted to mitigate against running up the score is the concept of mercy rules, which end lopsided games early. This is a very popular measure in youth sports. In Little League baseball, the games are called if a team has a 10-or-more-run lead after four innings or has a 15-or-more-run lead after three innings.

Parents and coaches have expressed varied opinions as to whether mercy rules are appropriate in youth and high school sports.

Coach Brian Schiff said in an email interview, "Mercy rules have good and bad. Winning games by huge amounts on one hand is not necessary and proves nothing in a game that's a mismatch, but then again in youth sports why should the better players, who put in lots of time and effort, be short changed in playing time. In Maccabi we have 'Rachmanus Rules' (means 'mercy' in Hebrew), which means if you have a team outclassed, you don't run up the score. Do things like don't run after rebounds, take 10 passes before you score, don't press, play a packed in zone and other things you can do to control the game, but not just pass the ball around which can be just as embarrassing to the opponent."[26]

Meaghan Keil, a high school girls softball coach in New York State, told the *Democrat & Chronicle* that she preferred a 10-run mercy rule, and that a 15-run mercy rule was too much. She said, "It's borderline unsportsmanlike. Up 15 [runs] you're already really beating up on somebody. You might be able to come back from eight or nine runs, but 10 is fine and sometimes [coaches whose teams are ahead] really push it try to get a five-inning game."[27]

However, the University of Michigan women's softball coach, Carol Hutchins, told the *Michigan Daily* that she opposed the mercy rule or thought that it should be raised from eight-run leads to 15. She said, "In what other sport do you stop playing because you're ahead? Eight runs isn't out of reach. You lose the opportunity to give some younger kids playing time."[28]

Another approach to mitigate excessive blowouts in timed sports like football and basketball is to use a running clock to speed up games, meaning that the clock will run after an incomplete pass in football or during foul shots in basketball.

From 2006 to 2016, the Connecticut Interscholastic Athletic Conference had a "score management" policy mandating football coaches to keep their margins of victory under 50 points or get a weeklong suspension. In 2016, that policy was changed to a running clock during blowouts.[29]

Mike Doto, Paramus Catholic boys basketball coach in New Jersey, told Greg Mattura of *NorthJersey.com* that he supported a running clock in blowout games, stating, "The running clock definitely makes sense because the competition is so lopsided that if you don't run the clock, teams are just going to have to pass the ball around, and nobody wants to see that at the end. Just dribbling around and passing to each other, that's almost more embarrassing for the team that's losing."[30]

While approaches such as mercy rules and running clocks can be used as effective tools to prevent embarrassing blowouts, one of their negative aspects is that subs on both teams might not get a chance to play in games and prove their abilities so that they can earn more playing time in future games.

Another way to prevent running up the score is via smart scheduling for out-of-conference games at the high school level. While playing overmatched teams in your own league is unavoidable, teams should try to avoid scheduling out-of-conference teams that they have a huge advantage over in talent. Such mismatches are an invitation to a blowout result.

Running up the score is a big issue in youth sports, high school sports, and college sports. It shouldn't be an issue in pro sports. Athletes are being paid large salaries and shouldn't complain that the other side is running up the score.

Tanking

Another gray-area ethical issue in sports that has been debated in recent years is the concept of "tanking" at the professional level.

In defining tanking, Joseph McManus wrote in the *Journal of Sport, Ethics and Philosophy*, "Tanking is an intentional strategy initiated by the management of a sports team in which the team is structured to avoid winning in the near term in order to accomplish the organization's longer term objectives (Motomura, Roberts, Leeds and Leeds 2016). Tanking managers adopt tactics that ensure over a full season of competition, the team fails 'to maximize the number of regular-season wins' it might otherwise achieve (Soebbing, Humphreys, and Mason 2013, 193). Tanking is a rational approach where sport leagues maintain an entry draft for new players and the league's draft order is set to favor teams with worse won-loss records (Borland, Chicu, and Macdonald 2009)."[31]

Regarding tanking, this technique drew the ire of many when the Philadelphia 76ers intentionally became bad for several seasons in order to gain high draft picks. The players and the coach were trying to win, but General Manager Sam Hinkie purposely avoided going after quality free agents and tried to have a noncompetitive team for four years in order to stock up on high-quality top draft picks. Supporters of this tanking adopted the mantra "Trust the Process," especially when the team acquired star players Joel Embiid and Ben Simmons in the NBA draft lottery. The process appeared to pay off during the 2017–2018 season when the Sixers earned the third seed in the Eastern Conference and reached the second round of the playoffs. They also reached the second round of the playoffs the following year, losing a heartbreaking seventh game to the eventual champion Toronto Raptors. The 76ers' process was a polarizing issue in Philadelphia among fans and media for several years, especially after the Sixers failed to advance past the first round in the 2020 NBA Playoffs and then lost a seven-game series to the Atlanta Hawks in the second round of the 2021 playoffs. At that point, many Sixer fans had stopped trusting the process and wanted to see many players, including Simmons, traded.[32] They got their wish when Simmons was traded to the Brooklyn Nets in 2022.

Many people nationwide had opinions regarding the approach of tanking.

Dallas Mavericks owner Mark Cuban was fined $600,000 for making comments that it was in his team's best interest to lose on purpose for the rest of the season in order to get a better draft pick. Shortly after the fine was imposed, NBA commissioner Adam Silver sent a memo to all 30 teams in which he said in part, "The integrity of the competition on the playing court is the cornerstone of our league. It is our pact with the fans and with each other, the fundamental reason we exist as a preeminent sporting organization, the very product that we sell. With everything else changing around us, it is the one thing in our league that can never change."[33]

Defenders of the tanking argued that in order to be really good in the NBA, you need to be really bad first in order to get the highest picks possible in the draft. Critics of the tanking argued that this technique went against everything that sports represent and that a team shouldn't intentionally try to lose.

Duke University basketball coach Mike Krzyzewski criticized the concept of NBA teams tanking, stating, "As an American, I wouldn't like to think that an American team would want to lose or create situations where you would want to lose…. I can't believe that that would happen. Maybe I'm naive and I'm going to go read a fairy tale after this."[34]

Glen Macnow, longtime Philadelphia sports talk radio host at Sports Radio 94 WIP, also is not a fan of the tanking years of the 76ers. He said in an email interview before the 2021 NBA Playoffs, "I could never buy into it. Cheating to lose is not better than cheating to win, in my book. It has worked—to an extent (we'll see how the Sixers fare this postseason)—but it cheapens it all, in my opinion."[35]

However, Hunter Felt wrote in *The Guardian* that fan acceptance of tanking in the NBA was a positive thing, "a sign that fans aren't solely invested in the sport for the immediate thrill of winning but are invested in their team's long-term health. Part of supporting one's team in the 21st century is exercising patience and taking the long view, which is why the 76ers could tank several seasons in a row without a fan revolt."[36]

Noting that fans with old-school values are more likely to find the practice of tanking to be unethical, Aiken et al. stated in their article in *Sports Marketing Quarterly*, "The implication here is that if management does not want to offend a major portion of their fanbase, they should not engage in tanking. However, if they do choose to tank, in order to avoid a fan backlash, they must figure out a way to distance the practice from judgments of ethicality. Likely, a public relations campaign must both frame their intentions as a rational short-term business strategy and convey futuristic visions of a winning team." They cite the 76ers' management use of the term "Trust the Process" as a way to convince their fan base that their tanking approach was a forward-thinking business decision.[37]

Eventually, in response to the concern about tanking, the NBA changed its rules regarding the NBA lottery to make tanking less effective. In 2019, it reduced the odds of the team with the worst record to getting the number one pick from 25 percent to 14 percent. Teams with the second- and third-worst records also have a 14 percent chance of getting the number one pick.[38] These new rules are likely to prevent the type of ongoing blatant tanking that took place during the 76ers' Trust the Process era.

Personally, I'm not a fan of tanking. There are many other ways to improve a bad or mediocre team, such as trades, free agency, and wise draft choices. Many great NBA players were drafted in the middle to late first round and even in the second round. Even if my favorite team, the 76ers, had won three straight NBA championships with Embiid and Simmons leading the way, I would be very happy that we won, but I would always wish that we had not reached this goal through tanking.

There have also been assertions in the NFL that some teams had engaged in tanking toward the end of the season in order to improve their draft status. Even though there is no draft lottery in the NFL, as the team with the worst regular-season record gets the first pick in the NFL draft, tanking in the NFL is rare. For one thing, unlike the NBA, one star player in football is unlikely to turn around a franchise. Some people alleged that the 0–11 New York Jets, after their last-second loss to the Las Vegas Raiders, were tanking toward the end of the 2020 season in order to be able to draft star Clemson quarterback Trevor Lawrence with the first pick of the draft.[39] After the Philadelphia Eagles put in a backup quarterback during a close game against the Washington Redskins in the last game of the 2020 season, angry New York Giants fans accused the Eagles of tanking, thus resulting in the Giants' failure to make the playoffs.[40]

Flopping and Intentional Fouls

Another gray area of sportsmanship is the frequent acts of diving or flopping in soccer and basketball. This is where a player overreacts to contact from another player, often in a dramatic fashion, in order to draw a foul on the other team's player.

In 2012, the NBA issued a press release defining flopping: "'Flopping' will be defined as any physical act that appears to have been intended to cause the referees to call a foul on another player. The primary factor in determining whether a player committed a flop is whether his physical reaction to contact with another player is inconsistent with what would reasonably be expected given the force or direction of the contact."[41]

In discussing the dive in soccer, Alejandro Chacoff wrote, "The dive and its immediate aftermath have gone from a cursory occurrence tinged with a little bit of acting to a true spectacle of excess. It now has the grandiloquence Roland Barthes attributed to wrestling. The scene is always punctuated with camp performances: the player's baffled expression on falling, the referee's slow, ponderous steps towards the player, the fiddling in the pocket for the card (red? yellow? so many options…)."[42]

Eric Levenson argued in his article in *The Atlantic (The Wire)* that Americans hate the concept of the flop because it is un-American and unsportsmanlike. "To the major practitioners of the flop—Europeans and South Americans—flopping is part of the game. In the States, however, it's often cited as one of the key aspects of soccer that keeps it from wider American acceptance."[43]

To their credit, soccer changed its rules so that a yellow card could be assessed against players who are deemed to have flopped or taken a dive intentionally.

What about flopping in basketball in order to try to draw an offensive foul against an opposing player? In 2012, the NBA instituted a rule that fined players for flopping.

NBA executive Stu Jackson supported the NBA's flop rule in a statement, according to ESPN: "Flops have no place in our game—they either fool referees into calling undeserved fouls or fool fans into thinking the referees missed a foul call."[44]

In a postgame press conference, DeMarcus Cousins criticized the practice of flopping to get calls, stating, "It kinda sucks. The competitive spirit of basketball is slowly leaking out. Taking pride in one-on-one defense is slowly leaking out. It's more about selling calls and flopping."[45]

The NCAA adopted a flop rule for basketball in 2019. In a controversial 2019 game, Missouri State was called for three flopping violations against Xavier, including a flopping call in the last minute of a tie game that resulted in a technical foul.[46]

Basketball has another gray issue of sportsmanship that arguably hurts the flow of the game—intentionally fouling players who don't shoot foul shots well. The intentional fouling of Shaquille O'Neal, a poor foul shooter, was dubbed "Hack-a-Shaq." The NBA revised its rules to state that intentional fouls committed in the last two minutes result in two shots and possession for the team that was fouled. That didn't stop teams from intentionally fouling poor free throw shooters before the last two minutes. A few teams started the "Hack-a-Ben" strategy to intentionally foul Ben Simmons of the 76ers to get him on the line due to his poor free throw shooting. The Atlanta Hawks successfully used that strategy against Simmons during the 2021 NBA Playoffs. San Antonio Spurs head coach Gregg Popovich told Jeff Zillgitt of *USA Today*, "On an intellectual or principle basis, I think you're on high ground," Popovich said of the tactic. "Now, visual-wise, it's awful. It couldn't be worse. I tend to side on the principle side where it's basketball, and if we have a guy who can't shoot and it's an important part of the game, I should probably get him off the court."[47]

Sometimes, there's nothing strategic about intentional fouls. Duke's Grayson Allen developed a reputation in college as a cheap-shot artist due to his tendency to trip other teams' players and commit flagrant fouls. Allen tripped opponents twice during his sophomore year, once during his junior year, and once in his senior year. After the incident in his junior year, he was suspended for a game and stripped of his captaincy. Allen was a very talented player who had a great college career and was drafted in the first round of the NBA draft. He also earned all-ACC Academic Honors four times. To Duke fans, he will be remembered as a hard-nosed, talented competitor who helped lead Duke to a national championship. It's unfortunate that many people outside of Duke will remember his college career for his multiple tripping incidents. To some people, he replaced Christian Laettner as the most-hated Duke basketball player ever.[48]

Trash Talking

Trash talking in sports is another polarizing gray area issue that is frequently debated. It's always been a pet peeve of mine, going back to Little League when kids would chant "We want a pitcher, not a glass of water." I've always felt that players should just play the game and not taunt other teams' players. Like Vince Lombardi and other coaches told players who had celebrated a touchdown, "Act like you've been there before."[49] I hated it as a player and I also hate it as a fan, even if it's a player from my favorite team doing the trash talking.

Arguably, one of the pioneers of trash talking was Muhammad Ali. He wasn't shy about his abilities, and he frequently belittled and humiliated his opponents. He would make predictions as to which round he would knock out his opponent. I felt that he went over the line when he called Joe Frazier ugly, a gorilla, and an Uncle Tom.[50] To others, however, Ali's trash talking was funny and entertaining.

Many sports fans cringed and ridiculed Seattle Seahawks defensive back Richard Sherman when he went ballistic during a postgame interview with Erin Andrews, bragging that he was the best cornerback in the NFL and bragging how he had shut down 49ers wide receiver Michael Crabtree.

Michael Cohen of *The Guardian* criticized Sherman's actions, stating, "At a time when middle and high schools are rolling out anti-bullying programs, trash-talking should not be given the 'boys just being boys treatment.' On the football field, talking trash is, for better or worse, part of the game. We're inured to its public displays. Off the field, it is the language of bullies—a tool that the strong use to terrorize the weak and the vulnerable. It's hardly an ethos for young people to embrace."[51]

Those who justify trash talking say that it's an effective way to get into an opponent's head and rattle them. They also claim that it's a way to continually psych themselves up during the game. While trash talking was a technique that I despised when I played sports, most of my sports ethics students have indicated that they like trash talking and that it's just part of the game that psyches them up to play harder.

Some athletes use trash talking from opponents as inspiration to play harder. Others just laugh it off as meaningless.

Nowadays, many athletes don't just do their trash talking on the field or the court, as they use social media to taunt opponents.

Refusing to Shake Hands

One of the great traditions of sports is how players shake hands and hug each other after games. After each playoff series, NHL players line up and shake hands. However, a gray area of sportsmanship arises when players refuse to shake hands with the other team after a hotly contested game.

The Detroit Pistons disregarded this tradition when they refused to shake hands with the Chicago Bulls after losing a series in 1991. The Bulls had swept the Pistons 4–0, eliminating the two-time defending champions by crushing them 115–94 in Game 4. Pistons star guard Isiah Thomas and several other Pistons walked off the court after the game without acknowledging the Bulls. Years later, Thomas expressed his regret about the incident to NBA TV, as noted by *Sports Illustrated*, stating that they did it because the Bulls had criticized the "Bad Boys" Pistons during the series, but he said that the team should have taken the high road.[52]

LeBron James was criticized when he failed to shake hands and stormed off the court when his Cleveland Cavaliers were eliminated from the NBA Playoffs by the Orlando Magic in 2009. James told the media that it didn't make sense for him to shake an opponent's hand and congratulate them after losing because he was a winner and a competitor. Noting the stain on Isiah Thomas's legacy for his handshake incident, Michael Wilbon criticized LeBron James in the *Washington Post*: "I'm hoping that Magic Johnson or Charles Barkley or Michael Jordan or Larry Bird, any one of the iconic players LeBron looks up to, will call him over the next week and very privately say: 'You can't do that again. There's no excuse. You lose, you shake hands, you own up, you do it graciously. And if you don't want to handle it that way, there's one way to avoid it: Don't lose.'"[53]

Unsportsmanlike Conduct in Football

Thus far, we've examined the gray area and debatable issues of sportsmanship. Now, let's look at some behaviors by teams and individual athletes that clearly go beyond the bounds of sportsmanship and hurt the reputation of themselves, their teams, and the sport.

The New England Patriots were involved in two of the most publicized controversies in NFL history. The first was Spygate, which involved the Patriots videotaping opponents' defensive signals. According to a Business Insider summary of an

ESPN *Outside the Lines* report, the Patriots sent scouts, posing as undercover media members, to film play signals of future opponents at their games. Some other techniques used by the Patriots: "Sending low-level Patriots employees to sneak into the visiting locker room during pregame warm-ups and steal the play sheet.... Sending employees through the visiting team's hotel to try to swipe playbooks and scouting reports ... 'Scrambling and jamming' opponent radio headsets to interfere with opponent communication."[54]

Several years later, the Patriots were involved in another scandal—Deflategate. That controversy took place when the Patriots allegedly deliberately underinflated footballs for use in their 45–7 playoff win against the Indianapolis Colts in 2015. The game officials replaced the 12 balls with replacement ones before the second half. After an investigation, the NFL suspended quarterback Tom Brady for four games; it also fined the Patriots $1 million and took away two future draft picks.[55]

Justice was served a few years later, when the Philadelphia Eagles beat the Patriots in the 2018 Super Bowl. (I'm an Eagles fan, so I had to get that in there.)

In 2010, there was a less publicized scandal in which the NFL fined the Denver Broncos and its coach, Josh McDaniels, $50,000 for failing to report the actions of Steve Scarnecchia, the Broncos' director of video operations, who videotaped part of a San Francisco 49ers walkthrough practice before the teams' 2009 game in London.[56]

Another clear and unambiguous unsportsmanlike act takes place when football players and coaches put bounties for intentional cheap shots against opposing teams' players. Bountygate was a scandal involving the New Orleans Saints in which there was an accusation of paying bonuses to Saints players who deliberately injured players on the opposing team through hard hits. The bounty policy existed from 2009 to 2011 and involved between 22 and 27 Saints players. The NFL found that the players and Saints defensive coordinator Gregg Williams had pooled their money to pay out the bounties, and that Saints head coach Sean Payton failed to shut the bounty system down. The league imposed a $500,000 fine on the team; took away draft picks; and suspended Williams, Payton, and two others.[57]

Williams apologized for the incident but later told Mike Claiborne of KMOX radio in St. Louis, according to CBSSports.com, "One of the things was it was on my watch, but there was nothing that hasn't been done in the last 50 years in the sport and there was nothing done to try to hurt somebody."[58]

Another highly publicized bounty incident took place with the Philadelphia Eagles during the so-called "Bounty Bowl." After the Eagles defeated the Dallas Cowboys, head coach Jimmy Johnson alleged that Eagles coach Buddy Ryan had put bounties of $500 on Cowboys quarterback Troy Aikman and $200 on kicker Luis Zendejas. Eagles linebacker Jessie Small leveled Zendejas during a second half kickoff, resulting in a wobbly Zendejas. "It's stupid to have a coach like that in the N.F.L., the fat little guy," Zendajas said after the game about Ryan. "He can't take you out himself so he pays somebody else to do it for him."[59]

Another famous incident of football unsportsmanlike conduct took place during a Thanksgiving Day game in 2012 when Detroit Lions nose tackle Ndamukong Suh stomped the Green Bay Packers' Evan Dietrich-Smith and was suspended for two games.[60]

Unsportsmanlike Conduct in Baseball

Baseball has had its share of controversy regarding sportsmanship over the years.

One of the most recent and most serious scandals took place when it was revealed that the Houston Astros had engaged in an extensive sign stealing operation during the 2017 and 2018 seasons. In executing their elaborate electronic sign stealing scheme, the Astros used a center field camera to steal signs, which were relayed by team staff members to the batter by hitting a garbage can. Despite their actions, Major League Baseball chose not to strip the Astros of their 2017 World Series title. MLB did impose a $5 million fine on the Astros and stripped the team of first- and second-round draft picks in 2020 and 2021. The league also suspended Astros Manager A.J. Hinch and GM Jeff Luhnow for one year before the team fired both of them. None of the Astros players were punished.[61] It said a lot that many Little League and youth baseball teams across the country stopped using the Astros nickname after news of the scandal broke.[62]

Mike Trout, star outfielder for the Los Angeles Angels, told ESPN in 2020, "It's sad for baseball. It's tough. They cheated. I don't agree with the punishments, the players not getting anything. It was a player-driven thing. … I lost some respect for some guys."[63]

In retaliation for the Astros' behavior, during the 2020 spring training season, opposing teams' pitchers threw beanballs at Astros players on several occasions.

George Brett was a Hall of Fame baseball player, but one of the things that he will be remembered for is the pine tar incident in a game against the New York Yankees at Yankee Stadium in 1983. Brett hit a home run to put the Royals up 5–4 in the ninth inning. However, the home plate umpire ruled that Brett used too much pine tar and called him out, resulting in Brett furiously charging out of the dugout to argue. American League president Larry MacPhail upheld the Royals' appeal of the ruling, determining that the home run should count and that the end of the game should be replayed.[64]

Brett's pine tar incident was the most famous one, but there are others. Yankees pitcher Michael Pineda was suspended for 10 days in 2014 for using pine tar on his neck in violation of Major League Baseball rules prohibiting pitchers from using foreign substances.[65]

Other incidents involving pine tar or other foreign substances involved Will Smith, Brian Matusz, and Joel Peralta.[66]

Noted Hall of Fame pitcher and spitball user Gaylord Perry, who used other foreign substances such as Vaseline, told Bill Madden of the *New York Daily News*, "Of course pine tar is a performance-enhancing substance," Perry said. "Why do you think so many pitchers are using it? It absolutely helps your sinkers to sink better and breaking pitches to break better."[67]

Michael Trueblood argued in his FoxSports.com article, "Pitchers don't need pine tar and sunscreen on the ball in order to pitch well, and if they do, they don't deserve to pitch well. We need a stronger enforcement system for the rules in place to stop them from using those substances, not a way around the rules that everyone can simply feel better about."[68]

In light of these sticky situations, in 2021, Major League Baseball instituted new rules cracking down on pitchers using foreign substances. If umpires find a foreign substance on a pitcher during a game, the pitcher gets ejected and also suspended for 10 games with pay.[69]

How about a pitcher using beanballs to intimidate a batter through inside pitches? Adam Felder advocated in his article in *The Atlantic* that Major League Baseball needed to get tougher on pitchers when it comes to beanballs. "For MLB not to crack down on pitchers intentionally throwing at batters is a profound oversight on its part at best, and a tacit endorsement of assault at worst. One can only hope the sport takes action before Ray Chapman's unfortunate status as the answer to a trivia question goes to another unlucky player."[70]

Unsportsmanlike Conduct in Other Sports

In addition to team sports, there are sportsmanship issues in individual sports. Boxing is a brutal, intense, and physical sport. However, there are rules and norms that boxers are expected to follow, such as the Marquess of Queensberry rules. Boxers are not expected to use low blows or head butts, and they can be penalized for doing so. One of the most notorious unsportsmanlike incidents in boxing history took place during the 1997 heavyweight championship bout between Mike Tyson and Evander Holyfield, when Tyson inexplicably bit off part of Holyfield's ear. Andrew Golota was disqualified for using several low blows in both of his 1996 fights against Riddick Bowe.[71]

Even the pristine and cultured sport of figure skating had an infamous occurrence of poor sportsmanship. "Whyyy? Whyyy?" That was the cry heard around the world after one of the most unsportsmanlike incidents in the history of sports took place. The Nancy Kerrigan–Tonya Harding incident shocked both sports fans and the general public. Kerrigan and Harding were the top American figure skaters preparing for the 1994 Winter Olympics in Norway. At the 1992 Olympics, Kerrigan received the bronze medal, while Harding finished fourth. While Kerrigan was practicing for the 1994 US Championships at a Detroit ice rink, Shane Stant attacked her by clubbing her in the knee. Stant had been hired by a man who had been contacted by Harding's former husband, Jeff Gillooly, to carry out the attack in order to eliminate Kerrigan from the competition.[72]

Fortunately, Kerrigan recovered in time to compete in the 1994 Olympics, where she won a silver medal. Harding came in eighth.

Harding pleaded guilty to conspiracy to hinder the prosecution of Kerrigan's attackers, was fined, and received three years' probation with community service. She was banned from the US Figure Skating Association for life and her 1994 US national championship was revoked.[73] Years later, Harding admitted to ABC that she had heard discussions regarding the pending attack of a competitor at the national championships so that she could make the Olympic team.[74] She also told ESPN that Kerrigan "was the cry baby who didn't win the gold. I'm sorry, I've never said this before but just shut up."[75]

When the movie *I, Tonya* was released, Kerrigan told the *Boston Globe* that "it's not really part of my life. As you say, I was the victim. Like, that's my role in this whole thing. That's it. It is weird, that's for sure. A bizarre thing."[76]

It's unfortunate that decades after this incident, some people view Harding as a sympathetic character and victim while viewing Kerrigan negatively. For instance, the headline to David Edelstein's *New York Magazine*'s *Vulture* article read, "*I, Tonya* Turns Tonya Harding from a Punch Line Into a Sympathetic Character."[77]

Another clear rule of sportsmanship ethics in another individual sport is that a runner should not pretend to have won a race that they didn't run.

In 1980, Rosie Ruiz took a shortcut to win the Boston Marathon. A few days after the race, witnesses who were spectators at the race came forward to report that Ruiz had run onto the course from the sidelines only a mile from the finish line. Boston police officers went to help her at the finish line when she pretended to be exhausted. She had taken a similar strategy in the New York Marathon by taking the subway instead of running most of the course.[78]

In 2015, Kendall Schler pulled a similar move, appearing to have won the St. Louis Marathon, but she had not run the entire race, sneaking onto the course after the final checkpoint.[79]

After Gregory Price, a 61-year-old runner, was caught cheating in a Marine Corps Marathon, he naturally caught a lot of criticism. Jim Hage, a two-time Marine Corps Marathon winner and member of the race's Hall of Fame, told the *Washington Post*, "A lot of running is about integrity and being yourself. The cliché is that there are no shortcuts to a marathon, and to have someone manufacture a shortcut is surprising…. I suppose non-runners might think it's sort of funny and a quirky thing. Runners might take more offense because we understand more what the sport's about, and it ain't about shortcuts."[80]

Sportsmanship has different meanings to different people. Most people would agree that players shouldn't intentionally injure other players via tripping in basketball, bounties in football, low blows and biting in boxing, or throwing beanballs at a batter's head. Other things such as tanking, running up the score, mercy rules, and trash talking are up for debate. Sure, winning is extremely important. Athletes at every competitive level give it their all and have a passion to win. But it's a hollow victory if you cheat to win. Sportsmanship needs to be taught and instilled at the youth sports level. Teach kids to play to win and to be competitive, but to do it within the rules. Pro athletes at the highest level need to set an example for kids as well. Winning is important, but so is playing the game the right way.

CHAPTER 3

Gambling

CONTROVERSIES INVOLVING GAMBLING have plagued collegiate and professional sports for generations. Shoeless Joe Jackson and the 1919 World Series, the college basketball point-shaving scandals of the early 1950s, Pete Rose betting on baseball in the 1980s, NBA referee Tim Donaghy feeding insider information to gamblers in the 2000s—what did it all do to the quality and business of sports? And with the 2018 Supreme Court decision ending the federal ban on states hosting sports betting, there is a brave new world of gambling taking shape. The explosion of gambling has led to many people suffering from gambling disorders, including college students. This chapter explores the forms, effects, and evolution of gambling in sports.

For decades, if people wanted to bet legally on sporting events, they needed to travel to Las Vegas to do so. In 2018, the United States Supreme Court ruled in *Murphy v. National Collegiate Athletic Association* that states could host legalized sports gambling.[1] Some states that adopted sports betting have required that such betting take place at casinos or racetracks. Other states are considering allowing legalized mobile phone bets.

In analyzing the impact of the court's decision in Murphy, Matthew Dziok noted in his *Western New England Law Review* article that after the Murphy decision, 26 states and the District of Columbia enacted laws legalizing sports betting as of May 2022.

Dziok argued that legalizing and regulating sports betting is better than the alternative of having people place illegal bets: "State-regulated sportsbooks provide a more effective way to monitor betting lines and are more likely to alert law enforcement authorities to suspicious betting trends. Conversely, because illegal operators are unlikely to divulge information about their books, regulatory officials are less likely to identify trends that would indicate potential match-fixing or point-shaving schemes."

In rejecting the views of some people who would like to see bans on betting on college sports, Dziok noted that many of the gambling scandals in college sports took place when there were no legal options for sports gambling. He wrote, "While protecting the integrity of college sports is a legitimate concern for college officials, completely banning college sports gambling fails to recognize that the integrity of college sports is also threatened, perhaps more severely, if the illegal sports gambling market continues."[2]

There are many pros and cons to sports gambling. It is an exciting type of entertainment. It gives some people a reason to watch the games. It can also be a socializing bond between friends, such as playing poker or getting together to draft their fantasy football teams. Some people go to a casino once a month with friends and family to gamble and have a nice dinner. Some people pay more attention to their fantasy football teams than the actual games themselves. It is also a way to show off your sports knowledge and to profit off it. Serious bettors follow trends and analytics and watch games and teams on a regular basis, which arguably makes their bets more informed and educated. People can gamble safely and responsibly as long as they know their limits. From an economic standpoint, legalized sports gambling can help states' economies. Furthermore, other types of legalized gambling are allowed, such as lotteries and casinos, so why not add sports gambling?

It can be argued that gambling on sports is more fun than pure games of chance such as a roulette wheel or a slot machine because the bettor is using their knowledge of sports to place bets. This could be reflected by picks in an NCAA March Madness pool or fantasy football teams, where the bettor gets to simulate an NFL general manager by drafting players for their own team. Many people take a lot of time to study trends and statistics of players' past performances when selecting their fantasy teams every season. Nowadays, people can not only bet on the results of entire games, but they can place bets on individual plays during a game, such as whether a kicker will make a field goal. Online sports betting websites such as DraftKings and FanDuel have made sports betting even more accessible and popular. Sports gambling commercials flood television airwaves on a regular basis.

A major trend in gambling in recent years has been the rise of fantasy sports, particularly fantasy football. In an email interview, Walter Cherepinsky, creator and operator of the popular sports website WalterFootball.com, said, "Fantasy football has normalized gambling. Prior to the emergence of fantasy football, gambling was taboo. None of the major networks talked about it, and if you wanted to place a wager, you'd have to go through a shady guy sitting in the back corner of a pizza parlor, or register online with a shady company located on some island in the Caribbean. Fantasy football's growth gave birth to daily fantasy Web sites, namely DraftKings and FanDuel, where you could innocently wager money on how players would perform. If this was OK, surely betting sides in sports would be fine. Now, DraftKings and FanDuel both have their own sportsbooks, and all of the major networks discuss the gambling to a degree. ESPN and CBS even have the point spreads next to teams on their ticker. This would've been unheard of 15 years ago."

Cherepinsky also said that gambling leads to more interest in watching games. "If you gamble on a team, you're more likely to watch them. Years ago, football fans would just tune in to watch their favorite team, and perhaps stick around for the nationally televised game later that night. Now, those who have invested their money into several teams on a football Sunday are more likely to either stream those individual games, watch NFL Red Zone, or follow closely online."[3]

The negative aspect of gambling is that it can be an addiction, resulting in personal bankruptcy and strained personal relationships. Gambling addictions can lead to marital strife, divorce, and the breakup of families. Gambling often affects lower-income people who see it as a way to break from poverty. Many people don't know their limits. Others are concerned about point-shaving scandals, especially at the college level where the players are not paid.

There have been many gambling scandals over the history of college and professional sports that tainted the reputation of a sport.

One of the most famous gambling scandals almost ruined professional baseball. In what is commonly known as the Black Sox Scandal, several members of the 1919 Chicago White Sox took bribes to throw games in the World Series against the Cincinnati Reds, leading to the Reds winning the best-of-nine series 5–3 (Major League Baseball briefly experimented with a best-of-nine format before permanently going back to the best-of-seven series). Even though star Chicago outfielder Shoeless Joe Jackson hit .375 during the series, committed no errors, and had six RBIs, he was implicated in the scandal. In 1920, an Illinois grand jury indicted eight members of the 1919 White Sox. Even though the players were acquitted by a jury on criminal charges that they had conspired to defraud the public by throwing the series, baseball commissioner Kenesaw Mountain Landis banned the White Sox players, including Jackson, for life.[4]

In a 1941 interview, Jackson said it wasn't so. He told *Washington Post* columnist Shirley Povich, "I know what you're going to ask me. It's what they all ask me when they get their nerve up. Well, Sonny, I'm as innocent as you are. I had no part in that fix in 1919."[5]

Decades after the incident, many people have asserted that Jackson should be eligible for the Baseball Hall of Fame. To this day, he remains ineligible despite his .356 lifetime batting average. The late 1980s movies *Eight Men Out* and *Field of Dreams* helped to spur public interest in Jackson and portrayed him in a sympathetic light.

Ted Williams and Bob Feller petitioned MLB commissioner Bud Selig in 1998 to allow Jackson to be eligible for the Hall of Fame. According to the *Sporting News*, Williams said, "He's served his sentence and it's time for baseball to acknowledge his debt is paid and the Hall of Fame Committee on Veterans to list him as a nominee. It's time and it's the right thing to do."[6]

However, Thomas Sowell argued against admitting Jackson and Pete Rose to the Hall of Fame, stating, "[T]he tangible things in major league baseball cannot exist without the intangibles of which the trust of the public is the most important. Once the public decides that it is all fake and crooked, this thriving sports empire collapses like a house of cards. Ballplayers who deal with professional gamblers jeopardize the whole game of baseball."[7]

In 2015, MLB commissioner Rob Manfred denied Jackson's case for reinstatement into the league, thus prohibiting his consideration for the Hall of Fame.[8]

According to MLB rules, "Any player, umpire, or club or league official or employee, who shall bet any sum whatsoever upon any baseball game in connection with which the bettor has a duty to perform shall be declared permanently ineligible."[9]

Despite these rules, I believe that, in light of Jackson's outstanding performance in the 1919 World Series and the inconsistent evidence against him, he should be eligible for Hall of Fame voting. Just like the steroid-era players, let the Hall of Fame voters decide regarding Jackson.

Another famous baseball-related gambling case involving an MLB legend took place in the 1980s. In 1989, MLB commissioner A. Bartlett Giamatti banned Pete Rose from baseball for life for gambling on MLB games while he was player-manager of the Cincinnati Reds. Rose denied the charges for several years, but in his 2004 autobiography he admitted to betting on baseball while managing the Reds. He claimed that he always bet on the Reds to win and never bet against his own team. In 2015, MLB commissioner Rob Manfred denied Rose's request for reinstatement.[10]

Like with Shoeless Joe Jackson, there is an ongoing debate as to whether Pete Rose should be eligible for the Baseball Hall of Fame. Eric Macramalla argued in *Forbes* in 2015 that Rose should never be admitted to the Hall of Fame, rejecting the view that Rose had already paid the heavy price of a 25-year ban. He wrote, "[I]n the face of MLB's indisputable need to have a highly effective deterrent in place to try and avoid the irreparable harm inflicted on the game as a result of gambling, it becomes very difficult to make an exception for Rose."[11]

However, as Stephen D. Mosher wrote in *Sociology of Sport Journal*, "The American public clearly is willing to grant Rose his wish. Public sentiment is overwhelmingly in favor of Rose being allowed into the Hall of Fame because of his baseball achievements." Mosher quoted Mark Harris, who wrote in the *New York Times*, "Fame and virtue are different things. I find it odd and unrealistic to hear to hear the commissioner of baseball demand of Pete Rose that he be the unblemished hero history has not recorded since the legend of Caesar's wife."[12]

I believe Rose should be eligible for election to the Baseball Hall of Fame in Cooperstown. Unlike the cases of players who used steroids, the on-the-field accomplishments of Rose were not affected by gambling. The 17-time All-Star remains baseball's all-time hit king with 4,256 career hits. It should be up to the Hall of Fame voters to determine whether his on-field accomplishments outweigh his gambling issues. Admittedly, as a Philadelphia sports fan, I have a partiality for Rose, who, along with other star players such as Mike Schmidt and Steve Carlton, led the Phillies to their first World Series championship in 1980.

Arguably, there is some precedent in allowing Rose into the Hall of Fame. Leo Durocher won World Series titles as a player for the New York Yankees and St. Louis Cardinals and as a manager for the New York Giants. He's famous for the quote "Nice guys finish last." In 1947, MLB commissioner Albert "Happy" Chandler suspended Durocher for a year for conduct detrimental to baseball by allegedly

Should Shoeless Joe Jackson, shown here as a player for the Cleveland Indians in 1913, be eligible for Hall of Fame voting? He was implicated in the 1919 Black Sox scandal, in which eight Chicago White Sox players, including Jackson, allegedly accepted money from gamblers to lose the World Series on purpose. However, Jackson had a great World Series, batting .375 with 12 hits and committing no fielding errors, and he has many supporters claiming that he should be admitted to the Hall of Fame in light of his .356 lifetime batting average, the third highest in Major League Baseball history (photo from Harris & Ewing Collection, Prints & Photographs Division, Library of Congress, LC-DIG-hec-02792 [digital file from original negative]).

associating with gamblers and other activities. Despite this gambling-related suspension, Durocher was voted into the Baseball Hall of Fame in 1994.[13]

Pro football has had a few gambling-related player suspensions. Star NFL players Paul Hornung and Alex Karras were suspended from playing in the entire 1963 season by NFL commissioner Pete Rozelle for betting on NFL games and associating with gamblers.[14]

In 2019, after Arizona Cardinals defensive back Josh Shaw bet on three NFL games for a few thousand dollars in a Las Vegas casino while he was sidelined with an injury, the NFL suspended him for the 2020 NFL season. In 2022, the NFL suspended wide receiver Calvin Ridley of the Atlanta Falcons for the entire 2022 season for betting on NFL games in 2021.[15]

Despite the historic concerns of professional sports leagues regarding gambling, major league pro sports have recently embraced the connection to gambling. For instance, in 2018, Major League Baseball entered into a sports betting agreement with MGM Resorts International, calling MGM its official gaming partner and giving MGM the right to use the MLB brand in its betting offerings in the United States.[16] Other pro sports leagues, including the NBA and NHL, have similar deals. Starting with the Denver Broncos in 2020, several NFL teams have entered into sports betting and fantasy sports partnerships.[17]

There have been numerous gambling scandals involving college sports. In general, college players are more susceptible to the temptation to accept money for point shaving since they are not receiving multimillion-dollar contracts like pro athletes.

One of the most famous incidents took place in 1951, when the New York district attorney indicted players from the City College of New York, Manhattan College, New York University, and Long Island University for point shaving during regular-season games dating back to 1947. Eventually, 32 players from seven colleges were arrested for fixing 86 games between 1947 and 1950. Seven CCNY players were arrested and charged with conspiring to fix games. At the time, CCNY was a national power that had won both the NCAA and NIT championships in 1950. However, the invention of the point spread in the late 1940s led to gamblers targeting college players. The scandal forced CCNY to drop to Division III.[18]

As noted by Dave Zirin in the *Los Angeles Times*, *New York Post* columnist and CCNY grad Maury Allen wrote, "That was the last time I really believed in pure idealism. For these guys to sell out their school and themselves and their careers for $800, for $1,000, for $1,500 was just such an emotional blow. It is a wound in your psyche that lasts all your life."[19]

Some University of Kentucky basketball players were also implicated in the gambling scheme, resulting in the NCAA suspending the Kentucky program for the 1952–1953 season via a basketball schedule boycott.[20]

In 1979, three Boston College basketball players were suspected of fixing nine regular-season games, resulting in one of the players, Rick Kuhn, serving prison time. Another player was acquitted and found not guilty, and the other was not criminally charged. The plan was to pay $2,500 for each game Boston College failed to cover the spread.[21] In 1996, 13 Boston College football players were suspended for betting on sporting events in violation of NCAA rules, with two of those players being dismissed from the team for allegedly betting against their own team in a blowout loss to Syracuse.[22]

In 1999, former Arizona State star basketball player Stevin "Hedake" Smith pleaded guilty to conspiracy to commit sports bribery and was sentenced to prison for shaving points during the 1993–1994 season. Smith fixed four games to erase a $10,000 gambling debt.[23] In 1998, two Northwestern basketball players were charged with fixing three games during the 1994–1995 season. Both players were sentenced to short prison time of one month each.[24] A point-shaving scandal involving five Tulane basketball players in 1985 forced the school to temporarily suspend its basketball program for three seasons.[25]

Will the rise of legalized gambling in the 2010s lead to the next big point-shaving scandal in college football or college basketball? Former Maryland congressman and University of Maryland basketball star Tom McMillen told the *Baltimore Sun* in 2019, "There is a 100 percent chance that there will be a major gambling scandal at an institution of higher education in the United States in the future. These kids are in a very vulnerable spot. You have one major scandal and it will be an enormous goodwill loss for these schools."[26]

Some states have implemented rules that ban betting on in-state college sports teams, rationalizing that such measures will protect their local student-athletes. For instance, people cannot bet on Rutgers football or basketball in New Jersey.[27]

The fact that college athletes are not paid means that they might be susceptible to gamblers and their agents reaching out to them to engage in point shaving. Many of these college athletes are from economically disadvantaged backgrounds and might accept money to help them and their family. The recent implementation of the cost-of-attendance stipends might help avoid this, since it provides some amount of funds to athletes for living expenses. In addition, new rules allowing college athletes to make money off their name, image, and likeness or get money from personal appearances or social media marketing could lessen the risk of athletes being susceptible to attempts to get them to engage in point shaving. Still, the temptation of accepting much larger amounts of money from gamblers to shave points would still be tempting. The pitch that gamblers make to players is that their team would still win the game, but that their team wouldn't beat the point spread. Due to the high salaries in major league professional sports, most pro athletes would not be susceptible to point-shaving offers, but college athletes might be more approachable.

Another group of sports-related people who could be susceptible to bribes are referees and officials. Fans will often yell at refs after a bad call, either urging them to go back to Foot Locker or alleging that they're being paid off. Unlike pro athletes who make multimillion-dollar contracts, referees and officials at the pro and college level do not make astronomical salaries. Referees have a great impact on the flow of a game, including their calls on penalties and fouls. If a referee calls two quick fouls against a star player early in a game, especially at the college level where five fouls in a game leads to disqualification of the player, it can affect the entire game, as the coach is likely to sit that star player for the rest of the first half. While some things are reviewable via video replay, such as goaltending or who hit the ball out of bounds, things like most fouls in basketball and holding in football are not reviewable. One of the most famous incidents of tampering with officials took place in the NBA when Tim Donaghy, a referee with 13 years' experience, was implicated in a scheme to fix NBA games. It was alleged that he placed bets on NBA games and gave gambling associates sensitive information as to which officiating crews would officiate games and how officials and players interacted. In 2007, he pleaded guilty to felony charges of conspiracy to engage in wire fraud and transmitting betting information through interstate commerce. An ESPN detailed investigation revealed the details of how Donaghy conspired to fix NBA games.[28]

Donaghy told Ashley Branca of *The Guardian*, "Any time that you have a sporting event with a Vegas line to it, there's always going to be somebody involved in organized crime trying to make a dollar off of it. So I think that they constantly are trying to get to that referee, to get to a player, to get to somebody, a trainer, or a coach who can give them inside information to where they can take advantage of it. So, I think it's always going to be there, and it is there."[29]

Should gambling on college sports be prohibited? A US Senate bill in 2000 that tried to do this never gained steam.[30] In theory, it's a good idea, but it's unlikely to ever happen due to the popularity of college sports.

NCAA rules prohibit NCAA athletes at all levels from participating in sports gambling. However, studies show that many athletes gamble. According to NCAA.org, a 2012 study commissioned by the NCAA showed that 57 percent of male student-athletes and 39 percent of female student-athletes had gambled during the past year.[31] Most college students are able to gamble responsibly and know their limits, but some might not. A 2010 University of Oregon study found that 34 percent of students who responded to a university-wide survey had placed bets from $10 to $100 on a single day, 10 percent of the students who responded had placed bets from $100 to $1,000 on a single day, and 1 percent had wagered over $1,000 on a single day.[32]

The National Council on Problem Gambling has established a Risk Education for Athletes Program, which seeks to educate athletes of all ages, but young people in particular, about the personal and professional risks of gambling.[33]

Gambling, especially sports gambling, has arisen as a serious problem for many other college students who are not athletes. While most universities have policies and education regarding alcohol and illegal drug use, only 22 percent of universities have formal policies on gambling addiction and 6 percent of university students have serious gambling problems, according to the National Center for Responsible Gaming.[34] In the past, most college gambling would consist of poker games and football pools. Now, many students go to online gambling extensively. In addition, fantasy sports among high school and college students have become immensely popular.

Holy Cross economics professor Victor Matheson told *The State News* in 2020 that over 75 percent of college students had gambled during the past year, and that sports gambling was particularly popular. According to Matheson, 6 percent of college students have a severe gambling disorder. Matheson indicated that confidence and the illusion of control puts young men at risk for a gambling problem, saying, "When you are a young college male, you think you are smarter than everyone else in the world. The combination of people that watch a lot of sports and people that think they're smart leads to a situation where you're thinking you are smarter than the house."[35]

Gambling is fun and exciting for many people, whether it be the lottery, casinos, fantasy football, NCAA March Madness pools, or horse racing. People spend hours inside a casino hoping to hit a jackpot in slots or a large winning hand in poker. People line up for hours when a lottery jackpot exceeds $100 million, knowing that the odds of winning are slim, but it provides a few hours or days of optimistic fantasizing as to what they would do with the money. Television and radio programs are flooded with ads promoting the lottery. Gambling has been normalized as a regular and accepted part of society. When sports commentators and analysts give their pregame predictions, they will often predict the outright winner of the game, the winner against the point spread, and whether to take the over/under for total points scored in the game. Even though there was no money involved, President Barack Obama would go on television and make his annual picks for the men's and women's NCAA Tournament brackets. Every March many people who don't even follow college basketball and haven't watched a game all year will make their bracket selections, sometimes picking teams based on mascots, team names, team jersey colors, or that their second cousin Jimmy went to Gonzaga. Some companies and organizations offer $1 million or other substantial prizes to anyone who picks all of the men's basketball NCAA Tournament games correctly. (As of 2022, no one has picked a verified perfect bracket.) I've watched many Philadelphia Eagles games with friends where some of them were much more focused on how the players in their fantasy teams were doing instead of how the Eagles were doing.

However, excessive gambling can turn into a disease or an addiction. The Mayo Clinic, for example, lists compulsive gambling, otherwise known as gambling disorder, as a disease.[36] Compulsive gambling can lead to extensive debt, bankruptcy, home foreclosure, divorce, alienation from family and friends, depression, and suicide. Art Schlichter is an example of how compulsive gambling can harm someone's life. Schlichter was a star quarterback at Ohio State and then had a pro career with the Indianapolis Colts. However, he developed a gambling addiction that led to multiple arrests and prison sentences for forgery, theft, and a million-dollar sports ticket scam. In 2009, he co-wrote the book (as told to sportswriter Jeff Snook) *Busted: The Rise and Fall of Art Schlichter* about his life of addiction and spoke out against casinos and gambling.[37]

Mike Robinson, psychology professor at Wesleyan University, wrote in *The Conversation* that up to 2 percent of Americans suffered from gambling disorder, stating, "It stands out as one of the few addictions that doesn't involve consumption of a substance, such as a drug. Like other forms of addiction, gambling disorder is a solitary and isolating experience. It's tied to growing anxiety, and problem gamblers are at greater risk of suicide."[38]

As to why it's a negative thing that sports gambling has become so pervasive and accepted in society, Virginia Commonwealth University associate professor in the Department of Rehabilitation Counseling Dr. Carolyn Hawley said in an email interview, "The concerns over the pervasiveness of sports gambling are not just its accessibility, but its normalization without subsequent protective safeguards in place. We know from past research that speed and ease of play may help fuel the addictive process and now we have a platform that for many, is available anywhere and all the time. Additionally, when we are inundated with constant advertising as well as teams and sports figures endorsement of these products, it normalizes its play and may reduce the perception of risk and harm involved."[39]

Regarding how easy it is for people to develop a gambling addiction, especially related to sports betting, Hawley said, "Our brains are wired for novelty, that is what makes gambling so attractive, we get bored with certainty and predictability. So this uncertainty with play, with a game's outcome, keeps us interested and excited and our brains release dopamine. These positive emotions then reinforce the behavior and can keep us gambling. And overtime our brains begin releasing dopamine just in thinking about or anticipating our gambling. This is why widespread education and awareness campaigns on gambling addiction are so important. We want to catch people early in the process before significant problems develop. So that someone who is beginning to spend more time as well as money than they had initially intended, and/or realizes that they are avoiding family, friends, and other leisure activities to gamble, may be developing a problem and needs to stop or scale back."

As to what society can do to help prevent gambling addictions, especially related to sports betting, Hawley said, "Gambling is always going to have some risk involved to it, similar to alcohol or other drugs, because we really enjoy it! So we need a widespread prevention approach that on one hand creates awareness of the risks and signs that you may be developing a problem, as well as an understanding of the disease process of addiction versus it being a moral issue, while also minimizing the dangers of play. And this is where implementing responsible gambling approaches are important such as parameters on how or if we are advertising for sports betting, slowing down the speed of play, enacting betting limits, and researching other methods and tools that operators can use to minimize harm."

Regarding how college students and young people are susceptible to sports gambling addictions, Hawley said, "There are numerous research studies that show an increased prevalence of gambling addiction in college students. We also see this for other risky behaviors such as alcohol and drug use demonstrating that this is a period of increased vulnerability to addiction. And considering how available and popular sports betting has become, we can expect as more of our college students play, more will develop problems."

While there are many federal and state government resources dedicated to fight alcoholism and substance abuse, not as much money or resources are dedicated to combating gambling addiction.

However, many resources are available for those with gambling addictions. March has been annually dedicated as Problem Gambling Awareness Month. The National Center for Responsible Gaming has published a fact sheet related to gambling disorders. Other national resources include the National Problem Gambling Helpline, Gamblers Anonymous, Gam-Anon, and the National Council on Problem Gambling. Most states also have resources and programs that are dedicated to gambling recovery services.

One of the most outspoken experts on the topic of gambling addiction is Arnie

Wexler, a certified compulsive gambling counselor and former executive director of New Jersey's Council on Compulsive Gambling. After the US Supreme Court legalized sports gambling, Wexler told *USA Today*, "You're going to have so many people addicted to gambling in the next couple of years, it's going to be crazy. We're going to have a volcano of gambling addiction in America."[40]

Gambling can be fun and exciting, but it's important for people to bet within their means. Gambling addiction is a serious disease and can ruin lives. Gambling scandals have plagued pro and college sports for over a century, and the potential threats of other gambling scandals act as a persistent Sword of Damocles hanging over the heads of those sports. The Black Sox scandal almost ruined Major League Baseball. No one wants to see anything like that occur again. Given the high salaries of pro athletes, it seems unlikely that a point-shaving scandal would occur with pro players. However, college players and referees at the college and pro level could theoretically be targeted to shave points. Sports gambling can be fun, and you can potentially profit off your sports knowledge, but it's important to know your limits. Gambling can become a serious addiction and lead to many financial problems. Young people in particular are at risk for gambling addictions and need to be careful.

Chapter 4

Media Coverage

Frequent debates take place as to how members of the media cover sports teams and athletes. While professional athletes are fair game as to criticism, to what extent should members of the media criticize athletes at the youth sports, high school, and Division I levels, particularly those who play at high-profile power conference programs? Another dilemma that sports reporters face is the extent that they should report on athletes' private lives. Another element of sports media is whether women's sports and nonrevenue sports like lacrosse and field hockey get sufficient media coverage. And female sportscasters have faced significant obstacles over the years, including the fight to get equal access to interview players in locker rooms and the struggle to gain respect and credibility. In recent years, the rise of social media in sports reporting has affected the profession. There is also the issue of bias and objectivity of sports announcers at the local and national level. Also, there have been times when athletes and coaches have lashed out at the media. The role and popularity of sports talk radio has increased significantly over the last few years, and hosts have to balance being entertaining and provocative with not crossing the line and deciding whether to discuss political and social issues. This chapter addresses the role of the media in covering sports and the ethical dilemmas that sports reporters face.

To what extent should the media criticize high school and college athletes? It would be rare for the local media to criticize high school athletes. A local paper is unlikely to say, "Bench the high school's quarterback; he's a bum." In contrast, criticism of professional athletes is fair game due to their huge salaries and high-profile celebrity status. Media outlets and sports talk radio frequently ridicule pro athletes who aren't performing well and will often mock them or question their heart, toughness, and motivation, and might give them derogatory nicknames, such as calling a defensive back "toast" for being burnt frequently on deep passes. College athletes probably are somewhere in between. Should the media avoid criticizing Division III athletes since they are not on scholarship? On the other hand, should big-time Division I college athletes, especially those who play in the high-revenue sports of college football and men's college basketball, be susceptible to media criticism?

High school sports get much more media coverage than they did years ago. National networks like ESPN will frequently televise individual high school football and basketball games, as well as high school basketball tournaments. There are other networks, such as the NFHS Network, that livestream high school games all over the country. People like to watch their local high school athletes, while many college fans like to watch potential recruits that their schools might be interested in. Numerous websites such as Rivals and Scout give very influential national and statewide ratings of high school football and basketball players. National signing day has become a huge media event on various sports networks like ESPN and the SEC Network. With increased exposure comes more scrutiny, but most media members realize that high school student-athletes should be treated differently from pro or college athletes when it comes to criticism.

Chris Goldberg, who covered high school sports for several years for the *Philadelphia Inquirer* and who operates PhillyLacrosse.com, which includes coverage of high school and college lacrosse, said in an email interview that the media should not criticize high school athletes. "I don't think there are any occasions—and we are talking ethically, because there are no set rules—where high school athletes should be 'criticized' or singled out on an individual basis. There are times of course when a play will be mentioned and just by describing the outcome of the play or situation a player's mistake can be noted. But there should not be any editorializing on a player mistake other than stating the facts of the play, High school athletes are on a different stage than professionals that are being paid or college athletes being given scholarship money; or even college players not receiving scholarship money."[1]

According to an article in AthleticBusiness.com, as high school sports have gotten more media attention and coverage, the athletes, coaches, administrators, and programs come under more media scrutiny. The article stated, "With recruiting violations, eligibility infractions, coaching improprieties, temperamental fans and a host of other off-the-field issues dominating high school athletics, preps reporters don't have to dig deep for fodder." Bob Goldring, director of informational services for the Ohio High School Athletic Association, told AthleticBusiness.com, "In a perfect world, I'd like to see less reporting on the negative aspects of high school sports. But I can't really blame a reporter for going with the story if an issue is out there, right in front of him. I'm more irritated by columnists who criticize officials, players and coaches than by someone reporting a scandal or something that's actually factual. That's just the nature of journalism today, and we're stuck with it."[2]

Regarding media coverage of high school athletes, Aaron Carter, sports reporter for the *Philadelphia Inquirer*, said in an email interview, "The increased media exposure of high school sports has both positive and negative implications for athletes, teams, and coaches. On the positive side, more exposure often means more opportunities for athletes to be seen by more college coaches, especially coaches from outside an athlete's immediate area of residence. Athletes are also able to create their own highlight videos or pay for highlight videos to be made so that they can send their exploits to college coaches. This likely gives high school athletes a greater sense of control during the recruiting process. In a sense, the playing field can be somewhat leveled if a player from a small school can still get exposed to college coaches. On the negative side, high school coaches often lament their athletes 'showing off' when they know a video camera is present. Coaches argue this can lead athletes to break from the team-concept, meaning athletes will be looking to make plays and 'go viral' for a highlight reel instead of playing for the team. There are also potential negative social side effects when an athlete is beaten badly or embarrassed on video, which can lead to bullying."[3]

To what extent should the media criticize college athletes, particularly those who play football or basketball at big-time Division I programs? Some people believe that Division I athletes are amateur athletes who don't get paid and therefore should not be criticized like the pros. In 2007, Mike Gundy, head football coach of Oklahoma State, received national internet fame when he went on a viral rant in a press conference, chewing out a reporter who had painted an unflattering portrayal of one of the players on the team. In particular, the reporter indicated that he was a coddled player, and included a scene of his mother feeding him chicken out of a boxed meal. Gundy famously yelled, "Come after me. I'm a man, I'm 40." Many people, including *New York Daily News* columnist Dick Weiss, criticized Gundy for losing his temper,[4] but as pointed out by Thayer Evans of the *New York Times*, many people praised Gundy for sticking up for his players and lambasting the media for criticizing amateur athletes who were acting the right way by going to class and being respectful to others.[5]

A less-publicized incident took place in 2015 when ESPN commentator Dan Dakich criticized Iowa basketball player Adam Woodbury for poking the eyes of multiple Wisconsin players, arguing that Woodbury's actions were gutless, intentional, and cowardly and that he should be punished for it. Iowa coach Fran McCaffery defended Woodbury and criticized Dakich, stating that Dakich was out of line for saying reprehensible things about an amateur athlete.[6]

On one hand, it can be argued that college athletes who go to big-time Power Five football and basketball schools know that they will be under a lot of scrutiny, especially in a small town or city, where the local media will give them more coverage than pro sports. They know that most of their games will be televised nationwide, and that their performances will be analyzed and dissected by cable sports network analysts and local sports columnists and sports reporters. If they get the benefits and perks of being a big-time college athlete, they should be able to handle the pressure and scrutiny that comes with it, especially during high-profile events like conference tournaments and championship games, as well as the NCAA Basketball Tournament in March. In addition, many Division I athletes will now be putting themselves out there advertising products and marketing themselves, in light of the new NCAA rules adopted in 2021 allowing college athletes to profit off their name, image, or likeness.

On the other hand, it can be argued that college athletes are amateur athletes and in most cases under age 21. They aren't pro athletes and aren't getting paid, and therefore criticism of them should be minimal.

The approach that most media outlets use is to criticize college athletes' on-the-field performance but to leave them alone when it comes to their private lives. The exceptions would be if the player is suspended, dismissed, or arrested. College players shouldn't be mocked, ridiculed, and eviscerated the way that pro athletes are.

As to whether the media should criticize college athletes, Chris Goldberg said in an email interview, "Most do feel that college scholarship players are open to individual criticism, especially at the Division I level in revenue-generating sports such as football and basketball. As you move down the ladder, to Divisions II and III and to non-revenue sports, there is a different view of criticism. Typically, only the revenue-generating teams at the Division I level are receiving the type of coverage that would even warrant criticism. Though today, newspaper coverage has been greatly reduced because of the demise of the industry and now social media posters and bloggers have made it easier for people to openly criticize athletes. I have seen a shift in how sports writers cover athletes because they are competing against the social media posters who are putting out more opinionated and partisan posts. Getting readers has become more important than ever so journalists have new factors to deal with."[7]

Regarding how the media should handle situations where there is a high school or college player involved with off-the-field controversies, Goldberg said, "I am very hesitant to report the name of a high school athlete that has gotten involved in an off-the-field incident. I will not print names unless an administrator/official signs off on that and also if the incident impacts a large group of people that would warrant posting a name. Sometimes the incident can be described without names; that's often what we do. It's different with a college athlete; names can be posted, but writers must confirm their information with authorities and sports information directors before posting anything,"

Another important social issue related to sports media coverage is the longtime struggle for women to emerge as respected sports reporters, analysts, sports talk radio hosts, and broadcasters. Women in the media have had to overcome many challenges over the years. Decades ago, they had to threaten a lawsuit to gain access to locker rooms to get postgame interviews of players. Among the early pioneers were Phyllis George and Jayne Kennedy, who were cohosts of *The NFL Today* on CBS in the 1970s and '80s. Traditionally, female reporters were assigned to be sideline or courtside reporters, making their on-air appearance minimal. The situation has improved in recent years, as more women are working as studio hosts and analysts and play-by-play and color commentators, especially in basketball. ESPN has had many female *SportsCenter* anchors, including Gayle Gardner, Linda Cohn, Suzy Kolber, Samantha Ponder, Laura Rutledge, and Hannah Storm. One notable female trailblazing announcer is Doris Burke, who frequently does play-by-play and expert color commentary on men's college and NBA games. Another is Beth Mowins, who has been calling college football games as a play-by-play announcer for ESPN since 2005. In 2017, Mowins became the first female broadcaster to do the play-by-play

Doris Burke, shown here interviewing NBA star Kyrie Irving, has become one of the top announcers covering the NBA. Burke, who received the Curt Gowdy Media Award from the Naismith Memorial Basketball Hall of Fame in 2018, has been a trailblazer for female sportscasters, acting as a play-by-play announcer, expert commentator, and sideline reporter for NBA and college games for over two decades (photo from Creative Commons. "Kyrie with Doris Burke" by SportsAngle.com is licensed under CC BY-SA 2.0).

announcing for a nationally televised NFL game, when she broadcast a *Monday Night Football* game. In 2022, Mowins did occasional play-by-play for NFL games on CBS. In 1987, Gayle Sierens had broadcast a regionally televised NFL game. In 2021, for the first time, an all-female broadcasting team broadcast a Major League Baseball game.[8] In general, most of the full-time sports talk show radio hosts across the country are men.

When I wrote a 2012 Huffington Post op-ed advocating for female play-by-play announcers in the NFL, I figured that it was only a matter of time for that glass ceiling to be shattered. However, as of 2022, there were no regular female play-by-play announcers in the NFL; Mowins was scheduled to call NFL games that season for CBS as needed.[9] I can understand why a woman wouldn't be an ideal expert color commentator for NFL games since no woman has ever played in the NFL, and expert commentators are usually former players who would have insight on what it's like to be on an NFL field or in a huddle. However, there's no reason why a woman couldn't be an effective play-by-play announcer. Most of the male play-by-play NFL announcers never played pro or college football and that doesn't affect their ability to call a game.

Beth Mowins, shown here in 2015, is another female trailblazer in sports broadcasting. She has done NCAA football play-by-play for ESPN since 2005. In 2017, she became the first woman to broadcast play-by-play for a nationally televised regular season NFL game and has broadcast many NFL games since then (photo from Creative Commons. "Groundbreaking sports broadcaster Beth Mowins '89" by Lafayette College is marked with Public Domain Mark 1.0).

Although there is a significant rise of women sports journalists, they still have an uphill climb to establish credibility. Many men still don't believe that women know about sports and women reporters are held to a higher standard. I remember hearing a sports talk show caller telling a female cohost that she didn't know anything because she was a girl. One prominent national incident that reflected this bias against female reporters took place when Carolina Panthers star quarterback Cam Newton laughed at a question from a female reporter, indicating that he found it funny for a woman to be talking about the route-running style of one of his receivers. The female reporter, Jourdan Rodrigue, said in a statement released to NFL Network Insider Ian Rapoport, "This afternoon, I did my job as an NFL beat writer and asked Cam Newton a question about one of his receivers. I was dismayed by his response, which not only belittled me but countless other women before and beside me who work in similar jobs."[10] Two days later, Newton issued a video apology, stating that his "word choice was extremely degrading and disrespectful to women."[11] Fortunately, many people called out Newton for his insensitive action, and Newton's expressions were an exception to the rule. Generally, most pro and college athletes and coaches treat female reporters with respect. They realize that female reporters are professionals who work hard and have considerable knowledge of the game.

As to whether people hold female sports reporters to a higher standard and whether women are under more scrutiny and skepticism, Leslie Gudel, a former sportscaster for ABC Sports and Comcast SportsNet in Philadelphia and the chief operating officer of Elevate Sports and Media, said in an email interview, "Yes, they're under more scrutiny and skepticism, but as far as I'm concerned, who cares. If you're good at what you do and you love it, the rewards are great and respect will be earned, not given. To me, that's more rewarding. I'm not like a lot of others who think the world should adapt to them. Go in, work hard, be the best you can be, respect the people around you and perhaps most importantly, learn how to tell people to go to hell and have them enjoy the trip. That may be the greatest advice my dad ever gave me. He never let me play the victim and always encouraged me to rise above it all by working hard and doing something I loved."[12]

As to whether people showed skepticism about her sports knowledge as a woman when she started on the air and whether that skepticism eroded over the years, Gudel said, "Yes, people showed skepticism about my sports knowledge my whole career and nothing was more gratifying than proving them wrong. My friends love to tell stories about random guys challenging my knowledge and me burying them and making them look silly. Be prepared and it will never be an issue. Be prepared for everything! Men will hit on you, who cares. Verbally sparring with someone is part of the fun. Establish boundaries … mine was, don't touch me. Nobody ever messed with me … at least not the extent I couldn't handle. If you know what you're talking about and make it clear you're not going to take any shit from anyone … in a way that isn't defensive or confrontational, but in how you carry yourself, you won't only survive in this business, you'll thrive."[13]

Female broadcasters often have to fend off sexual harassment. During a sideline interview in a preseason Jets game, an admittedly drunk Joe Namath repeatedly told ESPN's Suzy Kolber, "I wanna kiss you." Kolber acted professionally and took it in stride and Namath later apologized.[14]

After female reporter Ines Sainz was allegedly sexually harassed by New York Jets players and coaches, Jets owner Woody Johnson announced that he would fund a league-wide program to educate NFL players and teams about preventing sexual harassment.[15]

In 2009, a stalker posted nude videos online of prominent ESPN sports announcer Erin Andrews that he had taken in September 2008 through a peephole in an adjacent hotel room. Andrews sued the stalker and the hotel, and a jury awarded Andrews $55 million after a two-week trial. Andrews subsequently reached a settlement with the hotel.[16]

As reported by *Sports Illustrated*, until the late 1970s, female reporters did not have the same access to Major League Baseball players that male reporters had, therefore limiting their ability to interview players after the game. They would have to wait outside the locker rooms after the games. Most team officials, players, and male reporters were resistant to having women invade their boys' club. Some mocked female reporters, alleging that they just wanted to see naked male athletes. After 27-year-old female sportswriter Melissa Ludtke was barred from getting access to the New York Yankees locker room during the 1977 World Series, she sued Major League Baseball commissioner Bowie Kuhn in federal court to gain access to locker rooms to interview players. In defending the boys' club and questioning Ludtke, *Boston Globe* sportswriter Leigh Montville wrote, "Is she serious? Did she ever spit in a baseball glove? … Was her life absolutely dominated by sports as a kid?" During the course of the lawsuit, Kuhn argued that allowing female reporters in men's locker rooms would violate the high standards of integrity and morality of the game. Right before the 1978 World Series, federal judge Constance Baker Motley ruled in Ludtke's favor, pursuant to the 14th Amendment of the US Constitution.[17]

In describing the advances that female sports journalists have made over the last few decades, Leslie Gudel said in an email interview, "I think we've reached a point where people don't think twice when they see and/or hear a woman covering sports. That said, I think there is still a trial period for women that men don't have. Women have to earn respect. This never bothered me, because I was confident in my understanding of sports and often found this to work to my advantage, ultimately. Men would talk to me about things that they wouldn't talk about with my male counterparts. That works both ways, but it often meant that I got things out of my interviews that men wouldn't otherwise get. Also, the hardest ones to win over often became my biggest cheerleaders/supporters. Phillies 3rd base coach John Vukovich took me three years to win over after he told someone I should be home cooking a roast. Three years later, he told me he's not wrong very often but was wrong about me. A few months later, on his birthday, I cooked him a roast, potatoes, carrots and a chocolate cake, all from scratch, and served it up to him in the clubhouse after batting practice. I told him, 'For all the women you think can't cook and do their job, Happy Birthday.' We forged a wonderful friendship and he helped me secure interviews with people who otherwise wouldn't have talked to me, at that time."[18]

As to whether there is still a glass ceiling for female sports reporters, Gudel said, "I think the only glass ceiling is age…. I think a woman can get pretty much any job in sports TV now, but the question is, does she want it? Play by play is no easy task. I think *most* women get a later start at learning sports than men do. I personally believe the play by play role takes more time to develop and experience is important. The sacrifices that have to be made (moving to a small market to work for a minor league team) can create conflict for women who also want to have a family and I believe having a family is a barrier nobody talks much about when it comes to sports TV. At a certain point, I wanted to have children and once I did, I wanted to put them to bed at night and had to make a choice. I left the anchor desk and moved to a part time role covering the Phillies home games so I could put my kids to bed at night. That was a choice I made, nobody told me to or made me feel like I had to do that."[19]

Brisbane et al. analyzed the issue of gender bias against female sportscasters and noted the obstacles they faced but indicated that female sportscasters are gaining increased credibility among sports fans. They wrote, "While no evidence exists suggesting women perform worse than men as sports journalists, past studies have shown they have been subject to far more discrimination and sexism than in any other area of journalism" (Etling & Young, 2007; Schmidt, 2015; Schmidt, 2018).

However, the Brisbane study concluded that sports fans now accept women as sports journalists. It stated, "The analysis showed no significant difference between the participants' perception of the credibility and knowledge of the female sports journalist and their perception of the male sports journalist. There was also no interaction effect between the journalists' gender and type of reporting (objective versus opinion-based) when considering credibility and knowledge. Likewise, the participants' gender was not a significant predictor of either the female or male sport journalist's credibility and knowledge."[20]

Another issue that sports reporters often wrestle with is the extent that they should report on athletes' off-the-field activities. Reporters are often in a quandary when it comes to reporting on athletes' private lives. Back in the day, most reporters would turn a blind eye to athletes' off-the-field indiscretions, believing that it was their private lives. For instance, many in the media allegedly knew about Mickey Mantle's drinking problem but didn't report on it.[21]

These reporting dilemmas still exist today. Should the press reveal that an athlete is cheating on his wife, that he has a serious disease such as AIDS, that he has a drinking problem, etc.? What if a reporter sees or gets an eyewitness report that a star player was out drinking at a bar until 3 a.m. and left visibly intoxicated, even though they had a noon game that same day? For some reporters, the test is whether the athlete's indiscretion interferes with his performance on the field or his relationships with other players or coaches on the team. What if the athlete opens up about his own private life via social media or a reality television show?

Some reporters might choose to look the other way, believing that it's none of their business. Others might let the athlete know that they know about their indiscretions and will need to report on it if it affects the player's game performance. Others might just go ahead and report it. Reporters are in a tricky situation in these instances. On one hand, they are the watchdog for the public and need to report relevant information about the team and the players. On the other hand, it's important for reporters to have good relationships with players, coaches, and management, and writing a negative story about an athlete's private life might lead to that athlete and their teammates not wanting to talk to that reporter.

In 2015, the website SportsMockery.com reported that Chicago Blackhawks center Patrick Sharp was having an affair with his teammate's wife and other women. Even though the story was out there, most mainstream media outlets chose not to report about the rumor until Sharp denied the allegations to media members after a practice. *Chicago Sun-Times* columnist Rick Morrissey told the journalism website Poynter.org, "Just because you can write something doesn't mean you should. We [*The Sun-Times*] hold ourselves to a higher standard. We look at it harder than some of these websites that aren't held in the same journalistic standard."[22]

USA Today was criticized by many, including columnist Richard Cohen of the *Washington Post*, in 1992 for the way that it handled the situation of former tennis star Arthur Ashe being HIV positive from a blood transfusion, and that it in effect forced Ashe to hold a press conference announcing that he had the disease even though he wanted to keep that information private. *USA Today* had received a tip that Ashe was HIV positive, it asked him whether he had the disease, and it told him that it would continue to pursue the story. Ashe held the press conference because he believed that *USA Today* was going to print the story. In his press conference, Ashe questioned whether the media should intrude into his personal life. *USA Today* defended its actions, claiming that it was relevant for it to report on a public figure who had a fatal illness. However, many people, including Ashe, argued that this was a sensitive private matter, and that Ashe should have been allowed to keep his disease private if he wanted to. Arguably, his situation as a retired athlete was different from that of Magic Johnson, who announced in November 1991, at the beginning of the NBA season, that he had tested positive for HIV and would not play for the rest of the season and would retire from basketball.[23]

If Ashe would have wanted to go public to put a face to the disease and increase AIDS awareness, research, and funding, that should have been left up to him, not the media.

Mike Missanelli, a longtime sports talk radio host in Philadelphia at 97.5 The Fanatic and a former sports reporter for the *Philadelphia Inquirer* who now engages in sports podcasting, said in an email interview, "My rule on private lives is very simple. It's only ok to bring up private lives if it has been previously reported (and in this day and age of social media, it's pretty likely that that information is already out there), or if in your journalistic judgment or through proof sourcing, you can determine that the private life issues are negatively affecting the athlete's performance and hence cheating the fans they are playing for either financially or emotionally."[24]

In an email interview, Aaron Carter, sports reporter for the *Philadelphia Inquirer*, said regarding media coverage of athletes' private lives, "To the extent that a pro athlete's private life could affect their play, reporters must do such reporting. I would add, however, that reporters can and should use discretion when doing so. Reporters are truly the gatekeepers of information that's consumed by the public. In my opinion, the idea that a pro athlete makes a lot of money and therefore forfeits his/her privacy is a nonsensical fallacy that some fans and media members use as an excuse to delve into the salacious. An interesting question to pose of the most famous and wealthiest sports reporters would be: have they themselves made enough money or acquired enough fame to have their own private lives reported on? Who should make that decision? If an athlete's private life results in criminality, I would argue the public should be informed. A serious illness is another matter entirely. For me, that would depend on several other factors. Health information should be considered akin to personal property, in my opinion. I wouldn't rob someone of that either, regardless of whether they were a professional athlete or not."[25]

Some athletes were well known for their disdain for the media for various reasons aside from privacy issues, such as feeling that the media treated them unfairly or that they didn't like the attention and refused to do interviews.

Philadelphia Phillies Hall of Fame pitcher Steve Carlton refused to talk to the media for over a decade and earned the nickname "Silent Steve," because he felt that he had been unfairly treated by the Philadelphia press and he wanted to cut off distractions from the media.[26] Marshawn Lynch of the Seattle Seahawks was also well known for his reluctance to talk to reporters. Even though the NFL has a policy requiring its players to be available for media interviews after games and during the week after practice, Lynch frequently refused to speak to media members even though he suffered a $100,000 fine in 2014. During Super Bowl week in 2015, Lynch told the media why he didn't like to talk to reporters, stating, "I don't know what image y'all trying to portray of me. But it don't matter what y'all think, what y'all say about me because when I go home at night, the same people that I look in the face—my family that I love, that's all that really matter to me."[27]

Another aspect of being a sports reporter is the concept of bias and objectivity. There is a long-standing rule that there is no cheering in the press box, even for the home team. The goal is to have a professional working environment. At the national level, objectivity is important, as many fans often claim that certain announcers have it out against their team. One of the most famous examples of this is FOX Sports announcer Joe Buck, who has been criticized and hated by fans because of his alleged bias against their favorite teams. According to Mashable, there are many anti–Joe Buck Facebook groups and memes. In 2017, fans of the Green Bay Packers created an online petition that gathered over 25,000 signatures that insisted that Buck and his on-air partner, Troy Aikman, be banned from broadcasting Packers games because of their alleged bias against the team.[28]

In his defense, Buck has repeatedly told reporters that fans in almost every city feel that he is biased against their team. In 2012, he told the *San Francisco Chronicle/SFGate* regarding his alleged bias against the Giants, "Fans are used to hearing their hometown guys. When you come at it objectively, people aren't used to it. It gets frustrating. You want to say, 'No, I don't hate the Giants.'"[29]

The rules are more flexible when it comes to announcing a game as a broadcaster for the home team. These announcers sometimes get criticized as being "homers." Sometimes, it's comical to the extent that they root for the home team and complain relentlessly about fouls or penalties called by referees against their team. However, most viewers or listeners like it when their home team announcers get excited when the home team makes a great play or wins in dramatic finish.

Ari Bluestein is the cofounder and CEO of SFBN, which broadcasts high school and college sports, mostly in Pennsylvania and South Jersey. He is also a sportscaster for Drexel University women's basketball, Rider University sports, Pennsylvania Cable Network (PCN), ESPN3, and ESPN+. Regarding the issue of being a "homer," Bluestein said in an email interview, "As an announcer, I always cater to my audience. When I call high school state championships on the Pennsylvania Cable Network (PCN), I know the entire state of PA is watching including students, administrators and family members of both teams playing in the game. So on those broadcasts, I make sure to stay as objective as possible. On broadcasts like ESPN and NBC Sports Philadelphia, where I am technically hired by Rider and Drexel, I still try to be neutral knowing I have a fairly big local or national audience. However, when I am doing radio broadcasts for Drexel or Rider, and my audience is strictly the home team fans, I become the most homer announcer you can imagine!"[30]

Just like any other beat reporters, it's important for journalists to cultivate sources and be on a friendly basis, but not to be so friendly so that the reporter can't criticize the player, the coaches, or the team. The players, coaches, and the team have to understand that the reporters are not acting as public relations people who report only positive news and information.

Conflict-of-interest rules also apply to sports journalists and media outlets. Individual reporters get a free press pass to the game, access to the press box, and perhaps a free meal or inexpensive one in the press box area. However, it would be inappropriate for a news outlet to accept free tickets to games for reporters and employees who are not covering the game, because that could lead to an impression that the media outlet would not be able to report objectively about the team.

For the most part, the media tends to have a positive working relationship with head coaches and players. It's important to get their insight on the progress of the team. However, there have been times when that relationship has gotten contentious. Indiana University head basketball coach Bob Knight was notorious for his temper, at one point throwing a chair onto the court to protest a referee's call in a game against Purdue. In 2003, Knight launched into a tirade after an ESPN reporter asked about his relationship with his former player Steve Alford, who was now coaching the Iowa team that was playing Knight's Texas Tech team. According to the Associated Press, other incidents with the media involving Knight included when he tossed a *Basketball Weekly* journalist out of the team locker room, when he playfully fired a blank shot from a starter's pistol at a *Louisville Courier-Journal* reporter, when he barred a female Associated Press writer from the locker room, and when he was fined by the NCAA for an outburst at the NCAA Tournament postgame press conference.[31]

In 1978, former New York Yankees manager Billy Martin punched a reporter in the face. In 1993, Kansas City Royals manager Hal McRae went into an angry tirade at reporters and threw several objects, including a phone, after he was asked why he didn't use George Brett as a pinch hitter during the game. During a television interview, New Orleans Saints quarterback Jim Everett physically attacked announcer Jim Rome, after Rome questioned his toughness and called him "Chris," in a mocking reference to female tennis player Chris Evert.[32]

Another issue in sports media coverage is the extent that the media covers, or doesn't cover, women's sports and nonmajor sports. Does the media give enough coverage to women's sports and "minor" nonrevenue sports such as lacrosse, swimming, and field hockey? It's usually an economic decision that newspapers, sports talk radio, and television outlets have to make. Most have limited space or time and will decide to focus on the major sports that their audience cares about, mainly baseball, football, basketball, hockey, and college football and basketball. Regarding sports talk radio, the producers know that they are likely to lose listeners if they take calls on the WNBA, curling, or professional lacrosse. If you watch the five or so minutes of the sports coverage on your local nightly news, the announcers are likely to cover the local professional teams of the four major pro sports leagues and maybe some local major college football or basketball teams. The rare exception might be a human interest story when an athlete in a nonmajor sport has overcome substantial adversity. Some media outlets in some cities with MLS teams treat soccer as a major sport and give it significant coverage. In recent years, with the expansion of cable television sports channels, the Power Five television networks, and livestreaming, there has been a substantial increase in the coverage of both women's sports and nonrevenue sports. ESPN3 and ESPN+ are giving even greater access to these sports. During the Olympics, many women's events get just as much, if not more coverage, than the men's, including figure skating and gymnastics. In tennis, the women now get just as much coverage during the Grand Slam events as the men do. Soccer has emerged as a borderline fifth major sport, as there is extensive coverage of the men's and women's World Cup, Major League Soccer, and European soccer.

As to whether nonmajor sports like lacrosse get enough media coverage from major media outlets, Chris Goldberg, founder and operator of PhillyLacrosse.com, said, "Media outlets will cover what they can to satisfy their business pursuits so I don't think you can put rules on what they should cover. No major media outlets cover lacrosse unless their readership warrants it—such as in lacrosse hotbeds like Baltimore and Long Island. The newspapers there do cover lacrosse fairly heavily. But since lacrosse is generally a non-revenue sport, the coverage is minimal in most regions."[33]

Regarding whether women's sports get enough media coverage, Ari Bluestein said, "I have been the play-by-play announcer for Drexel women's basketball since 2009 and have also called numerous women's college sports and girls high school sports games. These are high quality athletic events that deserve more coverage from the media and these contests are extremely competitive. Even at the professional level, the WNBA does not get the publicity it deserves. I understand the NBA is going to be more popular no matter what, but the WNBA should have more television coverage and more publicity in general."[34]

Sports talk radio has become immensely popular over the last few decades. The shows tend to get very good ratings, and some cities, like Philadelphia, are able to support more than one major sports talk station. Many sports talk radio shows are also simulcasted on cable television, which increases their audience. Part of the reason for their success is their emphasis on local sports teams and athletes. "Sports is the ultimate escapism vehicle," Chris Oliviero, senior vice president of programming at CBS Radio, told the *Hollywood Reporter* in 2011. "No matter what's going on in somebody's life, they can take three hours to watch a game on Sunday and get away from all the negativity in the world. That's what sports talk does. It gives people that vehicle to just be a fan."[35]

As to why sports talk radio is so popular and influential, longtime Philadelphia sports talk radio host at Sports Radio 94 WIP Glen Macnow said in an email interview, "Sports talk radio allows fans to be in the arena even when they're sitting at home or driving in their car. The hosts are their friends and the callers are their peers. As the impact and relevance of print media declines, the hosts on sports talk radio become the columnists, the opinion makers. Just turn on my station the morning after an Eagles game. And fans want to know if other fans feel like them—do they see the QB's failures the same as I do? Why did the coach call that play? Sports talk works best when it evokes the feeling that the hosts are guys sitting around the bar over beers offering their (hopefully) informed opinions. The listeners are others in the bar, enjoying being pulled into listening to the conversation and, maybe, even offering their opinions."[36]

Sports fans have come to love sports talk radio. They like to call up the shows to get their points across and to either agree with the host or passionately disagree and argue with them. Sports talk radio has become the town square, where fans can celebrate together after a big regular-season win or championship or vent about the poor performance of the quarterback or coaching decisions. Some regular, colorful, and passionate callers of certain shows develop a certain amount of fame and recognition with that show's listeners. The comments of hosts and listeners can affect the public perception of players, coaches, general managers, and owners. An ongoing drumbeat of criticism could lead to the firing of a coach or the benching or trading of an underperforming quarterback or point guard. Many hosts are very influential in guiding these opinions. At times, the hosts get very personal when criticizing and mocking certain players, coaches, and general managers.

There have been many controversies involving sports talk radio. The hosts need to be controversial, opinionated, entertaining, and funny. Some hosts like to be confrontational and even insult their callers. Many hosts like to occasionally talk about themselves, things they do during their daily lives, their pet peeves, and their other interests outside of sports. If they're bland and boring, odds are they will get canceled due to poor ratings. Part of the process is to choose interesting topics and talking points that will stimulate calls to the show.

Regarding the balance of being edgy, provocative, controversial, and entertaining in order to get good ratings, versus being sure not to be boring or at the other end of the spectrum, crossing the line of being too insensitive, inappropriate, or controversial, longtime Philadelphia sports talk radio host Glen Macnow said in an email interview, "The bottom line is that you need to be true to yourself and your own beliefs. It's important to be entertaining, of course, but a host who gets caught in up having controversial takes is, eventually, going to lose credibility."[37]

Most sports talk shows nationally and in major cities will talk mostly about the four major professional sports—football, basketball, baseball, and hockey.

Occasionally, they will talk about major college sporting events, such as the College Football Playoff or the March Madness NCAA men's basketball championship. Sports talk radio in smaller markets, especially in college towns, might have more focus on the local university's teams.

Despite the pressure to stand out to get good ratings, sports talk hosts can't cross the line and be too offensive or insensitive in their comments. In November 2012, Dean Molberg, a Canadian sports talk show host in Calgary, was suspended when he joked that he wished that four members of a rival football team would die in a plane crash.[38] In 2013, hosts of an Atlanta sports talk show were fired when they mocked Steve Gleason, formerly of the New Orleans Saints, who was suffering with ALS.[39] In 2012, Dan Sileo lost his job at a Tampa radio station after he called Black NFL players "monkeys."[40]

Should members of the sports media transcend sports and discuss politics and social issues? Many fans want the media to just stick to sports because they see sports as an escape from the real world and the divisive nature of politics. They want sports talk hosts to focus on things like whether their favorite team has a chance to win a championship or whom their team should select in the upcoming NFL or NBA draft. However, there have been times when sports journalists have strayed into political commentary. In July 2019, ESPN's Dan Le Batard, host of *Highly Questionable* on ESPN and the *Dan Le Batard Show* on ESPN Radio, criticized President Donald Trump's political rally where Trump stood quietly for 13 seconds while the crowd chanted "Send her back" in reference to Minnesota congresswoman Ilhan Omar, a refugee from Somalia who became an American citizen. Le Batard also challenged ESPN's policy of avoiding any discussion of politics unless it intersected with sports.[41] FOX Sports' *First Things First* show host Nick Wright also condemned the "Send her back" chant as being racist, abhorrent, and dangerous on his Twitter feed.[42] In 2017, ESPN host Jemele Hill was criticized by some and praised by others when she called President Trump a white supremacist as well as an unfit, bigoted, incompetent moron on her Twitter feed, due to the president's reaction to the racial conflict in Charlottesville, Virginia. The following year, she left the network in a buyout of her contract.[43]

In an email interview, sports podcaster, former Philadelphia sports talk radio host at 97.5 The Fanatic, and former *Philadelphia Inquirer* reporter Mike Missanelli said regarding radio sports talk show hosts speaking out on political and social issues, "First of all, the sports talk host MUST have previously established a semblance of credibility to discuss political issues. (In my case, I come from a background where I was a newspaper reporter for many years who covered sports, but also general news issues. And that is a big breakthrough for me with an audience when I do branch out into these kind of non-sports discussions.) However, that kind of background isn't ESSENTIAL. If the issue is important enough, general intelligence can establish the kind of credibility it takes. In other words, if you can make logical sense in your presentation, you can be really effective. As a sports talk host, I have a simple rule that will trigger me to launch into political commentary: simply, if the political issue is more important than sports."

Missanelli added, "Now, that can mean that there is no sports issue that at the current time is that important (for example, during the pandemic, sports were completely shut down and there were, literally, no sports, to talk about; or it's between seasons and there is not really any interesting issues to talk about). The sports talk host must keep in mind that he STILL has a show to do and if he isn't talking about anything interesting, people are not going to stay with the show. But more likely, the issue is an important national public issue, and/or THE major news issue of the day or week. For example, the pandemic mayhem, stories that came from Ferguson Mo, or the George Floyd issue in Minnesota, or any of the Trump controversies as we approached the election. To ignore such issues as you do a daily TALK show, in my opinion would be cowardly and thus disingenuous to your listener. The talk show host, even, when doing sports, sometimes must be fearless and take some chances to make the show as interesting and talkable as possible, even though it can be risky."[44]

In addition to the mainstream media, there are issues and concerns regarding social media and athletes at all levels, including youth sports, high school sports, college sports, and pro sports. Social media can be a double-edged sword for many athletes who spend a significant amount of time on platforms such as Twitter, Facebook, TikTok, and Instagram. On one hand, athletes can bask in the glory of praise and adulation if they have a great game and help their team win. In contrast, if they have a bad game or transfer to another school, athletes can be subject to scorn, threats, anger, and ridicule from angry fans. Some schools and coaches have instituted rules and policies related to their athletes' use of social media. NBA All-Star Vince Carter told ESPN in an interview that it was common for NBA players to constantly be on their phones, checking their social media for fan reaction, including at halftime of games.[45]

Social media is replacing news outlets as places where news is announced. In the past, when high school senior athletes would announce where they were going to play in college, they would hold a press conference in the school gymnasium. Now, it's very common for high school athletes to announce their college destination by posting themselves in the school's uniform on Twitter. Same thing for when college athletes transfer from one school to another.

According to a 2020 article on fivethirtyeight.com, the NCAA's new rule of allowing athletes to make money off their name and likeness will likely come through the athletes' presence and branding on their social media. "Those who spoke with FiveThirtyEight were adamant that once NIL rights are permitted by the NCAA, influencer marketing via social media will be the primary money-making vehicle of the modern-day student-athlete, one that will dominate at least the initial wave of transactions. While other money-making avenues will open, including sponsorships with local business owners and appearance fees for autograph sessions, social media marketers can provide the widest reach and most immediate fiscal return."[46]

As to high school athletes and their use of social media, Aaron Carter, sports reporter for the *Philadelphia Inquirer*, said in an email interview, "The increased use of young athletes using social media isn't simply positive or negative. It is likely both. Young athletes are able to reach out to college coaches directly on social media. They can also reach out to media members. There could be a greater sense of empowerment and ownership of one's path when a young athlete can reach out to coaches on their own without waiting for coaches to contact them. On the flip side, social media has also become a haven for bullies young and old. Young athletes bully each other on social media, but are sometimes also bullied by adults. In some situations, social media 'beefs' can quickly escalate to violence and death."[47]

Reporters also need to be careful about how they use social media. Many reporters break stories on Twitter because it reaches their audience instantaneously. However, while there is a scoop mentality to be the first reporter to break an important story, the reporter still needs to make sure that their story is accurate. Accuracy must trump speed, even if you end up getting scooped by another media outlet.

The media plays a big role in sports. In addition to covering the games, reporters and commentators give reactions and opinions to the games themselves as well as the social issues that occur off the field. Oftentimes, how sports reporters act depends on whom they are covering. If they are covering youth sports and high school sports, reporters are less likely to get personal in their criticism of athletes and coverage tends to skew positive. At the other end of the spectrum are pro athletes who, for the most part, are susceptible to extensive scrutiny, criticism, and ridicule. In the middle are college athletes, where it might depend on whether they are Division I, II, or III, whether they play a revenue or nonrevenue sport, and whether they play in a major conference or school or a smaller one. Media coverage also depends on whether the announcers are hired by their home city or college teams where they would be expected to be favoring their teams, or are doing national broadcasts, where they would be expected to be more objective. Sports reporters also have to consider the extent that they are willing to report on athletes' private lives. Some reporters will do this only if it affects the player's performance on the field or court. Another issue in sports reporting is the emergence of female reporters and the struggles they have faced and the progress that they have made. There are issues related to sports talk radio and the balance that they have regarding being provocative, entertaining, and controversial, and crossing the line and going too far. Finally, the issue of whether sports reporters should comment on political and social issues has emerged in recent years. Some stations, media outlets, and networks are willing to let their sports reporters do this, while others want their reporters to focus mostly on the game.

Chapter 5

Athletes as Social Advocates

For many years, athletes just played the game and didn't comment on politics and social issues. That changed during the civil rights era of the 1960s, when Muhammad Ali spoke out against the Vietnam War and John Carlos and Tommie Smith raised their fists in the air during the playing of the national anthem at the 1968 Olympics. The concept of athletes as social advocates has resurfaced in recent years, when Colin Kaepernick took a knee to protest racial inequality and police abuse of Black people. Current athletes speak out frequently on social and political issues on social media as well. Most recently, especially after the death of George Floyd, many athletes spoke out after the repeated deaths of Black people killed by police officers. Some believe that athletes should just "shut up and dribble" while others support athletes being outspoken on issues. This chapter explores the role of athletes as social advocates and how they have been involved in other political issues such as ping-pong diplomacy in the 1970s and the allowing of Cubans to play Major League Baseball.

Should athletes use their platform and speak out on social issues and politics, or should they just "shut up and dribble," as Fox News host Laura Ingraham once said about LeBron James?[1]

In explaining why athletes are appropriate messengers for social justice, Yannick Kluch stated in his article in *Communication & Sport*, "It is the universal appeal of sport that allows sporting individuals to use sport as an arena to break cultural stereotypes and promote positive social change."[2]

For the most part, most prominent professional athletes during the first half of the 20th century were not outspoken or controversial and chose not to comment on social and political issues. There were some exceptions, such as boxing champion Jack Johnson. Also, Jackie Robinson became an outspoken advocate of civil rights after his retirement in the 1950s. However, the era of athletes being silent on social issues changed significantly in the 1960s.

One of the first prominent athletes to speak out on social issues was Muhammad Ali. He spoke out against the Vietnam War in 1967 and filed paperwork to excuse himself from service as a conscientious objector. He continued to refuse to fight in the war, stating that he had nothing against the Vietcong. His stance caused him to be stripped of his boxing heavyweight championship and he was banned from boxing for three years, right during the prime of his athletic career. In 1971, the United States Supreme Court reversed his conviction for draft evasion. Throughout his career, Ali spoke out against racism. In the 1960s, Ali was one of the most polarizing figures in America. Many people resented him and continued to call him by his original name, Cassius Clay, which he changed to Muhammad Ali in 1964. Others didn't like his trash talking and his brash, outspoken personality. Others found him honest, funny, courageous, and personable. Ali returned to boxing in 1970, won two of three slugfests against Joe Frazier, and stunned the world with his upset of George Foreman. Many people consider him to be the greatest boxer of all time. Decades after Ali was established as a controversial figure to some, most people came around to view him in a positive light and he emerged as a cultural icon. In 1996, despite displaying symptoms of Parkinson's disease, Ali was chosen to light the torch at the Olympic Games in Atlanta. In 1998 he became a United Nations Messenger of Peace and was awarded the Presidential Medal of Freedom in 2005.[3]

President Barack Obama issued a statement eulogizing Ali after his death in 2016, stating, "He stood with King and Mandela; stood up when it was hard; spoke out when others wouldn't. His fight outside the ring would cost him his title and his public standing. It would earn him enemies on the left and the right, make him reviled, and nearly send him to jail. But Ali stood his ground. And his victory helped us get used to the America we recognize today."[4]

Two other athletes who became polarizing and controversial figures at first for protesting about civil rights were US Olympic track and field stars John Carlos and Tommie Smith. Before the 1968 Summer Olympics, there had been widespread discussion among Black Olympic athletes as to whether to boycott the 1968 Summer Games in Mexico City due to the condition of civil rights in the United States. The discussed boycott fell through, but John Carlos and Tommie Smith took a stand in favor of civil rights when they accepted their medals. Smith had won gold in the 200 meters with a world record, and Carlos took the bronze. Both men bowed their heads and raised a fist covered with a black glove during the medals ceremony and the playing of the national anthem, representing the Black power salute and to protest injustice against Blacks. They also were shoeless to protest poverty and wore beads and a scarf to protest lynchings. Right after their protest, they were kicked out of the Olympic Village and sent home. At first, many Americans resented Smith and Carlos and saw them as radical and unpatriotic, and the two men received threats. Years later they were viewed as civil rights icons.[5] In 2019, both men were inducted into the US Olympic and Paralympic Hall of Fame.[6]

According to *Smithsonian Magazine*, "It was a polarizing moment because it was seen as an example of black power radicalism," said Doug Hartmann, a University of Minnesota sociologist and the author of *Race, Culture, and the Revolt of the Black Athlete: The 1968 Olympic Protests and Their Aftermath*. "Mainstream America hated what they did."[7]

In 2018, Smith told Reuters, "I knew it would have an impact but I didn't know

Muhammad Ali, at right, with baseball legend Mike Schmidt in 1975, was one of the greatest boxers of all time but he also became a prominent advocate on social issues. Ali put his boxing career on the line when he declared himself a conscientious objector to the Vietnam War and refused to serve in the United States military. He was stripped of his heavyweight title and banned from boxing for three years. Ali was given the honor of lighting the Olympic torch for the 1996 Atlanta Games, and he received the Presidential Medal of Freedom Award in 2005 (photo by Michael J.J. Maicher, courtesy Temple University Libraries, Special Collections Research Center, George D. McDowell *Philadelphia Evening Bulletin* Collection).

how far it would go.... It was a calling for me to do it.... A lot of people had died for the sake of equality. That was my chance. I had a platform."[8]

Dr. Ketra Armstrong is a professor of sport management and director of diversity, equity, & inclusion for the University of Michigan School of Kinesiology. She is also director of the Center for Race & Ethnicity in Sport (C-RAES), an affiliate faculty member in the Departments of Afro-American and African Studies and Women's Studies, and the U-M NCAA faculty athletics representative. As to how the public perception of Ali, Smith, and Carlos changed over the years, Dr. Armstrong said in an email interview, "What constitutes 'heroes and villains' is often a function of *time* and *place*. During the 1960's the country was in a period of social and cultural unrest, as African Americans were fighting for their human liberties and civil rights. So, the time was ripe for activism and protests. However, sport was not perceived to be the place. Sport was supposed to be the place of harmony, a cathartic escape for the problems of the world, and a means for Americans to come together on one accord. Sport was supposed to be the place where the only 'color' that mattered was the color of the uniform. Consequently, athletes who used sport a platform for protesting matters of racial injustice were maligned and denigrated."[9]

Armstrong added, "But, I believe that as more people—read: more White people and collections of people of Color—joined the struggle and began to understand and empathize with the horrors of anti–Black racism and the notable impacts of social inequalities, the protest movement gained wider acceptability, spawning an awakening of a slumbered social consciousness. I believe that as more of the masses began to acknowledge the indecency of racial injustice, the thinking around protests for racial justice changed—including protests in the context of sport, which has long been viewed as a powerful social institution. Consequently, while many athletes such as John Carlos, Tommie Smith, and Muhammad Ali were viewed negatively during the height of their activism (perhaps right time, but perceived to be the wrong place), in hindsight, these athletes were later honored as civil rights icons for the sacrifices they made for the human good (because of the time and because of the place)."

As to whether athlete protests at the Olympics should be allowed by the IOC, Dr. Armstrong said, "Yes, I believe that athlete protests should be allowed at the Olympics. Protesting is a human right, and forms of protest may occur in a myriad of subtle and profound ways. I do not believe that by virtue of being in sport (at the Olympics level or otherwise) athletes should have to forfeit their freedom of expression and their rights to address human injustices. However, I do believe that their gestures and forms of expression should be done in a manner that does not physically disrupt, infringe upon, or interfere with the actual participation of other athletes."

The debate and controversy over protests by athletes at the Olympics still exists over 50 years after Smith and Carlos's protest.

As of 2020, the IOC's long-standing Olympic Charter Rule 50 stated, "No kind of demonstration or political, religious or racial propaganda is permitted in any Olympic sites, venues or other areas." However, in December 2020, in light of the civil rights protests that took place in the United States during the summer of 2020, the US Olympic and Paralympic Committee announced that it would not punish or sanction US Olympic athletes who engaged in peaceful protest in support of racial and social justice. In 2021, the IOC revised its protest policy before the Tokyo Olympics to allow gestures of protest immediately prior to the athletes' competition but not on the podium during the medal ceremony. Prohibited gestures would include those that are disruptive or that target people, countries, or organizations. Some American athletes did end up protesting at the Tokyo 2021 Olympics, including shot put silver medal winner Raven Saunders, hammer thrower Gwen Berry, bronze medal-winning fencer Race Imboden, and most members of the bronze medal-winning US women's soccer team. Members of female soccer teams from other countries also protested racism and discrimination by kneeling during the pregame national anthems. After winning a silver medal in the shot put, Saunders raised her arms to form an X symbol during the medal ceremony as a symbol of support for oppressed people, including Blacks, LGBTQ people, and those suffering from mental health issues. After winning a bronze medal in fencing, Race Imboden drew an X mark on the back of his hand to protest the IOC's ban on political protests during medals ceremonies. Before her competition in the hammer throw, Gwen Berry raised her fist in protest of social and racial injustice.[10]

Aside from Ali, Smith, and Carlos, other prominent athletes began to find their voice, starting in the 1960s. NFL legendary running back Jim Brown, tennis icon Arthur Ashe, and NBA star Kareem Abdul-Jabbar were other famous athletes who chose to speak out on social issues. Abdul-Jabbar, then known as Lew Alcindor, chose to boycott the 1968 Summer Olympics in Mexico City as a protest for civil rights, and he continued to speak out frequently on social issues for decades. In the 1960s, Jim Brown established the Black Economic Union to help Black people advance economically, and in the 1980s, Brown established Amer-I-Can to help solve gang violence. Tennis star Arthur Ashe became the first Black male to win a Wimbledon title and he became an advocate on social issues after he retired, speaking out against apartheid in South Africa and about AIDS, after he was diagnosed with the disease. Bill Russell, who won two NCAA championships at the University of San Francisco, 11 NBA championships with the Boston Celtics, and five MVP awards, became a civil rights advocate beginning in the 1960s. In 2019, he was awarded the ESPY's Arthur Ashe Courage Award for his long-term social activism. In 1961, when the Celtics' Black players were denied service at a Kentucky hotel restaurant, Russell and other players left and decided not to play in a scheduled exhibition game. He spoke out in favor of civil rights legislation in the 1960s. President Barack Obama awarded Russell the Presidential Medal of Freedom in 2011.[11]

In 1967 in Cleveland, the "Ali Summit" took place. It featured some of the greatest Black athletes at the time, including Ali, Jim Brown, Kareem Abdul-Jabbar, Bill Russell, and Willie Davis, speaking out on civil rights issues. The summit was organized by former Cleveland Browns great running back Jim Brown, who had just retired. Brown asked other great Black athletes to meet together to support Ali's refusal to fight in Vietnam. The meeting was held at the offices of the Negro Industrial and Economic Union (later renamed the Black Economic Union), a Black empowerment organization founded by Brown.[12] At the meeting, the players asked Ali about his stance and then emerged to support him. According to the Associated Press, Jim Brown said the athletes were taking a risk by supporting Ali because of his unpopular stance at the time, saying, "It was the United States government that we were dealing with. Careers were at stake. And everybody that showed up at that meeting put all of that on the line. That was heavyweight stuff."[13]

For several decades after the turbulent 1960s, many athletes chose to stay fairly silent on social issues. That changed significantly in the 2010s. One of the most famous social advocates of this time was Colin Kaepernick, who became a hugely polarizing figure in American culture.

In 2016, San Francisco 49er star quarterback Colin Kaepernick decided to take a stand by refusing to stand for the National Anthem. He said that he did this in order to speak out against police brutality and racial injustice. Kaepernick became shunned by the NFL and effectively was allegedly blackballed, as no team signed him to play for several years.[14] Other NFL players around the league joined in the protest by either kneeling or sitting during the national anthem, or by raising a clenched fist in protest. The players' protests were controversial, as critics claimed that the players were unpatriotic and were disrespecting the American flag. Their actions became a political football, causing President Donald Trump to criticize the protesting players as well as the NFL, stating during a 2017 political rally in Alabama, "Wouldn't you love to see one of these NFL owners, when somebody disrespects our flag, to say, 'Get that son of a bitch off the field right now. Out! He's fired. He's fired!' Trump encouraged fans to leave an NFL game if they saw players protesting during the Anthem."[15] Trump later implied that Kaepernick should leave the country when he told the *Dori Monson Show*, "I think it's a terrible thing, and you know, maybe he should find a country that works better for him, let him try, it's not gonna happen."[16]

One of Kaepernick's 49er teammates, Eric Reid, began kneeling during the anthem in protest along with Kaepernick, and then continued kneeling when he joined the Carolina Panthers. He and Kaepernick sued the NFL for collusion in not signing them due to their anthem protest, and that lawsuit was eventually settled.[17] Other NFL players stood in solidarity with Kaepernick by raising a clenched fist during the anthem. Kaepernick eventually did commercials for Nike, and many athletes proceeded to take a knee during the national anthem after Minnesota police officer Derek Chauvin caused the death of George Floyd in 2020 by kneeling on his neck for over nine minutes. The NBA Black Lives Matter protests and boycott during the 2020 playoffs caused many people to view Kaepernick in a more sympathetic light, and many people advocated that he be signed by an NFL team, although that did not happen as of the end of the season in 2022. In August 2020, NFL Commissioner Roger Goodell apologized to Kaepernick about how the NFL handled his situation, telling Emmanuel Ocho in a YouTube interview, "I wish we had listened earlier, Kaep, to what you were kneeling about and what you were trying to bring attention to. We had invited him in several times to have the conversation, to have the dialogue. I wish we had the benefit of that, we never did. We would have benefited from that, absolutely." In 2020, New Orleans Saints quarterback Drew Brees apologized for saying that Kaepernick and others were disrespecting the American flag by kneeling during the national anthem.[18]

While many people felt that kneeling during the national anthem was unpatriotic and disrespectful to the flag, the players said that their intent was to raise social awareness, not to disrespect the flag. In fact, it was Nate Boyer, a former Army Green Beret who had played for the Seattle Seahawks, who advised Kaepernick to kneel during the national anthem instead of sitting down, which Kaepernick had wanted to do. Boyer said he felt that kneeling was more respectful than sitting.[19]

In 2017, Eric Reid wrote in the *New York Times*, "It baffles me that our protest is still being misconstrued as disrespectful to the country, flag, and military personnel. We chose it because it's exactly the opposite. It has always been my understanding that the brave men and women who fought and died for our country did so to ensure that we could live in a fair and free society, which includes the right to speak out in protest."[20]

In justifying the kneeling protest, Kaepernick told NFL Media after the game, "I am not going to stand up to show pride in a flag for a country that oppresses black people and people of color. To me, this is bigger than football and it would be selfish on my part to look the other way. There are bodies in the street and people getting paid leave and getting away with murder."[21]

Towler et al. wrote that Kaepernick had a great deal of influence and inspired many people, especially Black people, to get involved in social activism and political issues because of their identification with a celebrity athlete. They stated that in light of the attachment to famous athletes that sports fans have, "[B]lack sport stars who engage in political protest are especially well positioned to influence racial in-group members for at least two reasons: they are credible in-group messengers engaged in issue-congruent activism—that rooted in exposing racial grievances of the group—and their protest action often results in professional consequences."

Towler et al added, "Activism by black professional athletes matters to black political action. Our findings reveal a relationship between the social protests of sport stars like Colin Kaepernick, the corresponding Black Lives Matter (BLM) movement, and black political behavior. They generally suggest that black Americans who strongly approved of Colin Kaepernick and were highly identified with BLM were more likely to engage in several acts of nontraditional political engagement."[22]

President Trump's position on the national anthem protests and his other polarizing statements on racial issues led to many of the Super Bowl champion Philadelphia Eagles players deciding to not attend the planned White House ceremony in their honor. When it was revealed that only a handful of players would attend, Trump withdrew the invitation to the team. Other teams and individuals refused to visit the White House after winning championships during the Trump era or were not invited, including the Golden State Warriors, the Seattle Storm and Minnesota Lynx of the WNBA, the US women's World Cup championship soccer team, and some members of the Boston Red Sox.[23]

Some people believe that President Trump's criticism of professional athletes and his outspoken and polarizing manner led to athletes being more outspoken. As noted by Deena Zaru of CNN, CNN sports analyst Christine Brennan said, "Sports is really no longer an escape from the real world that it used to be. Sports is a mirror of our society. I think because Trump is so controversial and because the things he's saying and doing run counter to what many people believe … athletes are finding their voice in a way that is reminiscent of the 1960s."[24]

During the 1990s, many prominent athletes did not speak out on social issues for fear of being too controversial and possibly losing sponsors. Perhaps the greatest athlete of this era, Michael Jordan, regularly declined to speak out on controversial and political issues during his playing career. In the 2010s, Jordan became more outspoken in support of civil rights. In 2016, he donated $1 million each to two organizations that were working to promote trust between police and their local communities. Regarding his declining to speak out on social issues when he was a player, in the ESPN 2020 documentary *The Last Dance*, Jordan said, "I never thought of myself as an activist. I thought of myself as a basketball player. I wasn't a politician, I was playing my sport. I was focused on my craft."[25]

In 1991, Chicago Bulls guard Craig Hodges unsuccessfully approached Michael Jordan and Magic Johnson in an attempt to have the Lakers and Bulls boycott the first game of the NBA Finals as a protest against the lack of Black ownership and coaches in the NBA. After that unsuccessful attempt, Hodges wrote a letter to President George H.W. Bush urging more government attention to poor and disenfranchised communities, according to NBC Sports Chicago.[26]

"Maybe during the Michael Jordan era, there was the idea that sponsors would frown upon this sort of thing, but the consequences I think are a lot more complex," Roger Pielke, Jr., a political scientist and the director of the Sports Governance Center at the University of Colorado Boulder, told Christopher Clarey of the *New York Times*. "As athletes cross the lines that were maybe once taboo and they learn that the consequences are either not negative or, if you're LeBron James or Steph Curry, maybe even positive, I think we'll see more of it because that's the incentive structure."[27]

In recent years, many professional athletes have found their voice and are willing to speak out on social justice issues, especially through social media platforms such as Twitter, Facebook, and Instagram. They see themselves as role models and want to use their fame to their advantage in promoting causes that they believe in. Perhaps the fact that many of them now have large, guaranteed contracts has emboldened them to take the risk that some people will hold a grudge against them. Others may feel that the issues are too important for them to remain silent. Ever since the initiation of free agency in professional sports, there has been a shift in power toward the players as opposed to the owners. With this power has come more security to be able to speak out on social issues. Engaging in advocacy on social media reaches a large audience of followers and fans, many more people than athletes could have reached prior to the internet and social media. One powerful example took place in March 2012, when LeBron James of the Miami Heat tweeted a photo of members of the Heat wearing hoodies, with their heads bowed, in support of Trayvon Martin, an unarmed Black teenager who was shot and killed by George Zimmerman, a neighborhood crime watch volunteer. James's tweeted photo carried the hashtag "WeWantJustice." After a jury trial, Zimmerman was acquitted and found not guilty.[28] Another example of athletes using their voices to speak out took place when NBA players protested racist statements by Los Angeles Clippers owner Donald Sterling, forcing the NBA to oust Sterling from owning the team in 2014.[29]

In addition, many college athletes are speaking out on social issues via their social media. According to *Sports Illustrated*, in June 2020 Kylin Hill, Mississippi State's all-SEC running back, tweeted his objections to the Mississippi state flag, which contained the Confederate battle emblem. Threatening to sit out the upcoming 2020 football season, Hill Tweeted, "Either change the flag or I won't be representing this State anymore. ... & I meant that .. I'm tired."[30] Also in 2020, according to *USA Today*, Oklahoma State star running back Chuba Hubbard tweeted his objection to his coach Mike Gundy's wearing of a T-shirt that featured One America News Network, considered to be a far-right, pro–Trump cable news network. Hubbard tweeted, "I will not stand for this. This is completely insensitive to everything going on in society, and it's unacceptable. I will not be doing anything with Oklahoma State until things CHANGE."[31]

In discussing the results of his study on social justice activism of college athletes, Kluch wrote that they tend to express their voices through interpersonal connections and social media as opposed to participating in protests. "As an everyday form of activism, many of the participants saw their primary duty in educating the people around themselves, in intervening when discrimination occurred, and in raising awareness for social injustices through action and mentorship.... For these athletes, the image of an activist is not so much that of one walking in the streets anymore but rather that of one using the social power they have as an athlete to promote change in everyday situations such as in conversations, on social media, or in interpersonal settings."[32]

Many female athletes have spoken out on social issues. On the field, co-captain and star midfielder Megan Rapinoe of the United States Women's National Soccer Team is known for her goal scoring and her various hair colors. However, she has been both praised and scorned for her stands on social and political issues. During the 2019 World Cup, Rapinoe told the media that she was "not going to the fucking White House" if they won the championship. President Trump proceeded to criticize her, saying that "Megan should never disrespect our Country, the White House, or our Flag, especially since so much has been done for her & the team. Be proud of the Flag that you wear."[33]

In urging her teammates to avoid associating with President Trump through a White House visit, Rapinoe said, "I would encourage my teammates to think hard about lending that platform or having that co-opted by an administration that doesn't feel the same way and doesn't fight for the same things we fight for."[34]

In July 2022, Rapinoe did go to the White House to receive the Presidential Medal of Freedom from President Joe Biden honoring her accomplishments on and off the field as a social advocate, thus becoming the first soccer player to receive the award and only the sixth female athlete or coach to receive the award.[35]

Chapter 5. Athletes as Social Advocates 79

Megan Rapinoe, shown here in 2019, is known for her goal scoring and various hair colors, but she emerged as a vocal advocate on social issues related to gender, race, and sexual orientation, among other topics. As a member of the U.S. Women's National Soccer Team, she won an Olympic gold medal and two World Cup titles. In 2022, she received the Presidential Medal of Freedom at a White House ceremony (photo from Creative Commons. "Megan Rapinoe" by Lorie Shaull is licensed under CC BY-SA 2.0).

Rapinoe had been one of the first white athletes in any sport to kneel in solidarity with Colin Kaepernick's protest against racial injustice. After US Soccer instituted a rule requiring its players to stand during the anthem, Rapinoe protested by staying silent and not singing or putting her hand over her heart.[36]

In light of their success on the world stage, the US women's soccer team brought a lawsuit against the United States Soccer Federation (USSF), seeking equal pay and working conditions as the US Men's National Soccer team. In 2020, after a federal district court granted USSF partial summary judgment as to pay, the parties reached a partial settlement involving work conditions, including equality regarding charter flights, hotel accommodations, venue selection, and professional staff support. The women's team appealed the district court's grant of summary judgment to the Ninth Circuit.[37] As reported by ESPN, in February 2022, the parties reached a settlement as to pay, as the US Soccer Federation agreed to pay $24 million and "committed to providing an equal rate of pay going forward for the women's and men's national teams 'in all friendlies and tournaments, including the World Cup.'"[38]

There are many other notable female athletes who are committed to social causes. After disclosing that she was a lesbian, tennis superstar Martina Navratilova became an outspoken advocate for gay rights and AIDS research, among other social causes. Another tennis champion, Billie Jean King, has been an activist for social change and equality for decades, arguing for equal pay for professional female tennis players in the 1970s. In 1974, she founded the Women's Sports Foundation, which advances the lives of girls and women through sports and physical activity. In 2014, King created the Billie Jean King Leadership Initiative, a nonprofit organization that promotes inclusion and workplace diversity.[39]

One of the most notable examples of a female professional athlete who used their platform to fight racial and social injustice was Maya Moore. Moore, who starred at the University of Connecticut, won multiple WNBA championships, appeared in several WNBA All-Star Games, and won two Olympic gold medals in women's basketball, took a two-year break from playing in the WNBA at the peak of her career to fight Jonathan Irons's conviction and 50-year prison sentence for burglary and assault committed when he was 16 years old. Moore and Irons met in a prison ministry program, and her advocacy helped lead to a judge overturning Irons's conviction, determining that Irons should be freed because prosecutors in his case had not turned over fingerprint evidence that could have acquitted him, according to *USA Today*. Moore and Irons proceeded to get married.[40]

As reported by *The Undefeated*, Cheryl Reeve, Moore's coach with the Minnesota Lynx, said, "This is the epitome of using your platform. She's not dribbling up the court, not making a move, but the way she's given of herself is the same way she gave as a teammate, as a professional to her craft, that is really just who Maya is. If Maya is doing it, it's going to be excellent."[41]

There have been other instances where athletes became involved in political issues. Sports has been credited for easing the tensions between countries. Perhaps the most famous example was the ping-pong diplomacy that took place between the United States and China in the early 1970s. Ping-pong diplomacy started in 1971 at the World Table Tennis Championships in Japan when an American table tennis player, Glenn Cowan, went on a shuttle bus carrying members of the Chinese table tennis team and spoke with their best player, Zhuang Zedong, through an interpreter. The exchange went well, as Zedong gave Cowan a silk-screen picture of China's Huangshan Mountains, and Cowan reciprocated the next day by giving Zedong a T-shirt with a peace symbol and the phrase "Let It Be." The Chinese premier, Chairman Mao, hearing of the incident, proceeded to invite the United States table tennis team to China and the US players accepted. Later that year, 15 US table tennis players visited China for a 10-day visit. The players were treated like royalty with lavish banquets, and they toured the country. Shortly after their visit, President Nixon eased US travel bans and trade embargoes against China. The Chinese table tennis team then visited the US for an eight-city tour. In 1972, Nixon went to China to meet with Zhou Enlai and Chairman Mao, which was the first step in normalizing relations between the two countries.[42]

Reflecting on the success of ping-pong diplomacy, Robert Hormats, who had been a junior member of future Secretary of State Henry Kissinger's National

Security Council (NSC) staff and his adviser on international economic policy, wrote in *The Hill*, "Fifty years later, I've concluded that these visits had an impact far greater than we realized at the time. They personalized the relationship for everyday Chinese and Americans in ways that would have been hard to do through other channels."[43]

For many years, there has been a controversial issue related to Cuban baseball players who want to play Major League Baseball in the United States. In a deal initially negotiated under the Obama administration and designed to end the dangerous practice of Cuban players defecting and smuggling themselves out of Cuba with the help of human traffickers, MLB reached a deal with the Cuban Baseball Federation in 2018 that would allow Cuban players to join pro baseball teams in the US and Canada. The deal would have allowed players to return to Cuba during the offseason. In 2019, the Trump administration canceled the deal because it determined that the Cuban Baseball Federation was controlled by Cuba's communist leaders, and the Trump administration had chosen not to do business with them. In addition, the Trump administration opposed Cuba's support of Venezuela.[44] MLB hired lobbyists and the MLB commissioner met with Trump to change his mind, but to no avail. There were concerns that defecting Cuban baseball players put their lives at risk by hiring human smugglers and traffickers to leave the island.[45]

Star players who defected from Cuba to play in Major League Baseball in the United States include Yoenis Cespedes, Yasiel Puig, Jose Abreu, Aroldis Chapman, and Rolando Arrojo.[46] According to Reuters in December 2018, "More than 350 Cuban ballplayers have defected since the start of 2014, including more than 170 in 2015 alone, according to Cuban journalist Francys Romero."[47]

When MLB and the Cuban Baseball Federation had reached the 2018 agreement, Jose Abreu said in a statement released by MLB, "Knowing that the next generation of Cuban baseball players will not endure the unimaginable fate of past Cuban players is the realization of an impossible dream for all of us. Dealing with the exploitation of smugglers and unscrupulous agencies will finally come to an end for the Cuban baseball player. To this date, I am still harassed."[48]

In August 2020, one of the most significant incidents of athletes speaking out on social issues took place. After Jacob Blake, a Black man, was shot seven times by a police officer in Wisconsin, members of the Milwaukee Bucks decided that they would not play against the Orlando Magic in their second-round playoff game. The Magic players agreed as well, and the game was not played. The other NBA teams left in the playoffs followed suit, and playoff games for the next two days were canceled. The boycott/walkout spread to other sports, including Major League Baseball, Major League Soccer, the WNBA, and the National Hockey League. A poignant ceremony took place before a game between the New York Mets and Miami Marlins when the players took the field in a moment of silence for 42 seconds (representing Jackie Robinson's number), put a Black Lives Matter shirt over home plate, and walked off the field.[49] Some of the NBA players advocated considering canceling the rest of the playoffs, but they eventually decided to return to the court. A subcommittee of players, including LeBron James and Chris Paul, reached out to former president Obama for advice as to how to handle the situation. The NBA and the NBA Players Association reached an agreement to resume play and to take several initiatives "to promote voting access, combat social injustice and racial inequality, and advocate for police reform" according to ESPN's Tim Bontemps.[50] Many NBA players chose to kneel during the national anthem when the playoffs resumed.

Many athletes and sports teams got involved in the 2020 elections. LeBron James's More Than a Vote organization arranged with the Los Angeles Dodgers to make Dodgers Stadium available as a voting area for the November 2020 election. Many other pro teams followed suit, including the Atlanta Hawks, Charlotte Hornets, New York Knicks, Indianapolis Colts, Kansas City Chiefs, San Francisco 49ers, Baltimore Orioles, Boston Red Sox, New Jersey Devils, Tampa Bay Lightning, Seattle Sounders of the MLS, and Minnesota Lynx of the WNBA.[51] Members of the WNBA team the Atlanta Dream actively spoke out against their co-owner US senator Kelly Loeffler of Georgia, who had criticized the Black Lives Matter movement, and supported her opponent in the race for Senate, Raphael Warnock, who eventually won the runoff election.[52]

Not everyone supported the activism of the NBA players. President Trump said during a press briefing, "They've become like a political organization, and that's not a good thing. I don't think that's a good thing for sports or for the country."[53]

Other critics claim that the pro athletes are whiny, self-absorbed, and pampered, and shouldn't complain since they've benefited from the system and become multimillionaires. Some people say that they watch and follow sports as a distraction and escape from the problems and controversies of the real world. Others say that just because someone can dribble and shoot a basketball, throw a football, or hit or pitch a baseball better than anyone else doesn't mean that they should be listened to as experts on social and political issues. Others say that if athletes want to speak out, they should do it on their own time between games and on their social media, instead of right before games during the national anthem.

One of the most outspoken critics of athletes' protesting by kneeling during the national anthem was former Chicago Bears player and coach Mike Ditka. In July 2020, he told TMZ Sports, "If you can't respect our national anthem, get the hell out of the country."[54]

Many conservative pundits criticized the NBA players' social justice protests. As reported by *Forbes*, Turning Point USA founder Charlie Kirk tweeted, "Hilarious to see Black NBA players who make millions a year take a knee to try and tell us black people can't succeed in America. Kick them out of the league. Done watching the NBA."[55]

A few years ago, Fox News anchor Laura Ingraham made news when she quipped that professional athletes like LeBron James who speak out on social issues should shut up and dribble. Ingraham said, "It's always unwise to seek political advice from someone who gets paid $100 million a year to bounce a ball. Keep the political comments to yourselves. ... Shut up and dribble."[56]

During an NBA All-Star weekend press conference, James responded to Ingraham's criticism by saying, "The best thing she did was help me create more awareness.... We will definitely not shut up and dribble.... I mean too much to society, too much to the youth, too much to so many kids who feel like they don't have a way out."[57]

In supporting athletes speaking out about social issues, Dr. Harry Edwards told Kareem Copeland of the Associated Press, "Sports in modern societies really amount to secular religions. Athletes have a phenomenal megaphone. ... So that obligation to speak up, especially in regards to the African-American outcomes and interests, is critical."[58]

Dave Zirin wrote in *The Progressive* that there were some military veterans and veterans groups, such as Veterans for Peace, which expressed support for athletes who chose to speak out for social justice. He wrote, "Another hopeful sign is the number of vets who have stood up—or taken a knee—in support of these protests. They have fought to ensure that their time in the armed forces is not used as a shibboleth to bash players for exercising rights that are protected by both the Constitution and their collective bargaining agreements."[59]

As I wrote in my op-ed in *Real Clear Politics* in 2020, I think it's a good thing for athletes to speak out on social and political issues. I wrote that, even though many people view sports as a diversion from real-world problems, in light of the recent and frequent incidents of racial injustice, including the killing of George Floyd in Minnesota, athletes should continue to speak out. Athletes are role models and can be effective in raising issues and keeping certain issues prominent in the public mindset. I wrote, "Many professional athletes have found their voice and are speaking out on social justice issues, especially through social media. They want to use their fame and platforms to promote causes they believe in. In the next few months, their voices will be needed more than ever. This is a trend that should be celebrated as a slam dunk. Outspoken athletes can keep the conversation about the injustices of the criminal justice system going and eventually help move the ball forward."[60]

To this day, I still believe that athletes should continue to use their platforms to protest racial discrimination and speak out on other social issues—before and after games, if they choose to do so.

The last few years have proved that athletes should do more than just shut up and dribble. They have powerful platforms and many of them have used their fame to try to improve society by speaking out on important issues. While everyone in society now has a voice through social media, athletes still stand out as celebrities and role models that are able to influence their fans. They shouldn't feel obligated to speak out if they don't want to, but for those who do choose to address social issues, such as civil rights, they should be admired and encouraged to do so. People who disagree with these athletes' viewpoints should still respect their rights to opine on issues that they are passionate about. While athletes generally didn't speak out on social issues for the first half of the 20th century, social justice advocates and pioneers like Muhammad Ali, Tommie Smith, John Carlos, Jim Brown, Arthur Ashe, Bill Russell, and Kareem-Abdul Jabbar changed that narrative in the 1960s. While there was a period of time after that where many pro athletes were reluctant to speak out on social issues, that changed in the 2010s, when athletes like Colin Kaepernick and LeBron James started to raise their voices as social justice advocates. In Kaepernick's case, it likely cost him his football career. However, he helped to start a new era by emboldening other athletes to find their voices and use their platforms to speak out on social justice. That era is unlikely to end.

Chapter 6

Fan Obsession

Sports have a huge impact on our lives as fans, and fans have a huge impact on the sports we follow passionately. Most of these impacts can be positive, but others are harmful. There are many social issues related to being a sports fan, including why people become fans, the health and psychological benefits of being a sports fan, why people are so passionate about their favorite teams, the connection between athletes and fans, fan loyalty, why fans engage in violence, whether it is OK to boo high school or college athletes, court storming, the tangible effect that fans can have on a game, and racism by fans. This chapter will explore those issues.

Most people are exposed to sports at a young age and become fans of the teams that their family and friends follow. As a toddler growing up in Philadelphia, you are taught to love your Eagles and to despise the hated rival Dallas Cowboys. This early indoctrination often turns into a lifelong obsession.

This passion and obsession make us sit inside for three hours on a beautiful October Sunday to watch other people play football on television. It makes us go out in the streets to set bonfires and tear down light poles when our team wins a championship. It makes us stay on hold for 30 minutes to talk to a sports talk show host on the air for 40 seconds, knowing that the host might call us a dope or a moron and end the call abruptly.

This passion manifests itself when many of us wear our "lucky" team jerseys thinking that it will help our team win. We have sleepless nights the days before Selection Sunday for the NCAA Basketball Tournament when our alma mater's team is on the bubble. Many of us paint our faces and put team flags on our cars and homes. Fans travel across the globe to watch their country's team play in the World Cup.

Experts have expressed numerous reasons why we become sports fans, including benefits that we derive from it. Many of the reasons why we become and remain passionate sports fans revolve around the concepts of identity, self-esteem, and bonding with others.

Author Eric Simons wrote about these concepts in the *Washington Post*, stating, "[A] fan mirrors the feelings, actions and even hormones of the players. Self-esteem rides on the outcome of the game and the image of the franchisee. There are benefits to this: not just self-esteem but pride, identity, belonging." He added, "Athletic

Being a sports fan is a way to bond with friends, family, and total strangers in a shared passion for a local team. For example, Philadelphia sports fans turn out in droves for their sports teams' victory parades. Here, more than two million people attended a Flyers Stanley Cup parade in the mid-1970s; the team won two championships, in 1974 and 1975 (photo courtesy Temple University Libraries, Special Collections Research Center, George D. McDowell *Philadelphia Evening Bulletin* Collection).

teams offer not just a connection with the players and fellow fans, but also with regional pride, family relationships, color preferences, aesthetic tastes and even moral standards."[1]

Referencing results from a *Journal of Personality and Social Psychology* article by Cialdini, Borden, Thorne, Walker, Freeman, & Sloan, Dr. Susan Krauss Whitbourne wrote in *Psychology Today* about fan identification with their teams and "BIRGing" or "Basking in Reflected Glory." "Research shows that on the day after a team's win, people feel better about themselves." They say "we" won, and by "we," they don't mean themselves, personally. The closer you identify with the team, the more likely you are to BIRG. "People who BIRG also are more likely to wear their team's regalia on the day after a victory." As the Cialdini study observed, team fans always chant "We're number one," never "They're number one." The study concluded, "The tendency to employ appropriate apparel or language in a way that connects oneself to something good may involve an attempt to remind oneself of such connections and, thereby, positively affect self-esteem."[2]

Pursuant to what these experts indicate, being a sports fan is a way to bond with friends and family and to celebrate a shared identity. As a sports fan, you feel as though you're part of a group. It is an icebreaker for conversations with strangers.

You're not supposed to talk about politics and religion at holiday family dinners, but sports are fair game and most of the time you're on the same side. An NCAA March Madness pool can bring office workers closer. When a national icon like Usain Bolt wins multiple gold medals, it brings all residents of Jamaica together celebrating in pride. In reality, whether our favorite team wins or loses doesn't really affect our daily lives. However, in many ways, it does affect us psychologically. As Whitbourne and Cialdini indicate, basking in your favorite team's glory is a real phenomenon. Fans wear their favorite team's apparel after a big win as a way to brag to others. This boasting reflects our increased self-esteem and regional pride, as Simons notes. Listening to sports talk radio and chatting with others on social media after a local team's big win shows how emotionally involved other fans like us are in their teams. Sharing our joy and pain with others, even strangers online, helps us connect.

Sports are something that we are passionate about and follow religiously. People obsess over their NCAA bracket selections and fantasy football decisions for hours so they can get bragging rights against their friends. We frequently check the score of our favorite team's game if we're attending a wedding. Friends reminisce about a road trip that they took years ago to see their college team play in the NCAA Tournament. Fans of a team can share their joy or sorrow instantaneously via social media with other fans worldwide. We might even defend our teams even if they act irresponsibly or bend the rules. We are our teams, and our teams are us.

However, there are skeptics of fan identification with their favorite sports teams. Chris Jones ridiculed this concept of "we" when he wrote, "But no matter how much love and faith and belief you might have in something, you don't necessarily then become part of it. Put all your hopes in the stars if you'd like; that doesn't make you a constellation."[3]

Technically, Jones is correct in that we aren't technically part of a team. We don't suit up in our favorite team's jersey and actually go on the field or the court. However, fan identification is real.

According to NCAA.org, "A recent survey concluded that being identified with their favorite team is more important to people than being identified with their work and social groups, and as important to them as being identified with their religion (Smith, Grieve, Zapalac, Derryberry, & Pope-Tarrence, 2011)."[4]

There were several times when I engaged in the BIRGing and vicarious thrill of having my favorite teams win championships.

Perhaps the most memorable was when the Philadelphia 76ers won their last NBA championship.

As I wrote in the *Philadelphia Inquirer*, in 1983 I took a monthlong car trip out west with friends. By pure luck and good timing, we were in Los Angeles the night that Game 4 of the NBA Finals between the Sixers and Lakers was about to take place. The Lakers were down 3–0, and most of their fans had given up. Somehow, we were able to get tickets for the game at face value for $25 from a ticket broker. After the Sixers won the game to win the series 4–0, we joined other Sixers fans on the court to wave brooms and chant "Sweep!" We called our Philadelphia friends and relatives collect (to their parents' dismay) on a pay phone (younger people can Google that to find out what they were) to tell them that we were there.[5]

Since 1974, I've attended championship parades for the Phillies, Eagles, and Flyers.

There is also a vicarious thrill that sports fans experience when they attend a historic event, even if they don't have a rooting interest. When I was young, my relatives told me about their experiences watching Babe Ruth play against the Philadelphia A's and witnessing Sandy Koufax pitch a no-hitter against the Phillies. It's a badge of honor to attend historic events, like being able to say that you were there when the Berlin Wall came down or you saw the Beatles at Shea Stadium. I felt that thrill attending the 1996 Olympics seeing the Dream Team in basketball and Michael Johnson and Carl Lewis win gold medals in track and field, the 1994 World Cup when I saw Argentina's Diego Maradona score a goal in his last World Cup, and Christian Laettner's buzzer-beater for Duke against Kentucky in the Elite 8 classic in 1992 at the Spectrum in Philadelphia.

For a select few people, going to every Super Bowl was a badge of honor. As of 2016, there were eight fans of the "Never Miss a Super Bowl Club" who had attended every Super Bowl (Donald Crisman, Thomas Henschel, Larry Jacobson, Larry McDonald, Lew Rapoport, Alvin Schragis, Harvey Rothenberg, and Sylvan Schefler).

"We're devoted to each other, and we're devoted to the Super Bowl," Rothenberg told the *Today* show.[6]

In 2014, Jacobson told the *New York Post*, "My end is when they put me in a box."[7]

There can even be health benefits from being a sports fan.

As stated by Anna Almendrala of the *Huffington Post*, "Epic fandom is also linked to higher levels of well-being and general happiness with one's social life, as well as lower levels of loneliness and alienation, according to research by sports psychology professor Daniel Wann of Murray State University." According to Almendrala, the benefits of being a sports fan include having a built-in community that builds your sense of well-being, having a common language with other fans, having a safe space with others, and getting a vicarious thrill when your team does well. Wann told Almendrala, "We've known for years in psychology that feeling connections and affiliations with others is important for well-being. What fandom allows you to do is to gain those connections."[8]

In reporting about the psychological boost that Cubs fans had after they won the 2016 World Series, John Keilman and Genevieve Bookwalter wrote in the *Chicago Tribune*, "A vicarious win has been shown to increase a fan's testosterone level—losing does the opposite—and some scientists who measured these changes theorized that they could lead to larger effects, such as improving the health of one's immune system."[9]

For several years, an Ohio State fan could attest to the psychological benefits of being a sports fan, and he inspired many people with his courageous battle against cancer. When 11-year-old Ohio State football fan Grant Reed was diagnosed with cancer in 2012, he decided that he didn't want to use the word "cancer." Instead, he insisted on calling his cancer "Michigan." When his father, Troy, asked him why he wanted to call it that, Grant said, "Because Ohio State always beats Michigan." Troy said, "That was something he could understand and make it into a competition. He was going to beat this disease." A year after surgery and chemotherapy, Grant's tumor was gone. Sadly, however, the cancer reemerged, and Reed died from cancer in 2019.[10]

The psychological and physical benefits that Almendrala and Wann discuss is real for many people. Their discussion of the built-in community and common language with others shows how important sports are in connecting with others. For people who work long hours during the week, looking forward to NFL Sundays, where they get together with friends to watch games, makes their week more tolerable. This bonding during games with friends and family might be the highlight of our social lives and gives us a connection with others, thus increasing our psychological well-being and decreasing isolation or loneliness.

Sports can be helpful in psychological ways for communities faced with tragedies. The New Orleans Saints helped the city heal after Hurricane Katrina and the Red Sox rallied people after the Boston Marathon bombing. Saints linebacker Scott Fujita said, "[T]he community needed us. We needed the community.... This is why the marriage is so special between the team and the town, why the Saints are now so deeply rooted in the community and you just can't imagine New Orleans without the Saints."[11] Being at a sports event after a tragedy shows people in the community that they are not alone and that they will persevere together.

After the Boston Marathon tragedy, Boston residents found solace in bonding together at a Red Sox game at Fenway Park. Jon Terbush wrote, "Though sports may seem inconsequential when juxtaposed with such horrendous carnage and death, they can also serve as an effective way to combat grief, rallying people around one singular, local ideal."[12]

Many people have cited sports as a way to connect with their parents.

Columnist Mike Morsch wrote a column after Mark McGwire admitted to using steroids. Morsch wrote how he and his father had attended the game in St. Louis in which McGwire hit his record-tying 61st home run. Due to ticket demand, he and his father had to sit in separate sections 30 seats away from each other. Morsch indicated that despite McGwire's admission, it didn't spoil the magic moment that he shared with his father when their eyes met amid cheering fans. Morsch wrote, "The real magic of the day was between father and son and the game of baseball. McGwire's admission certainly taints the details of my personal story. But it can't take away anything from the memory of my dad and a love of the game we shared."[13]

Television talk show host Seth Meyers frequently talks about his father and their shared love for the Pittsburgh Steelers. He said that his father frequently walks up to strangers wearing Steelers hats and gives them tickets to his son's show. Meyers said the only time he saw his father cry was when his Steelers won the 2005 Super Bowl and he cried into a Terrible Towel.[14]

My love of sports came at a young age. My father was an avid sports fan. We had a distant relationship and didn't talk to each other much, but our one bond was sports.

Growing up in the early 1970s, I played catch with my father in our backyard and he coached my Little League team. My father took me to Phillies and Eagles games. He caught a foul ball hit by Larry Bowa that I still have today. My father took me to college basketball games at the Palestra, Temple football games, and two Flyers Stanley Cup parades. We would watch games together regularly on TV. These were experiences that my father and I shared and recalled years later.

While my mother wasn't much of a sports fan, she always supported my playing sports for school teams and would occasionally come to my games to root for me.

Part of being a passionate sports fan is identification with favorite players and teams. Kids scramble to get players' autographs. People go to autograph and collectible shows to meet famous current and former players and to buy memorabilia. Others buy items related to their favorite teams on eBay. According to a 2016 *Forbes* article, the market on trading cards and sports memorabilia could reach 67 million people, and that total is boosted by social media like Facebook, Twitter, Instagram, and Boxes, a social media company for sports collectors.[15] My sports memorabilia is low-tech, as I have a collection of *Sports Illustrated* magazines dating back to 1970. They don't have much monetary value, but they have sentimental worth to me and remind me of how I looked forward to getting each issue. Likewise with my collection of baseball cards and autographs from athletes when I was a kid.

Naturally, growing up in Philadelphia, I revered the local star players such as Mike Schmidt of the Phillies, Julius Erving of the 76ers, Bernie Parent of the Flyers, and Ron Jaworski of the Eagles. However, my connection wasn't always with the star players. I will always remember my opportunity to play tennis against Max Runager, who was the punter for the Philadelphia Eagles, when I worked at the Ron Jaworski Football Camp in 1980. As I wrote in the *Philadelphia Daily News*, the Eagles players who were at the camp frequently played tennis and I noticed that Runager was the best player. I played tennis for La Salle University, and I wanted to see if I could compete against Runager. I approached him at a bar and asked him if we could play. The next night we played a set and I was fortunate enough to beat him 6–4. Runager's fellow teammates were watching and heckling him during the match, and I became a camp hero for one night. Sadly, Runager died in 2017, but I'll always remember how nice he was in letting me play him.[16]

Part of being a true fan is the satisfaction of sticking with your team through thick and thin. It makes your joy more powerful. Citing a book by Jon Wertheim and Samuel Sommers, Tom Van Riper wrote in *Forbes*, "Just as refinishing your basement with your own two hands and your own sweat brings more satisfaction than paying a contractor to do it, sticking with the Cubs through years of futility would make a championship a lot sweeter than for a Yankee fan who's disappointed when his team doesn't win."[17]

Another long-suffering fan base was rewarded for their loyalty when the Boston Red Sox won the 2004 World Series, breaking an 86-year-old curse.

ESPN's Jerry Crasnick wrote about the fan connection with the Red Sox victory, stating that his friend, columnist Steve Buckley, "witnessed the impact of the 2004 World Series victory when he drove past the Cambridge Cemetery and saw countless Red Sox pennants, caps and jerseys adorning grave sites. The thrill of victory was so profound, the living were compelled to share it with the dead."[18]

As these writers indicate, there is something powerful and invigorating about sticking with your favorite team through ups and downs and it makes the psychological rewards greater when your long-suffering team wins. It validates your fandom and your loyalty. I experienced this as a Temple University football fan, supporting them through 18 straight losing seasons starting in 1991 and then enjoying their multiple bowl appearances and winning seasons in the 2010s. Likewise, long-suffering Philadelphia Eagles fans like me were rewarded for their loyalty when the Eagles finally won their first Super Bowl against the New England Patriots in 2018 (the Eagles had won three NFL Championships, in 1948, 1949, and 1960, before I was born and before the Super Bowl era started in 1967).

Regarding the psychological boost that long-suffering Eagles fans got when the Eagles won their first Super Bowl, Glen Macnow, longtime Philadelphia sports talk radio host at Sports Radio 94 WIP, said in an email interview, "Incredible. Sports in Philadelphia is a family thing—handed down from one generation to the next. When the Eagles won their first title since 1960, it was amazing how many fans talked about hugging their dads, or visiting grandparents' gravesites to share the moment. Philadelphians are a diverse lot, who disagree on most everything. But we all follow the same religion—we all worship the Eagles. Sports (all four local teams) are the entity that brings together city and suburb, rich and poor, Black and white, young and old. It's the unifying force."[19]

Fans can have a tangible effect on games, helping their hometown team win.

A 2015 study in the *Journal of Sports Economics* found that home crowds raise the likelihood of a home team's win by between 21 and 22.8 percentage points.[20] This study is validated by the trend of how point spreads in gambling tend to add several points to home teams. Arizona State's Curtain of Distraction is successfully used by fans in outrageous costumes to distract opposing teams' free throw shooting. Fan outrage can lead to a team firing a coach, benching or trading a player, or signing free agents. Fan apathy can force a team to make changes, such as when there are empty stands due to a losing record. The coronavirus pandemic of 2020 and 2021 that resulted in empty stadiums for games showed the importance of fans to sports and the energy that they bring. The Tokyo Olympics of 2021 had many great athletic performances, but the energy wasn't the same, as fans were not allowed to attend the events.

Another debate related to fan passion is storming the field or the court by college students after big wins. This is a long-standing custom, but recent incidents are causing many to question the practice. In 2016, the SEC fined Vanderbilt and Auburn $100,000 each for their failure to prevent court stormings after wins against Kentucky. The Big East can fine a member school $5,000 for a first-time court storming offense and up to $25,000 for a second offense. In 2017, the Pac 12 announced that it would fine its member schools $25,000 for the first court-storming offense, $50,000 for a second offense, and $100,000 for a third offense.[21] In 2017, a fan court storming with 0.5 seconds left on the clock cost host St. Bonaventure a technical foul, enabling visiting VCU to tie the game in regulation and win in overtime.[22] In 2015, after Houston won the AAC Championship, security guards reportedly tackled and hit fans who stormed the field.[23]

An article on Bloomberg.com argued that storming the court could lead to substantial lawsuits against universities and athletic departments.[24]

After a court storming in a road loss, Arizona basketball coach Sean Miller said that he was concerned that eventually one of his players would punch a fan in self-defense. He suggested that court storming be delayed until players leave the court.[25]

Writer Reid Forgrave argued that court storming should not be banned because it would eliminate magical moments that fans and players will cherish for the rest of their lives. "[L]egislating the fun out of college basketball—banning one of the things that makes this sport stand out in a crowded sports landscape—would take some of these great moments away from the players, too."[26]

Forgrave is right about the charm of court storming and how it makes college sports more exciting than pro sports. It's reflective of the passion that college students have for their teams. They're thrilled when their fellow students knock off a top 10 team. You don't see that same passion or court storming in pro sports. However, the Bloomberg.com article is correct in that the days of court storming could be numbered. More college teams and conferences will likely take measures to prevent it due to liability concerns.

Another issue is whether it's OK for fans to boo, heckle, or criticize high school or college players. In 2016, the Sportsmanship Guide for the Wisconsin Interscholastic Athletics Association released a list of cheers and chants that it considered inappropriate, including "Overrated," "Airball," and "Warm up the bus." The Kansas Association also listed similar unsportsmanlike cheers.[27]

Many high schools, school districts, conferences, and state associations are attempting to crack down on unruly fan behavior by adopting codes of conduct and sportsmanship initiatives through banners, signs, and public address announcements. Many state athletic associations, the National Federation of State High School Associations (NFHS), and the National Association of Sports Public Address

Announcers (NASPAA) provide guidelines to public address announcers at high school games to make announcements before the game, at halftime, and before the end of the game encouraging fans at the game to engage in good sportsmanship.[28]

Jack Kapenstein was a Pennsylvania Interscholastic Athletic Association (PIAA) official for over 30 years. He is also an assistant baseball coach at Northeast High School in Philadelphia and an announcer for SFBN, which covers high school and Division III college sports, mostly in Pennsylvania and New Jersey. In an email interview addressing fan behavior at high school and youth sports games, he said, "I certainly have heard some insults hurled from fans at opposing team players much more so than towards their own team. It usually occurs during quiet time such as dead ball periods following the calling of a time out or a foul, the administering of a free throw, or the calling of a violation. Additionally, this type of behavior can sometimes be heard when the fans sense a deficiency in a player's skill set, either real or imagined."[29]

Kapenstein indicates that this type of fan behavior takes place in both big contentious games and less well-attended lower-skill-level games, and both in the cities and suburbs. "It is mostly good spirited, but at times can become anywhere from personal to downright mean," he said.

He said that fan warnings from public address announcers generally don't work "because very few fans are paying attention during the reading, and will basically do what they want anyway." Kapenstein has witnessed game management at some schools stepping up to admonish individuals, or a whole section. "There was one game I officiated where a very large fan was continuing to edge closer and closer to the court while sharpening his invective. I could sense trouble coming. So could the head coach of the home school, being very experienced in quelling such situations; he asked that we stop play. He then walked across the gym with everyone watching and calmly explained to this rather robust looking fellow that he would need to tone it down a whole bunch of notches. It worked, and I was very thankful."

In another incident, Kapenstein recalled a suburban religious private school that had a raucous group of students that would sit together and be led in rousing epithets by a shirtless young man who was egged on by his cohorts. Kapenstein said, "The pack would all sit in one section, and the leader would turn to them, scream the comment out and then it would be repeated.... 'I could stop you, you have no handle, you can't shoot, you'll be working for us someday, my Mom could score on you, he's scared, he's shaking, etc.'"

Kapenstein noted that the fan insults had very little or no effect in intimidating the opposing team in most cases. The school with the pack did end up going 30–0, however, during that season, losing their only game in the state championship on a missed 35-foot desperation buzzer shot.

Kapenstein said the worst incidents took place many years ago in religious school games of opposing faiths. "Times have surely changed for the better, thank goodness. I've heard specific anti-religious statements and even seen fans throwing coins at [Jewish] players."

Expanding on Kapenstein's thoughts further, youth sports and high school sports should promote a positive atmosphere and fan sportsmanship is important. I think that fans shouldn't boo their own high school team, but mild razzing of the other team's players such as chants of "Overrated" and "Airball" are OK. Such chants are just made in fun and wouldn't be taken personally by players. Some sportsmanship guide rules regarding allegedly unsportsmanlike cheers such as "airball" seem to be overdoing it. Just don't get personal or racist in insults or throw things on the court. One extreme example occurred in New Jersey in 2017, when high school fans chanted racist and ethnic remarks at the opposing team's players.[30] Criticizing racist chants and taunts by fans and students at high school games, Bob Cook of *Forbes* stated, "[W]hile a little trash-talking is all in fun, being hateful doesn't cut it."[31]

As for colleges, Barbara Bruno argued in *Huffington Post* that it is wrong to boo college athletes, stating, "Many rabid fans point out that college sports can be big business. So what? The players are still not adults and they are (mostly) unpaid. You may 'live' to cheer for a university you graduated from 20 years ago, but the kids on the field (and their mothers in the stands) don't need to hear abuse rained on their heads."[32]

However, columnist Dave Solomon disagreed with those who criticize fans who boo college players, stating, "Booing has become a natural part of the culture in sports today and there's no genie who's going to put that back in the bottle.... I think we should be far more annoyed when fans think they're a participatory part of the action by throwing objects and creating a public nuisance—or using vulgarity."[33]

I believe that it's OK to boo college athletes, especially for Division I–level revenue sports like basketball and football when fans are charged admission. At Power Five schools in small towns, the local university team is the only game in town and receives extra scrutiny. Sometimes, fans are booing the coach, not individual players. Also, highly recruited players that choose to go to major programs should know that they will be under a microscope and subjected to intensive scrutiny by passionate fan bases that expect greatness. Along with the adulation and celebrity status that they get with being a star athlete on campus should come the realization that their actions on and off the field or court will be scrutinized. In addition, after the NCAA allowed athletes to profit off their name, image, and likeness in 2021, many athletes began to promote themselves and certain products, putting themselves out there as public figures.

There is a concern when it goes beyond boos. Recently, criticism of college players by fans has extended to social media. Sometimes, criticism crosses the line and gets too personal or offensive. In 2010, Kentucky's DeMarcus Cousins received numerous racist voice mails and texts from Mississippi State fans.[34] After Alabama kicker Cade Foster missed three field goals against Auburn in 2013, he received hateful Tweets such as: "You're the worst kicker in Alabama history." "Don't come back to campus." "Drink bleach." "I'm gonna kill you and your family."[35] After a disappointing loss to San Diego State in 2017, members of Arizona State's football team found numerous hate-filled, curse-filled, racist, homophobic, and stereotypical insults sent by their own fans.[36]

According to *USA Today*, assistant professors Blair Browning of Baylor and Jimmy Sanderson of Clemson found that student-athletes dealt with critical tweets by ignoring them, using them as motivation, blocking those who sent the tweets, or responding to critics through tweets or subtweets.[37]

Sanderson, director of Clemson's sports communications BA program, told the *StarTribune* in 2015, "When I was growing up, if I got mad at an athlete, by the time I sat down and wrote a letter to the newspaper or called into a radio show, I was generally cooled down. But with social media, man, as soon as an athlete makes a mistake, we just whip out our phones and send the message while we're still on that emotional high."[38]

These experts show that college sports fans need to act like adults. There's a big difference between criticizing an athlete and engaging in vicious personal attacks and threats. While some players could ignore or use it as motivation, as Browning and Sanderson suggest, others might be more sensitive and take it personally.

Many sports fans pride themselves on being knowledgeable about the sport, their favorite team, and players and coaches on those teams. Fans love to be Monday morning quarterbacks. Everyone has an opinion after their football team wins or loses on Sunday. People call sports talk radio to vent and criticize. Most fans believe that they know what's right for their team more than the coach or general manager. Anyone can start a blog related to sports and can rant and rave about teams and players on social media. People also like to show off their knowledge in their fantasy football selections and NCAA Tournament pools. Sports are a topic that many people feel they know a lot about. You don't need a PhD to be a hard-core sports fan.

One of my pet peeves is bandwagon sports fans. We all know someone who latches on to a team only because that team is successful. Some examples would include fans who wear gear representing the New York Yankees, Boston Celtics, Dallas Cowboys, Notre Dame football, and Duke basketball. I knew someone who grew up and lived in Philadelphia but became a Los Angeles Lakers fan when Kobe Bryant led the Lakers to several championships. When Bryant retired and the Lakers became lousy, he stopped being a fan.

Regarding bandwagon fans, Gus Turner of *Complex* stated correctly, "Please, dude, just stop. Being a true sports fan means sticking to one team, through thick and thin, in times of victory and in times of heartbreak. Once you start cheering for a different side, it's a slippery slope. Suddenly, you latch on to one championship team, and then another, and before you know it, you're supposedly a fan of half the franchises in the league."[39] I could understand a fan's loyalty to Duke if they went to school there or if they grew up in Dallas as a Cowboy fan. Otherwise, I don't get it. The investment of time by a diehard fan through tough times makes eventual success more satisfying than just jumping from team to team depending on its success.

While identification and psychological connections with professional athletes can be a positive experience, it can also be disappointing if it becomes hero worship. These players aren't perfect. Many of them can't live up to the perfect image that they've created. Many athletes that we idolize are caught up in scandals, such as Pete Rose and gambling, Lance Armstrong and doping, and Michael Vick and dogfighting.

There can be a dark side to being a sports fan, especially when it comes to violence.

There have been occasions of fights among fans as well as between fans and players. After Philadelphia Flyers fans allegedly threw beer at Toronto's Tie Domi in the penalty box and Domi squirted water on fans, one fan fell into the penalty box and had a skirmish with Domi.[40] The Malice at the Palace in Detroit featured a widespread brawl as the Indiana Pacers' Ron Artest, later known as Metta World Peace, and other players fought with fans after a fan threw soda on Artest.[41] In 1979, many Boston Bruins players went into the stands and pummeled New York Rangers fans at Madison Square Garden. After the game, 300 Rangers fans rocked the Bruins' bus.[42] In Chicago in 1979, Disco Demolition Night was a disaster. After disco records were blown up after the first game of a White Sox doubleheader, drunken fans stormed the field and the second game was canceled.[43]

A tragic incident occurred in 2011 outside Dodger Stadium, when two Dodgers fans assaulted Bryan Stow, a Giants fan and paramedic, fracturing his skull and rendering him severely disabled with long-term physical and cognitive damage after being in a coma for nine months. The reason for the attack was that Stow chose to wear a Giants jersey at an opposing team's stadium. It took Stow years to recover, but eventually he was able to throw out the first pitch at the Giants' home opener in 2021. The attackers were sentenced to prison.[44]

According to the *Washington Post*, in 2015, 6.34 fan arrests per game were reported leaguewide during the NFL regular season, with 126 arrests made in the 10th week of the season. Arrests increased when the home team lost. In 2015, a fan was shot and killed outside a Dallas Cowboys home game, while in 2013, a fan was beaten to death in the parking lot at Kansas City's Arrowhead Stadium. As a result, NFL teams have instituted a Fan Code of Conduct.[45]

A lowlight of sports fan passion took place at Wrigley Field. Steve Bartman, a lifelong Chicago Cubs fan, was vilified when he reached for a foul ball during the eighth inning of Game 6 of the 2003 NLCS and interfered with Cubs outfielder Moises Alou, preventing him from making the catch. The Cubs were five outs away from winning the NLCS, but that play sparked a Marlins' rally and they proceeded to win the game and the series. Bartman wasn't the only fan who reached for the ball, but he was the unlucky one who touched it. Bartman, who was booed and pelted with debris by angry Cubs fans, needed a disguise and a police escort to escape the stadium. He became public enemy number one and had to go into hiding. For years, he continued to receive threats and declined interview requests. To their credit, when the Cubs finally won their elusive World Series title in 2016, they gave Bartman an official championship World Series ring.[46]

Fan violence has been an unfortunate part of sports for decades. Fans fight among themselves and, at times, have fought with players. Here, police break up a fight that occurred in the stands during a Phillies-Cubs game in 1971 (photo by Anthony Bernato, courtesy Temple University Libraries, Special Collections Research Center, George D. McDowell *Philadelphia Evening Bulletin* Collection).

There have been many incidents of fan rioting after their teams won a championship. When the Montreal Canadiens won the Stanley Cup in 1993, fan riots resulted in $2.5 million in damages and 168 arrests. In 1984 when the Detroit Tigers won the World Series, fans looted local businesses and burned police cars. When the San Francisco Giants captured the 2014 World Series, their fans set fires and vandalized buses, police cars, and businesses, resulting in 40 arrests.[47]

Soccer fans are notorious for violence. During the 1985 European Cup, 39 people died when Liverpool fans fought with Juventus in Belgium. Other examples include fights between fans of England and Russia during the 2016 European Championships, fights between English fans and Tunisian fans during the 1998 World Cup, and over 500 arrests of fans that occurred during Euro 2000. In 2013, there were 18 soccer-related deaths in Argentina, 40 in Colombia, and 30 in Brazil.[48]

There is also a sad history of racism exhibited by fans. During a game, a fan at an opposing stadium threw a banana at the Philadelphia Flyers' Wayne Simmonds, who is Black. European soccer fans, who are notorious for racist chants, threw a banana at Barcelona's Dani Alves and called him a monkey during matches.[49] According to Richard Lapchick, there were 104 reported incidents of racism in sports internationally in 2016.[50] In 2017, Adam Jones of the Baltimore Orioles claimed that Boston Red Sox fans yelled racist slurs and threw peanuts at him.[51] After three Black players missed shootout penalty kicks for England in their 2021 loss to Italy in the European Championship, thousands of racist messages were posted on social media.[52]

ESPN's Mike Greenberg told *GOOD* that negative fan behavior can destroy the experience. "I know a lot of parents that don't want to take their kids to games. And I know a lot of kids that don't want to go. That's bordering on tragic. It is a delightful, communal experience and a rite of passage that I would hate to see any kids deprived of…. Just behave like a fan instead of behaving like a jerk."[53]

Greenberg is correct. We shouldn't be so obsessed with winning that we lose all perspective of what is right and wrong. These outrageous incidents show that fans who act like jerks can spoil the experience for everyone, especially for parents who are trying to bond with their kids.

What causes violence by sports fans?

Justine Gubar, author of *Fanaticus: Mischief and Madness in the Modern Sports Fan*, told *Forbes*, "[T]he right social circumstances enable people to act out in disturbing and inexplicable ways … an average fan in the wrong situation can turn into a knucklehead and rationalize bad acts like cursing out a kid or vomiting on his neighbor in the stands. With the hyped-up competition, the booze, the drive to stand out in a selfie, sports can provide a welcoming stage for fans to harness aggression, flaunt the usual ethical norms, and act out in obnoxious and sometimes violent ways."[54]

Christian End, an expert in sports fan behavior at Xavier University, told journalist Brian Handwerk of *National Geographic News*, "When we're less accountable we tend to behave in ways we wouldn't. If I'm among thousands of celebrating people and I were to throw a beer bottle against a brick wall, you'd have a hard time picking me out."[55]

Matt Beardmore wrote in *Psychology Today* that the desire to bully others with physical violence can be a factor in fan violence. "There are some people that identify with teams for maladaptive reasons, and that's so they can confront other people," Dr. Rick Grieve, coordinator of the Clinical Psychology Master's Program at Western Kentucky University, told Beardmore.[56]

As these experts indicate, peer pressure is to blame for many incidents of fan violence and misbehavior. It's the mob mentality and a feeling that acting like a numbskull is OK because everyone else is. Normally, most people wouldn't throw snowballs or beers at opposing players, but when one numbskull does it, other people want to join in the "fun." Normally, you wouldn't punch another fan wearing the visiting team's jacket or jersey if you were by yourself, but you might get your "beer muscles" if you think your home team's fans will cheer your actions. Violence might result from a perceived need to take out the frustration of a heartbreaking loss on an opposing team's fan, especially if that opposing fan is being obnoxious. Even then, that's no excuse. Odds are you wouldn't be violent against other fans at an opposing team's stadium if you were outnumbered.

Part of the problem is the extensive amount of alcohol consumed by fans tailgating before the game as well as during the game inside the stadium. As author Jerry M. Lewis stated in his book *Sports Fan Violence in North America*, "[D]rinking gives the violent fan permission to do what he wanted to do anyway. Because the celebratory fan is highly pleased with his team's victory, he wants to do an act that celebrates the victory and can be linked to the sport. Thus, he commits vandalism, throws missiles, sets fires, or fights with social-control forces, seeing these acts as feats of skill akin to the acts that take place on the playing field."[57]

What are some possible solutions to fan violence? According to the *Baltimore Sun*, alcohol sales at M&T Bank Stadium are cut off at the end of the third quarter. Fans are ejected for "drunk and disorderly behavior," according to the team's "fan code of conduct."[58]

Dennis Van Milligen, writing for *Gameday Security* and *Athletic Business*, cites the NFL's rule instituted in 2015 that implemented a temporary stadium ban for fans ejected for violating the NFL's fan code of conduct. "If a fan is banned from one NFL stadium, he or she is banned from all NFL stadiums." Also, opening stadium gates earlier could entice fans out of tailgate parties and have them engage in less drinking in parking lots. Milligen writes that technology can be useful to track incidents of violence in stadiums. It is also important to have adequate security and rapid response teams that can be deployed immediately in stadiums. He suggests creating peaceful environments such as the edible garden at AT&T Park in San Francisco.[59]

Bridget Fitzpatrick analyzed litigation by injured fans against stadium owners as a remedy, writing, "Despite efforts to curb this toxic relationship with alcohol by limiting tailgating and joining the TEAM coalition for standardized guidelines, the MLB has not gone far enough to protect fans and preserve the family setting of America's pastime. Therefore, fans must be legally enabled to recover if an overly intoxicated fan permanently disables another on stadium property. Some solutions suggest presumptions of duty and causation; however, these strategies, although potentially easier for plaintiffs, are unfairly burdensome to stadium owners. The goal should not be to punish stadium owners, but to create a safe environment that encourages responsible alcohol consumption, thereby lessening the need of future negligence litigation and bringing families back to the ballpark."[60]

I believe that it's a positive step for teams and leagues to take measures to cut off and limit alcohol sales and to create fan-friendly sections and to increase security, but the onus also falls on individual fans. Sure, have a few beers before and during the game, but know your limit. If you tend to be violent and get in fights when you drink, you should refrain from drinking before a game. Just because someone in front of you throws a snowball toward the field doesn't mean you should. There should be peer pressure from other fans to call out obnoxious fan behavior when it crosses the line. People can now do it anonymously, as many teams encourage using text messages to report fan misconduct. Also have a fan services location inside the stadium where people can report problems. Some fans lose perspective and see other teams, players, and fans as the "enemy" and not as human beings. Many people forget that it is only a game.

While there are negative aspects related to fan behavior, most of us have positive experiences when it comes to our fandom. We remember bonds created over the years with friends and family and living or dying over our favorite teams. That passion and dedication is rewarded when our teams win, even if it takes decades to occur. Sports have turned into the opiate of the masses. It gives us a valuable diversion that many people cherish and wouldn't trade for anything. I know I wouldn't.

CHAPTER 7

Medical and Psychological Issues

THERE HAVE BEEN MANY CONTROVERSIES that have arisen over the years related to medical and psychological issues in sports. For decades, the ongoing serious problem of concussions was ignored by teams, players, and coaches. Players were told to suck it up and get back out there, even though doing so jeopardized their long-term health. In the last decade, however, sports organizations are taking the issue much more seriously and have developed rigorous protocols and rules. Other medical issues in sports include whether athletes should have surgeries, playing hurt, and athletes' privacy. Body image issues, such as anorexia, bulimia, and other eating disorders related to wrestling, gymnastics, and body building, have become prevalent. In addition, there are other psychological issues that athletes deal with, such as anxiety, depression, and hazing. Another medical issue is the use of performance-enhancing drugs, such as steroids, human growth hormone, and blood doping, that has also led to serious long-term medical problems. Use of these substances hurts the sports, and it's up to coaches, players, officials, administrative bodies, and parents to prevent the problem. A minority viewpoint has arisen that steroids should be legalized to level the playing field; however, in the long run the dangers of steroids are too severe and use of them taints fair competition. Therefore, it is a positive development that organizations at all levels are increasing testing. Another angle related to medical issues is the issue of providing access and opportunities to disabled athletes. This chapter will address the medical and psychological issues of sports.

Most athletes at every level feel pressure to play even when they are injured or hurt. No one wants to come across as "soft" to themselves, family, coaches, fans, and teammates. Also, if you sit out for an injury, your replacement might end up playing better than you did, and you might be the one who is replaced permanently. No one wants to be another Wally Pipp, the longtime New York Yankee first baseman who famously sat out a game in 1925 due to a headache and was then permanently replaced by future Hall of Fame legend Lou Gehrig.[1] Even if you're hurt, you want to go out there and do whatever it takes to help your team win.

Players are heavily scrutinized as to whether they are willing to play hurt, whether the criticism is fair or not. In the 2011 NFC Championship game against the Green Bay Packers, some Chicago Bears fans were critical of quarterback Jay Cutler, who was sidelined for most of the second half due to a knee injury, claiming that he should have toughed it out and played through the injury.[2]

Some players expressed disappointment or outrage over criticism for their not playing due to injury. According to KNBR, in 2020 San Francisco 49ers running back Raheem Mostert took to Twitter to complain about criticism by fantasy football players and critics about Mostert's ongoing ankle and knee injuries during the season that forced him to miss some games and limited his effectiveness. Among the things Mostert tweeted were "Do you really think players get hurt on purpose?!! Like we want to spend MONTHS in rehab NOT doing what we love?" and "And for the millionth time, PLAYERS DON'T CARE ABOUT YOUR FANTASY FOOTBALL TEAM. This is our real life."[3]

In some cases, players choose not to play in certain games for fear of being injured. This has occurred recently where some star college football players opt not to play in their team's bowl games because they don't want to suffer an injury that could decrease their value in the upcoming NFL draft. In criticizing this increasing trend, Paul Zeise wrote in the *Pittsburgh Post-Gazette* in December 2022, "[L]et's stop with all of this hyperbole about 'career-ending injuries' because it is the ultimate example of a bogeyman. These types of career-ending injuries are so incredibly rare it is laughable that they are used as justification for players sitting out of bowl games."[4]

No injured athlete wants to be another Wally Pipp, shown here ca. 1921; he was permanently replaced in the Yankees' lineup by Lou Gehrig. When Pipp sat out a game in 1925 due to a headache, Gehrig took his spot and didn't relinquish it for more than a decade, playing in 2,130 consecutive games until he had to retire in 1939 due to his developing ALS (photo from George Grantham Bain Collection, Prints & Photographs Division, Library of Congress, LC-DIG-ggbain-33135 [digital file from original negative]).

In other cases, some professional players will sit out during some regular-season games, especially toward the end of the season, in order to stay healthy for a playoff run. That is common if a team has already clinched a playoff spot. In some cases, especially during a long NBA season in which teams play several games a week, teams frequently rest star players so that they don't have to play back-to-back games, or they restrict their players' minutes during the game. This practice of resting star NBA players has been dubbed "load management," and it often deprives fans of seeing these star players play. In discussing the load management issue, Criss Partee wrote in *Deadspin*, "In fairness, it isn't every player, but load management usually comes up with star players, who have the ability and freedom to pick and choose when they play. But that's who fans go to see—the stars in the NBA."[5]

Players who have played through pain and injury have been praised and viewed as heroes by their team's fans.

In 1986, All-Pro defensive back Ronnie Lott of the 49ers famously chose to amputate part of his crushed finger during the off-season so that he would be ready to play the next season.[6] During Game 7 of the NBA Finals in 1970 against the Los Angeles Lakers, Willis Reed of the New York Knicks took an injection to dull the pain of a thigh injury and famously limped onto the court at the beginning of the game to inspire his teammates. To the surprise of many, Reed started the game and scored the first two baskets. The Knicks ended up winning the game and the title.[7] In Game 5 of the 1997 NBA Championship series against the Utah Jazz, an exhausted and staggering Michael Jordan overcame flu symptoms from a virus or food poisoning to score 38 points to pace the Bulls to a key victory.[8] During the 1996 women's gymnastics competition at the Atlanta Olympics, Kerri Strug, encouraged by her coach, Bela Karolyi, yelling "you can do it," overcame an injured ankle to land the essential vault that clinched the gold medal for the women's team.[9] In 2002, Philadelphia Eagles quarterback Donovan McNabb fractured his ankle on the third play of the game against the Arizona Cardinals, yet he finished the game and led the Eagles to a win, throwing four touchdowns. Eagles head coach Andy Reid said that McNabb told Reid and the coaching staff at halftime, "Let's just move on, and go. It's not a big deal. Tape it up. You guys are making way too much out of it."[10] Boston Red Sox fans will always remember the "bloody sock game" when Curt Schilling pitched after having a tendon in his ankle sutured before Game 6 of the 2004 ALCS.[11] In the 1976 Montreal Olympic Games, Shun Fujimoto helped his Japanese men's gymnastics team win a gold medal when he competed on the rings with a broken kneecap and dislocated it when he landed.[12] These athletes and many others have been admired and glorified for their courage in persevering through injury and pain to take one for the team.

Not all of the instances where athletes played hurt turned out well. In some cases, it was a disaster. One of the most famous examples was during the NBA Championship Finals in 2019, when Golden State Warriors star Kevin Durant, arguably the best player in the NBA, attempted to come back to play in Game 5 against the Toronto Raptors after missing about a month of playing due to a calf injury. The Warriors were down 3-1 in the series and were facing elimination in a road game in Toronto. For weeks, some people had questioned Durant's toughness and his dedication to the team. During the second quarter of the game, Durant suffered another more serious leg injury in the form of a torn Achilles tendon that would keep him sidelined for a much longer period. Many people criticized the Warriors' medical staff and organization for letting Durant play.[13]

Charles Barkley told ESPN, "I don't think you can ever leave it up to a player. Players always want to play. But I think if you ask any rational player ... to put a guy who hasn't played basketball in over a month into Game 5 of the Finals, and have some type of move around the day before, I don't think that's fair to that man."[14]

Durant had been cleared to play by the Warriors' medical staff after Game 4 of the series, and Durant did play well during Game 5, scoring 11 points in 12 minutes. While Durant may have proved his toughness and competitiveness, it came at too high of a cost.

Sometimes regarding player injuries there can be many competing interests as to whether the athlete should return to playing, including those of the player, teammates, coaches, agents, family members, trainers, team physicians, consulting doctors, general managers, owners, athletic directors, members of the media, and fans. For instance, should the athlete have surgery right away and miss the rest of the season, or should they play hurt the rest of the year? The main goal for all should be to return the athlete to the field or court as quickly as possible, but more important when it is safe for them to return. However, the coaches' jobs are on the line every season due to the immense pressure to win. There aren't many coaches that have total job security. Those coaches want their best players to be on the field. Fans and media members will give intense scrutiny on athletes and when they will return to the field or court, oftentimes criticizing players who sit out many games during a season due to injury. Although the injured player is dying to get back on the field or court, their long-term health needs to be the ultimate consideration.

According to *Science Daily*, a 2016 Harvard Medical School study outlined legal and ethical recommendations involving the health of NFL players. Among the factors noted by the study were minimizing conflict of interest, adopting and improving ethical guidelines, adequate collection and access to data, and a patient bill of rights for NFL players.[15]

In discussing the use of risk-defusing operators (RDOs) in counseling injured athletes when they can return to playing, Mayer et al. wrote in *Frontiers in Psychology*, "[T]eam doctors and coaches should be very careful in offering RDO-related information." For example, if a team apparently needs support of an injured player, mentioning the option "to start competing and see how the pain develops" is an effective way to steer the athlete's decision toward "play." The same holds true for risk defusing recommendations like "play at less than 100%" or "stop playing when the pain increases." Offering RDOs like these trivialize health risks and promote playing hurt. "In contrast, players can be easily convinced to rest if they are told that choosing the medically safe alternative does not have severe sporting consequences, like the loss of a starting position."[16]

Since most athletes at all levels are fierce competitors, the issue of playing hurt will always be a part of sports. Another medical and psychological issue related to sports are eating disorders, which are common for athletes in many sports. According to the National Eating Disorders Association, a study revealed that over one-third of female NCAA athletes reported attitudes and symptoms placing them at risk for anorexia nervosa.[17]

Women's gymnastics is one of the most susceptible sports to eating disorders. Many gymnastics coaches insist that their athletes maintain certain weights. Olympic gold medalist Nadia Comaneci battled eating disorders, as did noted US Olympic gymnast Cathy Rigby.[18] According to the Associated Press, "One limited study by the American College of Sports Medicine found that up to 62% of female gymnasts have an eating disorder." Christy Henrich, a top American gymnast, suffered from eating disorders that led to her death at age 22 in 1994, weighing less than 60 pounds.[19]

Eating disorders are also an issue for men and boys. One of the main sports where this comes into play is wrestling. Young wrestlers often starve themselves and train intensely in small, hot workout rooms wearing heavy exercise suits in order to make the requirements for the lowest weight class possible. During wrestling season, they might try to exist on a regular diet of mainly carrots and celery. They do this to get an advantage over a naturally smaller opponent or to fill a weight class spot for their team. This attempt at weight loss often takes place in a short amount of time, such as a day or two. Some wrestlers use diet pills, laxatives, dehydration, and vomiting as methods to lose weight quickly. Severe dehydration can cause organ damage, and three college wrestlers died from dehydration weight loss in 1997.[20] Bonnie Taub-Dix wrote in 2012 in *U.S. News & World Report* that one-quarter to two-thirds of high school wrestlers use extreme weight loss techniques like dehydration, extreme exercise, and extreme dieting to make their lower weight class. She wrote, "Although most wrestlers look to their coaches or teammates for tips on how to cut weight effectively, that doesn't guarantee that the advice they receive encourages safe weight loss. If a coach suspects that disordered eating practices are endangering a player, he should be suggesting a referral to a pediatrician or recommending a consultation with a registered dietitian."[21]

Ice skating, boxing, UFC, and rowing are among other sports that have issues related to eating disorders.

Football is another sport that deals with this issue, especially in leagues where there is a weight requirement. According to a 1994 *Newsweek* article, "And a study of 131 Cornell University lightweight football players, completed this spring, found that 40 percent engaged in 'dysfunctional eating patterns' (mostly hinging or purging), with 10 percent classified as having outright eating disorders."[22]

Not all of eating disorders among athletes involve anorexia and weight loss. Some athletes suffer from obesity or binge eating. One of the most publicized athletes who struggled with this was Penn State kicker Joey Julius, who battled a binge eating disorder that started when he was nine years old. In November 2017, during his keynote speech at Mental Health and Wellness Week at Penn State, Julius told the audience that he gained 40 pounds during his senior year in high school and that he was embarrassed after people mocked his appearance online during a Penn State game and he became a viral sensation. He told the audience that he had told a trainer that he was contemplating suicide.[23]

In light of the many mental health issues that athletes must deal with, sports psychology has become an emerging and growing field. Sports psychologists adhere to a code of ethics and are expected to preserve confidentiality. According to the American Psychological Association, "Sport psychology is a proficiency that uses psychological knowledge and skills to address optimal performance and well-being of athletes, developmental and social aspects of sports participation, and systemic issues associated with sports settings and organizations."[24]

Sports psychologists can help athletes address anxiety and depression; fear of failure; poor concentration; performing in pressure situations; breaking out of a slump; dealing with negative criticism from fans and the media; dealing with teammates, coaches, referees, and opponents; the need for perfection; eating disorders; and substance abuse. In the past, athletes would have to turn to coaches, mentors, parents, teammates, teachers, or friends to help them deal with these issues, often resisting help from a trained mental health professional. Sports psychologists deal with athletes, coaches, and trainers. They can help a golfer with their swing, aid a baseball player in getting out of a hitting slump, help a field goal kicker deal with game-deciding kicks, help a pitcher focus on the strike zone, help a basketball player calm down while shooting free throws, give advice to soccer players on how to handle pressure involved in penalty kicks, and give advice to tennis players on how to win key points in a match. There are many undergraduate, master's, and doctoral sports psychology programs at universities across the country. A wide range of athletes at all levels are now consulting with sports psychologists to help them deal with their problems. Sports psychologist Dr. Chris Carr, who was hired on staff by the Green Bay Packers in 2020, told ESPN that in recent years, the NCAA was making sports psychology and mental health services a priority. Carr said, "In some ways this is a transitional shift in the culture of sports where we realize these are real issues and you need to have really good, competent providers to take care of those athletes."[25]

Many athletes have had to deal with and overcome psychological issues. In years past, this was something that most athletes would keep private. However, in recent years, many prominent athletes have come forward and admitted and described their mental health struggles. Perhaps the most prominent athlete to come forward was legendary Olympic swimmer Michael Phelps, who described his mental health issues for the first time before the 2016 Summer Olympics in Brazil. He continued to be an advocate for mental health issues, joining the board of Talkspace, an online company that provides access to therapists.[26] Philadelphia Eagles Pro Bowl offensive lineman Brandon Brooks went public with his anxiety disorder that forced him to miss several games.[27] Royce White starred at Iowa State and was selected as a first-round pick by the Houston Rockets in 2012. However, White struggled with anxiety issues, particularly his fear of flying. He never played for the Rockets. He did play briefly for two teams in the NBA Developmental League, played in one game for the Sacramento Kings, and played two successful seasons professionally in Canada.[28] According to *USA Today*, other prominent athletes who came forward to disclose their struggles with mental illness included former Los Angeles Laker legend Jerry West, New York Giants wide receiver Brandon Marshall, WNBA player Imani Boyette, tennis pro Mardy Fish, MLB pitcher and outfielder Rick Ankiel, and Olympic swimming gold medalist Allison Schmitt. In 2017, Phelps told *USA Today*'s Scott Gleeson and Erik Brady, "For the longest time, I thought asking for help was a sign of weakness because that's kind of what society teaches us. That's especially true from an athlete's perspective. If we ask for help, then we're not this big macho athlete that people can look up to. Well, you know what? If someone wants to call me weak for asking for help, that's their problem. Because I'm saving my own life."[29]

The issue of athletes and mental health received international attention when tennis star Naomi Osaka withdrew from the 2021 French Open due to her objections to having to do interviews due to her anxiety in talking to the media. Osaka was fined $15,000 and threatened with suspension for her failure to appear at French Open press conferences. After withdrawing from the tournament, Osaka revealed that she was suffering from anxiety and depression. A few months after that incident, star American gymnast Simone Biles stunned the world when she dropped out of the women's team finals competition at the Tokyo Olympics, in part due to pressure and stress and the belief that she would hurt her team if she continued to perform in the event. She subsequently proceeded to withdraw from the individual all-around finals and three individual apparatus events.[30]

Some people mocked and criticized Biles for her actions. Piers Morgan, a pundit and former British TV host, tweeted, "Are 'mental health issues' now the go-to excuse for any poor performance in elite sport? What a joke. Just admit you did badly, made mistakes, and will strive to do better next time. Kids need strong role models not this nonsense."[31] However, most people around the world, including athletes and celebrities such as Taylor Swift, Justin Bieber, Katie Ledecky, and Michael Phelps, were very supportive of Biles and praised her decision, citing her courage to come forward on this issue. Olympic gold medal swimming champion Katie Ledecky told *Us Weekly*, "She's such an amazing athlete. She's really shown a lot of bravery over the last week. [She] reminded everyone that mental health is a key part of health."[32] Biles returned to the Olympic competition in dramatic fashion a few days later, winning a bronze medal in the balance beam. "We're not just entertainment, we're humans," Biles said. "And there are things going on behind the scenes that we're also trying to juggle with as well, on top of sports."[33]

David Cassilo argued in his article in *Communication & Sport* that the media should focus on stories of athletes dealing with mental health issues to humanize them. "In prior research related to media coverage of mental health, there has been a call for more content focusing on the firsthand accounts of individuals who have mental health concerns (Wahl et al., 2002; Whitley & Berry, 2013). By hearing from people who actually have these conditions, it can humanize the experience. In sports, this challenges the stigma, as fans can see that even the top athletes in the world experience concerns like depression and anxiety."[34]

Concussion awareness and protocol is another medical issue in sports that has gotten increased attention in recent years. As noted in another chapter of this book, many concussions occur due to the violence in sports including football, ice hockey, boxing, UFC, and MMA. However, there also is increasing concern about concussions in soccer, mostly due to frequent heading of the ball during a game or a clashing of players' heads. According to James Ellingworth of the Associated Press, in May 2019, the UEFA, European soccer's governing body, announced that it wanted to revise its rules to allow doctors to assess players for head injuries during a game so that concussed players are not put back in the game. It also indicated that it might support rule changes regarding substitutions. In 2014, FIFA instituted a rule that allowed for three-minute breaks during a game to allow for concussion checks.[35]

Neurosurgeon Dr. Michael Cusimano of St. Michael's Hospital in Toronto stated in *Science Daily* in 2019 that in light of the high concussion rates in soccer, high-level players with potential concussions should be assessed appropriately. "Given the 'trickle-down' effect from professional levels to youth and informal play, the health and future performance of players at all levels demand that groups like FIFA and UEFA follow the protocols to which they were a signatory."[36]

Another medical and psychological issue in sports that occurred in recent years was a major controversy involving the sexual abuse of gymnasts. In 2018, Larry Nassar, the former national team doctor for USA Gymnastics, was accused of sexually assaulting hundreds of athletes. He pleaded guilty to multiple counts of sexual assault of athletes and was sentenced to a long prison sentence. One of the high-profile gymnasts who was sexually abused was Simone Biles, who won four gold medals at the 2016 Rio Games. In 2019, she criticized USA Gymnastics for failing to protect their athletes, telling the media, "[T]hey couldn't do one damn job. You had one job. You literally had one job and you couldn't protect us."[37]

One of the most significant medical issues in sports history took place in 2020. The world came to a halt in 2020 due to the coronavirus. In the United States, it wasn't until the sports world took the virus seriously that the entire country took the virus seriously. Sports screeched to a halt in March 2020 when NBA player Rudy Gobert tested positive for COVID-19.[38] The NBA promptly announced that it was suspending the season. Other pro sports leagues followed suit shortly thereafter. For a short time, the NCAA had contemplated playing the NCAA men's basketball tournament without fans, but it quickly changed its mind and canceled March Madness in its entirety. The next few months were a frustrating time for sports fans who looked to sports as a psychological and emotional release. It was also a devastating time for athletes at all levels, especially those playing youth sports, high school sports, and college sports.

The spring of 2020 was a desert as far as the absence of live sporting events around the world. For several months, sports fans had to settle for watching reruns of prior famous games. Things opened up on a slow gradual scale. First came pro baseball in South Korea, then came German soccer. In the United States, NASCAR, pro golf, pro tennis, UFC, and cornhole were the first sports to come back to live action. The NBA eventually renewed its season during the summer of 2020 with an eight-game regular-season conclusion and playoffs. The NHL went straight to the playoffs. Major League Soccer held a World Cup–style tournament to crown its season champion. After weeks of negotiations, Major League Baseball settled on a shortened season and held a World Series.

There were extensive precautions regarding the health and safety of the returning players. The NBA sequestered its players, coaches, and staff in a designated bubble area in Orlando, Florida, for the duration of its season and playoffs. Everyone entering the arena was tested for the virus. The players were holed up in the Walt Disney World hotels during the entire tournament, which lasted three months.

One of the big debates during 2020 and the beginning of 2021 was when and if fans should be allowed to attend pro or college sporting events. At first, there were no fans in attendance, as games were played in empty stadiums and arenas. During the summer of 2020, many people started to advocate that there should be fans at pro and college football games during the fall, perhaps with stadiums half-full of fans.

The New York Giants and New York Jets became the first NFL teams to announce that they would not have fans in the stands during the 2020 season. Most other NFL teams followed suit. It wasn't until late in the season that fans started to return to all NFL stadiums.

In a July 2020 op-ed that I wrote for *Street & Smith's Sports Business Journal*, I argued that it was a bad idea to have fans in the stadiums at sporting events during the pandemic. I wrote in part that even though fans are a huge part of the energy and passion of sports and give rise to a home-field advantage, it wasn't worth the health risk to have thousands of fans gather together in stadiums, even with a mask requirement. I noted that many fans would take their masks off during the games and would be maskless in many areas such as bathrooms and luxury suites. I wrote, "To many, a packed stadium of sports fans would be a symbol of normalcy. However, until there is a vaccine or a sufficient cure, it's a dumb idea. Right now, we're only in the first inning or first quarter of this struggle against the virus. We have to adapt to this new reality. Watching sports without fans should be a part of this new reality. It's like restaurants being open for takeout only. Yes, you don't get the full restaurant experience, but at least you're getting to eat the food."[39]

Toward the end of 2020 and the beginning of 2021, teams and leagues started to allow fans back into their indoor and outdoor stadiums. However, the coronavirus had an impact on the Tokyo Summer Olympics in 2021, as fans were prohibited from attending the Olympic events due to a large spike of coronavirus cases in Japan. Many athletes tested positive for the virus either right before or during the Olympics and were unable to participate in the Games. Some of the more prominent athletes to drop out of the Games due to the virus included emerging tennis star Coco Gauff, NBA star Bradley Beal, and pro golfers Bryson DeChambeau and Jon Rahm.[40]

Another coronavirus-related issue arose related to vaccinations. The NFL announced a new policy in July 2021 requiring that when a game was canceled due to a virus outbreak in a team's unvaccinated players, the result would be a forfeit by that team and players from both teams would not be paid for the canceled game.[41]

From 2020 through 2022 was not the first time that the sports world had to deal with a major health pandemic. In the late 1910s, the world suffered a major pandemic in the form of the Spanish flu, which killed between 50 and 100 million people worldwide, including around 675,000 Americans. According to the Baseball Hall of Fame, the disease killed several minor league baseball players, sportswriters, umpires, and Larry Chappell, a major league player who had played for the White Sox, Indians, and Boston Braves.[42] According to Yahoo Sports, Major League Baseball players, managers, and umpires wore protective masks during games. The 1918 regular season was cut one month short. College football teams played a condensed schedule in 1918, with at least 18 teams not playing any games at all. The 1919 Stanley Cup finals were canceled after players on both teams got the flu and were hospitalized. A major heavyweight boxing match between Jack Dempsey and Battling Levinsky was canceled.[43] Babe Ruth and boxer Tommy Burns were hit with the flu, but they survived.[44]

There have been many medically related tragedies that athletes have suffered. Among the tragic health-related deaths that received national attention were the sudden cardiac deaths of basketball stars Hank Gathers and Len Bias.

In the late 1980s, Hank Gathers was emerging as a major force in college basketball. The Philadelphia native moved to California to attend USC, but he transferred after one season and joined with Bo Kimble to help establish Loyola Marymount as one of the best teams in the country featuring its high-paced, high-scoring offense. During his college career, Gathers averaged over 23 points and nine rebounds. In his senior season in 1989–1990, the 6'7" Gathers was averaging over 29 points and 10 rebounds a game. He had established himself as one of the top college basketball players in the country, as well as a future NBA lottery pick. However, Gathers's promising basketball career and his life came to an abrupt and tragic end. During a West Coast Conference tournament game against Portland University, Gathers collapsed at midcourt and died suddenly of a heart condition. A few months earlier, Gathers had collapsed in a regular-season game against UC Santa Barbara. He was diagnosed with an irregular heartbeat and was prescribed a beta blocker. Doctors cleared Gathers to play while on the beta blockers but Gathers reportedly might have reduced his intake of the drug because it sapped his energy. The 23-year-old died from the heart muscle disorder hypertrophic cardiomyopathy. Remarkably, Loyola made an inspired run to the Elite Eight as an 11th seed in the NCAA Tournament, shortly after Gathers's death.[45]

Len Bias was one of the greatest college basketball players in the history of the

ACC. The 6'8" forward averaged over 23 points and seven rebounds per game during his senior season in 1985–1986. He was selected as the second pick in the 1986 NBA draft by the NBA champion Boston Celtics. However, only two days after the draft, Bias died of cocaine intoxication, which resulted in seizures and cardiac arrest. Larry Bird told a reporter that this was "one of the cruelest things I've ever heard." It was a shock to many people that someone as healthy and athletic as Bias could die from using cocaine.[46]

Another tragic medical-related death took place in 2018 when University of Maryland offensive lineman Jordan McNair died after suffering heatstroke during a team workout, and it took over an hour for the team training staff to call 911 after he showed heatstroke symptoms. According to CNN, "An independent medical report found several issues with his treatment, including failure to assess his vital signs, not having proper cooling devices and failure to recognize quickly he was having heat illness." McNair's family reached a $3.5 million settlement with the university.[47]

Another serious medical issue in sports relates to steroid use. The use of performance-enhancing drugs, such as steroids, human growth hormone, and blood doping, is a type of cheating that has tainted the sports world for decades. Steroid use by athletes is dangerous and taints fair competition. Fortunately, leagues and organizations at all levels are increasing testing.

For several years, Lance Armstrong was a feel-good story. He overcame testicular cancer to become one of the greatest cyclists in the world, winning seven consecutive Tour de France titles. However, this feel-good story turned out to be too good to be true. After Armstrong retired from cycling in 2005, a French newspaper reported that blood samples retested from a 1999 race showed EPO use that year. For several years, Armstrong vehemently denied the allegations, but in 2012, the US Anti-Doping Agency issued a lifetime ban on Armstrong after he did not fight allegations that he had cheated through doping. In 2013, Armstrong finally came clean during a highly publicized television interview with Oprah Winfrey in which he admitted to using performance-enhancing substances for years.[48]

Canadian sprinter Ben Johnson stunned the world when he demolished legendary sprinter Carl Lewis and the rest of the field in the 100-meter dash at the 1988 Seoul Olympics, shattering the world record at 9.79 seconds. For a very short time, Johnson was viewed as a Canadian national hero. However, it all came crashing down two days later when traces of a banned steroid were found in Johnson's urine, and he had to give his gold medal back to the IOC.[49]

Baseball suffered from the steroid era of the 1990s. In 1998, Mark McGwire and Sammy Sosa captivated the nation with their chase of Roger Maris's record of 61 homers in a season. McGwire set the regular-season record with 70 homers that season, but years later he admitted that he had used steroids.[50] In 2001, Barry Bonds, also suspected of using steroids, hit 73 home runs that season, breaking McGwire's record.[51]

One of the frequent debates regarding steroids in baseball are whether steroid users or suspected users should be eligible for admission to Baseball's Hall of Fame. Should those players be eligible for admission because their success was not due solely to the use of the steroids? Or should cheaters not be rewarded? Right now, the compromise seems to be that these players are on the ballot, but thus far, as of 2022, none of them have been voted in. Maybe there should be a separate steroid wing in the Hall of Fame with enlarged statues that are "swole" like Arnold Schwarzenegger.

In framing the debate of whether steroid users should be allowed into the Baseball Hall of Fame, Parsons and Stern wrote in the *Sociology of Sport Journal*, "Among baseball writers and fans, the issue of voting for players who were implicated as having used steroids is contested. Some argue that due to the widely held belief that anywhere between twenty and thirty percent of players were using some type of performance enhancing drug during this era, vote-casting sportswriters should simply treat the so-called Steroid Era as part of history and vote the best players into the Hall of Fame. Conversely, others (including the majority of baseball writers) believe players implicated in steroid use acted dishonorably, and are therefore undeserving of being collectively remembered and revered as part of the game's history."[52]

In 2017, Baseball Hall of Famer Joe Morgan wrote a letter to the Hall of Fame voters stating his objection to steroid users being eligible for the Hall of Fame. Morgan wrote, "We hope the day never comes when known steroid users are voted into the Hall of Fame. They cheated. Steroid users don't belong here. Players who failed drug tests, admitted using steroids, or were identified as users in Major League Baseball's investigation into steroid abuse, known as the Mitchell Report, should not get in…. By cheating, they put up huge numbers, and they made great players who didn't cheat look smaller by comparison, taking away from their achievements and consideration for the Hall of Fame. That's not right."[53]

In arguing that great players who used steroids during the steroid era should be in the MLB Hall of Fame, Tom Joyce argued in the *Washington Examiner* that the players assumed the physical risks in using steroids and that the Hall of Fame should not ignore those great players' contributions to the game. Joyce wrote, "The Hall of Fame should be about recognizing the achievements of the players, regardless of what it took for them to do it."[54]

In 2007, former US senator George Mitchell released his 409-page report identifying dozens of current and former Major League Baseball players who were linked to the illegal use of steroids and other performance-enhancing drugs such as human growth hormones. Among the star players named in the report were Roger Clemens, Barry Bonds, Andy Pettitte, Jason Giambi, Rafael Palmeiro, and Gary Sheffield. As reported by ESPN, the Mitchell Report stated, "Everyone involved in baseball over the past two decades—commissioners, club officials, the players' association and players—shares to some extent the responsibility for the steroids era. There was a collective failure to recognize the problem as it emerged and to deal with it early on."[55]

A very small minority of people have argued that steroids should be legalized so that the playing field will be level and individual players don't have to worry whether others have an unfair advantage. They also argue that taking steroids is an individual decision and that players decide to take steroids knowing the likely physical risks. Therefore, this informed consent makes the taking of steroids acceptable.

In advocating for the legalization of performance-enhancing drugs in sports, Chris Smith wrote in *Forbes*, "Not only would the playing field suddenly be even for all players, it would be at a higher level. A huge part of watching sports is witnessing the very peak of human athletic ability, and legalizing performance enhancing drugs would help athletes climb even higher. Steroids and doping will help pitchers to throw harder, home runs to go further, cyclists to charge for longer and sprinters to test the very limits of human speed."[56]

Ethics professor Julian Savulescu of the Oxford Centre of Neuroethics told *Wired* magazine,

"Doping is not against the spirit of sport. It has always part of the human spirit to use knowledge to make oneself better and doping has been a part of sport since its beginning. Doping should only be banned when it is significantly harmful relative to the inherent risks of sport, or against the spirit of a particular sport." He noted that while certain drugs would be inappropriate in archery and shooting to reduce tremors, or in boxing to reduce fear, "[B]lood doping up to a haematocrit [percentage of red blood cells in blood] of 50 percent is safe and not against the spirit of cycling."[57]

However, the detriment to the health of athletes who take steroids is overwhelming. Among the negative side effects are severe acne, increased blood pressure, weight gain, insomnia, blurred vision, heart disease, kidney disease, liver disease, and increased risk of aggression and depression. Players shouldn't have to be pressured to take steroids to keep up with the Joneses.

Rejecting the idea of legalizing steroids, Joe Valerio, a former NFL player for the Kansas City Chiefs and St. Louis Rams in the 1990s and an adjunct professor at Arcadia University's School of Global Business, said in a Zoom interview confirmed by email, "Steroids for athletic or casual use should not be legal. It's not good for the body, and it's not natural. It overshadows things like hard work, effort, blood, sweat, and tears. It's such an easy way out to get more strength. If they were legal, then you would have the issue of how much should or could be legal. It would be a slippery slope. How much would be enough? Steroids are proven to have some bad side effects like developing muscle mass too quickly or losing tendon strength. Sports aren't worth putting your body in harm's way by taking the easy way out. It's just unnatural to me."[58]

In arguing against the legalization of doping in sports under medical supervision, Marie Overbye stated in the *International Journal of Drug Policy* that this "might open a Pandora's box of uncertain outcomes, likely to lead to unpredictable games with unintended consequences for a greater number of athletes but without the capacity to truly ensure the protection of drug-using athletes' health.... Although the current drug regulation model faces a great variety of challenges, the solution of permitting strongly performance-enhancing and health-damaging doping substances under medical supervision would create new types of harms for athletes and that this trade-off between harms would be unwanted from the perspective of most athletes. Therefore, if the aim is to protect health and secure fairer competition for athletes in general, the legalising of certain 'doping' substances under medical supervision seems to be an inappropriate strategy."[59]

There have been many tragic incidents involving prominent athletes who used steroids. Lyle Alzado, a star defensive end in the NFL for 15 seasons, believed that his steroid use was responsible for his brain cancer. Alzado, who was one of the first prominent athletes to admit steroid use, died from cancer in 1992 at age 43. Baseball star Ken Caminiti admitted that he was on steroids in 1996 when he was named MVP of the National League. In 2004, he died from intoxication due to cocaine and opiates, with coronary artery disease and an enlarged heart as contributing factors.[60]

There can be a great deal of pressure for an athlete to take steroids and other performance-enhancing substances. This pressure can start at a young age. Freshmen and sophomores in high school might consider taking steroids so that they can get bigger and stronger so that they can make the varsity team. Once they make the team, there is the pressure to stay on steroids to keep their competitive edge. Juniors and seniors might be tempted to take steroids in order to get noticed by college football coaches and recruiters. The cycle and process then continues throughout college and then the NFL.

Joe Valerio said in a Zoom interview, "Fortunately, I didn't have any pressure to take steroids in high school or college. I went to a suburban school and steroids just weren't popular there, so there was no pressure. I didn't have access to steroids and I didn't need to do them. I also played multiple sports, so I was more focused on being a well-rounded athlete and didn't really need steroids. The pressures in college can be different though, where there's more pressure to succeed and to be on the field, and it might be harder to resist. I decided that steroids wouldn't be fair to me, my body, or my family. I would rather not succeed than use them to get ahead. It wasn't worth violating NCAA rules or laws. I understand, however, that peer pressure can be overwhelming, so it's important to surround yourself with people who want you to succeed the right way. In the pros, it would have been much harder to take steroids because the tests were too stringent and random. In the '80s and '90s some players performed really well in college due to steroids but then fizzled out in the NFL because they lost their edge when they couldn't do steroids anymore."[61]

In recent years, there has been an attempt at all levels to try to crack down on steroid use. At the high school level, the United States Supreme Court ruled in 1995 in *Veronia School District v. Acton* that random drug testing of athletes did not violate their Fourth Amendment right to privacy. Although testing is legal, most states do not have drug testing programs due to the high cost and infrequent positive test results.[62] In January 2019, an Indiana state senator introduced a bill that would allow for random drug testing of Indiana high school student-athletes.[63] In 2006, New

Jersey started steroid testing of high school athletes who qualify for postseason tournaments. During the 2016–2017 school year, only one student athlete out of 502 who were tested had a positive result, according to *MyCentralJersey.com*.[64]

In 2015, the American Academy of Pediatrics issued a policy statement that it opposed widespread implementation of drug testing programs for adolescents due to insufficient evidence that they were effective. Instead, they advocated for drug abuse prevention programs in schools, intervention programs and referral systems, and school-based services for students with substance use disorders. Regarding schools that decide to use drug testing, the AAP suggested that they monitor their programs for adverse effects, such as decreased participation in sports.[65]

Some school districts enact an opt-out policy. According to *Forbes*, pursuant to such a policy, in 2017 in a suburb of Columbus, Ohio, parents of 206 kids pulled their kids from drug testing, as opposed to 193 parents who consented.[66]

At the college level, the California Supreme Court ruled in 1994 in Hill v. NCAA that drug testing of college athletes did not violate plaintiffs' state constitutional right to privacy.[67]

At the end of the 1986 college football season, 21 players were ruled ineligible for playing in their teams' bowl games due to positive drug tests. The most high-profile player who tested positive and was suspended was Oklahoma All-America linebacker Brian Bosworth, who had to sit out the Orange Bowl. In his defense, Bosworth claimed that he had taken medically prescribed steroids to help rehabilitate his injured shoulder.[68] In 2008, Tony Mandarich, formerly known as "the Incredible Bulk," admitted to Showtime that he had taken steroids while playing at Michigan State, and that he had faked a drug test before playing in the 1988 Rose Bowl by providing a fake urine sample.[69]

In recent years, professional leagues and the NCAA have stepped up their drug testing measures.

The NCAA bans certain types of performance-enhancing drugs, including steroids. According to the NCAA's website, "The NCAA conducts testing at its championships, and year round on campus in Division I and II programs. In addition, the majority of institutions conduct their own institutional testing programs independent of NCAA drug testing. The NCAA spends more than $6 million annually on drug testing and education in an effort to deter the use of banned and harmful substances." The individual schools educate their student-athletes about the NCAA drug testing policies and about banned substances.[70]

While increased drug testing for banned substances has led to fewer incidents, they still occasionally occur. In 2019, two Clemson football players were suspended for the upcoming season after failing drug tests for ostarine, a banned substance.[71]

In 2014, Major League Baseball and the MLB Players Union entered into an agreement to strengthen the league's drug testing program by increasing the penalties for violation, requiring players to give two urine samples during the season, increasing the sophistication of the testing so that it can detect drug use from a two-week period, and random blood collections during the season.[72] The new rules had a positive effect. According to *USA Today*, positive drug test results dropped by over 50 percent from 2016 to 2017.[73]

The NFL began testing its players for steroids in 1987. In September 2014, the NFL and NFL Players Association agreed to testing for human growth hormone as well as an overhaul of the league's drug program.[74]

Pursuant to the NFL's drug testing policy, 10 players from each team are randomly tested each week during the season.[75] In 2019, Carolina Panthers safety Eric Reid, a staunch ally of controversial quarterback Colin Kaepernick, questioned the policy after he was selected to be tested six times during the 11 weeks that he was with the team.[76]

In 2015, the NBA started testing for human growth hormone.[77] It also tests for "drugs of abuse" that are not steroids. In May 2019, the NBA dismissed and disqualified Indiana Pacers guard and former rookie of the year Tyreke Evans from the league for a minimum of two seasons for violating the league's drug policy. In 2016, the league also banned guard O.J. Mayo for two years for violating the league's drug policy. These suspensions were for an unspecified "drug of abuse."[78]

Coaches should not ignore when certain players are showing symptoms of steroid use. They need to educate young athletes about the dangers of steroid use and that such use will not be tolerated on the team.

As reported by *Inside the Games*, a Scottish study found that coaches can play an important role in combating use of steroids and performance-enhancing substances, and that coaches and athletes should have anti-doping conversations.[79]

There is a debate among the major sports as to how to treat marijuana use. In 2016, former NBA player Jay Williams told Fox Business that he estimated that 75 to 80 percent of NBA players used marijuana and he encouraged the league to be more progressive in allowing athletes to use the substance, since it can help relieve pain.[80] In 2021, the United States Anti-Doping Agency decided to ban sprinter Sha'Carri Richardson from participating in the Tokyo Olympics because she had tested positive for marijuana after winning the women's 100-meter race at the US Olympic Trials in June. Richardson said she took marijuana to help her cope with her mother's death. While some people defended the decision, others felt that the punishment was too harsh.[81]

Another angle related to medical issues involves providing access and opportunities to disabled athletes. Many of us have been inspired by disabled athletes who have worked hard to overcome the odds to succeed in sports. The rise of the Paralympics, Special Olympics, and Invictus Games has given disabled athletes a forum to participate and display their skills, as well as to change society's views of disabled people. Many athletes have successfully competed against able-bodied athletes, such as Oscar Pistorius; pro golfer Casey Martin; and Anthony Robles, the one-legged NCAA wrestling champion. Unfortunately, there has been occasional controversy and debate whether certain disabled athletes actually have an advantage over nondisabled athletes.

One of the more notable incidents took place when professional golfer Casey Martin wanted to ride a golf cart during professional tournaments due to his debilitating leg disease, which limited his ability to walk. The PGA officials refused to grant Martin's request, alleging that walking was an essential part of the game of golf and that using a golf cart would grant Martin an unfair advantage. Martin proceeded to sue the PGA for violating the Americans with Disabilities Act and prevailed on appeal when the United States Supreme Court ruled in his favor in 2001.[82]

While the PGA felt that it should have the right to set the rules that govern the sport, their position toward Martin angered many people, including me. As I noted in my article in the *Chicago Tribune* at the time, "[T]he golf establishment looked foolish in defending the sport. If walking is a sport, maybe they should give 1st place medals to those who finish first in the Easter Day Parade."[83]

Martin played in the US Open using a golf cart in 1998 and 2012. The next pro golfer to get permission to use a golf cart during a major championship was John Daly, who was allowed to in the 2019 US Open due to osteoarthritis and a knee injury. Not everyone was happy with the decision, as Tiger Woods noted that he had won the 2009 US Open while walking with a broken leg.[84] However, Woods was supportive of Casey Martin. In general, most people viewed Martin positively as a pioneer and a trailblazer for the rights of the disabled. To many, the incident made professional golf look coldhearted. Martin eventually became the head coach for the University of Oregon's golf team.

Rejecting the argument that the Supreme Court decision in the Martin case would lead to an all-out modification of pro sports rules by the courts, Melissa Ann Resslar argued in the *Loyola University Chicago Law Journal*, "[G]olf is one of only a few sports that easily lends itself to modification under the ADA without changing the nature of the game. For example, using a strobe light during swimming or track and field meets will successfully, allow hearing-impaired athletes to compete, but will not have an effect on the hearing athletes' ability to be the fastest in their respective heat. However, not all sports can reasonably accommodate a disabled athlete without fundamentally altering the game. Casey Martin, for example, would not be able to request a modification of the rules of baseball, which require a player to run the bases. Waiving this type of rule in baseball is an extreme modification that would result in a fundamental alteration to the game."[85]

The sport of track and field faced a dilemma regarding the accommodation of disabled athletes when Oscar Pistorius inspired many people around the world as a world-class sprinter with two prosthetic legs. For years, the IOC denied Pistorius the chance to run in international events, claiming that his artificial legs below the knee, called Cheetahs, gave him an unfair advantage over able-bodied runners. Eventually, Pistorius prevailed on appeal and was allowed to compete for a spot in the 2008 Olympics, but he failed to qualify. Subsequently, he did extremely well in the 2012 Olympics, advancing to the semifinal round of the 400 meters. His performance inspired a worldwide audience. Pistorius subsequently was convicted in South Africa for killing his girlfriend in 2013.[86]

Before the 2012 Olympics, CBS Sports columnist Gregg Doyel argued that Pistorius should not be allowed to compete because it would be unfair to able-bodied athletes. While Pistorius wouldn't win that year, Doyel said, blade technology could improve enough to give him an unfair advantage by 2016.[87]

In fact, there is a phenomenon known as techno-doping, in which athletes use equipment to their advantage.[88] This has led to the debate of whether such a technique is appropriate.

In framing the debate regarding whether disabled runners like Pistorius should be allowed to compete against nondisabled runners, Burkett et al. wrote, "[T]he decisions about technology and sport are complex and must be based on a combination of scientific data and philosophical arguments pertaining to the nature of the challenge (articulated by the rules of every sport) and ethical ones regarding the un/fairness of the contest for victory therein."

The authors concluded, "The challenge for the future sports medicine and science research is to effectively 'match' the technology with the athlete and to ensure that it does so in a manner that preserves the integrity of sports contests and does so in a way that is accessible to all athletes at that level of competition in order to avoid Formula 1 style competition between engineers and technologists that are accessible to only wealthy individuals, teams, or nations."[89]

In supporting the decision to declare Pistorius ineligible for the 2008 Olympics, Lippi et al. wrote, "Technology is a great aid and the most favourable opportunity to overcome disabilities in daily life. It has nothing to do with traditional competitive sports, however, especially if 'cyborgization' is challenging to replace nature's own evolutionary scheme. If not, given the problems in controlling all potential aspects of athletic enhancement, it may be time to split Olympics and all sports further into traditional ('without enhancements') and open (doped, recombinant, bionic athletes …) categories."[90]

In opposing Pistorius's exclusion from the 2008 Olympics, S.D. Edwards wrote, "[F]irst it is not at all clear that the blades generate an advantage for OP. More likely, the opposite is the case. Second, even if they do confer an advantage, these abound in sport."

Edwards also wrote, "However, an argument of the kind just given will not succeed since it does not distinguish the kind of advantage (allegedly) possessed by OP from the advantages possessed by other athletes and regarded as unproblematic—such as those regarding athletes from the high plains of Africa, or from the USA. For just as the blades might not be available to other athletes, so being born and brought up in the USA or some other country is not available to other athletes."[91]

Another inspirational disabled sprinter is Hunter Woodhall, a double amputee who won two Utah high school state track championships, setting two state records, and became the first double amputee to get a Division I scholarship when he signed with the University of Arkansas. At Arkansas, he was part of a team that qualified for the NCAA Indoor Championships in the 4×400 and distance medley relays, and he was named a first-team All-American in both the indoor and outdoor 4×400 medley relay.

In addressing the controversy as to whether his blades gave him an unfair advantage, Woodhall told the *Deseret News*, "I've found it to be almost easier to just not focus on the negativity and the controversy and just do what I'm doing and put all my effort into what I'm doing rather than focusing on the negative things and especially things I can't change. If there ever comes a way for me to grow my legs back, until then, I'm going to keep doing what I'm doing and I'm not going to apologize for it."[92]

At the 2016 Paralympic Games in Rio, four visually disabled middle-distance runners ran faster times than the Olympic 1,500-meter champion Matthew Centrowitz.[93]

Some people, including disabled athletes, have argued that the Paralympics should be combined with the Olympics. A 2011 survey by the disability charity Scope showed that 65 percent of disabled people favored allowing disabled athletes to compete in the Olympics and to end the Paralympics, according to Will Heilpern of Business Insider. However, Heilpern wrote, "Paralympians do not necessarily need to be boosted by merging the Paralympics with the Olympics. Disability sport could simply be given more funding, more exposure, and respect, with increased media coverage."[94]

There was a rare scandal in the Paralympics, when it was found out that most of the Spanish men's gold medal basketball team in the Sydney 2000 Paralympics were in fact not learning disabled.[95]

By the way, Pistorius was not the only disabled South African to qualify for the Olympics. In 2008, swimmer Natalie Du Toit, who had her lower left leg amputated after a car collided with her scooter in 2001, qualified for the 2008 Beijing Summer Olympics. She finished 16th in the 10K marathon swim.[96]

Another disabled athlete who inspired many was Anthony Robles, who won an NCAA national championship in wrestling in his weight class even though he was born with only one leg. Some people argued that Robles had an unfair advantage in that his upper body was much stronger than the opponents in his weight class and there was one less leg for his opponents to grab. Most people, however, viewed Robles as an inspirational figure, as he was awarded with the Jimmy V Perseverance Award at the 2011 ESPYs. Matt Trowbridge of the *Rockford Register Star* criticized those who argued that the fact that Robles had one less leg to grab diminished his accomplishment, writing that Robles overcame his disadvantage through "determination, style, and smarts."[97]

Two other disabled wrestlers who achieved admiration and success were Dustin Carter and Nick Ackerman. Carter, a quadruple amputee, had a 41–2 record and advanced to the Ohio high school state championships in 2008 even though he did not have full legs or arms. In 2010, Carter was awarded the Medal of Courage Award from the Ohio Chapter of the National Wrestling Hall of Fame. Ackerman, a double leg amputee, won the 2001 Division III National Championship at 174 pounds for Simpson College in Iowa.[98]

Many other disabled athletes have accomplished great things. Even though Shaquem Griffin had part of one of his arms amputated as a child, he was able to go on to star as a linebacker for the undefeated Central Florida team that beat Auburn in the Peach Bowl. Griffin starred in the game and was named Defensive MVP. He wowed people at the NFL Combine with his speed and bench press and was then drafted by the Seattle Seahawks in the fifth round of the 2018 NFL draft. Griffin earned a roster spot with the Seahawks and played for three full seasons.[99]

Tom Dempsey was a kicker for the New Orleans Saints and Philadelphia Eagles. For several decades, he held the NFL record for kicking the longest field goal, 63 yards, which won a game against the Detroit Lions in 1970. Dempsey was born without a right hand or toes on his right foot. He wore a modified stub-toed shoe. Dempsey told ESPN that before he went out to kick his historic field goal, he heard one of his coaches say, "Tell Stumpy to get ready to go in and kick a long one." His record-setting shoe is on display at the NFL Hall of Fame. Nonetheless, some of his detractors, including Tex Schramm, the president and general manager of the Dallas Cowboys, alleged that his shoe gave him an unfair advantage over other kickers. Jason Elam of the Denver Broncos tied Dempsey's record in 1998. He rejected the suggestion that Dempsey had an advantage, telling ESPN, "An advantage? I don't know, I've never walked in his shoes. It could have easily been a disadvantage. He had a gift and talent for kicking the ball. More power to him."[100]

Rocky Bleier was another inspirational NFL player. Bleier was told that he would never play football again after his lower right leg was injured by shrapnel from a grenade during the Vietnam War. However, he went on to win four Super Bowl rings as a running back for the Pittsburgh Steelers during the 1970s.[101]

NFL player Samari Rolle of the Baltimore Ravens was another pro player who overcame medical adversity. In 2007, he announced that he had epilepsy and had suffered seizures.[102]

Jim Abbott inspired sports fans around the country as a Major League Baseball pitcher who was born without a right hand. In 1993, as a New York Yankee, he pitched a no-hitter against the Cleveland Indians. He also won a gold medal as a member of the 1988 US Olympic baseball team.

In 2012, Abbott told Peter J. Wallner of *MLive.com*, "There was never just a focus on trying to bring attention to my situation, but there extremely was the idea of being the best pitcher I could be. I became more and more appreciative of the role my playing could have to raise awareness to overcome a disability."[103]

Decades before Abbott, Pete Gray played one year of Major League Baseball as an outfielder for the St. Louis Browns during World War II when major league rosters were depleted. Even though Gray had lost an arm in a childhood accident, he

Disabled athletes like Tom Dempsey, who kicked an NFL record 63-yard field goal in 1970, have overcome substantial obstacles to achieve success in their sport. Dempsey, born without toes on his right foot and without four fingers on his right hand, wore a modified shoe. In 1971, Dempsey received the Most Courageous Athlete Award from the Philadelphia Sports Writers Association (photo courtesy Temple University Libraries, Special Collections Research Center, George D. McDowell *Philadelphia Evening Bulletin* Collection).

was able to hit .218 with 13 RBIs. The highlight of Gray's one-season career took place in May 1945 in a doubleheader against the New York Yankees. In the first game, Gray went three for five, driving in two runs and scoring another to pace the Browns to a 10–1 win. In the second game, Gray hit a single and scored the game-winning run in a 5–2 Browns win.[104]

Jim Eisenreich overcame Tourette syndrome to become a successful Major League Baseball outfielder, winning a World Series with the Florida Marlins in 1997 and a National League pennant with the Philadelphia Phillies in 1993. Jim Mecir overcame a club foot to become an MLB relief pitcher for 11 seasons. Mordecai "Three Finger" Brown overcame the loss of two fingers from a childhood farm accident to win 239 major league games and become a Hall of Fame pitcher. Curtis Pride was born deaf but enjoyed an 11-year MLB career.[105]

Other sports have featured successful disabled athletes. For instance, former World Super Welterweight Champion kickboxer Baxter Humby's right hand was amputated when he was a baby. Bethany Hamilton's left arm was bitten off by a shark in a 2003 surfing accident, but she went on to win the NSSA National Competition in 2005.[106]

The NCAA encourages disabled student-athletes to participate in NCAA sports, as long as the reasonable modification or accommodation does not give that athlete an unfair advantage, compromise other athletes' safety, or change the nature of the sport.[107]

Arguably, the most significant organization in advancing the cause and issues of people with disabilities is the Special Olympics. For centuries, many people with intellectual disabilities were shunned, misunderstood, neglected, ridiculed, and often hidden away in institutions.

The Special Olympics changed the way society viewed people with intellectual disabilities. Inspired by a summer camp for people with intellectual disabilities started by Kennedy Foundation director Eunice Kennedy Shriver, Special Olympics began in 1968 at Soldier Field in Chicago, where over 1,000 intellectually disabled athletes from the United States and Canada competed in more than 200 events. Today, Special Olympics involves over five million intellectually disabled athletes in over 170 countries.[108]

The Paralympics are also dedicated to promoting disabled athletes. The Paralympics began after World War II when Sir Ludwig Guttmann organized an archery competition in England in 1948 for British World War II veterans who were wheelchair athletes. Since the 1988 Summer Olympics and 1992 Winter Olympics, the Paralympics have been held at the same Olympic venues and have used the same facilities.[109]

The Invictus Games are another outlet for disabled athletes. They are an international competition for injured, wounded, and sick servicemen and women.[110]

High schools are evolving when it comes to accommodating disabled athletes. A significant lawsuit took place in Maryland, when Tatyana McFadden, a 16-year-old sophomore paralyzed from the waist down with spina bifida who had won medals at the Paralympic Games, brought suit seeking the right to be a member of her high school's track team and to compete alongside nondisabled high school athletes from other schools. In 2006, a federal district court judge in Baltimore issued an injunction in favor of McFadden and determined that she could use her wheelchair to compete in track alongside nondisabled athletes. McFadden and the school district entered into a final agreement allowing her to compete, and the Maryland state legislature subsequently passed a law that expanded the rights of students with disabilities to compete in school sports. After the Maryland legislature's actions, over a dozen states subsequently enacted laws allowing disabled athletes to compete alongside nondisabled athletes.[111]

Some of the federal statutes that have been relied on to get access for disabled athletes to compete in sports against nondisabled athletes include the Americans with Disabilities Act, Section 504 of the Rehabilitation Act of 1973, and the Individuals with Disabilities Education Act of 1990.

Part of the analysis of medical issues in sports includes psychological aspects of being an athlete. Hazing is one of the more concerning psychological issues in sports. Every athlete wants to feel that they are part of the team. But at what cost? Hazing takes place frequently among sports teams in the form of physical, sexual, and emotional abuse of athletes. This happens at all levels of sports, including middle school, high school, pro, and college athletes. During the last few years, there have been many hazing incidents that have led to the suspension of players and cancellation of team seasons. There are many reasons why athletes haze their teammates and there are debates as to what type of activities constitute hazing. Many states have instituted laws prohibiting hazing. While hazing occasionally occurs at the professional level, such as the Miami Dolphins' hazing incident, most serious hazing takes place at the youth sports, high school, and college level.

Hazing is typically associated with college fraternities, where pledges often perform humiliating challenges and rituals in order to be accepted into the group. However, hazing incidents are common at all levels of sports. These acts can include humiliation, substance and alcohol abuse, and physical and sexual assault.

According to a 2000 Alfred University study, 48 percent of American high school students who belonged to groups reported being subjected to hazing activities and 43 percent reported being subjected to humiliating activities.[112] Although there is no exact definition of hazing, one description, according to StopHazing.org, is "any activity expected of someone joining or participating in a group that humiliates, degrades, abuses, or endangers them, regardless of a person's willingness to participate."[113] According to StopBullying.gov, the US Department of Health & Human Services, and the Stop Bullying program, "Bullying is unwanted, aggressive behavior among school aged children that involves a real or perceived power imbalance. The behavior is repeated, or has the potential to be repeated, over time."[114]

A Vanderbilt University Medical Center report from 2016 stated that its researchers found that many hazing victims don't report hazing incidents or don't recognize the treatment as hazing. "One study revealed that of the 47 percent of student athletes who had been hazed, only 8 percent labeled the behavior as hazing. Another study found that college students perceived hazing as having more positive benefits than negative effects."[115]

Certain community building and initiation activities among teammates would arguably be acceptable, such as making freshmen collect baseballs or tennis balls after practice or making them be last in the cafeteria food line. Other activities might not be so clear cut, such as making freshmen stand up and sing the school's fight song or alma mater, making them run errands at midnight, and making them shave their heads. Other activities would clearly constitute impermissible hazing, such as physical or sexual abuse, making teammates eat a live goldfish while drunk, kidnapping them and dropping them off in the woods, paddling, forced excessive drinking of alcohol, forced nudity, or being forced to get a tattoo.

One of the most famous incidents on the professional level took place when three Miami Dolphins players subjected offensive lineman teammate Jonathan Martin to a pattern of harassment that included racial slurs and sexual taunts, causing

Martin to leave the team. He was traded to the San Francisco 49ers and retired from the NFL in 2015. One of the bullying players, Richie Incognito, was suspended by the team for the final eight games of the season. Five years after his suspension, Incognito apologized for his past actions and announced that he had become the national ambassador for Boo2Bullying, a nonprofit organization that works to eliminate bullying. In the video that he released on Twitter, Incognito said, "I've said some things in the past that I thought were edgy and funny, but really hurt people's feelings. Even though these were people I cared about and considered friends, I said things to them that affected them."[116]

The Martin/Incognito incident was a wake-up call and showed that bullying can occur at all levels and that even a 300-pound NFL lineman can feel that he can't fight back. It showed that bullying and hazing isn't just physical, but it can involve infliction of psychological harm.

The biggest concern is at the high school and youth sports level, where older teammates bully and haze younger and smaller teammates as part of the initiation process.

Several states have passed anti-hazing and anti-bullying laws. Many teams have preseason meetings and workshops in which anti-hazing policies are explained and emphasized.

One of the solutions to the problem is for schools, teams, coaches, and athletic directors to have a zero-tolerance policy when it comes to hazing and bullying. While coaches and administrators can't observe their players 24/7, they can set a culture that the team needs to follow. If coaches turn their heads and ignore hazing incidents, they can and should be fired.

Hazing is a serious problem in high school sports. *USA Today*'s online high school sports section includes a specific portion dedicated to stories nationwide regarding hazing incidents in high school sports.[117] This *USA Today* section reported dozens of hazing incidents in 2018 and 2019, pre–COVID. A 2017 *Dallas Morning News* survey revealed that nearly one in three high school coaches knew of hazing that occurred at his or her school. Twenty-two percent of those coaches "said they had stepped in to stop an occurrence of hazing, 12 percent said they had seen hazing turn into bullying or abuse, and 69 percent said more needs to be done to prevent the negative consequences of hazing."[118]

Sometimes, the more serious incidents result in juvenile charges. In 2023, three former Pennsylvania high school football players were charged with unlawful restraint, indecent assault and hazing and found delinquent in a juvenile court proceeding. The school's football program suffered a cancellation of one season due to the hazing incident.[119] In 2019, four former Oklahoma high school players accused of raping a teammate with a pool cue agreed to lesser juvenile charges of assault with a dangerous weapon and were ordered to pay $300 in restitution. Other times, hazing incidents can result in civil lawsuits.[120] In November 2018, an Illinois school district and six employees were sued for allegedly failing to stop a culture of hazing at a high school football team that led to one of the players being sexually assaulted. The claims against some of the defendants were dismissed.[121]

Some people argue that hazing is a positive activity, in that it can build bonding, camaraderie, and team unity. Others have the viewpoint that hazing freshmen is OK because the seniors went through it as freshmen, and they want to continue the tradition.

It's extremely hard for hazing victims to come forward and report incidents of abuse. Those who have the courage to do so risk incurring the scorn, criticism, and retribution of their teammates and their coaches. As the saying goes, "snitches get stitches." Similarly, it would be very hard for one of the upperclassmen who are hazing to speak out against this activity.

Many members of a school community might express anger if the reported hazing incidents result in star players getting suspended or kicked off the team, or having the entire season canceled. For instance, some angry parents spoke out after Sayreville High School in New Jersey canceled their football season in 2014 after a hazing incident. According to NBCNewYork.com, "Community members and parents expressed anger with the decision to end the season, while players decked out in blue and gray jerseys and letterman jackets made emotional pleas to the board."[122]

Organizations like StopHazing.org seek to stop hazing through education.

While there is no federal law specifically addressing hazing, it can come into play when hazing or bullying is based on race, ethnicity, color, national origin, sex, disability, or religion.

In 2007, the NCAA issued a report titled "Building New Traditions: Hazing Prevention in College Athletics" that addressed the roles of athletic administrators, coaches, athletes, and team captains in recognizing and preventing hazing on their teams. It distinguishes hazing activities from team-building activities and encourages development of alternative activities that reinforce team bonding. The report states that coaches should "Help your team develop positive traditions that are significant and meaningful and that contribute to their bonding and coming together as a group. This important strategy will help reduce the temptation to use hazing as a means of team bonding." The report also provides sample anti-hazing policies and programs from several universities, including Penn State, Southern Methodist University, Florida State, and the University of Vermont.[123]

The National Federation of State High School Associations has a website that provides resources on hazing education and prevention geared toward parents, school staff, principals, coaches, and students. Its website advises in an article by Jeff Jonas on September 6, 2017, that school officials who feel uncomfortable about how to approach dealing with hazing should seek outside help. "Many groups have been established to help high schools deal with the problem of hazing. Hazing is a widespread problem and the problems faced at their high school are not unique. The key is not to try and combat the problem alone; instead seek help, and make it a focus of the entire student body."[124]

Worcester Public Schools school safety director Robert Pezzella told Bill Doyle of the *Telegram & Gazette* in Massachusetts that people need to know how serious hazing is, whether it takes place on the field, the court, or the locker room, and that hazing will be punished severely. Pezzella said, "So we understand that there is still some primitive thinking from student-athletes. We have to change that thought process, we have to change that culture and that's why it's imperative for us as educators and professionals to make sure that they get the most necessary information in order to make good decisions as not only teenagers, but as student-athletes representing their schools and to have some school pride."[125]

In their article in the *International Journal of Sports Science & Coaching*, Johnson and Chin argue that adventure-based alternative team-building orientation activities such as rock climbing and canoe trips should be considered instead of traditional hazing, and that such activities could lead to "facilitating a greater sense of cohesion, diminishing team hierarchies, and shifting power relations, effectively democratizing the event and humanizing first year athletes." The authors argue, "This structure thus has a high potential to yield positive outcomes, contrary to traditional hazing which promotes a negative connection for membership. Ropes courses, rock climbing and all of the physical challenges seemed to meet the demand for a more rigorous, strenuous rite of passage for the participants, without the need or requirement for denigration or embarrassment."[126]

Medical and psychological issues play a large role in sports. Too often, problems are overlooked or not taken seriously. Sports leagues at all levels have gotten much better in dealing with these issues in recent years; however, there is always room for improvement and further evolving. Players want to tough it out and play hurt, but teams, coaches, and medical staffs shouldn't rush or pressure players to return to action. This is especially the case for concussions. For too many years, psychological issues were overlooked and ignored. It's a positive development that more high-profile athletes are coming forward to admit that they are struggling with anxiety, depression, or eating disorders and encouraging others to seek help for their conditions. Regarding steroids, testing has improved and increased over the years, especially at the professional level, thus making it harder for athletes to cheat the system. While a very small minority of people think that steroids should be legalized to guarantee a level playing field, this is a wrongheaded and dangerous idea that would lead to serious medical problems for many athletes. Disabled athletes continue to amaze and inspire us all to do better. Sports organizations and leagues should do their best to accommodate disabled athletes. Finally, hazing is an overlooked and serious problem that pervades sports, especially at the youth, high school, and college level. Peer pressure and the need to belong to a group, combined with older players attempting to assert their power and control, can be a dangerous combination. Coaches, schools, and administrators need to have zero tolerance for hazing, and more education on hazing needs to be provided to young people.

CHAPTER 8

Legal Issues

CONTROVERSIES INVOLVING LEGAL ISSUES have been a major issue in sports for many decades. News reports emerge almost daily about civil liability and criminal conduct of athletes, coaches, administrators, and organizations. Some people feel that athletes get special treatment under the law, while others believe that athletes like Michael Vick served their prison time and should get a second chance to play professionally. Another debated issue is whether fans injured at a sporting event can hold the team civilly liable for their injuries. The traditional "Baseball Rule" that absolves teams of liability is still the main legal rule, but a few courts in very rare occasions are choosing to chip away at the rule and allowing injured fans to recover damages. There are many business law aspects of sports, including the role of agents, and contractual issues in professional and amateur sports, including free agency. Title IX has been a huge legislative and legal success for girls and women, especially in providing opportunities to compete in sports. However, in recent years there has been controversy and debate about the law as many universities are cutting sports teams. Another legal issue relates to prayer at public high school football games. This chapter will explore the various elements of legal issues in sports.

Sports fans go to games expecting that they will have a great time rooting for their favorite team. They don't expect to get seriously injured. However, there are times when accidents happen. One legal issue in sports is whether teams can be held liable when a fan is injured during a game.

People go to games to watch and enjoy them, but once in a while, a fan is injured by things such as foul balls, broken bats, hockey pucks, errant football throws or kicks, or even objects shot out of a T-shirt or hot dog gun by a mascot. Sometimes the injuries can be serious and even fatal.

For over a century, courts have applied the "Baseball Rule," which acts to protect teams from liability if a fan is injured by a foul ball or thrown balls or bats during a game.[1] Over the years, teams have put disclaimers on tickets indicating that fans assume the risk of injury when they attend the game, meaning that the team cannot be held liable. While most courts have upheld the Baseball Rule over the years, some state courts, including ones in Georgia, Missouri, Indiana, and Idaho, recently declined to do so in certain situations.[2]

In a 1958 Wisconsin case, a fan who was injured in a scramble with 10 other fans to get a foul ball that was hit into the stands at a major league game sued the team for negligence. The court determined that an issue of fact existed as to whether the team was negligent in protecting the fan.[3]

In recent years, there have been many incidents of serious injuries to fans at professional games and leagues and teams have attempted to make stadiums safer, but are they doing enough to protect fans from harm?

In 2011, a New York man was injured at a Yankees game when a line drive hit his face, crushed his eye socket, broke his jaw, and permanently impaired his vision. In 2017, a line drive from Todd Frazier struck a two-year-old girl in the face at a Yankees game, causing bleeding on the brain.[4]

Bloomberg News published a statistical analysis in 2014 stating that over 1,700 fans per year are injured at Major League Baseball games, mostly by foul balls and broken bats. Part of the problem is that MLB teams built stadiums that had seats closer to the field and people are often looking down at their cell phones during games and not looking out for foul balls.[5]

In order to lessen the risk of fan injury, in 2015, Major League Baseball commissioner Rob Manfred issued a memo recommending all teams to extend protective netting down the foul lines to beyond the end of the dugouts to protect fans from foul balls.[6] By January 2018, all MLB teams complied with that recommendation. Camden Yards in Baltimore extended the netting to three sections beyond the end of the dugout.[7] While the netting is helpful in protecting fans, it is not foolproof. For instance, in 2018, a Dodger fan was struck in the head and killed by a foul ball that went over the protective netting behind home plate. In June 2019, another Dodgers fan was struck in the head by a foul ball and eventually hospitalized for her injuries.[8]

In May 2019, a young girl sitting in the stands on the left field line was struck in the head by a line drive hit by Chicago Cubs outfielder Albert Almora, Jr., in Houston's Minute Maid Park and was immediately taken to the hospital.[9] After this incident, many MLB players and others spoke out in favor of extending the protective netting at ballparks across the league. However, some fans object to protective netting, arguing that it impairs their view of the game and prevents them from the time-honored tradition of catching and keeping a foul ball that they can pass on to their children and grandchildren. In 2019, two US senators from Illinois, Dick Durbin and Tammy Duckworth, sent letters to Commissioner Rob Manfred urging MLB to extend protective netting for all of its teams' stadiums and to disclose to fans which sections of the stadiums were most at risk for fans to be struck by foul balls.[10]

The MLB Players Association twice recommended that there be protective netting from foul pole to foul pole. That is the policy of professional baseball teams in Japan. In 2019, the Chicago White Sox became the first MLB team to institute protective netting from foul pole to foul pole.[11] As of the start of the 2021 season, seven MLB teams had foul-pole-to-foul-pole netting. According to *Sports Illustrated* in August 2021, "Several teams have added at least some additional netting since then, but currently, only six big-league parks have fully extended netting, from foul pole to foul pole. Five other parks have netting that goes deep down the foul line, but not all the way to the foul poles, while 17 parks have nets that extend to the elbows, the area where the side wall changes direction and angles away from the field."[12] Fan injuries from foul balls and broken bats could also be an issue in college and high school baseball fields, since most teams don't have the resources to provide extensive netting to protect fans.

Nowadays, it's not just foul balls and broken bats that fans have to worry about. In 2018, a Phillies fan was injured at Citizens Bank Park by a hot dog fired by the Phillie Phanatic from an air-powered cannon. In 2009, a Kansas City Royals fan was injured by a hot dog that was thrown into the stands by Royals mascot Sluggerrr, suffering a detached retina. In 2019, a fan suffered a broken finger from a T-shirt fired from a cannon by Houston Astros mascot Orbit.[13]

In the NHL and other professional and amateur hockey leagues, fans have been injured by pucks flying into the stands. The most tragic incident took place in 2002, when a 13-year-old girl was struck in the head and killed by a puck at a Columbus Blue Jackets game.[14] After that incident, the league required protective netting behind the goals. In April 2018, a Tampa Bay Lightning fan was injured by a flying puck during a playoff game. She was sitting five rows away from the rink, just to the end of the protective netting.[15]

The NHL has mandatory leaguewide safety standards to protect fans regarding netting and minimum glass heights.[16]

Regarding injuries to football spectators, an Indiana court ruled for a fan who was injured during a scramble for a football that evaded the protective netting behind the goalposts and was kicked into the stands during a field goal attempt in a Notre Dame game in 1995. The court determined that Notre Dame owed the fan a duty to take reasonable steps to protect her from injury due to the actions of other fans.[17] In the last few decades, the NFL and colleges have put up protective netting behind the goalposts whenever there is an attempt for an extra point or field goal in order to prevent balls from going into the stands.

In noting the problem of applying the Baseball Rule in today's fan experience, Michael McCann wrote in *Sports Illustrated* that there are many more fan distractions than there were 20 years ago. "Now-a-days, many, if not most, fans routinely check their phones and go on the Internet while the game is taking place—especially given that some ballparks offer complimentary Wi-Fi. They also take photos of one another and post them on their social media accounts. Technologically advanced scoreboards, as well as various promotional activities that occur in between innings, also entertain fans."[18]

Agreeing that the Baseball Rule should be abandoned in light of the increased risk of being hit by a ball or bat at an MLB game, Nathaniel Grow and Zachary Flagel stated in the *William and Mary Law Review*, "[F]ans today frequently sit more than 20 percent closer to home plate than was the case throughout most of the twentieth century. This fact, along with a presumptive increase in the speed with which baseballs are being hit into the stands, has substantially reduced the reaction time that fans have to avoid errant flying objects heading in their direction. Indeed, in some cases it may now be virtually impossible for spectators to react in time to protect themselves from a particularly hard-hit foul ball. Consequently, wayward balls and bats present a much greater risk to fans today than at the time the Baseball Rule was first established in 1913." In light of this, the authors argued that the Baseball Rule should be replaced by a strict liability calculation.[19]

However, many experts, including sports law professors Peter Carfagna and Aaron Caputo, believe that the Baseball Rule is appropriate.

Peter Carfagna teaches sports law at Harvard University Law School and the University of Miami; is faculty supervisor of Harvard Law School's Sports Law Clinical Program; is chairman/CEO of Magis LLC, a privately owned sports marketing, management, and investment company; and was chief legal officer and general counsel of International Management Group (IMG). In a Zoom interview confirmed and revised by email, Carfagna said, "The Baseball Rule should remain intact with *very* rare exceptions. There is assumption of risk by fans, *very* broad/enforceable waiver language on the tickets, and public announcements before *and during* the game telling fans to be careful and to watch out for foul balls. Assumption of risk should protect venue operators and owners from liability in all but the most rare of cases."[20]

Aaron Caputo is executive director of legal and client services at the Superlative Group Inc., a sports marketing and advertising company, and he teaches sports law at Case Western Reserve University School of Law. In a Zoom interview confirmed and revised by email, Caputo said, "There is a long history and precedent to the Baseball Rule, which should be followed. It's consistent and has only a few limited and justifiable exceptions, such as distractions by venue operators."[21]

Can players be held civilly or criminally responsible for injuries that they cause during the course of a game? After the famous 2004 Malice at the Palace in Detroit during a game between the Indiana Pacers and Detroit Pistons, where players and fans ended up fighting each other, three Pacer players pleaded no contest to misdemeanor assault charges and were sentenced to a year of probation and were ordered to perform community service and pay fines.[22] However, criminal prosecution of players is rare. Usually, the result is a civil lawsuit or fines and suspensions imposed by the league. Even when Kermit Washington of the Los Angeles Lakers punched Rudy Tomjanovich of the Houston Rockets during a fight in a game and broke his jaw, fractured his skull, and broke his nose, Washington was not criminally charged for assault or battery. The NBA fined him $10,000 and suspended him for 60 days. Tomjanovich did get compensation for his injuries in a civil lawsuit against the Lakers' parent company.[23]

Ice hockey is a physical game that features checking and fighting, but criminal charges against NHL players are rare. Some exceptions included in 2004 when Todd Bertuzzi of the Vancouver Canucks attacked Colorado Avalanche forward Steve Moore from behind, resulting in Moore suffering three broken vertebrae and ending his career. Bertuzzi was suspended for the rest of the regular season and seven playoff games and was criminally charged with assault resulting in bodily harm. He pleaded guilty and was sentenced to one year probation and 80 hours of community service. Moore's civil lawsuit against Bertuzzi and the Canucks was settled out of court.[24] In 2000, Marty McSorley skated behind Donald Brashear and slashed him hard on the side of his head, rendering Brashear unconscious. The two had a fight earlier in the game. McSorley was suspended for the rest of the season and was later found guilty of assault with a weapon and sentenced to 18 months' probation.[25] Both of these cases were in Canadian courts.

In a minor league baseball game in 2008, Peoria pitcher Julio Castillo intentionally threw a ball toward the opposing team's dugout to prevent the other team's players from rushing the field during a brawl, but the ball struck a fan and resulted in a concussion. Castillo was arrested and eventually convicted of felonious assault and sentenced to 30 days in jail and three years' probation.[26]

Some courts have determined that athletes can be held civilly liable for damages for actions taken against their opponents. In 1973, Cincinnati Bengals running back Charles "Booby" Clark intentionally hit Denver Broncos defensive back Dale Hackbart in the back of his head in frustration. After it was determined that Hackbart had suffered a fractured neck from the blow, he subsequently sued Clark and the Bengals in federal court, alleging reckless misconduct. The district court ruled for the defendants, determining that football was beyond the realm of imposition of the law for tortuous conduct and that Hackbart assumed the risk of his injuries. The 10th Circuit Court reversed and remanded, holding that an intentional blow inflicted by one football player on an opposing player could result in liability in tort, because the intentional striking of a player in the face or from the rear is prohibited by the playing rules as well as the general customs of the game, even though there was no specific intent to injure Hackbart. The court determined that recklessness was the appropriate standard in determining liability in civil cases. The parties ended up settling the case in 1981. Many subsequent courts, in assessing similar incidents in sports injury civil cases, have also determined that recklessness, not negligence, is the appropriate standard to apply.[27]

In a subsequent football civil lawsuit for damages, a jury in 2005 ordered Oakland Raiders linebacker Bill Romanowski to pay Marcus Williams $340,000 for injuring the tight end during a practice in 2003. The case was later settled for $415,000. After Williams had blocked Romanowski during a practice drill, Romanowski grabbed Williams's helmet, ripped it off, and then punched Williams in the face, resulting in a broken eye socket, blurry vision, post-traumatic stress disorder, and depression.[28]

Generally, it is very rare for athletes to be held criminally or civilly liable for the actions that they take during games, even when it results in injuries to opposing players.

In a Zoom interview, Peter Carfagna said, "Civil or criminal liability for athletes for actions during games is very rare. There have been very few cases where there was malice aforethought, premeditated, or criminal intent that created civil or criminal liability or felonious assault and battery. There is assumption of the risk, as every pro player should know the risks and they agree to bring their grievances through collective bargaining. The recourse should be through the collective bargaining agreements, not the courts. If it were left to the courts, it could let the cat out of the bag and lead to unpredictable and unfair disruptions of the game—in contravention of the CBAs of the major leagues."[29]

Aaron Caputo added in a Zoom interview, "It's best served that these issues are addressed through collective bargaining, not the courts. Liability is very rare unless the conduct goes far outside the rules of the game."[30]

Another type of legal issue in sports revolves around sports agents, who serve an important role in representing professional athletes. They negotiate contracts and endorsement deals for their clients, but they also give financial advice and help manage their clients' money and investments. Agents don't need to be lawyers, but it helps to have a legal background, especially in contracts. Getting clients as an agent is a competitive endeavor. Agents, especially new or unestablished ones, scramble to get their first clients to get their foot in the door. There is also extensive competition to get a star college athlete who is projected to be a high first-round pick to sign with an agent. This competition has often led to unscrupulous conduct. In 2017, Terry Watson, a former agent for NFL players, pleaded guilty to criminal charges of violating North Carolina's sports agent law by improperly giving cash payments of around $24,000 and travel arrangements to three University of North Carolina football players to entice them to sign with him. Watson received probation, a $5,000 fine, and a suspended jail sentence of six to eight months.[31] Howard Porter was a three-time All American at Villanova who helped lead the Wildcats to the Final Four in 1971, where they eventually lost to UCLA in the championship game. Unfortunately, Villanova's Final Four appearance was vacated by the NCAA because Porter was found to have signed a professional contract before the NCAA Tournament. Marcus Camby led UMass to national prominence in the 1990s, leading the Minutemen to the Final Four in 1996, where they lost to Kentucky in a semifinal game. Camby was found to have violated NCAA rules by accepting cash and gifts from agents, which resulted in the NCAA vacating UMass's Final Four appearance.[32] Former USC star running back Reggie Bush had to return his 2005 Heisman Trophy after an NCAA investigation concluded that he had accepted $300,000 in cash and gifts from marketing agents while he was still in college. After the NCAA enacted a policy in July 2021 allowing college athletes to profit off their name, likeness, and image, many people, including Bush, advocated on social media that Bush should get his Heisman Trophy back. The Heisman Trophy Trust said that it could not give Bush his Heisman back unless the NCAA reinstated his 2005 Heisman Trophy award-winning season. In 2010, Josh Luchs, a former sports agent, admitted in *Sports Illustrated* that he had paid over 30 college athletes during the 1990s, including several players who ended up being first-round picks in the NFL draft.[33]

In 2017, a major fraud and bribery scheme was alleged by the US Attorney's Office in the Southern District of New York and the FBI, alleging that sports agents, sports clothing company representatives, college coaches, and college and high school athletes and their families had engaged in a massive pay-to-play scheme. Among the major programs implicated in the allegations and investigated for NCAA violations were Louisville, Auburn, South Carolina, Arizona, Oklahoma State, and USC. One of the alleged schemes involved coaches getting paid in order to influence players to choose certain sports agents after they decided to turn pro.[34]

In a Zoom interview, Peter Carfagna said, "At the college level, the schools involved are now trying to do everything they already should have done, although in some cases they responded too slowly by waiting for the NCAA to respond—which it has been woefully slow to do. In fact, the worst part of these college bribery cases is the NCAA's inaction and delay in handing down final sanctions on the guilty parties. By contrast, the courts' punishments of individual bad actors have been relatively swift and appropriate."[35]

Pursuant to the Revised Uniform Athlete Agents Act (RUAAA), many states have enacted laws that regulate sports agents and require them to register with the state, as well as prohibit agents from luring potential athlete clients through improper gifts or cash. At the federal level, the Sports Agent Responsibility and Trust Act (SPARTA) protects college athletes by prohibiting sports agents from signing them through false or misleading statements, promises, or misrepresentations, and giving gifts, cash, or loans to athletes or anyone associated with the athletes.[36]

As to the regulation of agents, Peter Carfagna said in a Zoom interview, "There is fairly sufficient regulation of agents, per the current player association regulations in the major leagues. However, they must be held more accountable in the financial arena where there is fraud, theft, misappropriation of funds, and self-dealing, and athletes must then be able to go to the court system. The fraud, theft, and embezzlement cases are legion, sadly. It is therefore important to have regulation of financial agents through the court system. Players associations have never been found liable to provide full recourse if millions of dollars of pro athletes' monies are misappropriated. It is therefore important to put players on notice as to their agents' financial management duties, and then for the athletes to be responsible for their own money management. There needs to be better education of pro athletes to monitor and look out for the charlatans who aim to steal their money."[37]

Aaron Caputo added in a Zoom interview, "There are many rules regulating player agents, such as the SPARTA, the RUAAA, and player association agent rules. These established rules help deter athlete agent misconduct, but many of the fact patterns and cases in this area are complex and the court system is more equipped to help to achieve the appropriate remedies for those who have been harmed."[38]

Another sports-related issue involves the ongoing attempts of women to participate in sports and to be treated equally to men. One of the most important legal developments of the 20th century was the passage of Title IX, which led to significant opportunities for women to participate in sports.

As to how Title IX is applied to athletics, the NCAA cites equal opportunities for participation, scholarships proportional to participation, and equal treatment as to other benefits, including equipment, travel, tutoring, and coaching, among other elements.

As to how institutions comply with Title IX, the NCAA states:

An institution must meet all of the following requirements in order to be in compliance with Title IX:

1. For participation requirements, institutions officials must meet one of the following three tests. An institution may:

   a. Provide participation opportunities for women and men that are substantially proportionate to their respective rates of enrollment of full-time undergraduate students;

   b. Demonstrate a history and continuing practice of program expansion for the underrepresented sex;

   c. Fully and effectively accommodate the interests and abilities of the underrepresented sex; and,

2. Female and male student-athletes must receive athletics scholarship dollars proportional to their participation; and,

3. Equal treatment of female and male student-athletes in the eleven provisions as mentioned above.[39]

While Title IX has resulted in many positive changes for girls and women in sports and society, the law has its critics. One of the main criticisms of Title IX is that in order to meet the requirements of Title IX, many universities are cutting men's varsity sports.

Before Title IX, female participation in sports was not emphasized to the extent it is today. In order to understand the ramifications and effects of Title IX, it's important to know the history of girls and women's sports and how they fought to overcome adversity.

One of the most famous early pioneers of female athletes was Babe Didrikson Zaharias, who won two gold medals in track and field at the 1932 Summer Olympics in Los Angeles, and then went on to have a very successful pro golf career in which she won 10 major LPGA tournaments. The Associated Press named her the greatest female athlete of the first half of the 20th century.[40]

Traditionally, baseball is thought of as a man's game, while softball is considered a women's game. However, according to the Baseball Hall of Fame, women started playing baseball in the 1860s at Vassar College in New York. The All-American Girls Professional Baseball League ran from 1943 to 1954 and was the inspiration for the popular 1992 movie *A League of Their Own*. The league, based in Midwestern cities, gave over 500 women a chance to play professionally and drew a total of around one million fans during the 1948 season. The league featured many talented players. The Cubs manager in the mid–1940s, Charley Grimm, said of Kenosha shortstop Dottie Schroeder that she would be a $50,000 player if she were a boy.[41]

Perhaps the biggest moment in women's sports took place when a woman beat a man at his own game. In 1973, Billie Jean King beat Bobby Riggs in a tennis match that she almost had to win. Earlier that year, Riggs had easily defeated Margaret Court, ranked number one in the world.

As I wrote in the *Philadelphia Inquirer* and the *Huffington Post*, the "Battle of the Sexes" occurred at the Houston Astrodome in front of 30,000 spectators and a television audience of over 50 million. The match had the ambience of an Ali–Frazier title fight. The 29-year-old King crushed the 55-year-old former Wimbledon champion 6–4, 6–3, 6–3. Despite Riggs's age, it was the biggest win of King's fabled career, even bigger than her 39 Grand Slam tennis titles, including 12 individual Grand Slam wins, because of its social significance. I wrote, "King's victory was a clarion call to young girls who wanted to participate in sports. Before the 1970s, women's sports were a tiny blip on the radar screen. Little League and youth sports were for boys only, and girls who dared to be athletic and play sports were tomboys or outcasts." After King's win, more girls felt comfortable to learn how to play tennis, take swimming and gymnastics classes, earn black belts in martial arts, and play on school basketball teams. King's victory also influenced how men perceived women. Boys growing up in the '70s and '80s began to see women as strong, independent people who didn't have to rely on men to support them financially. Young men started accepting women not only as athletes but also as working professionals.[42]

Women's tennis proceeded to become extremely popular and spawned many iconic players such as Chris Evert, Martina Navratilova, Steffi Graf, and Venus and Serena Williams, who were just as famous as the great male players of their eras.

Billie Jean King's win over Bobby Riggs in 1973 was significant in the growth and popularity of women's sports. Riggs, a 55-year-old former Wimbledon champion, had defeated Margaret Court, the number one player in the world, and he spoke out against the quality of women's sports. King's win over Riggs in a nationally televised match before 30,000 at the Houston Astrodome helped to launch a new generation of female athletes (photo courtesy Temple University Libraries, Special Collections Research Center, George D. McDowell *Philadelphia Evening Bulletin* Collection).

The WNBA began play in 1997 and is the most well-known and successful women's professional sports league. It was created by the NBA's Board of Governors. As of 2019, the WNBA had grown to 12 teams. The league featured superstars such as Cynthia Cooper, Rebecca Lobo, Sheryl Swoopes, and Lisa Leslie.

In general, women's basketball is becoming very popular at all levels. The NCAA started having a Women's NCAA National Championship Tournament in 1982. It started as a 32-team tournament, but expanded to a 64-team tournament in 1994. While Tennessee's program was dominant from the late 1980s to the 2000s, winning eight national championships from 1987 to 2008, it was surpassed by the University of Connecticut women's team, which won 11 national championships from 1995 to 2016, including four straight titles from 2013 to 2016. As of 2021, the UConn women had appeared in 21 Final Fours, while Tennessee had appeared in 18. UConn had an incredible 126-game regular-season winning streak lasting from 2014 to 2019. Their 111-game winning streak for all games was broken when UConn lost to Mississippi State in the NCAA Tournament in the 2017 semifinal game. Some critics complained that UConn's dominance was bad for the sport, but others claimed that it gave women's basketball more exposure. In 2017, the UConn women averaged 10,096 fans per home game, which was higher than the UConn men's basketball team's average attendance that fiscal year. In 2017–2018, the University of South Carolina averaged 13,239 fans per game, according to the *Post and Courier*. ESPN provides extensive coverage of the Women's NCAA Basketball Tournament, showing all of the games as well as extensive highlights on *SportsCenter*. The US women's basketball team has dominated international competition at the Summer Olympics, as they won their seventh straight gold medal in 2021 in Tokyo.[43]

Although attendance and television viewership for women's basketball games has increased significantly over the years, to some sports fans women's basketball still pales in excitement in comparison to men's college basketball and the NBA. There are various reasons for this, including the fact that men's basketball has a much longer tradition and established fan base. In addition, some people believe the athleticism of the men's game exceeds the women's game and allegedly makes it more exciting, as dunks occur every few minutes in a men's game but occur rarely in the women's game. The women's game tends to focus more on fundamental play and outside shooting, while the men's game is played above the rim most of the time.

Nonetheless, women's sports are exploding in popularity as far as participation. According to an article by Beth A. Brooke-Marciniak and Donna de Varona on August 25, 2016, in the World Economic Forum website, "Since 1972, thanks to increased funding and institutional opportunities, there has been a 545% increase in the percentage of women playing college sports and a 990% increase in the percentage of women playing high school sport."[44]

Title IX and its implementation has led to more resources, improved facilities, equipment, and training for girls high school sports and women's college sports in the last few decades. This has led to increased college scholarship opportunities for

Women's basketball has become very popular at the pro and college level. Here, the Drexel University women battle the University of Florida (photo by Jack Kapenstein).

female athletes. It has also led to Olympic success and an increase in women's professional sports. The women's NCAA basketball Final Four gets extensive coverage on ESPN, both as to games and postgame analysis. The US Women's National Soccer team has been far more successful than the US men in international competition, winning the World Cup in 1991, 1999, 2015, and 2019. Their 1999 World Cup victory drew over 90,000 fans.[45] Stars of US women soccer, such as Carli Lloyd and Megan Rapinoe, have become just as famous, if not more, than their male counterparts. There are more female athletes that have emerged as role models for young girls to emulate. Due to livestreaming and the explosion of cable television networks such as the Big Ten Network and ESPN+, women's college sports, including nonrevenue sports such as softball and volleyball, get extensive coverage.

The main complaint and controversy regarding Title IX is that in order to meet Title IX requirements, some schools have been eliminating many nonrevenue sports, mostly men's nonrevenue sports, such as baseball, tennis, rugby, and gymnastics. For instance, as reported by the Associated Press in 2020, Old Dominion discontinued wrestling; Cincinnati eliminated men's soccer; Florida International cut men's indoor track and field; Akron eliminated men's cross-country and golf, as well as women's tennis; Bowling Green eliminated baseball; Furman eliminated baseball and men's lacrosse; East Carolina cut men's and women's swimming and diving, and men's and women's tennis; and Appalachian State cut men's soccer, tennis, and indoor track and field. As reported by CBS News in December 2020, "This year at least 30 universities have cut almost 100 programs; soccer, squash, golf, gymnastics … more than 1,500 student-athletes, both men and women, will no longer have a team to compete for."[46] In some cases, such as with Clemson, Bowling Green, Stanford, and other schools, these cuts were reversed and teams were reinstated due to public pressure, student protests, threatened lawsuits, or alumni fundraising.[47]

After some women's college teams were cut, athletes at some universities, including Iowa, Michigan State, Fresno State, Dartmouth, and William & Mary, either brought or threatened lawsuits in order to have them reinstated. In many cases, the lawsuits and threatened suits were successful.[48]

According to *Sports Illustrated* in June 2020, 19 of the 30 Division 1 teams eliminated during the year at that time were men's teams. "Fearing Title IX violations, athletic directors can't risk discontinuing too many women's sports…. Football, and its 85 scholarships, can throw the numbers off kilter, forcing administrators to slash other men's sports. Since 1990, the top seven sports experiencing the most growth are female, while the top six having the least growth were male."[49]

Noting the problem that college athletic directors who are trying to do the right thing have in meeting Title IX requirements because of football, *ESPN The Magazine* senior writer Peter Keating told Bill Littlefield of WBUR's *Only a Game*, "You'd still be ignoring the devouring of college athletic resources that is taking place by football, which is a sport that women don't play. As long as 85 scholarships are being given out to the top football programs, you're going to have an enormous time demonstrating any kind of fundamental fairness in your athletic program."[50]

Dr. Ketra Armstrong is a professor of sport management and director of diversity, equity, & Inclusion for the University of Michigan School of Kinesiology. She is also director of the Center for Race & Ethnicity in Sport (C-RAES), an affiliate faculty member in the Departments of Afro-American and African Studies and Women's Studies, and the UM NCAA faculty athletics representative. In an email interview, Armstrong commented on how Title IX could be improved, stating, "The fundamental premise of Title IX—gender equity—does not need to be revised. What needs revising/improving is the accountability and creativity necessary to uphold and ensure that the ideals of Title IX are realized. When universities discontinue non-revenue sports to adhere to Title IX mandates, this is not a function of an inherent weakness in Title IX in and of itself. Instead, I believe that it is more often a function of mis-management and the strategic mis-allocation of resources."

Armstrong added, "We know that not all revenue sports boast balanced budgets. In fact, a great number of them operate at a deficit. Nonetheless, many universities will continue to expend a wealth of resources (personal, physical, informational, and thus, financial) on their non-profitable 'revenue' programs because of their tradition of offering them and the role they have historically played in the identity of the university. For instance, many universities will continually invest heavily in a football program that drains their financial coffers just to say that they offer football, it is critical to who they are, and it is an important part of their longstanding tradition. Such resources could be better served by being diverted to support a range of non-revenue programs. Therefore, I do not believe that Title IX is the blame for the dilemma of cutting non-revenue sports. Instead, the solution lies in a recalibration of values and budget priorities. The excessive, disproportionate, and often exorbitant amount of funds spent on some revenue sports should be revisited and revised to ensure a more equitable distribution of resources to promote optimal participation for male and female athletes. However, this will require universities to acknowledge and honor their 'financial truths,' challenge their traditions, and make some difficult and often unpopular decisions. This is the decision equity for which their student-athletes are 'entitled.'"[51]

Andrea Caporale Seiss, Title IX coordinator for Temple University, said in an email interview, "I do not think that Title IX needs to be revised in light of many universities cutting nonrevenue sports. The current regulation includes the elements that an institution must consider when evaluating equity within their programs. These guidelines have removed barriers and the percentage of women participating in sports has grown dramatically. However, equity within athletics is not just about the percentage of males and females that are on team rosters. Equity includes access to facilities, equipment, the provision of medical and training staff, academic support, marketing and promotion, travel allowance, and scholarships."

Seiss added, "It is not sufficient for a university to consider only player percentages in evaluating their Title IX compliance. They must consider the entire picture, regardless of whether the team is revenue generating. In order to accomplish this, a university can work collaboratively with their Title IX Coordinator to regularly evaluate their policies, procedures, and spending, ensuring compliance with all aspects of Title IX. Universities should examine their budget structure to determine fund allocation in a way that provides teams with access to what they need to be successful. Each team will not have the same financial needs, but the quality of what is needed should be equitable between teams. Athletic programs should consider ways to actively promote all teams, potentially leading to more revenue generating opportunities, but more importantly showing their student athletes that they believe in them and value them and their sport. The elements needed to create an equitable environment within athletics are provided in the current Title IX regulations and the onus falls on university leaders to actively consider all of these elements when making decisions about providing for or cutting teams from their programs."[52]

Recently, pay equity has been an issue in women's sports. In 2019, members of the US women's soccer team brought a gender discrimination class-action lawsuit against US Soccer regarding the inequities in pay and working conditions between the women's national soccer team and men's national soccer team. On the field, the women's teams have had much more success on the international level. The women have won four World Cup titles, while the men have never gone beyond the quarterfinals after their third-place finish in 1930. In 2020, a federal judge dismissed the women's claims regarding equal pay, but the women appealed that decision in

2021. In 2020, the parties reached a partial settlement of the lawsuit as to working conditions.[53] In 2022, the US men's and women's soccer teams reached a collective bargaining agreement with US Soccer that would provide equal pay structures for women as to appearances, tournament wins, revenue sharing, and World Cup prize money.[54]

Another legal issue related to sports is an ongoing debate as to whether athletes get special treatment from the judicial system and from teams when it comes to punishment and rehabilitation. One of the most debated issues took place after Michael Vick served jail time for his involvement in a dogfighting ring. Before his prison sentence, Vick was one of the most successful quarterbacks in the NFL. After his release from prison, many fans and dog lovers who were repulsed by Vick's actions didn't want their team to sign Vick even though he was a talented quarterback who could help their team. Eventually, the Philadelphia Eagles gave Vick a chance and he played five seasons for the Eagles and won the Associated Press NFL 2010 Comeback Player of the Year award. I believe that while what Vick did was terrible, he had served his time and should be given a second chance. Note the success of pro boxing champion Bernard Hopkins, who had served time in prison but reformed himself and had incredible success after his release.[55]

Whenever a high-profile athlete is charged with a crime or engages in violent behavior, it gains a lot of attention. Baltimore Ravens star running back Ray Rice punched his fiancée in an elevator, resulting in a two-game suspension from the NFL. This incident ruined his playing career, as NFL teams refused to sign him. Domestic violence charges against him were dismissed.[56] Minnesota Vikings running back Adrian Peterson hit his young son with a switch, resulting in a misdemeanor reckless assault no-contest, a fine, probation, community service, and a suspension from the NFL.[57] World champion boxer Floyd Mayweather, Jr., pleaded guilty to a misdemeanor domestic violence charge in 2010 and was sentenced to three months in jail. He was released after serving two months.[58] Baseball star Jose Canseco pleaded no contest to domestic violence in 1998 and was sentenced to probation.[59] In 2012, NFL wide receiver Chad Johnson pleaded no contest to a domestic violence charge and received probation.[60] Former Chicago Bulls great Dennis Rodman pleaded no contest to a misdemeanor charge of spousal battery in 2008 and received probation, road cleanup, and domestic violence counseling.[61] NBA great Jason Kidd pleaded guilty to misdemeanor spousal abuse in 2001, was fined $200, and was ordered to take anger management training.[62] Boxer Mike Tyson was convicted of rape in 1992 and served a little less than three years in prison.[63] After Aaron Hernandez of the New England Patriots was convicted of murder, he later killed himself in prison.[64] Baltimore Ravens star linebacker Ray Lewis and two of his friends allegedly got involved in a brawl outside a Super Bowl party at a nightclub that resulted in the stabbing deaths of two people. Lewis accepted a plea deal for misdemeanor obstruction of justice where the murder charges against him were dropped in exchange for his testimony against his friends. The two men were acquitted and found not guilty in a jury trial. Lewis was given one year of probation, was fined by the NFL, and later proceeded to win an additional Super Bowl.[65] In 2018, the Kansas City Chiefs released running back Kareem Hunt, after video surfaced of him physically attacking a woman. Hunt was not arrested or charged regarding the incident, and shortly after the Chiefs released him, the Cleveland Browns signed him.[66]

Probably the most famous incident of an athlete being criminally charged was O.J. Simpson, who was accused of stabbing his ex-wife Nicole Brown Simpson and her friend Ron Goldman to death in 1994. With the help of O.J.'s dream team of lawyers, Simpson was acquitted and found not guilty of murder. He was, however, found civilly liable for damages. In 2008, Simpson was convicted of kidnapping, assault, and robbery of two sports memorabilia dealers in Las Vegas. He served several years in prison before being paroled.[67]

In a 2013 ESPNW article labeling Simpson as the Patient Zero of athlete privilege in light of how his alleged repeated domestic violence against his wife was ignored or overlooked by friends and law enforcement, Sarah Spain wrote that this is a common occurrence when it comes to high-profile athletes. "Even when we see the abuse with our own eyes, hear the accounts of many or witness a conviction, when the criminals are beloved athletes, coaches and 'good guys,' we find ways to shame and blame the victims."[68]

Jeffrey Kluger's 2014 *Time* magazine article, citing the *San Diego Union-Tribune*'s NFL Arrests Database, indicated that 730 pro football players had been arrested between 2000 and September 2014. The *Time* article also cited Arrest Nation as reporting 47 NFL arrests in the first nine months of 2014. Kluger urged that leagues like the NFL should come down hard on athletes to prevent future incidents, stating, "You're likelier to stay the hand of the batterer when he knows he's swiftly and surely going to be battered in return—in the form of arrest, trial, suspension from play or even expulsion from professional football forever ... the league needs a sheriff, one whose penalties hit even harder than the players themselves do."[69]

In 2014, sports psychologist Mitch Abrams told Rachael Rettner of Live Science, "Athletes are not more violent than non-athletes, when they do transgress, it's big news." Rettner cited a statistic from the website FiveThirtyEight (which cited the *USA Today* NFL Arrests Database) that "the overall arrest rate (for any crime) for NFL players is just 13 percent of the national average arrest rate for men ages 25 to 29."[70]

Regarding college athletes and sexual assault, the NCAA issued a handbook to its member schools titled "Addressing Sexual Assault and Interpersonal Violence: Athletics' Role in Support of Healthy and Safe Campuses," which emphasized how athletic departments need to collaborate with other campus professionals to change the culture regarding sexual assault and interpersonal violence. The NCAA Executive Committee also issued a statement on sexual violence. The NCAA's website includes a sexual violence prevention toolkit, a best-practice guide for athletics administrators on recommended approaches to prevent or reduce incidents of sexual assault and violence on campus, and links to organizations and other resources related to preventing these incidents.[71]

In 2017, Indiana University instituted a policy determining that students who had been criminally convicted or pleaded guilty or no contest to a felony involving sexual violence would be disqualified from playing sports at the university.[72] In 2015, the Southeastern Conference adopted a policy that banned transfer student-athletes who had a record of domestic violence or sexual assault.[73]

A commonly asked question is whether athletes receive special treatment in the court system. In some cases, athletes are able to avoid jail time because they can afford good criminal defense lawyers, as opposed to average people who can't afford expensive defense attorneys and might be represented by overburdened public defenders.

An ESPN *Outside the Lines* investigation found, "From 2009 to 2014, male basketball and football players at the University of Florida and Florida State University avoided criminal charges or prosecution on average two-thirds of the time when named as suspects in police documents, a result far exceeding that of nonathlete males in the same age range." The report indicated that one of the main reasons for this discrepancy at these and several other universities with big-time sports programs was the access to high-profile attorneys. It also noted that athletic department officials frequently inserted themselves into the investigations of their athletes. Furthermore, it indicated that many cases were not prosecuted because of pressure from fans and the media on accusers and witnesses not to pursue charges.[74]

Similarly, as to pro athletes, Bethany P. Withers argued in the *New York Times*, "Combine selective enforcement of the league's policy and potential bias on the part of law enforcement and juries with the fame and glory of being a professional athlete, and we create a class of individuals who feel above reproach."[75]

One of the reasons why some people think athletes get off easy in the criminal justice system is the fact that they can afford good, expensive defense attorneys that average people or poor people can't afford. Public defenders work hard for poor people who can't afford an attorney, but their overwhelming caseloads put them at a disadvantage. Pro and college athletes also have support systems and advocates from teams that average people don't have.

After the arrest of San Francisco 49er player Ray McDonald for alleged domestic violence, it was reported that an off-duty police officer and 49er security employee, Sgt. Sean Pritchard, had gone to McDonald's home the night of the alleged assault. Jane McManus's ESPNW column questioned the appropriateness of pro athletes to call their team's head of security or one of the off-duty police officers employed by the team to go to the alleged crime scene allegedly to advocate for the athlete being investigated. McManus argued, "When the off-duty officer or security head arrives, that person is not there to ensure that the rights of an alleged victim are preserved. They are advocates for the player, in this case McDonald."[76] The district attorney eventually declined to file criminal charges against McDonald.[77] According to *USA*

Today, "Prosecutors described Pritchard's response as a 'side issue' and said his relationship with McDonald did not compromise the investigation or decision not to charge McDonald."[78]

Despite the criticism of alleged conflict of interest, some teams would argue that it's legitimate and appropriate to employ police officers as team security people to supplement their salary, and that it's OK to send a security representative of the team if one of its players is in legal trouble.

There have been disciplinary issues related to the abusive treatment of referees. Referees have a tough job. They can't please everyone. Unfortunately, they have been the target of violence. In January 2016, Calgary Flames defenseman Dennis Wideman gave a hard crosscheck to the back of linesman Don Henderson as he was skating toward his bench, resulting in a 10-game suspension of Wideman.[79] In 1996, Baltimore Orioles second baseman Roberto Alomar was suspended for five games for spitting in the face of home plate umpire John Hirschbeck after Hirschbeck called him out on strikes.[80] Delmon Young was suspended for 50 games when he threw a bat at an umpire after he was ejected for arguing a call during an International League game in 2006.[81]

In 2017, Pierluigi Collina, chairman of FIFA's Referees Committee, called for steps against violence and abuse toward referees. He warned that this could result in a worldwide shortage of soccer referees at all levels, and he told Sky Sports, according to Reuters, "[I]nstead of paying huge respect for these unknown heroes ... they are abused verbally, physically sometimes, this is a real threat."[82]

Another problematic issue is threats to athletes' personal security, and their response of hiring bodyguards or owning guns. Many athletes are concerned about their own and their families' safety, in light of incidents such as Washington Redskins safety Sean Taylor being shot and killed during a home invasion in 2007.[83] Former Saints defensive end Will Smith was fatally shot during a traffic altercation in 2016.[84] Due to social media, athletes are threatened often. In noting that he was considering hiring a bodyguard, Ben Wallace told ESPN, "Professional athletes, most of us came from the streets. We feel like we know the streets and can pretty much protect ourselves. But now we're in a position where we're being targeted, and the stakes are just too high. So, yeah, you might need that big guy standing next to you for a while."[85]

In 2012, *USA Today* reported that numerous NFL players told the paper that in their estimation, around 75 percent of NFL players owned guns.[86] This has led to some tragic or embarrassing incidents. Former Nets player Jayson Williams accidentally shot and killed a limousine driver at his New Jersey estate in 2002, was convicted of covering up the shooting, and pleaded guilty to aggravated assault. Plaxico Burress, a former receiver for the New York Giants, served a 20-month prison sentence after he accidentally shot himself in the leg at a nightclub and pleaded guilty to attempted criminal possession of a weapon.[87] In 2010, Washington Wizards players Gilbert Arenas and Javaris Crittenton brought guns to the locker room and confronted each other. Denver Broncos cornerback Aqib Talib accidentally shot himself in the leg in 2016.[88]

Just like all Americans, athletes have a Second Amendment right to carry guns. However, in criticizing athletes and gun use, Bob Costas told *Late Night* host Seth Meyers, "[T]here is in fact a gun culture, no matter how you feel about the Second Amendment or gun control…. There is a gun culture in sports."[89]

Over the years, there have been many famous incidents involving violence between athletes during a game, sometimes resulting in fines, suspensions, ridicule, criticism, or scorn. In 1977, Kermit Washington of the Los Angeles Lakers punched Rudy Tomjanovich of the Houston Rockets, breaking his jaw and dislocating his skull. Washington was fined $10,000 and suspended for 60 days.[90] In 1965, San Francisco Giants pitcher Juan Marichal hit Los Angeles Dodgers catcher John Roseboro over the head with a bat during a fight, after Roseboro had thrown a ball back to pitcher Sandy Koufax close to Marichal's face while he was a batter. Marichal was suspended for eight games and was fined $1,750. Years later, the two men became friends and Marichal was an honorary pallbearer and speaker at Roseboro's funeral in 2002.[91] In 1973 during Game 3 of the National League Championship Series, a brawl took place after Cincinnati Reds star Pete Rose slid hard into New York Mets second baseman Bud Harrelson, trying to break up a double play.[92] During the 2003 American League Championship Series between the Yankees and Red Sox, Pedro Martinez famously threw 72-year-old coach Don Zimmer to the ground after Zimmer headed toward him during a brawl between the teams.[93] In 1984, the benches were cleared three times and 13 players and coaches were ejected during a brawl between players and coaches of the Atlanta Braves and San Diego Padres.[94] The 1998 New York Knicks vs. Miami Heat playoff game featured a brawl and the enduring image of Knicks coach Jeff Van Gundy clinging to Alonzo Mourning's leg.[95] A New York Islanders vs. Pittsburgh Penguins game featured a lengthy fight in which 65 penalties were given out for a total of 346 minutes.[96]

While most of the publicity regarding legal issues relates to professional and college sports, there are many similar issues related to high school sports. There are many rules, laws, and regulations that guide the administration of high school sports. Some include regulation of homeschooled students who want to participate in high school sports and prayer at public school games.

An interesting emerging issue in high school sports is whether homeschooled students should be eligible to play varsity sports. Millions of high school students are now homeschooled, but some people believe that they should not be eligible to play high school sports, in part because they have chosen to be separate from the rest of the students. In 2004, a Michigan Appeals Court ruled that Michigan public schools did not have to allow homeschooled students on their sports teams.[97] Perhaps the most famous homeschooled student to play sports for their public high school was Heisman Trophy winner and NFL quarterback Tim Tebow. In 2021, Texas lawmakers introduced the "Tim Tebow bill," which would allow homeschooled students to participate in school sports teams and other extracurricular activities.[98] According to the Texas Home School Coalition, 35 other states have similar laws that allow homeschooled students to participate in school extracurricular programs.[99]

Michael Atkinson expressed support for Tim Tebow–inspired laws allowing homeschooled students to participate in school sports in his article in the *Journal of Law and Education*, stating, "Parents who choose to homeschool their children do so precisely because they do not wish their children to attend academic classes at a public school. Requiring them to do so in order to participate in sports defeats the purpose of homeschooling and constricts their athletic opportunities." He asserted that Kentucky should enact a Tebow law similar to ones in Tennessee and Florida, which "allow students to participate in public school athletics without taking classes, but still maintain academic accountability through annual submission of attendance records or academic portfolios."[100]

There is an ongoing debate as to whether public displays of faith should be taken out of sports, particularly at high school sports in public schools. People often interpret this as relating to the separation between church and state, even though the First Amendment does not use that phrase. The relevant First Amendment analysis relates to the Establishment Clause, which states that Congress shall not make laws that establish a religion, as well as the Free Exercise and Free Speech clauses.

The United States Supreme Court ruled in 2000 in *Santa Fe School District v. Doe* that a school policy permitting student-led and student-initiated prayer at high school football games violated the First Amendment's Establishment Clause. In the Santa Fe case, a student chaplain gave a Christian prayer over the public address loudspeaker before home varsity football games. The court determined that the prayers were public, not private speech. It determined that the school's sponsorship of a religious message was impermissible and constituted public speech. The court said, "The delivery of such a message—over the school's public address system, by a speaker representing the student body, under the supervision of school faculty, and pursuant to a school policy that explicitly and implicitly encourages public prayer—is not properly characterized as 'private' speech."[101]

In Washington State, high school football coach Joseph Kennedy was put on administrative leave in 2015 for kneeling in prayer at the 50-yard line after games. Many of his players had joined him in his postgame prayers. A Ninth Circuit panel rejected the coach's lawsuit that alleged that his First Amendment rights were violated, finding that the coach was acting as a public official by praying in full attire and in full view of the school's students and parents.[102] On appeal, the United States Supreme Court ruled in Kennedy's favor in a 6–3 decision in *Kennedy v. Bremerton School District* in 2022, finding that Kennedy's prayers were personal and constitutionally protected by the First Amendment's Free Exercise and Free Speech clauses. The court determined that Kennedy did not engage in prayer while acting within the scope of his duties as a coach. In distinguishing the Santa Fe case, the court stated, "The prayers for which Mr. Kennedy was disciplined were not publicly broadcast or recited to a captive audience. Students were not required or expected to participate."[103]

In another case, a Texas Appeals court ruled that cheerleaders at high school football games had a First Amendment right to write and display Bible verses on banners that the players would run through before the game. In 2018, the Texas Supreme Court declined to review the appeals court's decision.[104]

I believe that in many situations like those involved in the Kennedy case, having team prayers could be awkward for some players. In some cases, atheist players might not want to engage in any prayer at all because it invokes God. Since team prayers in the United States would often be Christian-themed prayers invoking Jesus, players of other religions, such as Judaism, Hinduism, Buddhism, or Islam, might feel left out. There would be implied peer pressure to join the rest of their teammates and their coach in a group prayer, but doing so would make them uncomfortable since they would be saying a prayer that they don't believe in. It might seem easy to say that they could choose not to join their teammates in the prayer, but that could lead to a sense of alienation for that player. This is especially the case at the youth sports or high school level involving young athletes who want to feel part of the group. There is also implicit pressure on those players to pray with their coach, since failing to do so could lead to a decrease in their playing time. While those players are not the exact equivalent of a captive audience like in situations involving prayers announced over a public address speaker, the implied pressure to join those prayers could be overwhelming.

Legal issues are a substantial part of society, and sports are no exception. In light of fan injuries at games, teams are taking more precautions, such as installing safety nets in stadiums. It will be interesting to see if the Baseball Rule, which has protected teams from liability for over a century, will continue to be adhered to. Regarding player liability for their violent actions on the field, criminal prosecution is unlikely, and the high standard of recklessness for civil cases makes lawsuits hard to win. Sports agent misconduct is an ongoing problem at the pro and college level and several agents have been punished for their misdeeds. Title IX is one of the most significant laws that have affected sports, as it has opened many doors for women and girls over the last few decades. Some feel that the law should be revised to avoid the cutting of nonrevenue sports teams, mostly men's, which have taken place to comply with Title IX. There is an ongoing debate as to whether athletes receive special treatment under the law and whether they deserve second chances. Public high schools face various legal problems in dealing with issues such as eligibility of homeschool students to play team sports and prayer at public school sporting events. You almost need a daily scorecard to keep up with legal issues in sports, whether it be state or federal legislation, athletes' conduct, administration of pro and amateur organizations, and court cases at the state and federal level.

Chapter 9

Youth Sports

In general, youth sports are great ways for kids to have fun, exercise, spend time with friends, and learn how to play a sport. However, many ongoing controversies have arisen over the years regarding youth sports in grades K through 12 and how they are influenced by parents, coaches, organizations, and players. Some controversies relate to gender, such as whether girls should be playing on boys teams or competing against them in sports like wrestling and football. There is also a less common issue of whether boys should play on girls teams, such as field hockey. Other issues include mandatory playing time and competition for playing time at higher levels of youth sports, overexposure and burnout, the pressure and time requirements for travel teams, the extensive costs of youth sports, college recruiting at an early age, pressure to perform, and pressure to specialize in one sport at an early age. Another hot-button issue is whether participation trophies are a good or bad thing. Some people hate them and argue that it gives kids a sense of entitlement, while others feel that they are appropriate for younger kids to encourage them to keep playing the sport. Unfortunately, youth sports are often spoiled by parents' misconduct in the stands and as coaches. This chapter will explore the issues of youth sports and the relevant controversies and debates.

For many people, playing youth sports is and was a huge part of their lives. Parents often try to expose their kids to playing sports almost right after they begin to walk. T-ball, youth soccer, basketball tournaments, and swim meets are a regular staple for many kids' weekends. There are many benefits to having kids play in organized youth sports leagues, including exercise, fun, learning teamwork and discipline, making new friends, learning skills needed to play a sport, boosting self-esteem and confidence, respecting coaches and referees, time management with homework, being persistent, and overcoming adversity when you're injured, your team loses, or you have a bad game. For many families, sports are the most common venue for parents to engage and be involved with their kids, whether that means teaching them how to throw a baseball or driving them every day to soccer practice.

In my case, growing up, playing sports was one of the most important things in my life. Many of these sports were organized teams, including Little League Baseball, junior high school tennis and wrestling, high school soccer, and college tennis. However, I spent just as much time playing unorganized pickup sports, including

The Little League World Series, held annually in Williamsport, Pennsylvania, is one of the most prestigious and popular competitions in youth sports. Playing youth sports has great benefits for kids but debates arise as to issues such as participation trophies, overscheduling, and specialization (photo from Creative Commons. "2012 Little League World Series—Williamsport PA 82593296" by samuelnabi is licensed under CC BY-SA 2.0).

street hockey in apartment parking lots, football at various local fields, and basketball at local parks and gyms. All of these sports, both organized and pickup, were events that I thought about all day, waiting in anticipation for practices and games. Trying to win and improve my skills were always important, but the most important parts of playing these sports were the friendships and a sense of belonging to a group.

The typical stereotype of kids today is that they are glued to their computer or phone screen all day, playing video games and going on social media. That's partially true, but many kids in grades K through 12 still engage in playing sports, especially organized youth sports. For many kids, that venue is the best chance for them to be with their friends and family.

According to the Aspen Institute, in 2018, 71.8 percent of kids ages six–12 played on a team or individual sport. Among the most popular youth sports are basketball and baseball. As reported by the Associated Press, "According to the Aspen Institute, which promotes youth sports participation and uses SFIA data, 13.6% of kids ages 6–12 played baseball in 2018, a 3% increase from 2015. Baseball was the second-most popular sport for kids in that age group, after basketball, which had a 14.1% participation rate."[1]

In addition to the physical benefits, science shows that participation in youth sports has substantial benefits related to mental health as well. A 2019 article in *JAMA Pediatrics* by Dr. Molly C. Easterlin, Dr. Paul J. Chung, and Dr. Mei Leng concluded, "In this study of 9668 individuals from a nationally representative database, among those with adverse childhood experiences, team sports participation during adolescence was significantly associated with better adult mental health outcomes, especially for males, including lower likelihood of having ever received a diagnosis of depression or anxiety and having current depressive symptoms. The findings suggest that participation in team sports is associated with better adult mental health outcomes among individuals exposed to adverse childhood experiences."[2]

An April 2021 segment of HBO's *Real Sports* documented the harmful effects that the cancellation of organized youth sports during the coronavirus pandemic had on the mental health of young teenage athletes. Kavitha Davidson's report detailed the incidents of severe anxiety and depression of young athletes due to their sports seasons being canceled. The report showed the importance of sports in young people's lives and how hard kids were hit when they couldn't play organized sports for over a year in some cases.[3]

Despite the many positives, many people criticize various negative aspects of what youth sports have become. One common criticism is the regular awarding of participation trophies to kids, whether their team won a championship or not.

Critics of awarding participation trophies argue that these trophies are making our country's kids soft and constitutes the wussification of America. They say that trophies should be earned and given only to the championship teams and players. This issue received a lot of attention in 2015 when James Harrison of the Pittsburgh Steelers announced on Instagram that he was returning his young sons' participation trophies, and that he would continue to return those participation trophies until they won real trophies and championships.[4] Some youth leagues across the country have started to do away with participation awards.[5]

In criticizing participation trophies, Dr. Vivian Diller wrote in *Psychology Today*, "Perhaps if we offered the gold, silver and bronze for actual achievements, kids would learn lessons that better served their needs as adults. Perhaps if we let them lose and teach them to congratulate those who win, we would help them build the motivation and endurance needed to face real life challenges—e.g., sustaining a long-term marriage or securing employment—two very elusive trophies in today's world."[6]

Those who defend participation trophies argue that it encourages young kids to participate in sports.

Lisa Heffernan wrote in Today.com, "Another reason to defend trophies for everyone is that, at a time when parents complain of the escalating competition in youth sports, they remind kids that we value their effort, regardless of ability or results. Participation trophies tell them that what matters is showing up for practice, learning the rules and rituals of the game and working hard."[7]

Gabriel Andrade also defended participation trophies as being beneficial to players on both the winning and losing teams. Andrade wrote in *Philosophia*, "John Rawls' theory of distributive justice (Heath, 2005) provides a strong rationale for participation trophies. While it is true that the brash delivery of participation trophies may be detrimental to youth sports and education as a whole, it is nevertheless important to consider that participation trophies can serve as educational means for important civic lessons in the development of a more just society."

Andrade added that participation trophies can teach sports competition winners that they shouldn't disrespect their competitors who lost, stating, "Participation trophies may be a relevant way of educating young athletes into accepting the dignity of losers. Contrary to conservative fears, a participation trophy would not necessarily be a venue for millennials' entitlement. Quite the opposite, it would be a recognition that, even as losers, they still deserve respect from the rest of competitors."[8]

Some leagues and competitions give trophies or awards to just the top three finishers, just like the Olympics. Other competitions, such as state wrestling or swimming championships, give awards to the top 10 finishers.

For some sports, there is great prestige even if you don't finish first, such as winning a bronze medal in the Olympics, finishing in fifth place at a state wrestling or swim meet, or making the NCAA basketball Final Four. Arguably, getting a varsity letter or letter jacket or a certification plaque for playing on a varsity high school or college team is the equivalent of a participation trophy. It's a tangible award acknowledging your participation on the team. For some athletes, just making the varsity team, especially at a large high school or at the university level where several people are cut and don't make the team, is a great accomplishment that they can cherish the rest of their lives.

My take is that participation trophies are mostly harmless and not a big deal to fret about, especially for very young kids. I see them as the equivalent of earning a varsity letter in a middle school or high school sports as an acknowledgment of participation. I think that most kids, especially older ones, realize that a participation trophy is not the equivalent of winning a championship trophy. It's unfair for older adults to criticize young people who grew up in this participation trophy era as being spoiled, soft, fragile, and entitled. It isn't the kids who came up with the idea that everyone should get a trophy, it was the adults. Many of these adults don't think negatively about the varsity letter jackets and certificates that they received in high school and middle school for being on a team, regardless of whether they got much playing time or whether their team won a championship. They look at those keepsakes as a source of pride.

Another controversial and debated issue in youth sports, especially in recent years, is whether the genders should compete against each other in the same sport, especially when they get older. Should girls be allowed to play on boys teams? Should girls be allowed to compete against boys in sports like wrestling? Should boys be allowed to play on girls teams? What about transgender athletes?

There has been an increase in girls participating on boys teams, especially football. A 2018 *New York Times* article cites a Sports and Fitness Industry Association statistic that girls make up nearly 11 percent of the 5.5 million Americans who play tackle football. In 2017, high school quarterback Holly Neher became the first girl in Florida history to throw a touchdown pass in a game. That same year, kicker K-Lani Nava became the first girl in Texas to score points in a high school state championship game. In some cases, girls can compete against each other in football. As of 2018, five states had sanctioned girls flag football as a varsity high school sport.[9]

There is some concern as to girls playing football against boys because of the physical nature of the sport and the risk of concussions. This is especially the case at the high school level, where most boys are bigger, stronger, and faster than girls. However, if a girl is willing to take the physical risk of getting injured, and her parents consent, then that should be sufficient to allow girls to play. Perhaps the best solution would be to increase female participation in youth football so that there would be enough players for girls to compete against other girls. In addition, girls could be encouraged to play flag football instead of tackle in order to decrease the risk of concussions and brain injuries. As girls and women become older and play at the high school and college level, many of them choose to be kickers, in which there is much less of a risk of physical injury than playing a regular position, such as quarterback, receiver, or defensive back.

There has been an increase in girls participating against boys in wrestling. In 2018 in Wisconsin, there were four wrestling tournaments in the state that featured girls-only divisions. The rest of the time the girls compete against the boys.[10]

Arguably, the best solution is to create more opportunities for girls to compete against other girls. According to USA Wrestling, as of 2018, six states have state championships for high school girls: Alaska, California, Hawaii, Tennessee, Texas, and Washington.[11]

Some girl wrestlers have thrived against boys despite the obstacles.

In 2006, Michaela Hutchinson became the first girl to win a state wrestling championship against boys, in the 103-pound weight class in Alaska. Prior to that, two girls, Erica Dye of West Virginia and Deanna Rix of Maine, had placed second in boys state championships. In 2010, Hope Steffensen became the second Alaska girl to win a state high school boys wrestling title. In 2019, two girl wrestlers placed for the first time at the Colorado state high school wrestling championships.[12]

Some people have religious and other objections to having boys wrestle against girls. Sometimes, boys choose to forfeit their matches against girls, even if it costs them a chance to win a state championship.

In the 2011 Iowa state wrestling championship, sophomore Joel Northrup, who had a 35–4 record, defaulted his first-round match against Cassy Herkelman because he felt that wrestling against a girl would go against his religious beliefs. In a statement to the media, Northrup said, "I have a tremendous amount of respect for Cassy and Megan (another female wrestler at the state tournament) and their accomplishments. However, wrestling is a combat sport and it can get violent at times. As a matter of conscience and my faith I do not believe that is appropriate for a boy to engage a girl in this manner. It is unfortunate that I have been placed in a situation not seen in most other high school sports in Iowa."[13]

For many boys, wrestling against a girl can be a no-win situation. If they win, it's no big deal because they're supposed to beat a girl. If they lose, they're likely to be embarrassed and teased by their teammates and fellow students. Given that choice, some boys choose to forfeit. For the girls, many will be at a physical disadvantage against the boys, or it might be frustrating if boys choose to forfeit or not wrestle against them. However, when this happens, it deprives girls a chance to compete in a sport that they love.

There have been incidents where boys attempt to play on girls teams. Generally, it involves situations when boys want to play sports like field hockey or volleyball, but their school offers the sports only to girls. It's a controversial issue that many state athletic organizations have wrestled with. Pennsylvania changed its rules to make it much harder for boys to participate on a girls high school team. It enacted a rule in 2014 that allowed boys to play on girls teams in certain situations where four criteria elements were met, but that having such a mixed-gender team would mean that team would be required to play against boys teams in playoff competition.[14] There are many countries around the world where men's and boys' field hockey are very popular. However, that popularity has not translated to the United States. Some boys want to play the sport so badly that they're willing to wear a skirt during games. A county athletics committee panel determined that Keeling Pilaro, a 13-year-old boy who grew up in Dublin, Ireland, would be allowed to continue playing for his Long Island high school's girls field hockey team, after it had been determined at first that Pilaro couldn't play on the team. Pilaro later transferred to a high school in Virginia where he did not play field hockey.[15]

Erin E. Buzuvis argued in her article in the *Texas Journal on Civil Liberties and Civil Rights* that segregation of the sexes in high school sports should be narrowly tailored and that sports should be integrated as much as possible. She argued that gender-free sports would "mitigate the stigma inherent in the protectionisms that female athletes are categorically inferior" and "equalize access to resources." She cited golf as a sport that would benefit from integration.

Buzuvis claimed that integrating the genders in sports would erode the perpetuation of gender stereotypes, stating, "Not only would integration of sports provide more opportunities to contextualize female athleticism, it is also possible that it would permit exploration of the possibility that segregation itself is contributing to differences in performance by perpetuating self-fulfilling gender stereotypes. Segregation sends the message that 'women are physically weaker' or that they 'will be badly beaten and emotionally crushed' if they participate alongside men."[16]

In a 2022 article in *The Atlantic*, Maggie Mertens also argued that athletes should be separated by ability rather than sex and that sex segregation of athletes should not be automatic, stating, "[As] long as laws and general practice of youth sports remain rooted in the idea that one sex is inherently inferior, young athletes will continue to learn and internalize that harmful lesson."[17]

While debates exist regarding boys playing on girls teams and girls playing on boys teams, a much more heated and politically polarizing issue has arisen as to whether transgender athletes should be allowed to compete against girls. In Texas, a transgender wrestler, Mack Beggs, who was in the process of transitioning from female to male and taking a low dose of testosterone, won two straight girls state wrestling titles, after his request to wrestle in the boys division was denied. While many people are supportive of transgender rights, some are concerned about the alleged unfair physical advantage that transgender athletes might have. A federal lawsuit was brought in Connecticut by three high school girls, alleging that allowing transgender girls to compete against cisgender girls violated Title IX. The lawsuit arose after two Connecticut transgender girls won several girls state championships in track and field. A federal judge dismissed the suit in 2021 on procedural grounds. The plaintiffs subsequently appealed the case to the Second Circuit.[18]

This has become a hot-button political issue in recent years, and several states have passed laws banning transgender girls from competing on girls teams, including Mississippi, Arkansas, Tennessee, and Alabama.[19]

In defending these laws, Mississippi governor Tate Reeves said at the bill signing, "This important piece of legislation will ensure that young girls in Mississippi have a fair, level playing field in public school sports.... It sends a clear message to my daughters and all of Mississippi's daughters that their rights are worth fighting for."[20]

In advocating for the rights of transgender athletes, tennis star Billie Jean King said, "There is no place in any sport for discrimination of any kind. I'm proud to support all transgender athletes who simply want the access and opportunity to compete in the sport they love. The global athletic community grows stronger when we welcome and champion all athletes—including LGBTQI+ athletes." Many organizations issued statements supporting the rights of transgender athletes to participate in sports.[21]

Elizabeth A. Sharrow argued that denying transgender athletes from participating in organized youth sports would have damaging psychological effects on those young people. She wrote, "Recently, a 2017 Human Rights Campaign Foundation report found that while sixty-eight percent of young people participate in organized sports, only twelve percent of transgender girls do (Johnson et al. 2018). This means that under the status quo, transgender students are less likely to reap the rewards of athletic participation, which include improved academic performance, better physical and mental health, meaningful and even life-changing social ties, and other benefits that help build healthy and fulfilling lives (Easterlin et al. 2019; Paluck and Clark 2020; Staurowsky et al. 2015)." Sharrow indicated that laws prohibiting transgender athletes from competing would deny them the chance to participate in sports and the chance to learn valuable life skills.

Sharrow added that allowing transgender athletes to participate in sports would lead to a reduction in transphobia. "This is especially crucial for transgender youth who are commonly harassed and excluded at school (GLSEN 2017). Involvement in sports can mitigate the vulnerabilities often experienced by trans kids (Goldberg 2021)."[22]

As opposed to the controversy over who should play sports against one another, additional issues exist at the youth level as to the manner in which kids play sports, how many sports they choose to play, and how much they should play.

A recent trend in youth sports is the extent of how organized they tend to be, and that fewer kids play unorganized pickup games at a park or local gym. A few decades ago, kids used to have pickup games of baseball, football, basketball, and street hockey. Growing up in the 1970s, my friends and I would spend countless hours and days playing street hockey and Wiffle Ball in our apartment complex's parking lots, touch football in the local park, or pickup basketball at various indoor and outdoor facilities. We would set up several orange cones in the park to delineate the end zones. We would play sports until it was too dark to see at night. There were times when we played during downpours and snowstorms. Many of us, including me, played on our junior high school and high school teams and had practice and games in the afternoon, but we still found time to play pickup games at night or on the weekends. Nowadays, kids still play sports, but it tends to be through organized leagues, intramurals, and travel teams. If kids tried to get a pickup baseball game at a local field or park today, they would likely strike out and not find enough players. If they're lucky, they might be able to organize a short pickup game during a 20-minute outdoor recess at school—if the school even has recess.

If you're a talented player as a kid, you're much more likely to be spending time on an AAU or travel team in order to showcase your skills, instead of playing a pickup game at a local playground.

According to an Alliance for Childhood policy brief from 2016, citing a study by Ginsburg et al., "The American Academy of Pediatrics links increases in depression and anxiety to a lack of unstructured playtime. It recommends that children spend at least 60 minutes each day in open-ended play."[23]

Dr. Esther Entin wrote in *The Atlantic* in 2011 that parents should encourage their kids to engage in free play. "The competing needs for childcare, academic and athletic success, and children's safety are compelling. But perhaps parents can begin to identify small changes—such as openings in the schedule, backing off from quite so many supervised activities, and possibly slightly less hovering on the playground that would start the pendulum returning to the direction of free, imaginative, kid-directed play."[24]

In response to this recent trend of organized sports, in 2010, Tim Donovan, director of the Youth Sports Institute at SUNY Cortland, started Sandlot Day, in which kids make the rules and decide which games to play.[25]

Another common trend in youth sports is the emphasis on specialization. In order to compete at an elite level, many kids have to give up playing other sports in order to focus on just one activity year-round. Many kids feel pressure from parents to get good enough in one sport to get a college scholarship. They also might get pressure from coaches from youth leagues, AAU teams, and varsity high school teams to specialize in their sport and play that sport the whole year and not play other varsity, intramural, or club sports. Their philosophy is that athletes need to show dedication to that specific sport.

One drawback of specialization at a young age is the increased risk of injury. In 2018, Dr. Mininder S. Kocher, pediatric orthopedic surgeon at Children's Hospital Boston, told the *New York Times* that he has seen an increase in elbow reconstruction Tommy John surgery on young baseball pitchers. A study of 12,000 kids by Kocher and his colleagues found that early specialization in sports resulted in increased risk of injury for boys and girls.[26]

Dr. Neal ElAttrache, an orthopedic surgeon at Kerlan-Jobe Orthopedic Clinic in Los Angeles, told ABC News that young baseball pitchers can be more likely to be injured due to the repetitive motions of pitching and chronic fatigue. ElAttrache said, "Early specialization into one sport, and year round participation…. The chances of overuse injuries and sometimes worse types of injuries are higher."[27]

There is evidence that being a multisport athlete can be beneficial.

Dr. Avery Faigenbaum is a full professor in the Department of Health and Exercise Science at the College of New Jersey. He teaches several courses, including health promotion, exercise prescription, and clinical exercise physiology. In a Zoom interview confirmed and revised by email, Faigenbaum said that multisport participation for kids has substantial benefits. "Data shows that multisport is the way to go before the high school years. Some sports like gymnastics or diving have an advantage in specializing early, but most sports show that being a multisport athlete leads to an increase in performance and longevity in sports. Most Division 1 athletes say that they played two or three different sports during childhood. Multisport participation early in life is the way to go, then it's OK to specialize in high school. It's nice to have a two- or three-month break to increase longevity. The hours played per week shouldn't exceed the kid's age. So a 10-year-old soccer player shouldn't exceed playing 10 hours of structured (i.e., practice and games) soccer a week. Do different activities, different sports, and outdoor active play. Do something else than your main sport."

Faigenbaum added, "Gladwell outlines the 10,000-hour rule, saying that you should play 10,000 hours at the youth level to be a Division 1 athlete. I don't think that's true. That amount of time has nothing to do with the quality of the practice. I think that 5,000 hours of quality practice is better than 10,000. It also depends on the quality of the coaching. You want to learn the technical skills and develop a passion for the game. It's important to develop athleticism, muscle strength, and fundamental movement skills like jumping and throwing. Make kids stronger for all sports and enhance their athleticism. Early specialization overlooks preparedness to play the game."[28]

In general, injuries are a major part of youth sports. According to CBS News in 2013, a study published by Safe Kids Worldwide found that kids get hurt playing sports every 25 seconds, and that around 1.35 million emergency room visits a year take place due to injuries in youth sports.[29]

Tackle football injuries are common for youth. Should youth football be banned due to concussions and other health risks? Dr. Avery Faigenbaum rejects the notion that football should be eliminated for kids under 12. "Physical inactivity is the fourth-leading cause of death. I want kids to be active. There is a risk of injuries in sports; the risk can never be lowered to zero, but we can make sports safer. Many soccer foundations have banned heading at the youth level, youth hockey has limited checking, Pop Warner football has eliminated kickoffs for kids under 10. If you eliminate certain sports like youth football, it could be a slippery slope. What about rugby, gymnastics, or cheerleading, where there are many injuries as well? Football is popular in the cities, where other sports like golf and tennis might not be an option. If a kid is 250 pounds, they're probably going to play football. We have to make the sport safer and continue the research. Maybe football can learn from soccer and hockey and implement rules at the youth level to make the sport safer. I don't think eliminating the sport is the best option. Modify the rules to make youth football more safe, so they can be prepared to properly play the game when they get older."[30]

As to the pressure on kids to play hurt, Dr. Faigenbaum said, "The pressure to play hurt usually arises at the high school or college level, not at the youth level. Most youth coaches are aware of the safety issues and won't ask an eight- or nine-year-old to play hurt. Some pressure to play hurt might come from the parents who tell their kid to walk it off or get over it. For kids age 12 to 14 undergoing growth spurts, it's important to be smart about training. In Europe, they value periods of less intense training (and recovery) more than the US. There isn't enough focus on rest and recovery in the United States when it comes to training young athletes. Kids get emotionally and physically tired after a hard game or workout. Kids should train hard on hard days and recover hard on the easy days. There is the concept of periodization, in which athletes systematically vary the intensity and volume of training over time. You shouldn't go hard every day. Some days should be very hard workout days, while other days should be easier workouts. It's important to educate kids that it's OK to have an easy workout day. High-intensity training is important, but less intense workouts can also be beneficial; maybe you emphasize techniques during lighter workout days. It's important to have those recovery days. Coaches and players should be educated as to less intense training and recovery strategies. There are other ways to avoid getting injured. Sleep is also a factor. Kids should get nine hours of sleep. There are also factors of good nutrition and hydration. There should be a holistic approach involving sensible training with qualified youth coaches."[31]

Regarding the pressure on athletic trainers and coaches at the youth and high school level to rush their players back on the field or court, Dr. Faigenbaum said,

"Athletic trainers in all 50 states must follow the rules. There are mandatory protocols for injuries like concussions and ACL tears. They get a four-year degree and perhaps a master's degree. Youth coaches are different. Some are certified. Others are well-meaning but misinformed parents. They don't understand when they tell the kid to brush off an injury; there could be an underlying injury. There needs to be better education of youth coaches. When in doubt, sit it out. You shouldn't care about the score. Kids play sports to have fun, make friends, and learn something new. It's the parents that care more about winning. You need the best coaches at the developmental level early in life. Right now, many youth coaches are volunteers and never had formal training. It's important to develop proper habits and a love of the game. You don't need a former Division 1 athlete to yell at the kids. Most kids drop out from playing sports by age 11. It's a tragedy. It's not fun anymore. It's important to plant the seeds at an early age that exercise and sports are important. You don't want kids to go down the inactivity road and gain weight and have poor cardiovascular health. Eighteen percent of kids are obese. It's not just about sports. Kids are getting turned off from physical activity. It's hard to get them back. When high school phys ed is optional, generally it's only the athletes that choose to do it. The other kids don't. It's a public health crisis."[32]

Dr. Faigenbaum indicated that pediatric exercise science can help prevent injuries in young athletes. "We can reduce the likelihood of injuries at the youth sports level if kids participate in an eight-week preseason conditioning program. Regular strength training and agility training can reduce injuries. The sooner we start, the better. There's too much sedentary behavior in kids, especially when phys ed is optional. It helps to have six to eight weeks of preseason conditioning. When the NFL didn't have their usual six to eight weeks of preseason training in 2020 due to COVID, you saw an explosion of injuries, especially ACL tears, which could have long-term effects later in life such as osteoarthritis. It's important to focus on strength, fitness, agility, balance, and coordination to prepare for the demands of a season. Preparatory conditioning works, especially at the youth level. It's important to educate parents, kids, and youth sports governing bodies about this. While year-round strength and conditioning is desirable, two months of preparatory conditioning before the start of the season is a minimum."[33]

Aside from physical injuries, another risk and potential psychological drawback of youth sports is burnout. Many kids get tired of constant practice and travel and want to do other things. According to the National Alliance for Sports and CNN, 70 percent of kids leave organized sports by age 13. John O'Sullivan, former college and pro soccer player and a longtime coach at the youth, high school, college, and pro levels, and the founder and CEO of the Changing the Game Project, told CNN, "We know all the benefits of activity from better grades to less drugs, less pregnancy, more likely to go to college and on and on and on and yet at the same age when most kids are walking away from sports is that critical age where if they're active then, they're likely to be active for life."[34]

In O'Sullivan's highly viewed TED talk on youth sports, he urges parents to be more positive toward their kids when it comes to sports and to not constantly criticize them or evaluate their performance after games. His mantra is that parents should constantly tell their kids, "I love watching you play."[35]

In a Zoom interview, Dr. Avery Faigenbaum said, "Maybe the term 'burnout' is exaggerated. Five to 10 percent of kids burn out from sports, but is it really burnout or excessive pressure from a coach, being yelled at by a parent, or not having the necessary motor skills to play the sport? Maybe playing sport just isn't fun anymore. There are many other factors. Kids growing up in the 1960s and '70s would play outside for several hours every day. This generation of kids aren't physically fit. They aren't accumulating a minimum of at least 60 minutes of daily moderate to vigorous physical activity. The 60 minutes doesn't have to be consecutive. Kids used to play outside, walk to school, and have daily recess and physical education. Kids today aren't physically prepared to play sports. Participation in physical activity shouldn't begin with competitive sports. Too many kids don't walk to school. Many only have phys ed once a week, their schools have deemed recess to be expendable, and they go home to engage in electronic media. Many kids are not prepared to play sports."[36]

Regarding the risk of overscheduling for youth athletes, Dr. Faigenbaum said, "Overscheduling increases the risk of injury. If a tennis or soccer player competes regularly and intensely for one to two hours for three straight days, that can be a setup for injury. Overscheduling can cause young athletes to pay less attention to getting adequate sleep and eating right. Kids should get eight or nine hours of sleep, but if they're overscheduled due to travel, they might only get six or seven. That leads to increased injury risk and poor performance. They also might not get the well-balanced meals that they would get at home, due to eating on the road. I blame the sports organizers that arrange four-day tournaments in August in a hot environment. I wonder if it's too much. Gymnastics tournaments last several days. Many injuries could be preventable with sensible scheduling. Instead of a yearlong schedule, it would be good to have three months doing other things and not playing in tournaments. Give young athletes a break."[37]

Faigenbaum added, "There's an unfitness epidemic with today's kids. They're weaker and slower than previous generations. That's the case in the US and globally. There are some amazing athletes, but there's also a lack at the physical fitness level. In the 1960s, there was an emphasis on calisthenics, such as push-ups, sit-ups, throwing and kicking a ball, and developing strength and skill. Now the focus is on accumulating at least 60 minutes of exercise at a predetermined target heart rate. Kids aren't learning the skills to success. They're not getting strong enough. There is a lack of physical literacy in kids today. That involves competence and confidence to move. If you're physically illiterate, you won't go out for sports and you'll watch TV at home. Physical education should be a part of schools, as well as recess and after-school programs. Just like reading literacy, it's important to get kids to start early for physical literacy. Don't wait until high school, when it's too late. It's like teaching kids to read in second or third grade."[38]

Another element of youth sports is the extensive cost and sacrifices that families may incur in order to have their kids to compete at a high level. A 2011 *CNN.com* article focused on these costs, giving an example of a 14-year-old quarterback named Nick Heras, whose parents paid over $50,000 a year for him to leave home in order to attend and train at IMG Academies, an elite athletic training program in Florida. Gabby Douglas, the first African American to win the all-around gold medal in gymnastics at the Olympics, moved to Iowa to train as a teenager with elite gymnastics coach Liang Chow.[39]

In 2010, USC offered a 13-year-old quarterback, David Sills, a scholarship. In recent years, it has become even more absurd, as the University of Nevada gave a football scholarship offer to nine-year-old Havon Finney, Jr., and the University of Illinois offered a football scholarship to 10-year-old Bunchie Young.[40] These scholarships were not binding, as these kids were too young to sign their National Letters of Intent, but they still raised eyebrows nationwide.

Perhaps the worst part about youth sports isn't the kids, it's their parents. Dr. Jim Taylor wrote in *Psychology Today* that expectations and pressure from parents are some of the reasons why many kids cry after games and often don't enjoy playing sports.[41]

Most parents are supportive of their kids when it comes to playing sports. However, there are many incidents of rogue parents who can't control themselves at their kids' sporting events and need to be ejected from the stands or be banned from attending all of their kid's games in the future. Some of the more serious and outrageous incidents of parents' misbehavior included a parent who in 1999 paid $2 to a Little League pitcher to intentionally hit a batter on the other team with a pitch, a youth hockey father who killed the father of another player during an argument and a brawl after their sons' youth hockey practice, and a hockey coach who intentionally tripped a 13-year-old player on the other team during the handshake line after the game.[42] In June 2019, a nationally publicized incident of parental misbehavior took place during a youth baseball game involving seven-year olds in Colorado, when parents stormed the field due to a call on the field by a 13-year-old umpire and then brawled among each other. Several people were cited for disorderly conduct.[43]

According to *USA Today* in 2018, a referee of youth sports in Oklahoma is fighting back against parental misbehavior at events by trying to publicly shame them. Referee Brian Barlow created a Facebook page in which he paid people $100 to post cell phone videos of parents' serious misconduct at youth sports games.[44]

"They need to remember that many of the officials at this level are doing it to give back to the kids, remember that the kids don't play a perfect game, coaches don't coach a perfect game and certainly our officials aren't going to officiate a perfect game," NFHS executive director Bob Gardner told NBC's *Today* show.[45]

The high dropout rate of kids playing youth sports could be partially attributed to the pressure that is put on them by their parents, some of whom might be living vicariously through their kids to achieve what they didn't on the field or the court.

Little League Baseball has a parent code of conduct that emphasizes six core principles of sportsmanship: "trustworthiness, respect, responsibility, fairness, caring, and good citizenship." Parents agree, among other things, not to force their kids to play sports; to be a positive role model by showing positive support for players, coaches, spectators, and umpires; not to boo, taunt, or use profane language or gestures; and to not yell at or ridicule their own kid or other players.[46] Many youth sports leagues have imposed codes of conduct that parents must adhere to. It is common for abusive parents to be thrown out of games or in some cases be banned from coming to future games. Most parents are well meaning and want to be strong advocates for their kids but act as helicopter parents by getting too involved by insisting that their kid get more playing time or trying to get their kid's coach fired or replaced.

In dealing with parents who complain about their kids' lack of playing time, USA and Philadelphia Maccabiah juniors basketball head coach Brian Schiff said in an email interview, "Basically, unless a kid plays every minute of every game, you can almost never satisfy parents, but treat them with respect and just try, if you are put in that situation, to explain yourself the best you can. Ultimately, you are in charge and have to let them know and realize that. Sometimes you have to be real and say others are at this point better than your child and here's what they have to do to get better and reach that level. Some will get it. Most, sadly, won't."[47]

Rules related to grooming and personal appearance have caused controversy in youth sports. In December 2018, there was an outcry when a wrestling referee insisted that a Black high school wrestler in New Jersey would have to immediately cut his long dreadlocks in order to avoid forfeiting his match. Video of the wrestler getting his haircut while on the mat went viral and raised outrage. The incident resulted in investigations by the New Jersey Interscholastic Athletic Association and a state civil rights investigation. After the investigation, the referee was suspended for two years, and his lawsuit for defamation and other claims against the school district was dismissed. New Jersey then passed a law banning discrimination based on hair style or texture.[48] In 2021, a Black high school sophomore softball player in North Carolina was forced to cut off her hair braids that had beads at the end during a game in order to comply with a mandatory rule governing softball.[49]

In 2014, a Seventh Circuit court ruled that a junior high school could not force a male basketball player to cut his hair, because there was no rule requiring girl players to cut their hair. The rule had been in place to promote team unity and a clean-cut image.[50]

As mentioned earlier, playing time is another issue debated in youth sports. It's no fun for a kid to sit on the bench for the whole game watching the other kids play. It's also no fun for a parent to pay for their kid to play on a team and then not get to see their kid play. Decades ago, this would happen all too frequently. In addition, nepotism and favoritism would occur, as coaches would favor their own kids and their own favorite players at the expense of other players. When kids don't get playing time in games, they're likely to stop playing the sport. Times have changed, as most youth sports leagues have playing time requirements for players. Little League Baseball requires that each player must play a minimum of six defensive outs and bat at least one time during the game. USA Hockey recommends equal playing time for all players at the 12 and under level unless it's a one-goal game in the last minute or if a player is misbehaving. Youth football leagues across the country have various requirements regarding playing time. For instance, the Harrisonburg, Virginia, youth football league requires that each player play a minimum of eight plays per game, either on offense or defense, and not including special teams.[51]

In the book *The Ethics of Coaching Sports: Moral, Social and Legal Issues*, Scott Kretchmar argued in a chapter that youth sports coaches should play all players, including benchwarmers, because they are learning the sport and should be given a chance to compete. He stated, "In youth sports settings, education, development, opportunity, healthful exercise, and play are basic benefits that should trump any concerns over winning, excellence, financial gain, and the like. Everybody should play, and everybody should play for significant portions of the game."[52]

As kids get older and start playing for competitive AAU or travel teams there is an expectation that the better players will get more playing time and there is more emphasis on winning. The same thing goes for playing varsity sports in high school. Most coaches want to get everyone on the team playing time, but those coaches' jobs often depend on having a winning record, so they want to play the best players most of the game.

Coach Brian Schiff said in an email interview, "Playing time is ultimately the only real thing a coach has over a player." Of course, all situations are different. If you are in a rec or house league or even in a lower or middle school level, all players should play equally, as at those levels it is not about winning but about development and having fun. However, as you get higher or advance, it is a competitive activity and winning is a part of it. I have a line that I say to my players at the higher levels: "Our team will be good so everyone will play. However, 'crunch time' players will get to play in the 'crunch' by listening, working hard, knowing what to do and where to be (my teams tend to run a lot of plays), and doing what the coaches ask."[53]

Travel teams have become an important part of youth sports over the last few decades. Oftentimes there is pressure on young athletes and their parents to compete on travel teams in order to get the experience of playing at a higher level. However, there are costs and time commitments involved in being on a travel team. Parents have to drive their kids long distances, many times out of state, for games and tournaments. There are tryouts and no minimum guaranteed playing time. It can be a valuable experience for kids who are standouts at the recreational league level and who want to play with and against better competition. They will also get access to more expert coaching. It can be a great way to meet new friends and for parents to spend time with their kids. However, the time commitment can be extensive, with a game or tournament every weekend. It might not be worth it to the kid or to the parent if the kid is getting to play only for five minutes in a basketball game or one inning in a baseball game. It is helpful if travel coaches are up-front with players and their parents about the team's playing time policy and give an honest assessment as to how much time the kid is likely to get on the team. Some kids would rather be a star player on their rec or intramural team than a benchwarmer on a travel team.

Aaron Carter, sports reporter for the *Philadelphia Inquirer*, said in an email interview, "The pressure on high school athletes and their parents to get noticed by colleges is most likely the result of the prohibitive cost of higher education in America. Financially, youth sports has become a billion dollar industry. If it's not equipment or travel teams, parents sometimes must decide whether to pay for private coaches. As the cost of tuition rises so too does the importance of scholarship monies. For example, a young baseball player could have a hitting coach, a separate pitching coach, a separate speed and agility coach, and a separate strength coach. The dilemma for parents becomes, if they cannot pay for these coaches and another parent can, their child might fall behind and miss out on scholarship opportunities. Rating services such as Scouts, Rivals, as well as AAU team and summer camps have also become increasingly more important in the youth sports industry. 'Prestigious' camps, rating services, and teams build reputations for finding and producing top-tier talent, which can mean fierce competition between services, camps, and teams, all of which can mean parents willing to spend money for such services. As a result, not only could there be pressure to perform well, there could also be pressure to join the 'right' teams, be invited to the 'right' camps, and be talked about positively by the 'right' scouts."[54]

There are many reasons for kids to play sports, including exercise, making friends, and learning teamwork and responsibility. The positives clearly outweigh the negatives. Ideally, more kids would play pickup games, but being involved in leagues and teams is a lot better than staying home and watching television, being online, or staying glued to the phone. Parents and coaches should do their best to make sports fun for kids and not a chore. They also should try to avoid putting too much pressure on the kids, which often leads to burnout and quitting organized sports altogether. Participation trophies are mocked and ridiculed by many, but if it helps to boost kids at a young age to show them appreciation for coming to practice and games, there's no harm to awarding them. Regarding girls playing on boys teams and boys playing on girls teams, ideally in the future there would be enough participation and opportunity so that there would be more girls football and wrestling teams and boys field hockey and volleyball teams so that it doesn't become an issue. In the meantime, it should be up to the girl if she wants to accept the challenge and physical risk of playing on boys teams, especially at the high school level and beyond. Other issues that have arisen in youth sports, such as the emergence of travel teams, sufficient playing time, specialization in one sport, and the high cost of participating in some sports, have become concerning to many. Despite complications from these issues and debates, youth sports are important and should continue to thrive in the future.

Chapter 10

College Sports

College sports, especially at the Division 1 level, are immensely popular to watch among sports fans. Many people prefer watching college sports over the pros because of the passion of the student-athletes, fans, and alumni. However, there are many controversies regarding college sports. In recent years, one of the most frequent debates involves whether college athletes should be paid and whether the one-and-done rule for college basketball players should be abolished. Part of the analysis of this issue involves cost-of-attendance stipends; athletes being able to profit off their name, image, and likeness; and the attempt by Northwestern University football players to unionize. Other controversies happen frequently in college sports, including recruiting violations and ethics, educational standards, graduation rates, the rise of the Power Five conferences, the shifting membership of conferences, how the college football championship is determined, and the Penn State Jerry Sandusky scandal. There are other issues as to how the NCAA, athletic directors, compliance officers, and coaches administer and enforce NCAA rules. This chapter will explore how college sports, the NCAA, its teams, and its athletic directors have dealt with the social issues involved in their sport.

The NCAA and its member schools, especially those schools in the Division I Power Five conferences, are making a ton of money. As of 2022, the Power Five football conferences were the Southeastern Conference (SEC), Big Ten, Atlantic Coast Conference (ACC), Pacific-12 (Pac-12), and Big 12, and the Group of Five football conferences were the American Athletic Conference (AAC), Mountain West, Sun Belt, Conference USA, and the Mid–American Conference (MAC). According to *USA Today*, the SEC made $721 million during the 2019 fiscal year, resulting in an average of $45.3 million per 13 of the 16 members that were eligible to receive full shares of revenue. During the 2018 fiscal year, the Big Ten Conference distributed around $54 million to each of the 12 member schools eligible to receive full revenue shares.[1] In August 2022, the Big Ten reached a seven-year media rights deal with FOX, CBS, and NBC that would pay a total of over $7 billion.[2] According to ESPN, the Pac-12 generated around $530 million in revenue in 2019 and distributed around $32.2 million per school, and the ACC generated around $455 million and $29 million per school in 2018–2019.[3] According to the Associated Press, the Big 12 reported around $37.7 million per school for the 2019–2020 school year.[4]

Major Division 1 college sports, such as the University of Michigan's national powerhouse football program (shown here in a 2012 game), are immensely popular. Fans have a passion for college sports, as they go to games in droves and watch them on television. Many interesting issues have arisen related to college sports, such as whether the athletes should be paid (photo from Creative Commons. "University Of Michigan Football Images from Air Force Game" by missycaulk is licensed under CC BY-SA 2.0).

In addition, many people are making a lot of money off the players. For instance, according to *USA Today, Alabama,* head football coach Nick Saban made $9.3 million in 2020, LSU head coach Ed Orgeron made $8.9 million, and Clemson head football coach Dabo Sweeney made $8.3 million.[5] As of 2020, there were at least 12 university athletic directors that made $1 million or more per year, headed by Chris Del Conte of the University of Texas at $2.08 million and Danny White at the University of Tennessee with a base salary of $1.8 million.[6] Conference commissioners also do well. According to Steve Berkowitz of *USA Today* in 2020, Pac-12 commissioner Larry Scott earned $5.4 million in 2018, Big 12 commissioner Bob Bowlsby earned just over $4 million, and ACC commissioner John Swofford earned nearly $3.8 million.[7] Some people would argue that these successful coaches, athletic directors, and conference commissioners deserve these large salaries, because their leadership and success can lead to increased prestige and revenue for their universities and conferences.

In light of all of this money being generated, many people have advocated for years that college athletes in revenue-producing sports, namely football and basketball, should be paid a salary or receive other type of compensation for their efforts.

Those who oppose paying athletes believe that student-athletes are already receiving substantial benefits in the form of free tuition and room and board, which in some cases can amount to a value of over $200,000 over four years.

All of the NCAA Division I schools offer athletic scholarships, except for the Ivy League, which does offer financial aid from other parts of the university.[8]

In arguing against paying college athletes, Horace Mitchell wrote in *U.S. News & World Report* in 2014 that students are amateurs, not career professional athletes. "They are students receiving access to a college education through their participation in sports, for which they earn scholarships to pay tuition, fees, room and board, and other allowable expenses. Collegiate sports is not a career or profession. It is the students' vehicle to a higher education degree."[9]

While athletes receive a great deal of benefits, they are expected to follow many rules and regulations to keep their scholarships. They are expected to attend practice and go to games, and often miss many classes due to playing away games. They are often shepherded into certain majors and classes that are conducive to fitting into the football or basketball team's schedule. Many Division I athletes come from poor or economically challenged backgrounds and wouldn't be able to afford a college education without a scholarship. Even with full scholarships, many college athletes have difficulty in paying for basic needs.

Acknowledging this problem, the NCAA instituted cost-of-attendance stipends in 2015 to help college athletes with their living expenses, such as money for gas, groceries, and travel expenses to go home. This money is additional to the benefit of a scholarship and can range up to $7,000.[10] For example, according to the *Atlanta Journal Constitution* in 2015, the University of Tennessee had the highest stipend for SEC schools at $5,666, followed by Auburn at $5,586.[11] The rule was approved by the Power Five conferences and has also been adopted by most Group of Five conferences and teams. According to a 2017 *Washington Post* article, many Power Five schools are giving the stipends to scholarship athletes in all sports, while some schools in non–Power Five conferences are choosing to give the stipends only to basketball players.[12]

Praising the cost-of-attendance stipends, North Carolina State offensive lineman Garrett Bradbury told the Associated Press, "I think it's phenomenal. I think it's tremendous. I think the interesting thing about a college football team is there are so many different guys from so many different situations and backgrounds. At one end of the spectrum, you have guys that might be financially OK from their home situation and they can put that money toward saving or buying little things that they need. Then there are some guys that might be sending home money for an electric bill."[13]

Fran Dunphy, men's basketball coach at La Salle University who previously coached men's basketball at the University of Pennsylvania and Temple University and served as interim athletic director at Temple, said in a phone interview confirmed by email, "I think cost of attendance is a way of giving student-athletes compensation. The concern I have is that the payouts are not equal throughout all levels of Division I. I also think that the Pell Grant is a great thing. If you come from a disadvantaged background you qualify for as much as $6,000 a year, which is a great help to so many families."[14]

There was a significant development starting in 2019 regarding the compensation of college athletes. In September 2019, California governor Gavin Newsom signed a bill that allowed college athletes in California to profit from their own name, image, or likeness, starting in 2023. The bill had passed unanimously through the California House and Senate. Colorado subsequently passed a similar law. In response, the NCAA initially asserted that California's law was unconstitutional, and it opposed similar laws in other states because it wanted to have a uniform set of rules and level playing field for student-athletes nationwide. It was concerned that a patchwork system would lead to athletes choosing schools primarily based on where they could make the most money and that certain states would have unfair recruiting advantages.[15] However, due to public pressure, the NCAA did start to initiate a process that would allow NCAA student-athletes to profit off their name, image, or likeness. In April 2020, the NCAA board of governors outlined specific categories in which student-athletes could profit off their name or likeness. The proposed rules would allow compensation for third-party endorsements related to athletics, without school or conference involvement. It also would allow compensation for other opportunities such as social media, new businesses that they start, and personal appearances. The NCAA clarified that the schools should not be able to pay their student-athletes for their name, image, and likeness activities.[16] In June 2020, Florida governor Ron DeSantis signed a bill that allowed college athletes to earn money from endorsements, starting in 2021.[17] Members of Congress have introduced legislative bills intended to help the financial situation of college athletes, including a bill introduced in February 2021 by Democratic senator Chris Murphy of Connecticut and Democratic congresswoman Lori Trahan of Massachusetts that would make it illegal for the NCAA to restrict endorsement deals that college athletes could sign and would prohibit the NCAA from preventing athletes from organizing under collective representation to sell their licensing rights as a group, including media rights, jersey sales, and video games.[18] In May 2021, Senators Bernie Sanders and Chris Murphy introduced the "College Athletes Right to Organize Bill," which would allow NCAA athletes to form a union and become employees of their schools.[19]

Many experts have varied opinions when it comes to athlete compensation and name, image, and likeness opportunities for college athletes.

Fran Dunphy said in a phone interview, "The NIL is the hottest topic we talk about these days in college athletics. Where this issue will be seen by all of college athletics in the future will be fascinating. How student-athletes will be compensated is being talked about by the NCAA, legislators, universities, athletic departments, and athletes. So much is unknown but as always we will figure out how to make it work. The hope is that it won't hurt the overall world of athletics and will give many people the opportunity to be on teams and to compete."[20]

Jay Bilas, a longtime advocate of compensating college athletes, wrote in the *New York Times* in 2012, "Athletes do not need to be paid by the university as employees. But barriers to athletic compensation outside of the university should be removed."[21]

In noting the distinction between universities paying college athletes and allowing them to profit off their name, image, and likeness, Joe Valerio, a former NFL lineman in the 1990s for the Kansas City Chiefs and St. Louis Rams, said in a Zoom interview confirmed by email, "Athletes should not be paid from their schools. It's disparaging to the term 'student-athlete.' If you're lucky enough to get free tuition through a scholarship, I'm all for that. It helps attract good athletes to schools in a positive manner. However, I'm for the name and likeness payments. If players can strike a deal outside of college endorsing a product, that's no different from a regular student who holds a side job like working at a restaurant or running a company. A player should be able to make money outside of school. Tuition and scholarships should be enough from the school, though, as it's very generous."[22]

Fran Dunphy said in a phone interview that athletes should not get paid aside from name, image, and likeness opportunities. "As far as paying the players, aside from the NIL, I would think that would hurt the game. There are already great gaps between the 'haves' and the 'have-nots,' and the schools who get the most attention will get even more. I also think we are not emphasizing enough the value of the college education."[23]

In 2014, Northwestern University football players attempted to form a union, seeking employee status and the ability to collectively bargain. Northwestern refused to grant employee status to the players. A regional director of the National Labor Relations Board in Chicago ruled that the Northwestern players were university employees and could hold an election to form a union, citing the extensive benefits that the players' efforts brought the school as well as the school's extensive control over the athletes' lives, according to ESPN.[24] However, on appeal, a full NLRB board dismissed their union election petition, declining to assert jurisdiction to hear the players' clams to form a union, thus ending the Northwestern players' attempts to unionize. According to *InsideHigherEd*, the board reasoned that, if it granted the claims of players at a private school like Northwestern, it could have negative ramifications for state universities, over which the NLRB did not have jurisdiction. Although the NLRB did not reach the merits of the players' claims, their ruling would likely have a chilling effect on future claims.[25]

The issue of compensating college athletes is constantly evolving. In June 2021, the United States Supreme Court, in a 9–0 ruling in *National Collegiate Athletic Association v. Alston*, determined that student-athletes could receive education-related payments, such as scholarships for graduate school or paid post-eligibility internships. A concurring opinion in the Alston case by Justice Brett Kavanaugh argued that the NCAA's remaining compensation rules raised serious antitrust questions and arguably suggested that a future lawsuit by NCAA athletes could challenge those remaining compensation rules.[26]

Shortly after the US Supreme Court ruling in *Alston*, the NCAA announced an interim policy that starting on July 1, 2021, college athletes in all three divisions would be allowed to profit off their name, image, or likeness. Many players and companies reacted quickly to benefit from the new rule, announcing sponsorship deals within the first two weeks that the new rule was instituted. Dan Lambert, the owner of American Top Team, a Florida-based chain of mixed martial arts gyms, announced that he would offer each scholarship player on the University of Miami football team a monthly payment of $500 to promote his gyms on social media. University of Miami quarterback D'Eriq King signed four endorsement deals, including one with College Hunks Hauling Junk along with his teammate Bubba Bolden. King also partnered with Florida State quarterback McKenzie Milton to form Dreamfield, a company that would help NCAA athletes book live events. According to ESPN, as of July 2021, Alabama quarterback Bryce Young had over $800,000 in NIL endorsement deals. The new rule has benefited men and women, as well as athletes from nonpower conferences and nonrevenue sports. Twin sisters Hanna and Haley Cavinder, basketball players for Fresno State's women's team, signed endorsement deals with Boost Mobile and Six Star Pro Nutrition, in part due to their social media audience of millions of followers. After Mississippi State won the 2021 NCAA men's baseball national championship, senior star outfielder Tanner Allen began selling his own autographed trading cards and other personal merchandise on his website, with a portion of the proceeds going to the Mississippi State Foundation.[27]

Kunkel et al. wrote in *Sport Management Review* that many college athletes will be able to benefit from their social media presence to brand themselves and engage in this new NIL world, stating, "For the individual athlete, social media represents a cost effective and wide-reaching mechanism to communicate with large volumes of consumers (Geurin, 2017)."

Kunkel added, "The power of social media is arguably more profound at the collegiate level where athletes generally do not have access to widespread media coverage or marketing consultants and must rely on their inherent brand value and more organic means of promotion (Geurin-Eagleman & Clavio, 2015)."

Indicating that while athletes from larger schools have a bigger platform, social-media-savvy student-athletes who can build a large online following can increase their brand whether they are male or female or go to bigger schools or smaller schools, Kunkel wrote, "Thus, athletes who present a compelling image, which is generally multi-faceted and includes dimensions related to their athletic performance, attractive appearance, marketable life, and their sport (cf. Doyle et al., 2020; Kunkel et al., 2020), can resonate with consumers and attract valuable brand partnerships as NCAA NIL policies change."[28]

Will NIL payments go mostly to high-profile Power Five athletes in the revenue sports of football or basketball? Will the payments go mostly to the high-profile players, such as star quarterbacks? In her analysis in *CQ Researcher*, Bethany Bradsher wrote that people like John Shuman, athletic director and former head football coach at Fork Union Military Academy, and L.J. Goolsby, a director and head coach of a top youth basketball program, indicated that such discrepancies related to NIL will exist as to high-profile schools and the positions played by the athletes. "But Goolsby and Shuman say prospective players know early in the recruiting process which schools have deeper coffers, recognizing that significant extra money is available to them only if they catch the eye of the big-time programs—schools that earn the greatest share of television and endorsement revenue. So, even if the courts and legislatures end up allowing NIL compensation, discrepancies will still exist, Shuman says. For instance, players in high-profile positions, such as football quarterbacks or wide receivers, will almost certainly receive more opportunities for NIL profits than linemen, he says." However, Bradsher noted that, according to statements by college basketball analyst Jay Bilas to the *News-Gazette*, players in all NCAA sports would benefit from NIL due to social media and other digital platforms. "Bilas said, 'You can have softball players, soccer players, you name it, especially in the local markets.'"[29]

Some people are concerned about the discrepancies in state laws regarding NIL and are encouraging a consistent standard on the federal level.

Christopher Palmieri argued in his *Touro Law Review* article, "To date there have been four congressional proposals made regarding college athletes' rights to NIL compensation. Each of the four proposals differ, and some of them are very far apart. Nevertheless, with the variation seen among state legislation, as well as the different stances taken by some universities, one thing is clear: there is a need for standardized legislation." He added, "Thus, the best solution is a standardized federal act. This act would theoretically take away any of the recruiting issues that can arise from the lack of uniformity of state acts and remove the power from the NCAA's hands which have a clear bias in the outcome." Palmieri asserted that provisions from three of the proposed federal statutes should be combined so that athletes could profit from their NILs, and universities and the NCAA could avoid conflicts of interest with the brands or companies they are contracted with.[30]

A related issue to paying college athletes is the rule that prohibits athletes from going to the NBA right out of high school. The one-and-done rule for college basketball players has been a source of controversy in college sports. For several decades, players could come right out of high school and make themselves eligible for the NBA draft. Notable success stories included Kobe Bryant and LeBron James.

In 1971, in a lawsuit brought by Spencer Haywood, the United States Supreme Court ruled in *Haywood v. National Basketball Association* that the NBA's requirement that a player must wait four years after high school graduation before being allowed to enter the NBA would be overturned. Haywood ended up playing 12 years in the NBA and was selected to Basketball Hall of Fame. Pursuant to the hardship rule regarding financial or other challenges, there were some notable basketball players who went straight from high school to the pros without playing college basketball. Moses Malone became the first player to do this in 1974 when he signed with the Utah Stars of the ABA. Two years later when the ABA merged with the NBA, he went to the NBA and became one of the greatest players in NBA history, winning three MVP awards and an NBA title with the Philadelphia 76ers in 1983. Other early players to go straight to the pros were Darryl Dawkins and Bill Willoughby, who took advantage of the hardship rule in 1975 to join the NBA. There were many notable NBA players who were drafted right out of high school, including LeBron James and Kobe Bryant.[31]

Spencer Haywood (number 42) successfully brought a lawsuit challenging the NBA's requirement that players had to wait four years after graduating high school to enter the NBA. Haywood, shown here in a 1976 game, went on to be a four-time NBA All-Star. He won a championship with the Lakers in 1980 and was elected to the NBA Hall of Fame in 2015. Number 20 is Doug Collins (photo by Albert F. Schell, courtesy Temple University Libraries, Special Collections Research Center, George D. McDowell *Philadelphia Evening Bulletin* Collection).

In 2005, the NBA, with the support of the NBA players' union, instituted the one-and-done rule, which mandated that a player had to be 19 years old and one year removed from high school graduation to be eligible for the NBA draft.[32] Most players chose to go to college to play for one year, although a few went overseas to play. Many people criticize the rule, indicating that it hurts the quality of college basketball, where teams have a star player for only one year. They also feel that it is unfair to make highly talented players wait a year to become eligible for the NBA.

In 2018, Detroit Pistons head coach Stan Van Gundy told reporters, "People that were against [players] coming out [of high school] made a lot of excuses, but I think a lot of it was racist. I've never heard anybody go up in arms about [minor league baseball or hockey]. They are not making big money, and they're white kids primarily and nobody has a problem."[33]

It was reported that the NBA is considering ending the one-and-done rule in the next collective bargaining agreement with the players' union.[34]

In a phone interview, Fran Dunphy said, "Ending the one-and-done rule is the direction that we're going. I support that. There's not a lot of players that it will affect. Half a dozen players might be good enough to be drafted right out of high school. Particular players will be told in advance where they're likely to be drafted, whether it's the first round, second round, or not drafted. If you're told that you're going to be a second-round pick with no guaranteed contract, is that what you would want? That player might be better served playing in college for a year."[35]

Some recent high school graduate athletes have taken an alternative approach to spending the obligatory one year of playing college basketball. A few high-profile high school grads chose to go overseas to play professionally, including Jeremy Tyler, who opted to play in Israel and then Japan; R.J. Hampton, who chose to play for a New Zealand pro team; Brandon Jennings, who played in Italy; Emmanuel Mudiay, who played in China; and LaMelo Ball and Terrance Ferguson, who both played in Australia.[36] Other recent high school grads chose to play in the NBA's G League right away, including top prospects Jalen Green and Isaiah Todd in 2020. In 2020, the NBA

Moses Malone (with the ball) and Darryl Dawkins, shown here in 1978, were among the first players to jump directly from high school to the professional leagues without playing in college. Malone had a Hall of Fame career, winning an NBA championship in 1983 with the Philadelphia 76ers. Darryl Dawkins played for several years with the Sixers and acquired fame for shattering backboards with thunderous dunks on two occasions in 1979 (photo by Salvatore C. DiMarco, Jr., courtesy Temple University Libraries, Special Collections Research Center, George D. McDowell *Philadelphia Evening Bulletin* Collection).

formed a G League team called The Ignite, in which players can earn up to $500,000, train with NBA-level coaches, and play in a league against older, veteran players.[37] In 2020, University of Texas men's basketball coach Shaka Smart told *Forbes* that in the future, he could see 10 to 12 high school grads per year choose to skip college to go straight to the G League.[38] Other options for young star basketball players emerged in 2021. The media company Overtime announced that it would be forming a pro basketball league starting in September 2021 for high school and college students age 16 to 18, paying the players at least $100,000 per season, and the Professional Collegiate League established a league that paid players $50,000 to $150,000, plus education expenses.[39]

All these new options have given talented high school seniors more options than going to college for the mandatory one year. This will benefit the individual players, but it could hurt the quality of the college game. On the other hand, it might make college basketball more of an amateur-focused sport where more players stay for four years and graduate with a degree. I believe that these are good approaches and are somewhat like developing a minor league farm system similar to Major League Baseball, where high school graduates could choose to either play college ball or sign professionally and likely spend time in the minor leagues.

As for the NFL, the league mandates pursuant to the collective bargaining agreement with the NFL Players Association that players must be three years removed from high school before being eligible to play in the NFL as a rookie. Part of the rationale is that younger players should have time to grow physically and in maturity before being ready for the NFL.[40]

Ohio State running back Maurice Clarette attempted to challenge the rule in 2004. He prevailed in the lower court, but that decision was reversed by an appeals court, and the United States Supreme Court declined to review the case.[41]

After 19-year-old freshman quarterback Trevor Lawrence led Clemson to win the national championship game over Alabama in 2019, many people started to question whether the NFL should change its rule. Just as in basketball, some freshmen will be physically developed and have enough talent to go pro.

NFL player agent David Canter told *Sports Business Journal* that college football players should be allowed to turn pro earlier. "If a team wants a player and that player is deemed good enough by that team to sign or draft, what's his age matter?"[42]

Former NFL player Joe Valerio said in a Zoom interview, "The three-year rule is a tricky question. Players only have a certain amount of time to make money in the NFL. If they have an opportunity in front of them to make a certain amount of money from their physical skill, they will want to maximize their earning potential while they're young and before they get injured. I would almost rather see them go right from high school to the NFL instead of forcing them to go to college for a year or two. It's patronizing to the term 'student-athlete.' On the other hand, it's hard to go right from high school. In football, they won't be physically ready to go to the NFL; the players are more physically mature and the game is more violent so

I think we could profit from a minor league farm system like baseball that bypasses college."43

In an email interview, Walter Cherepinsky, founder and operator of WalterFootball.com, which is one of the top websites in the country that analyzes the NFL draft, argued that the NFL should keep its current rule of mandating that players wait three years due to the physical nature of the sport. "I think college players should wait three years to enter the NFL following high school. The NBA once allowed high school athletes to enter the league following graduation, and now they've adopted a one-and-done system. This works in the NBA because basketball is not nearly as physical of a sport as football happens to be. It would be very difficult for an 18- or 19-year-old to compete with grown men in a sport where one hit can end a career. There would be some exceptions, of course, but opening the floodgates for high school athletes to enter the NFL would create an uptick in injuries and shortened careers."44

Age eligibility for the NFL and NBA are much more of a debated issue than for other sports. As for the NHL, the league changed its rule to allow 18-year-olds to be drafted, after a lawsuit by Ken Linseman.[45] Major League Baseball allows teams to draft high school graduates who have not yet attended college.[46]

Another debated social issue related to college sports is academics, both in terms of college admission and athlete academic performance once the student-athletes are in college. A major controversy and debate regarding college athletes and academics took place in the 1980s when the NCAA enacted Proposition 48, which required that a student athlete get a 2.0 GPA in core courses as well as a minimum SAT score of 700 or ACT score of 15 in order to be eligible to play college sports as a freshman. Opponents of the rule claimed that the use of standardized test scores unfairly discriminated against minority student-athletes from poor neighborhoods. Georgetown head coach John Thompson got national attention in 1989 when he walked off the court in protest of Proposition 48 and the subsequent Proposition 42 rule, which required universities to deny athletic scholarships to incoming freshmen who failed to meet the minimum academic standards, before the beginning of a game against Boston College.[47]

Other vocal critics of the rule included John Chaney, head coach at Temple. In 1991, Chaney told the *News & Record*, "Higher education is already costly. That deprives enough kids. Now there are more and more kids finding that they are being outdistanced by education. Many people are being fooled by the statements of the NCAA that due to Prop 48 graduation rates have gone up. Graduation rates of athletes have always been higher than the regular student body. The only reason they are even higher now is there are less blacks attending school. It doesn't mean people are being educated better. We're simply taking fewer risk students."48

Nowadays, it's pretty much accepted by most people that if an athlete doesn't qualify academically for their freshman year that they will most likely go to a junior college or a prep school at first and then apply to a Division I school.

In response to the coronavirus, in 2020, the NCAA announced that it temporarily would be making standardized test scores optional for incoming freshmen to meet initial NCAA eligibility policies. That policy was extended in 2021.[49]

The NCAA measures the academic progress of student-athletes through the Academic Progress Rates (APR), which tracks the graduation rates of university student-athletes. Scholarships can be limited if a school fails to meet the minimum APR. APR can also be a factor in bowl selection, in that teams with 5–7 regular-season records will be selected based on higher APR scores. In May 2020, the NCAA announced that 15 Division I teams would face postseason ineligibility due to low Academic Progress Rates.[50]

In 2020, a class-action suit was brought against the NCAA, alleging that its academic rules and penalties discriminated against historically Black colleges and universities (HBCUs). Attorney Beth Fegan told NPR that the HBCUs' traditional mission is to enroll low-income, first-generation, and at-risk students. "And so HBCUs are already starting at lower graduation success rates, lower Academic Progress Rates," Fegan said, "and yet they're being held to the same benchmarks as predominantly white institutions who don't have the mission [HBCUs do]. The NCAA should be supporting the mission of HBCUs, not penalizing them for it."[51]

Other concerns relate to how universities are educating their student-athletes. A highly publicized alleged academic fraud scandal took place at the University of North Carolina, where dozens of athletes, along with regular UNC students, took a sham course in the African and Afro-American Studies Department that required no attendance and submission of just one paper. After an extensive investigation, the NCAA chose not to impose any penalties against UNC because the NCAA's academic rules were not broken. One critic of the NCAA's decision not to punish UNC, Gerald Gurney, a University of Oklahoma professor and past president of the Drake Group, told the *New York Times*, "If ever there was a case of academic fraud, North Carolina would have to be the poster child—the longevity and the outrageous behavior to keep athletes eligible through systematic fraud. And it leads one to the absolute conclusion that this finding sanctions academic fraud among our institutions for the purpose of keeping athletes eligible."[52] The UNC academic controversy was a black eye and an embarrassment for both UNC and the NCAA and fed the perception that athletes go to high-level Division 1 schools just to play sports, not to get a college education.

Some high-level recruits come into college knowing that they plan to spend only a year at the school before entering the NBA draft. That diminishes the incentive to attend classes. Other students realize that the odds of them making a pro roster are slim, so they focus more on school and take advantage of their academic scholarship. Some coaches and athletic departments put a high priority on academics, while that's not the case for some schools that simply want to keep their star players academically eligible. Players are often steered into easy classes or easy majors that don't require as much academic rigor. Unfortunately, the pressure for college coaches is immense, and even if they have an outstanding record as far as graduating players, they're likely to be fired if their teams have a poor record on the field or the court. This pressure to win does not exist to the same extent at smaller Division I schools, Division II and III schools, and nonrevenue sports.

College athletes do get the advantage of having tutors and mentors along with extensive administrative oversight of players to check with professors to monitor the athletes' progress in the class. As a professor at Division I Temple and Division III Arcadia, I am contacted frequently by the athletic department to report on how athletes are performing in my classes. In many cases, I've noticed that many athletes tend to be very good students.

Fran Dunphy said in a phone interview confirmed by email that universities and coaches do care about the academics of their student-athletes, that schools give athletes a great deal of academic support, and that the APR matters to coaches and athletic directors. "The APR is sufficient. I don't know any coach who doesn't want their athletes to do well in school. It matters to us as coaches and athletic directors. It helps the student-athletes when their careers are over. It helps them in the real world when they are pursuing their way of making a living. The student-athletes are supported by the athletic departments, which have many more resources than in the past. To be an athlete in college is a great opportunity, but it isn't easy. It's hard work. It takes great focus to be a good student and a good athlete. In many ways, it's a full-time job."[53]

Recruiting violations are always a concern when it comes to major college sports. There is tremendous pressure on universities, athletic departments, and coaches to have winning programs. This pressure to win often leads coaches to break the rules when it comes to recruiting star players. One of the more embarrassing incidents took place at the University of Louisville. In 2017, the NCAA vacated the University of Louisville's 2013 national men's basketball championship as part of its penalties imposed from a sex scandal involving players, recruits, and strippers. Although head coach Rick Pitino denied knowing about the incidents, the NCAA determined that Pitino had allegedly failed to monitor his staff for compliance with NCAA rules and it suspended him for five games. Louisville was also involved in another alleged recruiting scandal as part of a federal investigation concerning recruit bribery in an attempt to steer players to certain schools and shoe companies. These scandals eventually caused Louisville to fire Pitino in 2017.[54] Subsequently, Pitino was hired to coach Iona and he brought them to the NCAA tournament in 2021. In 2023, he was hired as head coach at St. John's University.

University of Arizona associate head coach Emanuel Richardson was arrested and pleaded guilty to bribery as part of a scheme to steer players to agents, managers, and financial advisers. He was sentenced to three months in prison. In 2019, the NCAA announced that it was officially investigating the Arizona men's basketball program, and in 2021, it charged Arizona with five rules violations, including academic misconduct and failure to monitor.[55]

One of the measures used to punish coaches, albeit rarely used, is the show-cause penalty. This penalty has been imposed on several prominent college basketball coaches, including Todd Bozeman, Bruce Pearl, Clem Haskins, Kevin Ollie, and Kelvin Sampson. In college football, among the coaches receiving show-cause penalties were Chip Kelly and Jim Tressel. It's a scarlet letter designed to make college coaches who violate NCAA rules hard to employ by other schools in the future. If the NCAA imposes a show-cause order against a coach, that means that NCAA penalties imposed on that coach will stay with him for a number of years and could be transferred to a new school that decides to hire that coach. In order to avoid those NCAA penalties, the new school must prove to the NCAA Committee on Infractions and show cause why the new school should not be penalized and how it planned to monitor the coach.[56] Pearl and Sampson are examples of coaches who managed to have successful comebacks from show-cause violations, as Pearl's Auburn team reached the Final Four in 2019 and Sampson's Houston team reached the Final Four in 2021.

According to *USA Today*, "But many schools are hesitant to give second chances to those who have received show-cause penalties. There are plenty of administrators who wouldn't consider hiring someone implicated in major NCAA violations, multiple athletic directors said." George Washington athletic director Patrick Nero told *USA Today*, "There's a higher percentage of schools that would say, 'We're going to take a pass because of the reputation.' There's 340 Division I basketball jobs; maybe there are 320 that would say we're not going to hire someone with that history. That's a high, high percentage who would say no. But that means there are shots for them."[57]

Fran Dunphy said in a phone interview, "Show-cause violations are appropriate. The hit you take to your reputation is devastating. We all need to do the right thing and make sure the people in your athletic program know that we will do our very best but do it without compromising our principles."[58]

One of the biggest college sports scandals took place at Penn State University, when longtime assistant football coach Jerry Sandusky was criminally convicted in 2012 of child sexual abuse of boys that he had met as part of his Second Mile program. When told of one of the incidents, legendary head coach Joe Paterno reportedly informed only the Penn State athletic director. Paterno and other Penn State officials received criticism for not doing more to stop Sandusky's actions and for failing to contact the police. The Sandusky incident caused Penn State to fire Paterno as well as the school's president, Graham Spanier, and the school's athletic director, Tim Curley, and senior vice president of finance and business Gary Schultz resigned. In July 2012, the NCAA issued a $60 million fine against Penn State, banned the football team from postseason bowls for four years, vacated all of its wins from 1998 to 2011, and removed 20 scholarships for four seasons. The penalties were harsh, but some people, such as Tony Manfred of Business Insider and INSIDER, believed that Penn State football should have been given the death penalty. Manfred wrote in BusinessInsider.com that the only way to change the culture at Penn State was to eliminate the football team. Others felt that the penalties were too severe, in that they were punishing players who weren't at Penn State when the incidents occurred. Political pundit James Carville suggested on an ABC News *This Week* panel that Penn State's football program should be allowed to continue, but that the proceeds generated by the program should be used to compensate Sandusky's victims. In 2014, the NCAA ended Penn State's postseason bans and limits on scholarships.[59] The Nittany Lions recovered quickly and became a national powerhouse again a few years later. The Sandusky incident did raise a national debate about institutional culpability and the pressure to field a big-time college football program.

Anne Neal, president of the American Council of Trustees and Alumni, told the *Wall Street Journal*, "What happened at Penn State is emblematic of a pervasive culture on college campuses where reputation is more important than academic quality, transparency, ethics and accountability. It also underscores the distressing fact that, in too many places, the academic mission has taken a back seat to athletics."[60]

At one time, Southern Methodist University was a national power in college football. At its peak, it featured the Pony Express star backfield of Eric Dickerson and Craig James in the early 1980s. SMU went undefeated in the 1982 season, won the Southwest Conference, finished second in the national polls, and won the Cotton Bowl. Two years later, it won the Southwest Conference championship again. But due to the school's repeated violations of payments to its athletes, the NCAA instituted the death penalty upon SMU in 1987, canceling its 1987 football season and resulting in SMU choosing to cancel its 1988 season. To this date, it is the only time that the death penalty was imposed on a Division I school. The death penalty sanction was devastating to SMU's football program, as it had only two winning seasons from 1989 to 2008.[61]

In arguing that the NCAA's death penalty rule should be dead and not applied to alleged NCAA violations by Louisville, Mike DeCourcy of the *Sporting News* wrote in 2018, "The assessment of the death penalty has the potential to interfere with many businesses related to college athletics…. There are broadcasts contracts in which U of L is engaged, and there may be deals arranged for outside tournaments and events. There is the commitment to play home games at the city's KFC Yum! Center, an arena that already has fiscal issues even with roughly 20 dates a year from its primary tenant."[62]

The NCAA, as a governing body, takes its rule enforcement seriously. It has a detailed handbook of numerous pages with the relevant governing rules. Each NCAA division has its own compliance manual, and each school has its own compliance director. The NCAA also holds an annual convention in which new rules are debated and adopted. The NCAA's website has compliance forms for each division. The NCAA enforcement department has various elements, including an infractions process, development, investigations and processing of potential violations, processing secondary infractions, and a unit that promotes and protects academic integrity. The NCAA also established a Division 1 men's basketball ethics coalition. The NCAA membership resources includes Division I enforcement operating procedures and charging guidelines and academic misconduct guides.[63]

Sometimes, a school will self-impose a postseason ban on bowl games or NCAA Basketball Tournament appearances. For instance, in 2020, LSU self-imposed a one-year postseason bowl ban on its football team for NCAA violations. LSU also imposed reductions in recruiting visits, communications, and evaluations.[64]

In criticizing Arizona's self-imposed ban for the 2021 NCAA men's basketball tournament, Fran Fraschilla told *Sports Illustrated*, "I'm against self-imposed bans, period. Obviously, it's the equivalent of plea bargaining. But if the NCAA is doing its job—which is often questionable—they should be the ones meting out the penalties. I think on the whole it's a terrible idea. To do it in the middle of the season is even worse."[65]

Another controversial issue that has always existed in Division I college football is how the sport crowns its national champion. During most of the 20th century, the college football national champion was decided by the polls. Usually, there was one consensus national champion, but a few times, there were co-national champions due to disagreements in the polls. This subjective method of crowning a national champion resulted in controversy on several occasions, especially when undefeated teams such as Penn State were denied a share of the national championship by the pollsters. While Joe Paterno led the Nittany Lions to two national championships, in 1982 and 1987, their undefeated teams in 1968, 1969, 1973, and 1994 did not win the national championship. In 1969, after Texas rallied to beat Arkansas, President Richard Nixon visited the Longhorns' locker room and declared the Longhorns the nation's number one team. This was later ratified in the final polls.[66]

To try to help resolve the national championship controversy, the NCAA came up with the Bowl Championship Series (BCS) system starting in 1998, in which a combination of polls and computer rankings would rank the teams, with the top two teams playing in the BCS National Championship. While this system was better than crowning a mythical national champion, public pressure led to expansion of the playoffs. In 2014, the College Football Playoff began, in which a committee met and selected the top four teams to play in the College Football Playoffs. Again, this system was an improvement over the BCS in that it added two more teams to the playoffs, but the system remained flawed. The worst part of the CFP era was that it favored the same national powers and continued to exclude the underdogs—mostly teams from the Group of Five conferences that had gone undefeated during the regular season. On several occasions, teams from Power Five conferences with two losses would be ranked ahead of undefeated Group of Five teams, which were left out of the College Football Playoff. This happened to Central Florida twice. It also happened to Cincinnati in 2020, but the next year, the Bearcats became the first Group of Five team selected for the College Football Playoffs.

In 2021, the NCAA considered a proposal that would expand the number of teams in the playoffs from four to 12. The field would consist of the six highest-ranked conference champions and the six highest-ranked at-large teams as chosen by the selection committee. No league's conference champion would automatically qualify for the playoffs, and more than one team per conference could qualify, meaning that theoretically, high-profile leagues like the SEC and Big Ten could have four or five teams make the field.[67] In September 2022, the College Football Playoff's board of managers voted unanimously to expand the CFP field to 12 teams starting in 2026 or even earlier.[68]

I believe that this will be a positive development for college sports, as it gives more teams a chance to compete for a championship, especially teams from the Group of Five conferences that were basically shut out of the playoff systems despite having undefeated seasons. The one exception was when Cincinnati was selected to the CFP in 2021. Teams from the Group of Five conferences now will be able to tell recruits that they will have a legitimate chance to make the championship playoffs and compete for a national championship because a minimum of at least one Group of Five team will make the playoff each year. Odds are that the teams from the Power Five conferences will continue to dominate, but at least it gives the Group of Five conferences a chance. Hopefully, the fact that there will not be a guaranteed playoff spot for Power Five conference champions will mean that fans and the media stop the artificial labeling of Power Five and Group of Five conferences. Expansion is also good for the Power Five conferences because it means that many of them will likely get multiple teams into the playoff field. Despite this, hopefully, the artificial and arbitrary labels of Power Five and Group of Five conferences will disappear. A major part of the charm and popularity of the NCAA men's basketball March Madness championship tournament is the fact that every year, at least one underdog team from a small conference pulls a surprising upset. Expansion of the College Football Playoff will lead to underdog teams from smaller conferences to have an opportunity to prove that they can play with the major schools.

While it would be impractical to hold a tournament similar to the 68-team NCAA men's basketball tournament, the NCAA is taking a positive step by expanding the College Football Playoff field. Actually, I think the NCAA should expand its Division I FBS playoff system to include 16 teams. Critics of a 16-team playoff claim that it's too many games for the athletes to play during a season; however, for several years the FCS football playoffs has had 24 teams in the championship tournament. Due to the coronavirus pandemic, the FCS football national championship tournament was moved to spring 2021 and the field was temporarily reduced to 16 teams.[69] Expanding to 16 teams at the Division I FBS level would give even more teams an opportunity to play for a championship. It also could help to ensure that undefeated teams from smaller Group of Five conferences would not be left out of the field. It would also likely mean that fewer star players would choose to sit out bowl games due to injury concerns because the bowl playoff games would have more meaning than the non-playoff bowl games.

Will the expansion of the College Football Playoff have an adverse effect on the student-athletes' academic performance?

Starcke and Crandall wrote in the *Journal for the Study of Sports and Athletes in Education*, "In short, teams spending three weeks in playoff contention suffer academically compared to teams not participating in the playoffs when GPA is the dependent variable, but excel academically at week three when APR is used."

They added, "Overall, the findings of this study are mixed, reinforcing the need for additional research. While limited by a lack of institutional data, analyses using fall-term team GPA reveal football student-athletes may pay a price academically when competing in the playoffs for three weeks—a period of time encompassing finals week for many colleges and universities. The opposite effect appears when looking at APR, yet questions remain as to usefulness of relying on APR as a measure of academic performance."[70]

I believe that the expansion of the College Football Playoff would have an overall minimal effect on academics because it would apply only to the few teams that advance to the semifinals and championship game. In addition, most of the playoff games would be played during winter break.

A somewhat related issue is the ongoing shift in conference realignment in recent years, as many college teams have moved to a different conference. One of the most recent seismic shifts took place in 2021, when Texas and Oklahoma announced that they would be leaving the Big 12 to join the SEC.[71] Subsequently, UCF, Houston, and Cincinnati left the American to join the Big 12, along with independent BYU, and UCLA and USC announced in 2022 that they planned to leave the Pac-12 to join the Big Ten.[72] They were followed by Oregon and Washington in 2023. There is ongoing speculation that the Big Ten and SEC will continue to expand, which will have a domino effect on the other conferences. This ongoing version of musical chairs has led to anxiety for the conferences whose teams have been poached or rumored to be poached.

Major college sports has its flaws, scandals, debates, and controversies, including whether and how to pay college athletes; when college athletes should be allowed to turn pro; scandals in academics, eligibility, and recruiting; conference realignment; and how to decide the national champion in football. However, college sports remain among the most exciting types of sports to watch. The NCAA March Madness basketball tournament is probably the most exciting event in sports. Personally, I like watching college sports over the pros because of the passion of the players and the fans. For college students, it's a lot easier to identify with players whom you see on campus and in class, as opposed to highly compensated professional players. Fans at college games frequently storm the court or field after a top 10 win. How often do you see that at the pro level?

Chapter 11

Professional Sports

Professional sports get the most attention of sports fans, since they involve the best athletes playing at the highest level. With this attention comes increased scrutiny as to how professional leagues deal with issues and controversies involving their players, coaches, and organizations. Issues that professional leagues have needed to respond to include medical matters such as violence in sports and concussions, high salaries and free agency, the building of stadiums, moving teams and franchises to new cities, and dealing with racial issues by adopting hiring protocols such as the NFL's Rooney Rule, which requires NFL teams to interview minority candidates for head coaching positions. There are many causes and forms of violence in sports, such as in boxing, hockey, football, and mixed martial arts. This chapter will explore issues related to professional sports and how they deal with social issues.

One of the frequent complaints about professional sports is the high salaries of the athletes. Are the astronomical salaries of pro players hurting their sports? Or are the players being fairly compensated for their unique skills?

Labor relations in professional sports is a major issue that encompasses free agency, high player salaries, team salary caps, collective bargaining agreements, duty to bargain in good faith, arbitration, regulating agents, establishing minimum age requirements for players in the league, and the rising power and influence of players associations.

In the past, owners had most of the bargaining power with players and could keep salaries low. One of the main suspected reasons for the Chicago White Sox gambling scandal of 1919 was that the owner Charles Comiskey was allegedly stingy in paying his players.[1] For decades, it was common for professional players to hold second jobs and to take the subway or buses to games. One of the rare exceptions was Babe Ruth, who made headlines when he got the then astronomical salary of $80,000 a year in 1930. When reporters asked Ruth whether he should have a higher salary than President Herbert Hoover, Ruth said, "Why not, I had a better year than he did."[2]

Things changed with the Curt Flood case, which eventually led to player free agency. After the St. Louis Cardinals traded the All-Star outfielder Flood to the Philadelphia Phillies, Flood refused to go. After Major League Baseball commissioner Bowie Kuhn denied Flood's request to become a free agent due to the reserve clause in Flood's contract, which bound players to their teams for their entire careers unless they were traded, Flood brought a $1 million lawsuit against Kuhn and Major League Baseball in 1970. According to CNN, Flood wrote a letter to Kuhn in which he said, "After 12 years in the Major Leagues, I do not feel that I am a piece of property to be bought and sold irrespective of my wishes." In an interview, Flood told sportscaster Howard Cosell, "A well-paid slave is nonetheless a slave."[3]

The United States Supreme Court ruled against Flood in its 1972 decision, but due to the pressure that Flood's suit brought to MLB and its owners, the players union was able to bargain for arbitration on grievances by players. This led to pitchers Andy Messersmith and Dave McNally being able to become the first MLB free agents in 1976. However, the lawsuit basically ended Flood's baseball career.[4]

Flood may have lost his battle in the lawsuit, but he won the war for other professional athletes to follow. Surprisingly, as of September 2022, Flood is not in the Baseball Hall of Fame. In 2019, people including his family and notable sports figures such as Billie Jean King and Martina Navratilova advocated for Flood's admission to the Hall of Fame by the Golden Days Committee, according to CNN.[5] Several members of Congress in 2020 also advocated for Flood's admission to the Hall of Fame. Flood had a great baseball playing career, winning seven straight gold gloves, with a .293 career batting average in 12 seasons and two World Series titles, but it is his off-the-field efforts that make him Hall of Fame worthy.[6]

Regarding the effect that the Curt Flood case had on professional sports and free agency, Dr. Jun Kim, associate professor and program director of sport management in the School of Global Business at Arcadia University, said in an email interview, "I remember the Flood v. Kuhn (1972) case was a catalyst to free agency in pro sports. Before the free agency era, players had to battle against the reserve clause, and they were often traded to other teams on an owner's whim. Free agency enables pro athletes to negotiate their contract with the teams of her or his choosing instead of being retained by one team. It's common the teams allocate a significant portion of their payroll on a few players. That is, star players account for big chunks of team payroll. To stay profitable teams need to win, which leads to more viewers as well as higher revenue from the merchandise and sponsorship selling. Income inequality, a disparity of income destructions, obviously exists in sports, while those highly paid athletes are valued more since they drive the team's business profitability forward. As a result, they deserve to earn more."[7]

Other professional sports initiated free agency as well in the late 1900s.

The NBA's collective bargaining agreement with the players union in 1988 created unrestricted free agency rules. All-Star Tom Chambers of the Seattle Supersonics became the first unrestricted free agent and signed with the Phoenix Suns for a five-year, multimillion-dollar contract.[8] Ever since then, many NBA stars became free agents and signed with other teams, including Shaquille O'Neal, LeBron James, Ray Allen, Steve Nash, and Kevin Durant.[9] Other developments that helped increase player salaries were the concept of Bird rights, unrestricted free agency, and maximum salary contracts.[10]

Curt Flood, shown here sliding into second base in 1966 against the Phillies' Cookie Rojas, had a great career in Major League Baseball but he is best known for challenging the league's reserve clause in court when he objected to his trade from the Cardinals to the Phillies. His lawsuit helped lead to free agency in baseball as well as other pro sports (photo by Richard Rosenberg, courtesy Temple University Libraries, Special Collections Research Center, George D. McDowell *Philadelphia Evening Bulletin* Collection).

As for the NFL, after years of disputes related to free agency, in 1993 the NFL and NFL Players Association agreed to a settlement on Reggie White's class action related to free agency, according to *Sports Illustrated*. Two months after free agency began, 82 players had switched teams.[11]

In comparing free agency in Major League Baseball with the NFL and NBA, in a Zoom interview confirmed by email, Peter Carfagna (see short bio in earlier chapter) said, "In Major League Baseball, the fact that there is no hard salary cap has allowed big-market teams to go crazy. A hard cap will never happen in baseball because of the Players Union's historical refusal to consider it—for good self-interested reasons. The extraordinarily high salaries are hurting the 'level playing field' of Major League Baseball, however, in my opinion. Players bounce around during free agency, and teams can't keep their best players forever. In the NFL and NBA, the teams have a better chance to keep their players than in MLB. In MLB, it's very rare for one player to stay with one team for his entire career. It hurts the sport, as the rich get richer. The big-market teams have an advantage in payroll and more margin for error. The smaller-market teams can't make mistakes in their roster maintenance and free agent signings."[12]

Aaron Caputo (see short bio in earlier chapter) added in a Zoom interview confirmed by email, "It's not that player salaries are too high. It's that Major League Baseball's lack of a hard cap has led to a lack of competitive balance between the teams. The NFL and NBA have more competitive balance than Major League Baseball because of their salary caps."[13]

While there has been a great deal of scrutiny toward high salaries and free agency, another social issue related to pro sports that has garnered much attention in recent years is player safety, particularly when it comes to violence, fighting, and concussions. Pro sports and leagues affected the most by this issue include the NHL, NFL, boxing, and mixed martial arts.

One ongoing debate is whether the NHL should outlaw fighting. Comedian Rodney Dangerfield used to joke that one night he went to a boxing match and a hockey game broke out.[14] Fighting in the NHL has been a long-standing tradition that has been condoned and championed for decades. Most fans and players see it as an essential part of the game, and they don't want it to go away. It is a way for the players to police themselves against chippy, dirty play and cheap shots. It's also a way to protect star players from getting injured by hits from other teams' players. A fight can inspire and motivate a team, shift momentum in a game, and get the fans engaged. Many fans find the fighting to be entertaining and fun. In some games, the most excited that fans get is when a fight breaks out. In my decade or so of teaching social and ethical issues in sports, I've had very few students who felt that fighting in hockey should be banned.

However, while advocates of fighting assert that fighting is an essential part of the game, it should be noted that there is almost no fighting at Olympic hockey games, college hockey, and high school hockey. With a ban on fighting in hockey, there would be no need for goons or enforcers who are in the league solely for their ability to fight and protect other players. It also might make the sport more family friendly. There is also the issue of the rise of concussions and CTE in sports. Derek Boogaard was a hockey enforcer who developed CTE brain damage and died from an accidental overdose of oxycodone and alcohol.[15] Another argument against fighting in hockey is that no other sport condones fighting as part of the game even though many of those sports, such as football and basketball, also involve physical contact between players. If a rare fight occurs in other sports, the referees act quickly to break it up and separate the players. In the NHL, the referees stand back and let the players duke it out.

In recent years, the NHL has taken steps to minimize fighting and to encourage more speed and skill in the game. The emphasis has led to a significant decrease in fights in NHL games over the last few years. Goons and enforcers are becoming an endangered species. However, fights still do occur and are still cheered by most fans in the arena.

One of the most vocal critics of fighting in hockey is former Montreal Canadiens goalie Ken Dryden. In his 2017 book, *Game Change*, Dryden argued for an end to hits to the head in hockey games. In 2013, he wrote in the *Globe and Mail*, "Fighting is supposed to be an escape valve to release pent-up feelings that might otherwise find expression in far more dangerous stick-work. Different somehow from football, baseball, basketball and every other major team sport, different somehow from hockey played everywhere outside Canada and at every level except major junior or pro, it is supposed to be unavoidable. It is supposed to be harmless. It is none of these things."[16]

Plassche et al. argue in their 2022 article in *The Physician and Sportsmedicine* journal that, even though fighting has decreased in the NHL in recent years, the league should take stricter measures to limit fighting even further, especially in light of concerns about concussions. "Although the era of the enforcer seems to be behind us, fights are still happening, with a spike seen recently in the COVID-19 bubbles. Disillusionment with the proposed benefits of fighting, as well as concern for the monetary costs, integrity of the game, and the well-being of its players calls into question whether fighting should remain a part of this great game. We propose a change to the rules, in line with those used in international and Olympic play, to make fighting a game misconduct penalty."[17]

The NHL has had its regular share of fights over the years, but one of the more brutal incidents took place in a 1968 game between the Philadelphia Flyers and Boston Bruins. Flyers defenseman Larry Zeidel and Bruins wing Eddie Shack engaged in a vicious stick-swinging battle, and both players suffered head wounds.[18]

The Flyers were legendary for their physical play, especially in the 1970s, when they established their reputation as the Broad Street Bullies. Their intimidating tactics helped them win two Stanley Cups, in 1973–74 and 1974–75. The team had talented players like Bobby Clarke, Bill Barber, Rick MacLeish, and Bernie Parent, but it was the team's enforcers, Dave "The Hammer" Schultz, Don Saleski, Andre "Moose" Dupont, and Bob "The Hound" Kelly, which struck fear in opposing teams.

Former Flyer Gary Dornhoefer told *Sports Illustrated*'s *The Hockey News*, "Well, Schultzy, he could throw 'em. He's such a mild-mannered guy, you would never associate Dave Schultz with a guy that when he got on the ice he was a terror. But it didn't matter who, he had some fights that he also lost. He just went out there and if it was time to do something, he would do it. A tremendous team player." Bobby Clarke added, "We took a lot of pride in the way we played the game. Not only were we winning, we were playing the game properly and the fighting was part of the personality of the team. There are lots of teams in the league who had as many tough guys as we did, but our reputation became so big that it was intimidating to other teams."[19]

Naturally, the city of Philadelphia looks back fondly on the Broad Street Bullies era, especially since it produced two Stanley Cup victories.

Not everyone looks back fondly on that era. In 2010, Scott Altman of Bleacher Report named the 1970s Broad Street Bullies as the second-dirtiest sports team in

The Philadelphia Flyers' Broad Street Bullies, shown here in 1973, dominated the NHL and struck fear in other teams during an era when fighting in hockey was pervasive and popular. Fighting in the NHL has decreased in recent years and some people believe that it should be banned due in part to concern about head injuries. Others believe that fighting in hockey is a tradition worth keeping. From left are Donald Patrick Saleski, Dave Schultz, Andre Dupont and Bob Kelly (photo by Joseph Tritsch, courtesy Temple University Libraries, Special Collections Research Center, George D. McDowell *Philadelphia Evening Bulletin* Collection).

history, ranking only below the Detroit Pistons' Bad Boys.[20] In 2010, Phil Mushnick wrote in the *New York Post*, "The Flyers were so down, dirty, dastardly, despicable, demonized and detested, Bruins and Rangers fans found common ground, bound by their visceral hatred for the Flyers."[21]

In recent years, the NHL started cracking down on fighting and violence. There is more emphasis on skilled players as opposed to enforcer goons. According to Stephen Whyno of the Associated Press in 2018, the past four NHL playoffs had included a total of 39 fights, compared with 46 fights in the 1978 playoffs and 85 fights in the 1988 playoffs.[22] One of the few enforcers left in the league, John Scott, lamented the fact that while he played for the Chicago Blackhawks, opponents would turn down fight requests. He told the *Chicago Tribune*, "It has gotten even harder these days. It's hard to find fights."[23]

I'm glad to see the recent trend of the decline of fighting in the NHL. I think fighting cheapens the sport and makes it look silly. It's the only major team sport where the referees stand back and let players fight. It's not essential to have fighting to play the sport of ice hockey—just look at the Olympics and college hockey.

Violence is also a big issue in the NFL. Will the NFL continue to exist 20 years from now? This seems like an absurd question, given the immense popularity of the league. However, the league faces an existential crisis due to the increasing realization of the damage done to players' brains via concussions. Over the last few years, many kids are migrating from playing football to soccer. If this continues, the talent pool for pro football could diminish in the future.

Youth football participation is down, and some states are contemplating banning tackle football for kids under 12 years old. In a discussion commentary for the medical journal *Pediatrics*, Dr. Lewis Margolis, a pediatrician and epidemiologist at the University of North Carolina, argued, "Pediatricians should advocate for the discontinuation of high school football programs until, and more importantly unless, we can be assured that it does not have long-term detrimental consequences."[24]

In 2018, a survey by the National Federation of State High School Associations showed that boys' participation in 11-player football fell 6.5 percent from its 2009 peak to 2017, dropping from 1.11 million to 1.04 million.[25]

Star quarterback Brett Favre indicated that if he had a son, he would be hesitant to let him play football. Favre told WDAM in Mississippi in 2014, "It's a violent sport, and for two reasons I don't know if I'd let him play. The pressures to, you know, live up to what your dad had done, but most importantly the damage that is done by playing." In August 2021, Favre said in a public service announcement on behalf of the Concussion Legacy Foundation, "Having kids play before high school is just not worth the risk. CTE is a terrible disease, and we need to do everything we can to prevent it for the next generation of football players."[26]

According to an April 2018 *Sports Illustrated* article, four states—New Jersey, California, New York, and Illinois—were considering legislation that would ban tackle football for players younger than age 12. In March 2018, the Maryland state legislature rejected a bill that would have barred youth tackle football.[27]

In defending these proposed laws and the government's role in protecting children, the *Los Angeles Times* editorial board wrote on February 2, 2018, "It's becoming increasingly clear that exposing children to repetitive head hits can lead to significantly compromised cognitive abilities later in life, with impacts on, among other things, the demand for healthcare, the incidence of domestic violence and the stability of families."[28]

Football leagues at all levels have instituted player safety rules, including outlawing helmet-to-helmet hits, targeting, blows to the head, strict concussion protocols, and reducing contact in practice. There is talk of eliminating kickoffs. College football now allows the receiving team to use a fair catch during kickoffs. Safer helmets are being developed. After two years of development and almost $10 million in funding, Vicis released its Zero1 helmet in collaboration with the University of Washington. In 2016, the Ivy League's football schools instituted a rule that banned regular-season tackling in practice, and in 2017, the NCAA instituted a rule banning two-a-day practices.[29]

Over the last decade, the NFL has initiated new rules and protocols regarding concussions, including eliminating blindside blocks, prohibiting players from lowering their head to initiate and make contact with their helmet against an opponent, protecting defenseless receivers, limiting overtime periods, and prohibiting chop blocks and horse collar tackles.[30] In 2017, the NFL established medical examination tents on the sidelines to provide an immediate evaluation of players to identify and review injuries, with a specific focus on concussions.[31]

Joe Valerio, who played five years in the NFL for the Kansas City Chiefs and St. Louis Rams in the 1990s, said in a Zoom interview confirmed by email that concussion protocol has improved significantly since he retired from the league. "Concussions weren't taken as seriously back then as they are now. I am not sure the coaches knew the full implications, unless a player's injury was really serious and they were unconscious. It would be said that 'you got your bell rung' and they would ask you simple questions like, how many fingers they were holding up and 'where are you now?' As long as you weren't vomiting it didn't seem too serious and they might also ask someone to wake you up every few hours to make sure you were conscious."[32]

Valerio added, "I agree with the stricter targeting rules. It's great for the game. The sport can be played in a manner that doesn't take away from an action-packed game. You can tell when it's an obvious target hit. At the NFL and major college level, the players are athletic enough and skilled enough so that they can control their bodies so that they're not going after someone's head. They're too good as an athlete to get out of control. I think the rules are strict enough today, but maybe they could be even stricter."[33]

According to ESPN, Dartmouth developed a unique technique to try to eliminate concussions via the use of virtual reality and a 190-pound vinyl robotic tackling dummy, called the MVP Drive. Dartmouth's approach proved successful, as its football team's injury rate fell 80 percent the first season that it banned tackling in practice in 2011, and its concussion rate declined by 58 percent in the second season. The team still went on to win 76 percent of its games for the next five seasons. Other teams have adopted the MVP Drive tackling dummy, including the Pittsburgh Steelers, Dallas Cowboys, and Notre Dame.[34]

Some fans and players hate the new rules, alleging that it constitutes the "wussification" of America. They long for the old days when "men were men" and if you took a big hit, you just "had your bell rung" and would be shoved right back on the field. They believe that NFL players are grown men and understand and assume the risks of serious head injuries when they play the sport. In criticizing the NFL's new rule in 2018 that penalized players for leading with their helmet to make a hit, Minnesota Vikings safety Andrew Sendejo wore a hat that stated "Make Football Violent Again."³⁵ Video reviews of dangerous hits have also been criticized by some as being too time-consuming and that they slow down the pace of the game.

It wasn't until the early 2000s that football started taking concussions and head injuries more seriously. Dr. Bennet Omalu, a pathologist, was a pioneer in changing societal views of concussions. The 2015 movie *Concussion*, starring Will Smith, told his life story and described his efforts to publicize the tragedy of brain damage in retired NFL players. Omalu told *The Guardian*, "There is no equipment that can prevent this kind of injury."³⁶

Former NFL players sued the league, claiming that it had hid the risks of brain injury. The lawsuit was settled, resulting in awards of up to $5 million each to players who retired before July 7, 2014.³⁷

The issue of concussions in the NFL and when players should be allowed back on the field after a head injury received increased scrutiny in 2022 when Miami Dolphins quarterback Tua Tagovailoa was allowed to continue to play despite suffering what appeared to be a head injury during a Sunday game and then taking another hit to the head a few days later in a Thursday night game, suffering a concussion and ending up being treated at a hospital. This led the NFL to change its concussion protocol to keep players who demonstrate ataxia, which "is defined as abnormality of balance/stability, motor coordination or dysfunctional speech caused by a neurological issue," from returning to play in games.³⁸

Shortly after this incident, the sports world was shocked again during an NFL game in January 2023 when Buffalo Bills defensive back Damar Hamlin suffered cardiac arrest and collapsed after making a tackle. Medical personnel immediately administered CPR to Hamlin while players from both teams were in tears and kneeling in prayer for him. Hamlin was taken to a hospital in critical condition, and the game was canceled. Hamlin's condition improved significantly in the next few weeks, but this shocking incident reminded people how dangerous football can be. After the Hamlin incident, people such as Georgetown University professor Jacques Berlinerblau suggested that it might be best if football fans divest themselves from the sport due to its violent nature, stating in his MSNBC opinion article, "[F]ootball can't really ensure player safety because of the passion it instills in us, the fans. Until we stop cheering, tweeting about, gambling on and watching these games, horrific injuries are going to occur."³⁹

Some NFL players who had suffered multiple injuries, including concussions, have chosen to retire early, including Chris Borland, Luke Kuechly, and Andrew Luck. In the future, this could become a trend. NFL players might decide to make significant money by playing three or four years in the league and then retiring before they sustain serious injuries that include brain damage.⁴⁰

Former NFL player Joe Valerio said in a Zoom interview, "I think you'll start to see more players make financial and health decisions to retire early. They'll have to balance how much money they've made with suffering a career-ending injury that might plague them for the rest of their life. It's a cost-benefit analysis in deciding whether it's worth it or not. Several concussions might make that cost-benefit analysis easier. This type of analysis will be made at all levels, including pro, college, high school, and youth football, and be made by the players and their family members."[41]

Another issue related to violence in sports is whether fighting-specific sports, such as MMA, UFC, and boxing, should be banned due to the health risks to its participants, especially repeated blows to the head.

Mixed martial arts, or MMA, which includes events staged by Ultimate Fighting Championship (UFC), has emerged as a hugely popular spectator sport worldwide. After Joao Carvalho died in the ring during an MMA fight, Peter McCabe argued in his April 15, 2016, article in *The Guardian* that MMA fighting should be banned. He wrote, "At a time when responsible sports bodies are rightly taking action to improve their concussion protocols to ensure participants are properly cared for when accidental collisions occur, it seems perverse that MMA can be allowed to continue to encourage trauma to the brain. There is no conceivable way in which MMA can even remotely be considered safe."[42]

After Canadian UFC fighter Tim Hague died in the ring, the Edmonton City Council imposed a one-year ban on combat sports.[43]

Defenders of MMA argue that the fighters engage in these sports in free will and that they know the risks. They warn of a nanny state that is too protective of its citizens.

In defending MMA and criticizing the longtime New York ban on MMA, Matthew Doarnberger wrote in 2015, "Not only are the dangers of MMA overblown, but there's actually even more danger in not legalizing the sport. Just as alcohol prohibition resulted in death, blindness and increases in organized crime, prohibition on MMA has similar consequences. Fighting of this nature has been driven underground in New York where it is unregulated and far more dangerous. Many politicians never seem to learn the lesson of unintended consequences that come from banning voluntary activities in high demand."[44]

In 2016, New York State ended its 20-year ban on MMA and became the 50th state to legalize the sport.[45]

Daniel Neyra argued in his article in *Family Court Review* that MMA should not be banned but that there should be stricter and more consistent regulation of children's MMA in light of safety and health concerns.[46]

Boxing has been one of the most popular sports in the history of humanity. For decades fans waited with bated breath for major bouts that captivated the world, including Dempsey–Tunney, Louis–Schmeling, Ali–Frazier, and Duran–Leonard. However, the sport of boxing started to see a decline after the 1980s.[47]

Some believe that the violent nature of the sport could threaten its future.

There have been several tragic deaths during boxing matches over the years. Ray "Boom Boom" Mancini was a great lightweight boxer who unfortunately might be most remembered for the fight that resulted in the death of his Korean opponent, Duk Koo Kim, in 1982. In a fight televised live on CBS, Kim collapsed at 19 seconds of the 14th round. He died a few days later from a blood clot and brain damage that resulted from blows that Kim had taken from Mancini.[48] In 1962 at Madison Square Garden, boxer Emile Griffith pummeled world welterweight champion Benny Peret, who was knocked out in the 12th round and died after 10 days in a coma.[49] Ed Sanders, a 1952 Olympic boxing gold medal winner, died shortly after a 1954 fight with Willie James.[50] Leavander Johnson, the lightweight champion of the world, collapsed in the locker room after his 2005 fight with Jesus Chavez and subsequently went into a coma and died.[51] American featherweight champion Davey Moore died due to injuries sustained in a 1963 fight.[52] In 1933, heavyweight boxer Ernie Schaaf went into a coma and died after a knockout loss against Primo Carnera.[53] CNN stated in 2019 that according to a survey started by Manuel Velazquez, "Between 1890 and 2011, it's estimated that 1,604 boxers died as a direct result of injuries sustained in the ring…. That is an average of 13 deaths a year."[54]

After boxer Scott Westgarth died in February 2018, the brain injury charity Headway demanded that the sport of boxing be banned. "Boxing is a senseless waste of life and the time has come for it to be banned," Headway's chief executive, Peter McCabe, said.[55]

Howard Cosell, one of the most famous sportscasters of his time, was well known for his boxing coverage, including his classic interviews of Muhammad Ali. However, a brutal fight caused Cosell to retire from calling future boxing matches. After heavyweight champion Larry Holmes pummeled Randall "Tex" Cobb into a bloody pulp in 1982, Cosell called for the end of professional boxing due to its brutality. He told the *New York Times*, "The Cobb fight did it for me. I was leaving the ring and people were shouting, 'Hey, Howie, that Texan sure can take a punch, can't he?' I said, 'Don't they realize what's happening here? Four days or four weeks or four months or four years later, that man is going to pay for the pounding he took.'"[56]

Many doctors and medical organizations have called for a ban on boxing due to its violence. Since 1983, the American Medical Association has called for a ban on boxing due to safety concerns.[57] As noted by Tony Sheldon in the *British Medical Journal*, the Dutch Health Council advised the government that "professional boxing should be banned unless its rules can be tightened quickly to reduce the risk of brain injuries."[58]

D.K. Sokol argued that the medical profession should not get involved in the debate by calling for bans in boxing but instead should stick to providing advice and information on how to improve the safety of the sport, such as reducing the number of rounds in fights, increasing intervals between rounds, improving headgear, and having referees stop fights earlier. Sokol wrote, "[T]he medical profession should inform boxers and those involved in the sport (coaches, referees, and so on) of the potential dangers of boxing, as well as suggesting ways to minimize the risks. The obligation stops there. The role of the profession should be no more than advisory and informational—the changes need to be made within the sport itself."[59]

Boxing's supporters argue that it doesn't need to be saved and that its decline in popularity is overblown. In 2017, noting the anticipated crowd of over 90,000 at Wembley Stadium for the Wladimir Klitschko and Anthony Johnson match, ESPN boxing writer Nigel Collins wrote that the sport just needed a superstar champion to revive its popularity.[60]

Those who would not want a ban on boxing would argue that the fighters are adults and can make an informed decision as to whether they want to risk serious head injuries by engaging in the sport.

Arguably, pro boxing should require fighters to wear headgear and have fewer rounds to make the sport safer. As Sokol observed, in the 1980s, professional boxing changed the length of bouts from 15 three-minute rounds to 12 three-minute rounds.[61]

However, with society gaining an increased sensitivity to the danger of concussions, I wonder if boxing will decline even more if another prominent boxer dies in the ring or shortly after a fight from a head injury. It's possible that boxing is the type of sport that just can't be engaged in safely, no matter what type of safety measures are implemented.

Another social issue in professional sports throughout the years relates to race and ethnicity regarding coaches, administrators, teams, and athletes. Minority pioneers in pro sports included Jack Johnson, Joe Louis, Jesse Owens, and Jackie Robinson. In recent years, the NFL has attempted to address the lack of Black head coaches in the league by implementing the Rooney Rule. Over the years, there have been hardships, such as the quotas and limits on Black players in the 1950s and '60s and racism in European soccer. There was also the controversy over the Washington Redskins' nickname and continuing use of American Indian/Native American/Indigenous Peoples' mascots and names at the high school, college, and professional sports level.

The Washington Redskins went many decades without much of an outcry about their name. However, that changed in the early 21st century. Many people started to speak out against the nickname, alleging that it was racist and demeaned Native Americans. Many urged the team to change its nickname. In 2014, 50 United States senators signed a letter urging the NFL to force the Redskins to change their name.[62] For years, owner Daniel Snyder refused to change the name, and many defended him, saying that the name was not racist and was part of a long tradition. In January 2018, NFL commissioner Roger Goodell said that the league would not pressure the Redskins to change their name.[63]

A 2014 *Sports Illustrated* poll of over 500 NFL fans showed that only 25 percent said that the Redskins should change their name and that 79 percent said that the name was not offensive.[64] A 2016 *Washington Post* poll of 504 Native Americans showed that 90 percent were not bothered by the team name and that 73 percent did not find the term "redskin" to be disrespectful.[65]

In arguing that the Redskins should ignore the politically correct culture and keep their name, Naomi Schaefer Riley wrote in the *New York Post*, "Critics of the Redskins name are mostly folks who know nothing about American Indians but think their problems can be solved by more money and greater cultural sensitivity."[66]

However, according to the *New York Times*, "A decade ago, the American Psychological Association recommended the immediate retirement of Native American mascots and symbols, in part because they appear 'to have a negative impact on the self-esteem of American Indian children.'"[67]

Finally, in 2020, the Redskins bowed to public and corporate pressure and changed their name temporarily to the Washington Football Team.[68] In 2022, the team announced that their new name would be the Washington Commanders.

Some states have passed laws prohibiting the use of Native American nicknames and mascots in high schools. Over the years, several college and pro teams changed their nicknames and mascots (St. John's Redmen became the Red Storm, St. Bonaventure Brown Indians became the Bonnies, Stanford Indians became the Cardinal, Marquette Warriors became the Golden Eagles). As far as mascots, in 2007, the University of Illinois discontinued its mascot Chief Illiniwek.[69] In the 1980s, the Atlanta Braves got rid of Chief Noc-A-Homa, who had a teepee in the left field bleachers and set off smoke signals and did a celebration dance when a Braves' player hit a home run. While the Cleveland Indians removed the Indian Chief Wahoo logo from their uniforms after the 2018 season, the Indians still sold merchandise featuring Chief Wahoo in 2019. Due to public pressure, in July 2021, the Cleveland Indians announced that they would change the team name to the Cleveland Guardians, which refers to the Guardians of Traffic statues in Cleveland.[70]

Many people believe that some Native American nicknames that aren't pejorative, such as Chiefs or Seminoles, could be considered acceptable. However, the history and traditional use of Redskins is a pejorative term that was meant to demean Native Americans, and it's a good thing that Washington finally changed its name. Also, there should be an end to Native American mascots that come across as a joke or a caricature. In addition, use of the Tomahawk Chop by Florida State and Atlanta Braves fans could also be interpreted as offensive and should be eliminated.

Despite criticism of the Tomahawk Chop, during its April 2021 home opener, the Atlanta Braves encouraged its fans to do the chop and chant by showing digital Tomahawk Chop images and playing a drumbeat during pivotal moments of the game.[71] However, I think that it's inevitable that in the near future, these teams will stop the practice.

There has been a long struggle for Black athletes, coaches, and administrators when it comes to professional sports. There has been progress, but there still is a long way to go.

In response to the decades-long exclusion of Blacks from professional sports, Blacks formed their own professional leagues and teams, such as the Negro Leagues, the Harlem Globetrotters, and the New York Renaissance. Today, the Globetrotters are known as the Clown Princes of Basketball, with funny stunts throughout the game, combining comedy, trick shots, and athleticism. However, the Globetrotters were pioneers that helped to integrate basketball. Founded in 1926, the Globetrotters have played over 26,000 games in over 123 countries, entertaining over 148 million fans and being pioneers of the slam dunk and fast break. The team started in Chicago and was given its name by its manager, Abe Saperstein. In their early years, the team played serious basketball. They even beat the Minneapolis Lakers, champions of the all-white National Basketball League, in 1948 and 1949. Several Black early players in the NBA had played for the Globetrotters, including Nat "Sweetwater" Clifton, Earl Lloyd, Chuck Cooper, and Wilt Chamberlain. In the early years of the NBA, NBA teams featured doubleheaders with the Globetrotters in order to boost attendance.[72]

Between 1920 and the late 1940s, the Negro Leagues were the premier organization for Black baseball players who were banned from Major League Baseball. Some of the great players included Josh Gibson, James "Cool Papa" Bell, Satchel Paige, Judy Johnson, and Buck Leonard. The annual East-West All-Star Game in Chicago's Comiskey Park would frequently draw over 50,000 fans. Once Major League Baseball started signing great Black players, including Satchel Paige, Jackie Robinson, Larry Doby, Hank Aaron, and Willie Mays, the Negro Leagues started to decline.[73]

The feats of Jesse Owens in the 1936 Berlin Olympics and Joe Louis's boxing prowess helped pave the way to integration in sports and in society. Pro football became integrated in 1946 with the NFL signing of Kenny Washington, and Jackie Robinson debuted in Major League Baseball with the Brooklyn Dodgers in 1947. In 1950, Earl Lloyd became the first Black player in the NBA. In the next decade, Black superstars like Bill Russell, Wilt Chamberlain, and Oscar Robertson emerged. Willie O'Ree became the first Black player in the NHL in 1957.[74]

While almost everyone is familiar with how Jackie Robinson broke MLB's color barrier, many people are unaware of the unofficial unspoken quotas or limits on the number of Black players on college and professional teams in major sports in the 1950s and '60s. For instance, in the early 1950s, the NBA was suspected to have had an unofficial agreement to limit the number of Black players per team to two or three.[75]

One sad incident of racial discrimination involved Cleo Hill, who starred at Winston-Salem State University and then became a first-round pick of the NBA's St. Louis Hawks. However, in the 1961–1962 season, team management told Coach Paul Seymour to freeze out Hill on offense to favor white players on the team, leading to Seymour resigning because he wanted to play Hill more. The move allegedly resulted from Hill's boycott of a preseason game with other Black players after being denied service at a Kentucky hotel restaurant, as well as the dislike of the Hawks' three main stars at being upstaged by a rookie who they felt shot the ball too much. Hill never played in the NBA after that season. Kenny Benton, Hill's college roommate, told the *New York Daily News*, "He doesn't like to talk about it, but Cleo Hill got blackballed in the NBA. He never got a chance to project his skills—he had to watch guys who

The Harlem Globetrotters have entertained fans for decades but at one time they played serious basketball and beat the best pro teams of their era. Their success helped lead to the integration of the NBA. This 1953 photo shows Reece "Goose" Tatum with the ball moving past the Warriors' Mark Workman in a game played between the Globetrotters and the U.S. All-Stars in Connie Mack Stadium (photo by Elwood P. Smith, courtesy Temple University Libraries, Special Collections Research Center, George D. McDowell *Philadelphia Evening Bulletin* Collection).

couldn't hold his jock become stars." Hill's story was featured in a 2008 ESPN documentary, *Black Magic*.[76]

For decades, there was an unwritten rule in football that Black players couldn't be successful quarterbacks due to an alleged lack of intelligence. Black quarterbacks had to overcome the stereotype that Black quarterbacks were athletic and white quarterbacks were smart and savvy. These terrible stereotypes were enforced for many years by coaches, general managers, scouts, and members of the media. Successful high school and college Black quarterbacks were usually converted to play other positions, such as wide receiver or defensive back. Eventually, that mindset began to change. In 1988, Doug Williams of the Washington Redskins became the first Black quarterback to win a Super Bowl. Five Black quarterbacks guided their teams to the NFL playoffs in 2000, but it wasn't until 2001 that Michael Vick became the first Black quarterback to be drafted with the first pick in the NFL draft. In 2006, Warren Moon became the first Black quarterback to be inducted into the Pro Football Hall of Fame.[77] As of 2022, there were many star Black quarterbacks in the NFL, including Russell Wilson, Patrick Mahomes, Jalen Hurts, Dak Prescott, Kyler Murray, and Lamar Jackson.

Conservative commentator Rush Limbaugh opened up old wounds on this issue in 2003 when he said as a member of ESPN's *Sunday NFL Countdown* show that Eagles quarterback Donovan McNabb was overrated due to his race. Limbaugh said, "I don't think he's been that good from the get-go. I think what we've had here is a little social concern in the NFL. The media has been very desirous that a black quarterback do well. There is a little hope invested in McNabb, and he got a lot of credit for the performance of this team that he didn't deserve." Amid the controversy over his statements, Limbaugh resigned from his ESPN position.[78]

Despite the integration of the NFL and the fact that most of the players are Black, there are still very few Black head coaches. In order to address this discrepancy, in 2003 the NFL instituted the Rooney Rule, which required its teams to interview minority candidates for head coaching and senior football operation jobs.

In 2016, Tony Dungy told ESPN, "[I]t seems like in the last few years, people haven't really done what the rule was designed for. It has become, 'Just let me talk to a couple minority coaches very quickly so I can go about the business of hiring the person I really want to hire anyway.'"[79] After the 2020 season, only one Black coach, David Culley, was hired that offseason as an NFL head coach.[80] As of September 2022, there were only four Black head coaches in the NFL: Todd Bowles, Lovie Smith, Mike Tomlin, and Mike McDaniel, who identifies as biracial.[81]

I interviewed several people to get their opinions on diversity and the Rooney Rule and how it could be improved.

As to pro sports diversity and the Rooney Rule, Peter Carfagna said in a 2021 Zoom interview, "There have been little steps, bits and pieces of improving diversity. There has been more diversity in upper-level management and front-office positions in recent years, such as with the Washington Football Team and the Miami Marlins. Social justice issues nationwide have illuminated this issue, and it's evident that the higher offices in sports need to become more diverse. The situation can be improved, as far as hiring more minority head coaches, as individual merit determines in each case. It should hopefully become a situation where it's color-blind and the best person available is hired. Thankfully, there are many minority coaches who are the best qualified. However, hiring a winning NFL head coach is getting to be more of a 'win now' litmus test—can you coach the team to victory? You need to win now."[82]

In a 2021 Zoom interview, Aaron Caputo added, "It starts at the lower levels, such as coordinators, position coaches, and all the way down the line. That's where it starts, and the NFL has done a decent job of expanding the Rooney Rule to reach these levels. However, if the Rooney Rule is to create meaningful change, more work is needed."[83]

As to how the Rooney Rule has been insufficient and how it can be improved, Dr. Ketra Armstrong, sport management professor at the University of Michigan, said in a 2021 email interview, "The Rooney Rule is a well-intentioned endeavor, in that it requires NFL hiring committees to include individuals of Color in their applicant pools. However, the Rooney Rule does very little in 'moving the needle' in the hiring of individuals of Color in the NFL leadership ranks because it cannot legislate prejudices or remove the biases and other ideologies that often marginalize candidates of Color—adversely impacting their sport leadership opportunities and experiences. As such, the Rooney Rule has become a performative 'look good/feel good' measure, with limited impact in addressing the problem it was designed to combat."

Armstrong added, "Changing the racial composition of NFL leaders, requires system level change. As such, improving the Rooney Rule requires improving the systemic/organizational culture of the NFL, and the reliance on practices and procedures (both expressed and implied) that have perpetuated the need for such a rule. Changing the organizational culture must be intentional, authentic, comprehensive, and involve actions with accountability. It also involves acknowledging the social and ethical ills of a lack of racial and ethnic diversity. Such an organizational culture change should include (but is not limited to) the following: (a) establishing a substantive office of Diversity, Equity, and Inclusion in the leadership structure of NFL teams, (b) requiring and holding accountable each NFL team to develop 'measurable and movable' culturally diverse recruitment plans and human resource pipelines for their coaching and other leadership positions, (c) requiring unconscious bias training for all individuals involved in the NFL hiring process, and a willingness to 'think outside the box' of traditional expectations of the 'right' skills or the 'right' pedigree, (d) requiring each NFL search committee to document the ways in which they actively and intentionally sought to create diverse applicant pools—beyond token representation to meet the letter of the law of the Rooney Rule—and summarize the strengths and weaknesses of all of the candidates relative to the positions of hire, and (e) most importantly, commit the personal and financial resources to ensure real change—i.e., notable increases in the racial and ethnic diversity throughout their organizations. Such measures would give real meaning to the Rooney Rule and allow it to have an earnest impact."[84]

Marcus Hayes is a longtime sports columnist for the *Philadelphia Inquirer*. In a 2021 email interview, Hayes said regarding the insufficiency of the Rooney Rule, "The root of the failure of the Rooney Rule involves three truths, all of which revolve around NFL owners and their white coaches and general managers, as well as NCAA college presidents and their white athletic directors and head coaches, ignoring the imbalance of power in football. They want to keep their fans and boosters comfortable. First, NFL owners are almost exclusively white, old, male, and obscenely wealthy—a demographic largely that usually has little interest with any sort of change, since the existing system has served them so well. Progress that profits them usually is the only progress that interests them. For most owners, if they believe a

Black man as head coach is much more likely to help them win more games than the pool of white coaches, they will consider the Black coach. Otherwise, they will hire someone that they, their front office, and their fan base feel more comfortable with to act as the face and voice of the organization, which usually is a non–Black man. Second, you cannot change the ethnicity of the owners or the fan base, but owners are able to change the demographic of who works in the front office. Theoretically, this would influence owners to better appreciate what Black men can do. However, the successes of Jerry Reese with the Giants and Ozzie Newsome with the Ravens—Black general managers with two Super Bowl wins apiece—have done little to influence owners' hiring practices regarding top decision-makers. Only two GMs in 2020 were Black, though three of the seven vacancies filled this year were filled by Black men. Of those five teams with Black GMs, only one—the Dolphins—has a Black head coach. Again: Owners hire head coaches.

Finally, the preponderance of successful head coaching hires in the past 15 years, both in the NFL and the top levels of the NCAA, involved coaches with offensive backgrounds rooted on the offensive side of the ball. The ideal has become an offensive coordinator, and preferably one who will call his own plays, thereby ensuring he will stay if the team wins. More often than not, offensive coordinators have also been quarterbacks coaches. Which is the nub of the whole discussion."

Hayes added, "NFL head coaches and owners, as well as NCAA head coaches and athletic directors simply will not hire, develop, and promote Black men to coach their quarterbacks and run their offenses. Why? The only plausible explanation is racism. Considering the NFL and NCAA's atrocious record of defending racist mascots, traditions, and symbols, neither institution has any real defense. Not hiring, developing, and promoting Black men for the most valuable assistant coaching jobs limits the number of attractive candidates in the pipeline. Certainly, plenty of viable candidates already exist—new Texans coach David Culley has been a head coaching candidate for 15 years—but the more candidates that exist, the better chance the Rooney Rule has to actually work. This is not coincidental. This is not a mistake. Overwhelmingly, neither NFL owners, white coaches, or general managers, nor NCAA college presidents, white athletic directors, or white coaches have any interest in filling the pipeline with people who don't look like them. Until this changes, the Rooney Rule has no chance."[85]

The issue of the insufficiency of the Rooney Rule drew even more scrutiny when former Miami Dolphins head coach Brian Flores brought a class-action lawsuit against the NFL and four of its teams in 2022, alleging racial discrimination in their hiring practices.[86]

Sadly, racism still exists in sports today. Adam Jones of the Baltimore Orioles said that Boston Red Sox fans called him a racial slur and threw peanuts at him during a game in 2017.[87] A hockey fan threw a banana at the Philadelphia Flyers' Wayne Simmonds, a Black player, during an exhibition game in Ontario in 2011.[88] Right before the NBA Finals of 2017, a racist slur was spray-painted on the front gate of the home of LeBron James.[89]

In 2017, Richard Lapchick wrote in ESPN.com, "According to research from the University of Central Florida's Institute for Diversity and Ethics in Sport, acts of racism in sports in the U.S. increased from 31 in 2016 to 41 in 2017. Internationally, there were 79 racist acts in sports."[90] The same organization's 2018 study recorded 52 acts of racism in the United States and 137 incidents of racism internationally.[91]

Racism is a major concern in European soccer. In 2019, Juventus forward Moise Kean was subjected to racist chants from fans after scoring a goal.[92] In 2014, Barcelona star player Dani Alves ate a banana that was thrown at him by a racist fan during a match.[93] In an attempt to lessen racism, the English Football Association in 2018 instituted a Pursuit of Progress program that sought to bring diversity in coaching staffs to English soccer.[94] However, racism took place again after the European Championship final in July 2021, when numerous racist social media posts berated three Black English soccer players who missed penalty kicks during a shootout in a loss to Italy. The online racist abuse was condemned by England's Football Association, the England team and its players, UK Prime Minister Boris Johnson, and Prince William, among others.[95]

The racial integration of professional ice hockey has been a very slow process. The main reason is likely cultural, in that ice hockey was traditionally a Canadian sport and that most young American Black athletes were playing other sports like football, basketball, and baseball. Willie O'Ree became the NHL's first Black player in 1958. Perhaps the most accomplished Black NHL player was Grant Fuhr, who was the five-time Stanley Cup–winning goalie for the Edmonton Oilers and was the first Black player inducted into the NHL Hall of Fame. Other Black players who won a Stanley Cup include Eldon Reddick and Dustin Byfuglien. Hall of Famer Jarome Iginla was a six-time NHL All Star.[96]

Perhaps the first major Black athlete in the United States was Jack Johnson, who became the first African American world heavyweight boxing champion in 1908. Many white Americans resented Johnson and openly rooted for a "great white hope" to come along and defeat him. After Johnson beat a white fighter in 1910, white men in New York set fire to a Black tenement building and white mobs chased Black people in Atlanta. After driving across state lines with his 19-year-old white girlfriend, Johnson was convicted of violating the Mann Act, an anti-prostitution law, by an all-white jury in a racially related conviction in 1913. He temporarily fled to Europe and then lost his title to Jess Willard in 1915. In May 2018, Johnson received a posthumous pardon from President Trump.[97]

Americans were much more receptive to two of the major Black sports stars of the 1930s, Jesse Owens and Joe Louis. Owens won four gold medals (100 meters, 200 meters, long jump, and four-by-100-meter relay) at the 1936 Olympic Games in Berlin, Germany, shattering the narrative of white Aryan supremacy set forth by Adolf Hitler. After the Olympics, Owens was feted with ticker-tape parades in New York City and Cleveland.[98]

Americans were tuned to their radios in earnest to hear Joe Louis knock out

German boxer Max Schmeling in the first round of their rematch in 1938 in front of over 70,000 fans at Yankee Stadium to earn the world boxing heavyweight championship. Historian Bert Sugar called it "The greatest sporting event of the 20th century," according to ESPN.[99]

The most famous trailblazer regarding race in sports is Jackie Robinson, who broke Major League Baseball's color barrier in April 1947 at Brooklyn's Ebbets Field. Robinson was Rookie of the Year in 1947, league MVP in 1949, ended up playing 10 seasons for the Dodgers, and led the team to six National League pennants and a World Series title in 1955. While he was a great player, it was his courage and inner strength in the face of ongoing resistance and racism that made Robinson a social icon. Since 2004, Jackie Robinson Day has been celebrated annually by Major League Baseball every April 15 to commemorate the day that Robinson broke the color barrier, and all MLB players are requested to wear number 42 in honor of Robinson.[100]

Another social issue related to professional sports is the pressure to build new stadiums and the threats to move professional franchises to different cities. There have been many instances where pro teams moved to other cities for various reasons. For instance, in baseball, the Brooklyn Dodgers moved to Los Angeles, the New York Giants moved to San Francisco, and the Milwaukee Braves moved to Atlanta. In football, the Baltimore Colts moved to Indianapolis, the Cleveland Browns moved to Baltimore, the St. Louis Cardinals moved to Arizona, and the Oakland Raiders moved to Las Vegas. In basketball, the Seattle SuperSonics moved to Oklahoma City, the Philadelphia Warriors moved to California, and the Minneapolis Lakers moved to Los Angeles. In the NHL, the Atlanta Flames became the Calgary Flames, the Colorado Rockies became the New Jersey Devils, and the Minnesota North Stars became the Dallas Stars.[101]

Pro sports teams' owners frequently threaten to move their franchise to another city if the city fails to build the team a new stadium or substantially renovate the existing one. Sometimes there is pressure for teams to keep up with other franchises and hot trends in stadiums, whether it be domed stadiums, stadiums with retractable roofs, all-purpose stadiums with AstroTurf that could host baseball and football teams, and baseball-only stadiums. For instance, the Baltimore Orioles' construction of Camden Yards in 1992 led to a slew of MLB teams seeking to have similar old-fashioned-style parks with modern amenities. There is huge prestige and economic benefits for cities to have professional teams, so many cities will bend over backward to try to accommodate teams' requests for new stadiums. Most stadiums are publicly funded and paid for by taxpayers, often through municipal bonds, while some are funded through a mix of public and private funds. In many cities, sports teams' requests and demands often lead to a public debate as to whether building a new stadium is worth it.

In criticizing public funding of stadiums, Richard Florida wrote in *Bloomberg*, "As the 2015 NFL season kicks off and all the excitement that comes along with it, let us not forget that U.S. taxpayers are bearing a large part of the cost. In the past 15 years alone, over $12 billion of the public's money has gone to privately owned stadiums—constituting essentially a massive transfer of wealth from everyday Americans to the super-rich owners and players involved in these billion-dollar sports franchises."[102]

Arguably, it is advantageous for cities to do everything they can to accommodate their sports teams when it comes to building new stadiums because of the construction jobs and boon to the local economy. There is also an element of civic pride and a sense that having professional teams in a city is a sign that it is a major city. In most cases, stadiums don't just host their own teams' games, they also host major events such as all-star games, Super Bowls, college bowl games, local college and high school games, major concerts, World Cup Soccer or US Soccer games against foreign teams, political conventions, Olympic events, and other major gatherings. To some people, a city isn't considered a major city unless it has professional sports teams. New stadiums usually result in higher attendance, including visitors from other cities. Oftentimes, a new stadium leads to the rise of new businesses, such as restaurants and bars, near the stadium.

Among the arguments that those who oppose public funding of stadiums make is that cash-strapped cities and states should be spending their money on other and more important public priorities such as health and education.

As noted by the *Berkeley Economic Review (BER)* in 2019, a Roger G. Noll and Andrew Zimbalist study on new stadiums paid for by taxpayers through public financing shows that they have a limited and possibly negative local impact. The *BER* article stated, "This is because of the opportunity cost that goes into allocating a significant amount of money into a service like a stadium, rather than infrastructure or other community projects that would benefit locals. Spending $700 million in areas like education or housing could have long-term positive consequences with the potential for long-term increases in the standard of living and economic growth."[103]

As to whether cities should continue to build new stadiums for team owners under the threats to move their team to another city, in an email interview, Dr. Jun Kim, associate professor and program director of sport management in the School of Global Business at Arcadia University, said, "Teams owners and NFL should be responsible for the stadium financing, not taxpayers. When St. Louis Rams moved to Los Angeles back in 2016, Stan Kroenke left significant debt payments on the 23-year-old Edward Jones Dome, a stadium that no longer had a tenant. The Rams paid $500,000 annually to play in the old stadium, which they don't have any obligation to pay anymore. In 2019, Missouri still owed over $47 million on bonds issued to build the Rams' old stadium. The stadium still sits empty and is scheduled to host a few events (e.g., Saint Louis Auto Show) for the remainder of the year. This is a clear sign that using public funds to finance new stadiums doesn't work."[104]

Despite various controversies, professional sports continue to thrive in the United States and worldwide. People like to watch pro sports because they feature the best athletes. They are also a source of civic pride that people can bond over and latch onto. Among the main concerns about pro sports are the increasing salaries, especially for star players. Until free agency emerged, players were underpaid and had no freedom to leave their teams. Now, the players have much more bargaining power, causing teams to pay star players huge contracts. In Major League Baseball, this hurts the small-market teams, which generally can't afford to pay and keep star players. Team owners make a ton of money, but some of them still play hardball with cities to build new stadiums, sometimes threatening to move their teams if they don't get one. Several pro teams have relocated over the years, for various reasons, thus breaking the hearts of fans that supported and followed their team for decades. Race and ethnicity is another issue that pro sports have dealt with over the years. It took a long time to integrate pro sports, and there are still issues related to race and ethnicity today. After years of public and corporate pressure, the Washington Redskins finally gave in and changed their offensive nickname. The NFL's adoption of the Rooney Rule was a positive development, but the league still has fallen short when it comes to hiring minorities for coaching and management positions, especially head coaches. Violence and concussions are a serious issue for pro sports, as fewer kids are playing football and some NFL and college players are retiring early due to concussion concerns. Some people have called for elimination of violent sports like boxing and MMA due to frequent blows to the head, and even though the NHL now emphasizes skilled players and has turned away from using enforcers, fighting is still allowed. Despite these flaws and controversies in pro sports, fans still go to the games in droves and watch games on television or online. Most of us are willing to give up three hours of a beautiful fall afternoon to watch NFL games. That's something that most of us will never punt away.

Chapter 12

Olympic Sports

Every four years, the world's greatest athletes gather to participate in the Olympics. There are many great aspects of the Olympic Games, including the competition and the spirit of camaraderie among athletes and fans from numerous countries. However, at every Olympic competition, disputes and controversies arise. One of the most controversial incidents involved the 1972 US vs. USSR men's basketball championship game, in which referees and officials gave the Soviet team three chances to win the game at the end, depriving the US team of a gold medal. Many Olympic sports, such as boxing, gymnastics, and figure skating, have seen controversy due to the nature of subjective judging, which often favors athletes from the host country. Unfortunately, the Olympics have been a target for terrorists, most notably in Germany in 1972 and Atlanta in 1996. Political controversy has arisen over the years, as there were boycotts of the Olympics that took place related to apartheid and the Soviet invasion of Afghanistan. Other issues arise frequently, including athletes playing for other countries, the benefits and problems for host countries, and the controversies involved in Olympic bids. This chapter will explore the positive and negative elements of the Olympic Games.

The Olympics are one of the few events that bring the world together. I attended the 1996 Olympic Games in Atlanta as a spectator. I arrived the day after the Olympic Park bombing, amid sorrow, fear, and apprehension. At the time, no one knew if this would be a one-time event, and it briefly crossed my mind whether to stay in Atlanta. Fortunately, I decided to stay. I was lucky to have gotten many coveted tickets via the lottery system and saw Michael Johnson's two gold medal races, Carl Lewis's fourth consecutive goal medal performance in the long jump, and the second version of the men's basketball Dream Team, among other events. It was great to see and interact with people from all over the world. People who spoke different languages traded Olympic pins and other memorabilia. Many people with extra tickets just gave them away for free outside the venues. It was also interesting going to obscure sporting events that I had never attended before, such as team handball and weightlifting. The only negatives were the long security lines to get into the venues, and the fact that most of the venues played the "Macarena" incessantly.

The original Olympic Games took place in Olympia, Greece, from 776 BC through 393 AD.[1] Under the leadership of Baron Pierre de Coubertin, the Olympics were revived in Athens, Greece, in 1896. The Winter Olympics were established in 1924 in Chamonix, France.² The Summer and Winter Olympics used to take place in the same calendar year but starting in 1994 they are now staggered two years apart, with the exception of the Tokyo Summer Games, which were postponed from 2020 to 2021 due to the coronavirus. With the exception of World War I and World War II, the Olympics have been held consistently.³

The Olympics provide a showcase for athletes to test themselves every four years and prove that they are among the best in the world. They can settle debates as to who is the fastest runner or swimmer, the strongest weightlifter, or the most talented gymnast. Most of the Olympic athletes are not famous professionals and the Olympics are usually the only time that the world is focused on relatively obscure sports like Greco-Roman wrestling, curling, archery, and table tennis. For the most part, the competition is fierce but friendly, even among athletes from countries that are considered adversaries. For two weeks, athletes from all over the world mingle and interact with each other in the Olympic Village. As exemplified in the elaborate opening and closing ceremonies, it's a way for many of the greatest athletes in the world to unite and perform for a worldwide audience on television.

Olympic success and gold medals can lead to national pride, especially among smaller countries that don't get much time in the limelight and aren't considered world powers. As noted in a *Rolling Stone* article, Usain Bolt became a legend and a

Usain Bolt's Olympic success made him a national icon in Jamaica. Arguably the greatest Olympic sprinter ever, Bolt (shown here in 2012) won eight gold medals in three Olympic Games, including wins in the 100-meter and 200-meter dashes in 2008, 2012, and 2016 (photo from Creative Commons. "Usain Bolt—The Bolt!" by Nick J Webb is licensed under CC BY 2.0).

hero in Jamaica, rivaled perhaps only by Bob Marley. Morgan Jerkins wrote in *Rolling Stone*, "Bolt's representation for Jamaica is overwhelmingly great. He has shown Jamaicans that they can compete on the world stage and can stimulate their country from the inside out, whether it's through advertisements being shot on the homeland or charitable foundations."[4]

As to how Bolt has increased national pride, Dennis Boothe, a lawyer who grew up in Kingston, told Jerkins, "I think he is very significant in expressing how Jamaicans feel about themselves. Almost like validation that we all can excel on the world's stage despite being such a small country."[5]

As great as the Olympics are, they often lead to controversy and criticism on many levels, both before and during the event itself.

Among the major issues and controversies related to the Olympics are boycotts and threatened boycotts.

As detailed by Berg et al., in light of political pressure domestically and from American diplomats in Europe, the United States considered a boycott of the 1936 Berlin Olympic Games due to the Nazis' discriminatory and repressive policies. However, the Roosevelt administration ultimately decided against a boycott due in part to the American position of neutrality and a decision that it would be more advisable from a political standpoint to focus on domestic problems associated with the Great Depression.[6]

The first Olympic boycott took place during the 1956 Melbourne Games when three countries boycotted as a result of the Soviet Union's crushing of the Hungarian revolt and three countries boycotted due to the Suez War. In 1976, 22 countries boycotted the Montreal Olympic Games as a protest of apartheid in South Africa.[7]

In 1980, the United States and several other Western nations decided to boycott the Moscow Summer Olympic Games. President Jimmy Carter made his decision to boycott the Moscow Games on March 20, 1980, due to the Soviet invasion of Afghanistan in 1979 and its failure to withdraw its troops from that country by Carter's imposed deadline of February 1980, according to History.com. The US boycott was joined by Canada, Japan, and West Germany, but other Western nations, including Great Britain, Australia, France, and Greece, chose to send their athletes to the Moscow Games.[8] According to the US State Department archives, 65 nations chose to boycott the Moscow Games, while 80 nations participated. It was the first and only time that the United States boycotted the Olympics.[9] According to *USA Today*, there were 466 members of the US Olympic team in 1980, and an attempted lawsuit by some team members against the USOC was unsuccessful.[10] For many of these athletes, the 1980 Games were a once-in-a-lifetime opportunity. According to *USA Today*, over 200 of the 1980 US Olympic team members did not make the 1984 Olympic team.[11]

Carter told the members of the US Olympic team at the White House, "I can't say at this moment what other nations will not go to the Summer Olympics in Moscow. Ours will not go. I say that not with any equivocation; the decision has been made. The American people are convinced that we should not go to the Summer Olympics. The Congress has voted overwhelmingly, almost unanimously, which is a very rare thing, that we will not go. And I can tell you that many of our major allies, particularly those democratic countries who believe in freedom, will not go.

"I understand how you feel, and I thought about it a lot as we approached this moment, when I would have to stand here in front of fine young Americans and dedicated coaches, who have labored sometimes for more than 10 years, in every instance for years, to become among the finest athletes in the world, knowing what the Olympics mean to you, to know that you would be disappointed. It's not a pleasant time for me."[12]

Some people praised Carter for the boycott, saying that the Soviets should not be rewarded on the world stage due to their aggression. Others criticized the boycott decision because it denied athletes a chance to compete, and in retrospect, the Soviets ended up remaining in Afghanistan for several years after the boycott.

In 1984, many of the Soviet bloc nations reciprocated by boycotting the Los Angeles Olympic Games. According to the *New York Times*, although the Soviets had hoped to convince over 100 countries to boycott the 1984 Los Angeles Summer Games, only 14 countries ended up doing so.[13] Nonetheless, it was frustrating that in certain sports, athletes weren't able to test themselves against Soviet bloc athletes that were among the best in their respective sports.

In subsequent years, some people suggested that the United States and other countries should boycott the 2008 Beijing Olympic Games due to human rights abuses in China. Some suggested that countries boycott the Sochi Winter Olympic Games due to Russia's harsh treatment of LGBTQ people. In 2017, U.S. United Nations Ambassador Nikki Haley suggested that it was an open question whether the United States would send its athletes to the 2018 Winter Olympic Games in South Korea due to tension with North Korea regarding nuclear weapons and missile tests.[14] In a February 2021 Fox News column, Haley argued that the United States should boycott the upcoming 2022 Winter Olympics in China, due to China's ongoing human rights violations.[15] According to the CBC, several Canadian politicians were also arguing for a boycott of the 2022 Winter Olympics.[16] In addition, 17 academics and activists outlined China's human rights abuses in the *Journal of Emerging Sport Studies* and issued a call for an international full or diplomatic boycott of the 2022 Winter Olympics.[17] They also urged, among other items, that sponsors withdraw from the Games and that international broadcasters should not televise them.

In light of these calls, several countries, including the United States, United Kingdom, Canada, India, and Australia, declared a diplomatic boycott of the 2022 Beijing Winter Games, deciding that they would send their athletes but not the representative ministers or officials.[18]

Arguing in support of boycotting the 2008 Beijing Summer Olympics, Anne Applebaum wrote in *Slate*, "The boycott of South African athletes from international competition was probably the single most effective weapon the international community ever deployed against the apartheid state."[19]

Dr. Ketra Armstrong, sport management professor at the University of Michigan, said in an email interview regarding Olympic boycotts to protest human rights violations or other offensive conduct by the host nation, "Yes, I believe that entities (individuals, organizations, nations, cities, etc.) that violate human rights and/or are engaged in offensive conduct of that or a similar nature should be barred from hosting the Olympics. After all, such behavior is incompatible with the Olympic spirit and counters the fundamental values (of opportunity, fairness, human decency, integrity, honor, and others) the Olympic Movement espouse. However, due to the commercial success of the Olympics and the amount of financial and in-kind support offered by sponsors, media, and others, many Olympic organizers have tended to get myopic, look the other way, and/or explain why the human rights offenses are 'not so bad' in context."

Armstrong added, "It takes real courage and sacrifice to stand in the face of human indignities and challenge wrong-doers to do right. Unfortunately, given the mass appeal of the international sport enterprise, Olympic organizers have not been willing to make sport events the source of such sacrifice. Consequently, in absence of the Olympic governing bodies taking such a stand, many Olympic athletes have taken it upon themselves to protest human rights violations in their own unique way. In fact, I like seeing athletes in various domains of sport reclaim their power—as producers of the sport enterprise—and engage in activism to hold sport entities more accountable to being more socially and culturally responsible to their stakeholders and the communities from which their athletes hail. The Olympics should not be exempt from such accountability, and their commercial objectives should not supersede social and ethical imperatives."[20]

Rejecting the method of Olympic boycotts, Nicholas Sarantakes wrote in the *New York Times*, "If you are going to have an international Olympic movement that is truly inclusive in its membership, then you need to be prepared to compete against teams and play in nations that do not share your values."[21]

In opposing the proposed boycott of the 2022 Winter Olympics in Beijing, David Shoemaker and Karen O'Neill argued in an op-ed in the *Globe and Mail* that countries like Canada should use other tools to address China's human rights violations, such as diplomacy through its ambassadors and other measures, stating, "We have billions of dollars in annual bilateral trade. We court billions of dollars in investment from China. And we encourage Chinese students to study in Canada.... Boycotts don't work. They punish only the athletes prevented from going, those they were meant to compete against and those who would have been inspired by them."[22]

On one hand, Olympic boycotts are arguably appropriate, because it is appropriate to send a message to the host country and the world that the host country's egregious behavior should not be tolerated. Going to the host country's Games allegedly gives legitimacy to that nation and its controversial policies. In retrospect, maybe a boycott of the 1936 Olympics in Berlin could have sent Hitler a message that the rest of the world objected to Nazi Germany. On the other hand, one of the positives of American athletes attending the Berlin Olympics was that victories by Black athletes such as Jesse Owens shattered Hitler's myth of Aryan supremacy.

Although the Olympic boycotts related to South African apartheid did not result in immediate change, it arguably was part of a cumulative ongoing pressure campaign on the South African government, which after decades of world scorn, finally decided to end apartheid in the early 1990s.

The strongest argument against Olympic boycotts is that it is unfair to punish athletes who had trained for four years for their one moment of glory on the world stage. In some sports, such as gymnastics, most athletes peak at a young age and have only one, maybe two, realistic chance to make an Olympic team. Most Olympic sports, such as curling and water polo, get media attention only every four years during the Olympics.

My take is that full Olympic boycotts that result in countries not sending their athletes to the host nation to participate are generally a bad idea because the athletes have worked too hard and should not be the ones who are punished. They should not be used as political pawns. An Olympic boycott could deprive many athletes who have trained their entire lives of their one and only chance of competing on the Olympic stage. Other methods of worldwide government pressure, including sanctions, diplomatic boycotts, threats to move the Games to another host city, and diplomacy, should be used as tools to curb an Olympic host country's human rights abuses. For the most part, Olympic boycotts have not been successful. In addition, this issue could be avoided in the future if the IOC decided not to choose host countries that have current and ongoing records of severe human rights abuses.

Judging and officiating is often a matter of controversy in Olympic competition. One of the most controversial officiating fiascos took place during the 1972 Olympic gold medal men's basketball game between the United States and the Soviet Union. Prior to 1972, the United States had won every gold medal in men's basketball, dating back to 1936. However, there were warning signs that the Americans' streak could be in jeopardy prior to the 1972 Games, when several star American players were not available to play, including the top college player in the country, UCLA center Bill Walton, who chose not to play; Julius Erving, who had gone to play professionally in the ABA in 1971; and Swen Nater, who left the team before the Games, according to ESPN.[23]

In the 1972 gold medal game, the US team stormed from behind to take a 50–49 lead after Doug Collins made two clutch foul shots with only three seconds remaining. The Soviets inbounded the ball and time ran out, leading to a US celebration, but the Soviet bench was improperly awarded a time-out with one second left. Dr. William Jones, the British secretary of the International Basketball Federation (FIBA), intervened and ordered that three seconds be put back on the clock. When play resumed, a Soviet pass went astray, the clock ran out, and the Americans celebrated again. However, the court was cleared, and three seconds were once again put back on the clock because the clock operators did not have the right time when the ball was inbounded. During the ensuing chaos, Jones warned the American coaches that they would forfeit the game if they refused to play out the remaining three seconds. The third time was the charm for the Soviets when Alexander Belov caught a long pass from Ivan Edeshko, evaded two American defenders, and made the winning layup. The Soviet team rejoiced, while the Americans were stunned in disbelief and anger. The Americans' appeal was denied by a 3–2 panel vote, and the US team refused to accept the silver medals. It was the first American men's basketball team loss at the Olympics after 63 straight wins and seven straight gold medals.[24]

In 2012, Collins told *The Guardian*, "People say, 'Why didn't you leave?' We were told that if we left we would forfeit so we were pushed out on the court."[25] To this day, all of the American players on the team have refused to accept the silver medal and have vowed never to do so. The fiasco is still considered one of the worst displays of officiating in any sport. Some people claimed that Jones exerted his influence at the end of the game because he thought that total American dominance in Olympic basketball was bad for the sport and he wanted to see more parity. US forward Mike Bantom told ESPN, "With some hindsight and some perspective, you realize that bad decisions happen quite frequently in the Olympics. You've seen it happen in gymnastics, track and field, boxing. It happens all over the place. It was pretty personal to us that it happened, but looking back it's not that unusual that something like that happened. In 1972, it just so happened that we were the people who got screwed."[26]

Another ongoing Olympics controversy involves subjective judging. Unlike sports like track and field and swimming, where there is a clear winner due to precise time metrics, certain sports like gymnastics, rhythmic gymnastics, diving, figure skating, boxing, moguls, half-pipe, and ski jumping are all subject to the subjective whims of the judges, where factors such as artistry and execution are considered in the scoring. In some cases, the judges might be influenced by politics. In other cases, there can be an honest debate as to how to award style points. These judges are highly trained and experienced, but they are still capable of harboring bias and making mistakes. A fraction of a point can mean the difference between winning a gold medal and finishing fourth, off the medal stand. Unlike team sports like baseball, football, basketball, soccer, and ice hockey, the Olympic subjective sports do not use instant replay to correct referee errors.

Every four years, all of us armchair athletes who never went on a balance beam or laced up a pair of skates become critics of the judges, especially if they penalize or don't reward an athlete from our own country. These are sports that we never pay attention to until they are shown during the Olympics. Most of us wouldn't know the difference between a double axel and an axle wrench. We shake our heads in disbelief when a skater from a foreign country falls during their Winter Olympics routine yet gets a higher score than American skaters who didn't fall. For most of us the only diving we do is a cannonball in our backyard pool, yet during the Summer Olympics we think we can tell the difference between good and poor dives in platform diving.

One of the factors in scoring ice skating is projection, which is radiating energy resulting in an invisible connection with the audience.[27] This could give a home ice advantage to a skater from the host country. The only criterion for scoring snowboarding's half-pipe competition is overall impression.[28]

In the 2002 Salt Lake City Winter Olympics, controversy emerged when a Russian figure skating team was awarded a gold medal over a Canadian pair due to alleged fixed judging. A few months after the Games, after hearings and testimony, the International Skating Union determined that a French judge voted for the Russian pair as part of an alleged vote-swapping deal between France and Russia to fix the outcomes of the Olympic pairs and dance competitions. During the Games, the International Olympic Committee determined that the Canadian skaters would share the gold medal with the Russians.[29] It's been said that a tie in sports is like kissing your sister, but in this case, it seemed like a fair result.

In criticizing the increase of subjectively judged sports to the Winter Olympics, John Branch wrote in the *New York Times* in 2014, "But Olympic evolution has taken sports increasingly into subjective territory, where winners are not determined by clocks and measuring tapes. Even in the wake of judging scandals in figure skating, most of the events that have been added to the Olympics over the past 20 years, and most of those that will debut in Sochi, Russia, require a panel of judges to determine the winners—an exercise that might seem ripe for exploitation and controversy."[30]

One of the biggest judging controversies took place in the 1988 Seoul Olympic Games when judges awarded the light middleweight gold medal to the host country's Park Si-hun over American Roy Jones, Jr. Jones landed 86 punches to Park's 32 and Park took two standing eight counts, but three of the five judges awarded the fight to Park. As the referee raised Park's hand as the winner, he whispered to Jones, "I can't believe they're doing this to you."[31]

According to *Sports Illustrated*, one of the fight's judges said, "It was a terrible thing. The American won easily; so easily, in fact, that I was positive my four fellow judges would score the fight for the American by a wide margin. So I voted for the Korean to make the score only 4–1 for the American and not embarrass the host country."[32]

In discussing the home advantage of the Olympic host countries, Marshall B. Jones wrote in *Psychology of Sport and Exercise* that studies show that home advantage in Olympic sports is more common in subjectively judged sports. He stated that past studies of Olympic sports have found "whatever advantage the home country has in overall performance can be attributed to subjectively evaluated sports or to elements of subjective evaluation in otherwise objectively evaluated sports (Balmer et al., 2001, 2003)."

Jones noted that prior to the Balmer studies on biased Olympic judging,

"[J]udges were known to give inflated marks to athletes from their own countries and, in some cases, deflated marks to athletes from closely competitive countries (Ansorge & Scheer, 1988; Park & Werthner, 1977; Seltzer & Glass, 1991). This bias, however, did not necessarily imply a home advantage. The host country's judges might favor their own competitors, but visiting judges might favor theirs. Balmer et al. hypothesized that a bias in favor of the home country would nevertheless exist, mediated primarily by the influence of the home-country crowd on the judges."[33]

One positive trend in some of these subjective sports is more openness in the judging factors, such as disclosing that a certain amount of deductions are made for things like a fall from a balance beam or a bobble in gymnastics. Another factor that usually weighs into subjective judging is the degree of difficulty of the elements that the athlete performed in their routine, such as the number of triple jumps performed during an ice-skating routine. In some judged sports, the outlying scores are discarded.

After the 2002 scandal, the International Skating Union instituted a new set of guidelines that gave numeric base values to jumps, spins, and other elements in skaters' programs.[34]

According to Dr. Craig Wrisberg of the University of Tennessee, athletes who compete in subjectively judged sports like figure skating often have to deal with added stress and have to wonder, "'How a judge might evaluate me represents a potential distraction which, if I let it, can take my focus off what I need to do in order to skate my best.'"[35]

Ice-skating coach Rafael Arutunian told NBC Sports that ultimately, it's up to the individual athletes in subjectively judged sports like figure skating to do their best and try to stand out from the rest of the field, and that in the end, "Our sport has always been subjective, regardless of the accepted system of judging. I don't believe in complete objectivity in cases where people, with or without the assistance of machines, are making the decisions. A figure skater must be a head taller than the rest and just deal with it."[36]

Another controversy and social issue related to the Olympics is the competition among cities around the world to host the Games and the decision of certain cities to spend the time, money, and effort to become an Olympic host. There are benefits and detriments in being a host city or country. On the positive end, the Olympic Games can be a two-week public relations coup for the host country and city, which can entice tourists to come there. One of the biggest examples would be Barcelona, Spain, which hosted the 1992 Summer Olympics.

According to *The Guardian*, Barcelona had an increase of passengers to its airport from 2.9 million in 1992 to 21 million in 2002, and tourism accounted for 12.5 percent of the city's GDP, compared with less than 2 percent in 1992. In addition, the city invested $8 billion in infrastructure and revitalized its harbor and port.[37]

Justin Clark wrote in the *Los Angeles Times* in 2015, "Barcelona converted its waterfront into a center of nightlife and tourism and became the rare major

European city to offer an enjoyable sand and surf experience. It also constructed a ring road, and brought its airport up to international standards, eventually becoming the fifth-most visited city in Europe and halving its unemployment rate in the process."[38]

The 1992 Games also bolstered Spain as a power in international sports. Sportswriter Juan Jose Paradinas told Allen Barra of *The Atlantic*, "The Barcelona Olympics unleashed a torrent of money from both the government and private sources to build sports facilities all over the country and support sports which had not previously had support in Spain. By the end of the decade, we saw the results. Now Spanish sports *make* money. Real Madrid may be the most profitable football [soccer] club in the world."[39]

Montreal, Canada's Olympic experience and the aftermath was not as successful, as the city ran up a $1.5 billion debt. The Olympic Stadium, once nicknamed the "Big O," became known as the "Big Owe." The stadium endured years of rips in its roof and falling concrete.[40]

As to whether it is worth it for cities to bid on hosting the Olympics, Dr. Jun Kim, associate professor and program director of sport management in the School of Global Business at Arcadia University, said in an email interview, "It is only worth for cities that are able to rely on already existing infrastructure. Previous hosting countries such as China, Russia, Brazil, and South Korea invested massive sums to create infrastructure. The amount of money invested in Olympic Games hosted by those countries ranges from $13 billion to $50 billion. More problems occur after the event. Operational costs for those newly built facilities and stadiums will contribute to annual deficit due to unused and under-used properties. The hosting cities and government must be considered opportunity costs of public spending that could have been spent on other priorities. Of course, the debt left over after hosting the games can burden public budgets for decades like Greece. The 1984 LA Olympics was the only Olympic Games that produced a profit because the required infrastructure already existed."[41]

One of the ongoing controversies of the Olympics is the bidding process of host cities and countries to acquire the Games. There were reported investigations into the alleged bribing of voters and IOC members regarding the awarding of the Summer Olympics in Rio in 2016 and Tokyo in 2020.[42] This issue also dogged the awarding of the 2002 Winter Olympics to Salt Lake City.[43] In 1999, the IOC voted to expel six IOC members and other members resigned after it was disclosed that Salt Lake City Olympic organizers had given them hundreds of thousands of dollars in cash, gifts, trips, medical expenses, and scholarships.[44]

According to the Council on Foreign Relations (CFR), "In 1972, Denver became the first and only chosen host city to reject its Olympics after voters passed a referendum refusing additional public spending for the games." CFR also cites the high costs of hosting the Games—"Cities invest millions of dollars in evaluating, preparing, and submitting a bid to the IOC. The cost of planning, hiring consultants, organizing events, and the necessary travel consistently falls between $50 million and $100 million. Tokyo spent as much as $150 million on its failed 2016 bid, and about half that much for its successful 2020 bid, while Toronto decided it could not afford the $60 million it would have needed for a 2024 bid."[45]

There have been instances where the safety of athletes has been an issue in the Olympics. One of the most controversial and tragic incidents took place at the Winter Olympics in Canada in 2010 when Nodar Kumaritashvili, a luge athlete from Georgia, died during a practice run when he flew off the track and hit a steel pole. According to CNN, the course was the fastest in the world by around 15 to 20 mph, and some athletes had complained before the incident that the track was too fast. The last time that a luge athlete had been killed during the Olympics was in 1964. That same year, an Olympic skier was killed during a training run. As for the Summer Olympics, a marathon runner died in 1912 and a cyclist died in 1960.[46]

Unfortunately, the Olympics have been used as a platform by terrorists, who know that the entire world is watching for two weeks. The most tragic incident took place at the Munich games in 1972, when eight members of the Palestinian terrorist group Black September took 11 Israeli Olympic athletes hostage and later killed them. The terrorists had called for the release of 234 Palestinian prisoners. A 24-hour standoff took place between the terrorists and German police. When the terrorists and their hostages were taken by helicopter to the Munich airport, a shootout took place, and the hostages were killed.[47]

Terrorism struck again at the Atlanta Olympic Games in 1996 when two people were killed and over 100 people were injured by a 40-pound bomb filled with nails and screws in Centennial Olympic Park. After a seven-year search, domestic terrorist Eric Rudolph was arrested. In 2005, Rudolph pleaded guilty to the Olympic bombing, two other Atlanta bombings, and a bombing of an Alabama abortion clinic, resulting in Rudolph receiving four consecutive life sentences plus 120 years in prison.[48]

The Olympics and all international competitions are a potential target for terrorists who want to promote their message through violence. This is especially the case after the terrorism attacks of September 11, 2001. As noted by a *Wired.com* article before the Winter Olympic Games in South Korea, in addition to the traditional concerns of kidnapping or bombings, new concerns included drones and computer cyberattacks. There was concern that drones could deliver bombs or chemical weapons, and computer hackers could steal credit card data, contaminate scoring systems, alter drug test results, or blackmail athletes with stolen personal information. Security analyst Peter Singer told *Wired*, "What's different now from past Olympics is increased use of unmanned systems and the cyber domain to stage attacks. The attacker doesn't even have to be onsite. They can do it from afar."[49] According to CNBC.com, over 60,000 security forces and interceptor drones were deployed to protect the South Korea Games.[50] According to Reuters in 2018, the Tokyo Olympics were expected to be the first to use facial recognition technology to aid in security by identifying everyone who entered the 40 venues, including athletes, staff, volunteers, and media members.[51] The *Asia Times* reported in 2019 that hundreds of security cameras had been deployed in Tokyo streets and parks.[52] As it turned out, security and the threat of terrorism became less of an issue during the 2021 Tokyo Olympics, because spectators were banned from attending events due to the coronavirus.

The Olympics have also been a target of political protests. An example was the attacks and protests on the Beijing Games Olympic torch relay around the world. Starting in March 2008, protestors seeking independence from China for Tibet and condemning human rights violations in China tried to disrupt an initial torch lighting ceremony in Greece. Protests then followed the next few months in London, Paris, San Francisco, New Delhi, Bangkok, Nagano, and Seoul. At times, protesters tried to capture or extinguish the torch despite extensive security.[53]

Should the concept of athletes competing for nations be abolished? Would this make the Games less political? In recent years, there has been an increase in athletes applying for dual citizenship so that they can compete in the Olympics for another country, oftentimes because it might give them a better chance of making an Olympic team. Are these athletes being disloyal and unpatriotic or are they just giving themselves a better chance of participating in the Olympics since country affiliation shouldn't matter? According to a 2018 CNN.com article by Rob Hodgetts, 178 athletes at the 2018 Winter Olympics in South Korea were competing for nations that they were not born in, which amounted to about 6 percent of the total number of athletes competing at those Games. Of those 178 athletes, 37 American-born athletes were competing for other nations, followed by 21 from Canada and 19 from Russia. Three countries at those 2018 Games, Nigeria, Kosovo and Eritrea, made their first appearance at a Winter Games as a result of having a non-native athlete compete for them.[54]

An example of one of those non-native Olympic athletes was bobsledder Jazmine Fenlator-Victorian, who had raced in the 2014 Sochi Olympics for the United States but decided to race for Jamaica in the 2018 Winter Olympics in order to embrace her diversity and inspire Jamaican kids to pursue their dreams, which could include being a Winter Olympian. She grew up in New Jersey, but her father was Jamaican.[55]

In arguing for free agency for Olympic athletes so that they can compete for other countries, Peter Spiro wrote in *Slate*, "It makes more sense to allow free Olympic association, with athletes playing for any team that will have them. The Olympic Charter notes that 'the Olympics are competitions between athletes in individual or team events and not between countries.' That's exactly right. We don't require our major-league ballplayers to hail from the cities they play for, so why should we demand anything different of our Olympic athletes?"[56]

In 2015, the IOC created the Refugee Olympic Team, which competed for the first time in the 2016 Summer Olympics in Brazil. That team consisted of 10 athletes from four countries. The team was created to allow athletes who had been forced to leave their countries to compete in the Olympics.[57] In the 2021 Tokyo Summer Olympics, there were 29 athletes from 10 countries on the Refugee Team, competing in 12 sports.[58]

The Olympics has its controversies and flaws, ranging from boycotts by countries; protests by athletes; biased judging, especially in subjectively judged sports; the ongoing threat of terrorism and the need for extensive and expensive security; controversies in the Olympic bidding to become the host country; the expensive cost to host the Olympics; and whether athletes should be allowed to compete for other countries. Despite all of the controversies, scandals, and political issues, the Olympics are still one of the greatest sporting events in the world and are worth preserving. They bring athletes and fans from all over the world together. The athletes get to prove who the best are in their respective sports. Nations and their people, especially in the smaller countries, get a boost of national pride when their athletes get a medal. I've attended many great sporting events over the years but attending the 1996 Olympics was one of the greatest experiences that I've had as a sports fan. It's an event that everyone should try to experience in person at least once in their lives.

Conclusion

WHY SHOULD I CARE ABOUT social and ethical issues in sports? That's what some sports fans might think. They have busy lives, and they just want to watch the games at night or on weekends. However, as sports fans we are inundated with the dilemmas and controversies of social and ethical issues in sports on a daily basis. These issues affect how we feel about sports and can also have a huge effect on society as a whole. Oftentimes, there are no clear-cut answers to the questions that arise. Nonetheless, it's important to be aware of what those issues are, since they affect the sports that we love.

While debates about what constitutes a sport may seem esoteric, the results can have real-life implications, such as whether a purported sport actually qualifies as a sport for purposes of Title IX at the NCAA level or consideration as an Olympic sport. Sports like baseball and football are obviously sports, but what about activities like esports, Quidditch/Quadball, competitive eating, and poker?

How we play sports determines a lot about the value and benefits of sports. Winning is important, extremely important, but how we as athletes go about trying to win is also important. Sports have rules and customs, and athletes need to follow those rules in order to have a fair competition. Some behaviors are clear cut, such as don't use low blows in boxing, but other behaviors are ambiguous and debatable, such as whether running up the score or using mercy rules are appropriate, whether professional teams tanking to get better draft picks is acceptable, whether flopping in sports like soccer and basketball should be punished, and whether trash talking by athletes is acceptable.

Gambling has become socially acceptable and more and more popular in recent years. It's almost impossible to watch television without being exposed to a commercial for a gambling-related phone app or website. While gambling can be fun and exciting, it's important for gamblers to know their limits to avoid an addiction. Another dark side to gambling is the long history of point shaving, especially at the college level. Some people are concerned that the US Supreme Court decision in *Murphy v. NCAA*, which allowed states to conduct legalized sports gambling, could lead to the temptation to get college athletes to shave points.

There are many social and ethical issues related to media coverage of sports, including whether to criticize high school or college athletes, the historical struggles of female sports reporters trying to gain respect, whether sports reporters and other media professionals should speak out on political and social issues, and whether the media should report on athletes' private lives.

Ignoring the call by some for athletes to "shut up and dribble," many male and female athletes are finding their voice and becoming advocates for social justice. Continuing the tradition of activism started in the 1960s by athletes such as Muhammad Ali, Bill Russell, Jim Brown, Kareem Abdul-Jabbar, Tommie Smith, and John Carlos, current-day athletes such as LeBron James, Colin Kaepernick, and Megan Rapinoe are speaking out on social justice issues. Many athletes are finding their voices on social media, as opposed to engaging in street protests.

Fan obsession is another important element regarding sports. While some people are casual or even bandwagon sports fans, many fans derive self-esteem and vicarious thrills from watching their favorite team win. Sports have turned into the opiate of the masses, as many people would go crazy if they couldn't watch sports. There can be health and psychological benefits when your favorite team wins, but when your favorite team loses it can ruin your whole week. There have been many instances of fan violence over the years, such as when teams win championships or when fans have too much to drink at the stadium.

There are many social and ethical issues related to medical and psychological aspects of sports. Debates and controversies occur as to whether athletes should play hurt. While steroid use seems to have declined in recent years due to athletes becoming more aware of the long-term harm they can do to your body as well as an increase in testing, steroid use is still a concern. Some people have called for steroids to be legalized to institute a level playing field, but this is still a minority viewpoint and it's a bad idea. Many athletes also deal with psychological issues, such as eating disorders, anxiety and depression, and having to endure hazing by teammates. Disabled athletes such as Jim Abbott, Anthony Robles, and Shaquem Griffin inspire sports fans through their ability to excel and overcome and compensate for their disabilities. Controversies have emerged, however, as to the extent that disabled athletes should be accommodated, such as incidents involving golfer Casey Martin and sprinter Oscar Pistorius.

Regarding legal issues in sports, the Baseball Rule has been applied over the last century to prevent fans injured at a sporting event from suing the team, but courts have recognized some limited exceptions to the rule. For the most part, athletes will not be held civilly liable or criminally charged for their conduct on the field. Some people feel that athletes get special treatment under the law due to their celebrity status. There was a debate as to whether athletes like Michael Vick who served their prison time should get a second chance to play professionally. There have been many incidents of misconduct by agents for professional athletes, which has led to NCAA violations and increased regulation of agents at the state and federal level. Title IX has led to increased opportunities for girls and women to participate in sports, but many universities are cutting sports teams, especially in men's sports, to comply with Title IX. At the high school level, legal issues have arisen as to prayer at public high school football games and whether homeschooled students can participate in school sports.

While youth sports have many positives, they often involve controversy and debate. Should girls be allowed to play on boys teams like wrestling, golf, and football? Should boys be allowed to play on girls teams like field hockey, lacrosse, or volleyball? This is something that states and athletic associations are having to decide. In light of competitive travel teams, there are issues of sufficient playing time, burnout, injuries, costs, specialization, and pressure to perform. The rise of awarding participation trophies has caused adults to mock the younger generations for being spoiled and entitled. However, blame the parents for giving them out, not the kids. Also, participation trophies are equivalent to varsity letter jackets and certificates that adults received over 50 years ago and are still proud of. While most parents are positive supporters of their kids, there are many instances of parents' misconduct in the stands and as coaches.

College sports are great and exciting for the players and fans, but they have become a big moneymaking business. Schools, teams, conferences, coaches, and athletic directors make huge amounts of money due to television contracts, bowl revenue, and NCAA March Madness appearances, but for years, the student-athletes were not profiting at all. While college athletes cannot be paid directly by the schools, they are now allowed to market themselves and profit from their name, image, or likeness. In addition, schools can provide cost-of-attendance stipends to help athletes pay for living expenses. Debates continue as to whether the NBA should abandon its one-and-done rule, while some believe that the NFL should allow younger players into the league. In light of the pressure to win or be fired as a coach or athletic director, there are ongoing scandals related to academics, eligibility, and recruiting violations. The rise of television money has led to frequent conference realignment that is unlikely to stop in the near future. To its credit, the NCAA will expand its College Football Playoff to 12 teams, which is a positive development, since it will give the underdog, Cinderella schools from Group of Five conferences a legitimate chance to be selected for the playoffs and compete against the big boys.

Professional sports are the most watched and scrutinized by most fans and the media since they involve the most elite athletes. With that scrutiny comes many controversies and debates, such as how professional leagues are dealing with medical issues including concussions and violence in sports. The NFL has increased safety protocols as to better equipment and more rules to protect players from head injuries. While fighting has decreased in the NHL as teams are favoring more skilled players as opposed to the less skilled enforcers or goons, some people want the NHL to abolish fighting altogether. There are also racial issues and controversies, such as the use of Native American/Indigenous Peoples' team nicknames and the lack of Black head coaches in the NFL, which has led many to question the usefulness of the Rooney Rule. Ongoing economic issues persist, such as high salaries and free agency, the building of stadiums, and moving teams and franchises to new cities.

Every two years, we are enthralled by the great athletic performances of elite athletes around the world at the Olympic Games. Despite the pageantry, sportsmanship, camaraderie, and record performances, the Olympics have their flaws and controversies, including biased and subjective judging, the high costs of hosting an Olympics, and the bidding process to host the Games. Politics are often unavoidable in the Games, as there have been boycotts, protests by athletes, and the specter of terrorism. Despite these flaws, the Olympics remain of the greatest sporting events in the world. If you've never attended the Olympic Games, it's an experience that you should experience at least once.

So, whether you're a quarterback at the high school, college, or pro level, or an armchair quarterback who watches 18 hours of football on television during the weekend, being informed and knowledgeable about social issues in sports can make you a better athlete and a better sports fan.

Chapter Notes

Chapter 1

1. Bernard Suits, "The Elements of Sport," in *Ethics in Sport*, ed. William John Morgan (Champaign, IL: Human Kinetics, 2007), 9–19.
2. Ronald B. Woods, *Social Issues in Sport*, 2d ed. (Champaign, IL: Human Kinetics, 2011), 5–9.
3. Felix Lebed, "Physical Activity Is Not Necessary: The Notion of Sport as Unproductive Officialised Competitive Game," *Sport, Ethics and Philosophy* 16, no. 1 (2022): 111–129, https://www.tandfonline.com/doi/abs/10.1080/17511321.2021.1874044.
4. Nicholas Stoll, "Nicholas Stoll: Cheer Isn't an NCAA Sport, and Title IX Just Might Keep It That Way," *Michigan Daily*, October 13, 2020, https://www.michigandaily.com/sports-society/nicholas-stoll-cheer-isnt-an-ncaa-sport-and-title-ix-just-might-keep-it-that-way/.
5. Kristi Dosh, "Is Cheerleading a Sport? The IOC Ends the Debate," *Forbes*, December 21, 2016, https://www.forbes.com/sites/kristidosh/2016/12/21/is-cheerleading-a-sport-the-ioc-ends-the-debate/#1f4003804526.
6. Madison Peyser, "What the IOC's Recognition of Cheerleading Means for the Sport and Its Athletes," FOX Sports, August 7, 2021, https://www.foxsports.com/stories/olympics/international-olympic-committee-recognizes-cheerleading-international-cheer-union-sport.
7. Elisabeth Sherman, "Why Don't More People Consider Competitive Cheerleading a Sport?" *Atlantic*, May 2, 2017, https://www.theatlantic.com/entertainment/archive/2017/05/why-dont-more-people-consider-competitive-cheerleading-a-sport/524940/.
8. Jennifer Allen, "The Athlete on the Sidelines," *New York Times*, February 20, 2004, https://www.nytimes.com/2004/02/20/opinion/the-athlete-on-the-sidelines.html.
9. Hunter McKay, "Cheer: Owls Win National Championship at 2018 NCA Collegiate Nationals," KSUOwls.com, April 7, 2018, https://ksuowls.com/news/2018/4/7/general-cheer-owls-win-national-championship-at-2018-nca-collegiate-nationals; Ed Brennen, "Peak Performance: Cheerleaders Take Fourth at Nationals," UMass Lowell (official website), June 8, 2018, https://www.uml.edu/News/stories/2018/Cheerleading-nationals.aspx.
10. Jake Kobersky, "Texas A&M Cheer Squad Wins National Championship," KBTX News, April 10, 2018, https://www.kbtx.com/content/news/Texas-AM-Cheer-Squad-wins-national-championship-479282193.html.
11. "UCA Competitions," Varsity.com, accessed October 7, 2022.
12. Matt Bonesteel, "Is Cheerleading a Sport? The American Medical Association Thinks So," *Washington Post*, June 10, 2014, https://www.washingtonpost.com/news/early-lead/wp/2014/06/10/is-cheerleading-a-sport-the-american-medical-association-thinks-so/?utm_term=.55f8bfbd96da.
13. Wayne Drehs, "Athletes Are Cheerleaders Too," ESPN, April 3, 2016, http://www.espn.com/espn/page2/story?page=drehs/040316.
14. Luis Gude and Gillian Hotz, "Concussions in Cheerleaders Reported from a Countywide Concussion Injury Surveillance System," *Practice (The Sport Journal)* 24, no. 96 (November 15, 2019), https://thesportjournal.org/article/concussions-in-cheerleaders-reported-from-a-countywide-concussion-injury-surveillance-system/; Zachary Y. Kerr, Avinash Chandran, Aliza K. Nedimyer, Alan Arakkal, Lauren A. Pierpoint, and Scott L. Zuckerman, "Concussion Incidence and Trends in 20 High School Sports," *Pediatrics* 144, no. 5 (2019), https://doi.org/10.1542/peds.2019-2180; Luis Torres, "Is Cheerleading a Sport? Some Concussion Experts Say It Should Be Classified as One," *Cronkite News*, March 23, 2020, https://cronkitenews.azpbs.org/2020/03/23/cheerleading-concussions/.
15. Alyssa Roenigk, "Sorry, Cheerleading Is Not a Sport," ESPNW, July 7, 2014, http://www.espn.com/espnw/news-commentary/article/11128302/espnw-former-college-cheerleader-says-sorry-cheerleading-not-sport.
16. Associated Press, "U.S. Appeals Court: Cheerleading Not a Sport," CBS News, August 7, 2012, https://www.cbsnews.com/news/us-appeals-court-cheerleading-not-a-sport/.
17. Jill P. Capuzzo, "In Person: Athletes with Appetite," *New York Times*, January 19, 2003, https://www.nytimes.com/2003/01/19/nyregion/in-person-athletes-with-appetite.html.
18. Gabriel Muller, "The High Art of Com-

petitive Eating," *Atlantic*, June 9, 2014, https://www.theatlantic.com/health/archive/2014/06/is-competitive-eating-a-sport/ 372172/.

19. Marielle Mondon, "Following Eagles Super Bowl Victory, Wing Bowl Is Officially Over After 26 Years," *PhillyVoice*, October 30, 2018, https://www.phillyvoice.com/eagles-super-bowl-victory-wing-bowl-wip-officially-over/.

20. K. Jeanine Congalton, "Competitive Eating as Sport," in *Sporting Rhetoric: Performance, Games, and Politics*, ed. Barry Brummett (New York: Peter Lang, 2009), 175.

21. Jon Yates, "Sport Has 'Eating Athletes' Bursting with Pride," *Chicago Tribune*, June 16, 2004, https://www.chicagotribune.com/news/ct-xpm-2004-06-16-0406160209-story.html.

22. Associated Press, "Some Find Competitive Eating Hard to Swallow," NBC News, November 21, 2007, https://www.nbcnews.com/health/health-news/some-find-competitive-eating-hard-swallow-flna1c9463761 (link no longer available); Associated Press, "Iowa Regains its Corn Contest," *Columbus Dispatch*, September 9, 2008, https://www.dispatch.com/article/20080909/NEWS/309099739; Mike Downey, "Man-Bites-Dog Show Ghastly," *Chicago Tribune*, July 5, 2007, https://www.chicagotribune.com/news/ct-xpm-2007-07-05-0707050058-story.html.

23. Mariel Soto Reyes, "Esports Ecosystem Report 2021: The Key Industry Companies and Trends Growing the eSports Market Which Is on Track to Surpass $1.5B by 2023," *Business Insider*, January 5, 2021, https://www.businessinsider.com/esports-ecosystem-market-report.

24. Lindsay Poss, "Poss: Virginians Should Be Excited About Esports Betting," *Roanoke Times*, May 5, 2021, https://roanoke.com/opinion/columnists/poss-virginians-should-be-excited-about-esports-betting/article_113f59a2-9e00-11eb-a8a1-6b62462d55aa.html; Dean Cooke, "What ESports Games Can You Bet On?" *Telegraph* (London), May 14, 2021, https://www.telegraph.co.uk/betting/esports-betting-games-markets/.

25. Kyle Winters, "ESports: The New Path to an Athletic Scholarship," *USA Today*, January 31, 2018, https://usatodayhss.com/2018/esports-the-new-path-to-an-athletic-scholarship.

26. Sarah E. Needleman, "Are High School E-Sports the Next Friday Night Lights?" *Wall Street Journal*, April 19, 2018, https://www.wsj.com/articles/are-high-school-esports-the-next-friday-night-lights-1524162330.

27. "What Is NACE?" National Association of Collegiate Esports (NACE), accessed February 12, 2021, https://nacesports.org/about/.

28. Janek Speight, "Germany to Recognize ESports as an Official Sport," Deutsche Welle (DW), August 2, 2018, https://www.dw.com/en/germany-to-recognize-esports-as-an-official-sport/a-42509285.

29. Bryan Armen Graham, "Esports Could Be Medal Event at 2024 Olympics, Paris Bid Team Says," *Guardian* (London and New York), August 9, 2017, https://www.theguardian.com/sport/2017/aug/09/esports-2024-olympics-medal-event-paris-bid-committee.

30. Liana B. Baker and Rory Carroll, "Esports Get a Cool Reception at Winter Games," Reuters, February 7, 2018, https://www.reuters.com/article/us-olympics-2018-esports/esports-get-a-cool-reception-at-winter-games-idUSKBN1FR13Y.

31. Vlad Savov and Sam Byford, "ESports Are like Email: The Digital Equivalent of Something We've Been Doing for Centuries," *Verge*, July 11, 2014, https://www.theverge.com/2014/7/11/5890907/can-video-games-be-sports.

32. Nicholas David Bowman and Gregory A. Cranmer, "Can Video Games Be a Sport?" in *Understanding eSports: An Introduction to a Global Phenomenon*, ed. Ryan Rogers (Lanham, MD: Lexington, 2019), 15–30.

33. "Quidditch Is Being Renamed. But the Sport Will Never Lose Its Magic, Say Players," CBC Radio, August 13, 2022, https://www.cbc.ca/radio/day6/quidditch-canada-name-change-1.6549672.

34. "About U.S. Quidditch," U.S. Quidditch, accessed September 2, 2020, https://www.usquidditch.org/about/mission; "What Is Quadball?" U.S. Quadball, accessed October 14, 2022, https://www.usquadball.org/getting-started/what-is-quadball.

35. "Could Quidditch Be an Olympic Sport?" BBC, July 10, 2012, https://www.bbc.co.uk/newsround/18785407.

36. Sian Cain, "Australian Dropbears Defeat U.S. Team to Win Quidditch World Cup," *Guardian* (London and New York), July 25, 2016, https://www.theguardian.com/books/2016/jul/25/australian-dropbears-triumph-in-quidditch-world-cup-jk-rowling.

37. Hallie Grossman, Rebecca Nordquist, and Alyssa Roenigk, "Olympics Confidential," ESPN, April 27, 2016, http://www.espn.com/espn/feature/story/_/id/15355659/us-olympians-weigh-rio-2016.

38. "Harry Potter Sport Quidditch Aims for Olympic Glory," *Telegraph* (London), July 10, 2012, https://www.telegraph.co.uk/culture/harry-potter/9390023/Harry-Potter-sport-Quidditch-aims-for-Olympic-glory.html (link no longer available); Darin Pike, "The Weirdest Events in the Summer Olympics," *Bleacher Report*, https://bleacherreport.com/articles/1255728-the-weirdest-events-in-the-summer-olympics; Darin Pike, "The Weirdest Events in the Summer Olympics," *Atlantic*, July 13, 2012, https://www.theatlantic.com/entertainment/archive/2012/07/the-weirdest-events-in-the-summer-olympics/259800/.

39. Ollie Williams, "Quidditch Is Real and It Wants to Go Pro," CNN, November 21, 2014, http://edition.cnn.com/2014/11/21/sport/quidditch-mudbloods/index.html.

40. Belinda Goldsmith, "Olympics-Quidditch Nerds Target Games to Promote Their Sport," Reuters, July 9, 2012, https://www.reuters.com/article/oly-quidditch-tournament/olympics-

quidditch-nerds-target-games-to-promote-their-sport-idUSL5E8HF8O320120709.

41. Email interview with Mary Kimball, October 19, 2020. Mary Kimball is the executive director of U.S. Quidditch (Quadball).

42. Constance Gibbs, "Pole Dancing Could Be on Track to Be an Olympic Sport," *New York Daily News*, October 17, 2017, https://www.nydailynews.com/life-style/pole-dancing-track-olympic-sport-article-1.3569892; Rosemary Black, "Pole Dancing Could Be Recognized as a Sport and Headed to the Olympics," *New York Daily News*, February 23, 2010, https://www.nydailynews.com/life-style/pole-dancing-recognized-sport-headed-olympics-article.1.198909.

43. Rachel Moss, "Should Pole Dancing Be Classified as a Sport? Two Women Go Head to Head on the Debate," *Huffington Post UK*, October 17, 2017, https://www.huffingtonpost.co.uk/entry/should-pole-dancing-be-classed-as-a-sport-women-on-either-side-of-the-debate-share-their-views_uk_59e5f470e4b0a2324d1dbf9b.

44. Shawn Smith, "Tokyo Olympics 101: What Are the New Sports?" NBC Olympics, April 6, 2021, https://www.nbcolympics.com/news/tokyo-olympics-101-new-sports.

45. Chris Chase, "Jimmie Johnson Isn't an Athlete? So What?" *USA Today*, November 18, 2013, https://ftw.usatoday.com/2013/11/jimmie-johnson-donovan-mcnabb-nascar-athlete.

46. Joshua David Stein, "Can We Really Call Motorsport a Sport?" *Daily Beast*, February 1, 2017, https://www.thedailybeast.com/can-we-really-call-motorsport-a-sport.

47. Seth Koenig, "Science Proves It: Racecar Drivers Are Athletes," *Motorsport Safety*, March 1, 2016, https://www.motorsport-safety.org/media/news/science-proves-it-racecar-drivers-are-athletes (link no longer available). Article reprinted at https://abigailui.com/blog/race-car-drivers-athletes-774.html.

48. Larry Atkins, "Sorry, Golf Is Not a Sport," *Chicago Tribune*, April 19, 2002, https://www.chicagotribune.com/news/ct-xpm-2002-04-19-0204190149-story.html.

49. Peter McCleery, "Are Golfers Really Athletes?" ESPN, May 2, 2007, https://www.espn.com/golf/news/story?id=2857006.

50. McCleery, "Are Golfers Really Athletes?"

51. Mosi Secret, "Poker Is More a Game of Skill, than of Chance, Judge Rules," *New York Times*, August 21, 2012, https://www.nytimes.com/2012/08/22/nyregion/poker-is-more-a-game-of-skill-than-of-chance-a-judge-rules.html.

52. Lydia Smith, "Pole Dancing and Poker Could be Included in Olympic Games," *Independent* (London), October 22, 2017, https://www.independent.co.uk/sport/football/news-and-comment/pole-dancing-poker-olympic-games-observer-status-recognised-sport-a8013686.html.

53. Gary Wise, "Poker in the Olympics?" ESPN, February 17, 2010, https://www.espn.com/espn/poker/columns/story?columnist=wise_gary&id=4918780.

54. Associated Press, "Breakdancing Gets Olympic Status to Debut at Paris Games in 2024," ESPN, December 7, 2020, https://www.espn.com/olympics/story/_/id/30470282/breakdancing-gets-olympic-status-debut-paris-games-2024.

55. Bill Chappell, "Breakdancing in the Olympics? Paris 2024 Organizers Say 'Oui, Garcon!'" NPR, February 22, 2019, https://www.npr.org/2019/02/22/697009844/breakdancing-in-the-olympics-paris-2024-organizers-say-oui-garcon.

56. "Breakdancing Will Be an Olympic Sport in 2024," NPR, December 20, 2020, https://www.npr.org/2020/12/20/948315555/olympic-breakdancing.

57. Stephen Smith, "Olympic Dreams: Six Unlikely Sports Vying to Make It to the Games," CBS News, June 26, 2012, https://www.cbsnews.com/media/olympic-dreams-six-unlikely-sports-vying-to-make-it-to-the-games/.

58. "Top N. American Athletes of the 20th Century," ESPN, https://www.espn.com/sports century/athletes.html, accessed May 22, 2021.

59. SI Staff, "Sportsman of the Year," *Sports Illustrated*, December 24, 1973, https://www.si.com/vault/1973/12/24/618484/sportsman-of-the-year.

60. Tim Keown, "Calvin Borel Among Greatest Athletes," ESPN, May 4, 2010, https://www.espn.com/espn/commentary/news/story?id=5161226.

61. PETA, "Cruel Sports," PETA.org, accessed December 10, 2022, https://www.peta.org/issues/animals-in-entertainment/cruel-sports/.

62. "Portuguese Lawmakers Reject Proposal to Ban Bullfighting," Associated Press, July 6, 2018, https://apnews.com/article/7ac950ad34244f25897b9827390d6ca2.

63. "Bullfighting," *Humane Society International*, accessed November 6, 2020, https://www.hsi.org/news-media/bullfighting/.

Chapter 2

1. "Welcome to the Ancient Olympic Games," *International Olympic Committee*, accessed March 14, 2021, https://olympics.com/ioc/ancient-olympic-games.

2. The Editors of Encyclopaedia Britannica, "Marquess of Queensberry Rules," *Britannica.com*, accessed March 15, 2021, https://www.britannica.com/sports/Marquess-of-Queensberry-rules.

3. Joseph Doty, "Sports Build Character?!," *Journal of College and Character* 7, no. 3 (2006): 1–9, https://doi.org/10.2202/1940-1639.1529.

4. Jay D. Goldstein and Seppo E. Iso-Ahola, "Promoting Sportsmanship in Youth Sports: Perspectives from Sport Psychology," *Journal of Physical Education, Recreation & Dance* 77, no. 7 (2006): 18–24, https://doi.org/10.1080/07303084.2006.10597902; National Collegiate Athletic Association, Report on the Sportsmanship and Fan Behavior Summit, 2003, http://www.ncaa.org/sportsmanshipFanBehavior/report.pdf (link no longer available).

5. Adrian Glass-Moore, "Runners From Devils Lake, Fargo South Appear on the Ellen Show, Given Trip," *Grand Forks Herald*, October 29, 2014, https://www.grandforksherald.com/sports/3602525-runners-devils-lake-fargo-south-appear-ellen-show-given-trip.

6. Gene Marks, "Why Did This German Olympian Help Jesse Owens While Hitler Watched?" *Entrepreneur*, February 14, 2019, https://www.entrepreneur.com/article/328050.

7. James Hetherington, "When Sportsmanship Was the Winner," *Advertiser*, May 20, 2015, https://www.adelaidenow.com.au/sport/when-sportsmanship-was-the-winner/news-story/68b6a7e047225a8695e9af41b09c8b20.

8. Joel Beall, "17 Golf Rules You Definitely Need to Know When Playing in a Tournament," *Golf Digest*, May 26, 2016, https://www.golfdigest.com/story/18-golf-rules-you-definitely-need-to-know-when-playing-in-a-tournament.

9. ESPN.com News Services, "Phil Mickelson Penalized for Using Different Type of Golf Ball on 7th Hole," ABC News, October 9, 2015, https://abcnews.go.com/Sports/phil-mickelson-penalized-type-golf-ball-7th-hole/story?id=34375811.

10. Jim Thomas, "How to Get Disqualified in Golf," *Golfweek*, accessed March 22, 2021, https://golftips.golfweek.usatoday.com/disqualified-golf-20551.html.

11. Cathal Kelly, "Canadian Coach's Act of Kindness in Cross Country Skiing at Sochi Olympics Reflects All of Us: Kelly," *Toronto Star*, February 11, 2014, https://www.thestar.com/sports/sochi2014/skiing/2014/02/11/canadian_coach_lends_helping_hand_to_russian_skier_in_cross_country_skiing_at_sochi_olympics.html.

12. Sally Jenkins, "Vince Lombardi: The Coach That Still Matters 40 Years After His Death," *Washington Post*, September 7, 2010, https://www.washingtonpost.com/wp-dyn/content/article/2010/09/06/AR2010090603019.html.

13. Email interview with Brian Schiff, May 28, 2021. Brian Schiff was the head coach for eight gold medal United States Maccabiah 16 & Under Boys basketball teams, a former assistant coach at Abington Friends School and middle school head coach at AFS, and a member of the Philadelphia Jewish Sports Hall of Fame.

14. "Sportsmanship," *Pass It On/The Foundation for a Better Life*, accessed September 22, 2021, https://www.passiton.com/inspirational-stories-tv-spots/106-basketball.

15. Sam Borden, "Uruguay's Suarez, Known for Biting, Leaves Mark on World Cup," *New York Times*, June 24, 2014, https://www.nytimes.com/2014/06/25/sports/worldcup/apparent-bite-by-luis-suarez-mars-uruguays-victory-over-italy.html.

16. Ron Dicker, "No One Wins When the Final Score Is 161–2," *Huffington Post*, January 11, 2015, https://www.huffpost.com/entry/arroyo-valley-bloomington-161-2_n_6451192.

17. Nicholas Dixon, "On Sportsmanship and 'Running up the Score,'" *Journal of the Philosophy of Sport* 19, no. 1 (1992): 1–13, https://doi.org/10.1080/00948705.1992.9714491.

18. Alun Hardman, Luanne Fox, Doug McLaughlin, and Kurt Zimmerman, "On Sportsmanship and 'Running up the Score': Issues of Incompetence and Humiliation," *Journal of the Philosophy of Sport* 23, no. 1 (1996): 58–69, https://www.tandfonline.com/doi/abs/10.1080/00948705.1996.9714531?journalCode=rjps20.

19. "Is Running up the Score a Problem?" ESPN, November 17, 2010, https://www.espn.com/espn/commentary/news/story?id=5816279.

20. Dave Clark, "Coach Luke Fickell Apologizes after No. 7 Cincinnati Runs Fake Punt up 32 Points in Fourth Quarter," *Cincinnati Enquirer*, November 13, 2020, https://www.cincinnati.com/story/sports/ncaaf/2020/11/13/luke-fickell-cincinnati-fake-punt-ecu/6292284002/.

21. Zach Pekale, "9 of the Craziest Comebacks in NCAA College Basketball History," NCAA, July 7, 2020, https://www.ncaa.com/news/basketball-men/article/2020-07-07/college-basketballs-9-craziest-comebacks; Chris Johnson, "Nevada Upends Cincinnati with Epic Comeback, Leaving Bearcats Stunned and Done," *Sports Illustrated*, March 18, 2018, https://www.si.com/college/2018/03/19/ncaa-tournament-nevada-comeback-victory-cincinnati; Nick Bromberg, "UCLA Stuns No. 19 Washington State 67–63 Despite Anthony Gordon's 9 TD Passes," *Yahoo! Sports*, September 22, 2019, https://www.yahoo.com/now/ucla-stuns-no-19-washington-state-6763-despite-anthony-gordons-9-td-passes-063047766.html; Jordan Alexis, "10 Best Bowl Games in the History of College Football," *Fansided*, December 10, 2019, https://fansided.com/2019/12/10/best-bowl-games-college-football-history/3/.

22. Schiff, email interview.

23. Evan Barnes, "Basketball: Are Blowouts Signs of Bad Sportsmanship," *Los Angeles Daily News*, January 8, 2015, http://blogs.dailynews.com/preps/2015/01/08/basketball-blowouts-signs-bad-sportsmanship/.

24. Mike White, "Mike White's Xtra Points: Calling Out Coaches for Running up the Score," *Pittsburgh Post-Gazette*, September 17, 2015, https://www.post-gazette.com/sports/highschool-football/2017/09/15/Mike-White-running-up-the-score-sportsmanship-Imani-Christian-California/stories/201709150030.

25. ESPN.com News Services, "Coach: Team Didn't Run Up 100–0 Score," ESPN, April 12, 2009, https://www.espn.com/highschool/rise/basketball/girls/news/story?id=4062181; Associated Press, "In the Wake of a 100–0 Win, a Texas Coach Loses His Job," *New York Times*, January 25, 2009, https://www.nytimes.com/2009/01/26/sports/26fired.html.

26. Schiff, email interview.

27. Jeff DiVeronica and James Johnson, "Section V Mercy Rule: Does it Protect Athletes From

Injury, Embarrassment," *Democrat & Chronicle*, May 4, 2018, https://www.democratandchronicle.com/story/sports/high-school/2018/05/04/mercy-run-rule-section-v-baseball-softball/576871002/. Article partially reprinted: Jeff DiVeronica and James Johnson, "Does the Mercy Rule Protect Athletes From Injury, Embarrassment?" *USA Today*, May 5, 2018, https://usatodayhss.com/2018/does-the-mercy-rule-protect-athletes-from-injury-embarrassment.

28. Alex Hermann, "'M' Players and Coach Reflect on Softball's Eight-Run Mercy Rule," *Michigan Daily*, April 19, 2010, https://www.michigandaily.com/content/softballs-eight-run-rule-plague-or-promise.

29. Owen Poole, "CIAC Eliminates 50-Point Rule in High School Football," *Norwich Bulletin*, June 27, 2016, https://www.norwichbulletin.com/sports/20160627/ciac-eliminates-50-point-rule-in-high-school-football.

30. Greg Mattura, "Does NJ High School Basketball Need a Mercy Rule? Here's What Coaches, Refs Have to Say," *NorthJersey.com*, January 28, 2020, https://www.northjersey.com/story/sports/high-school/boys-basketball/2020/01/28/nj-high-school-basketball-mercy-rule-running-clock-rule-needed/4535309002/.

31. Joseph McManus, "Ethical Considerations & the Practice of Tanking in Sport Management," *Sport, Ethics and Philosophy* 13, no. 2 (2019): 145–160, https://www.tandfonline.com/doi/abs/10.1080/17511321.2018.1483418; Jeff Borland, Mark Chicu, and Robert D. Macdonald, "Do Teams Always Lose to Win? Performance Incentives and the Player Draft in the Australian Football League," *Journal of Sports Economics* 10, no. 5 (2009): 451–484, https://journals.sagepub.com/doi/abs/10.1177/1527002509331615; Akira Motomura, Kelsey V. Roberts, Daniel M. Leeds, and Michael A. Leeds, "Does It Pay to Build through the Draft in the National Basketball Association?" *Journal of Sports Economics* 17, no. 5 (2016): 501–516, https://journals.sagepub.com/doi/abs/10.1177/1527002516641169; Brian P. Soebbing, Brad R. Humphreys, and Daniel S. Mason, "Exploring Incentives to Lose in Professional Team Sports: Do Conference Games Matter?" *International Journal of Sport Finance* 8, no. 3 (2013).

32. Evan Macy, "Eight Years after the Start of the Process, the Sixers Are Still Mediocre," *PhillyVoice*, June 21, 2021, https://www.phillyvoice.com/the-process-sixers-hawks-game-7-ben-simmons-trade-rumors-joel-embiid-sam-hinkie-daryl-morey/; Carron J. Phillips, "As Expected, 'The Process' Failed," *Deadspin*, June 21, 2021, https://deadspin.com/as-expected-the-process-failed-1847141354.

33. Sam Amick, "Adam Silver Cautions NBA Teams to Protect Integrity of Game," *USA Today*, February 28, 2018, https://www.usatoday.com/story/sports/nba/2018/02/28/adam-silver-cautions-nba-teams-against-tanking-protect-integrity-game/380197002/.

34. ESPN.com News Services, information from the Associated Press was used in this report, "Coach K Can't Fathom Tanking," ESPN, November 13, 2013, https://www.espn.com/mens-college-basketball/story/_/id/9971131/mike-krzyzewski-duke-blue-devils-coach-says-fathom-nba-teams-tanking-games-better-draft-position.

35. Email interview with Glen Macnow, May 25, 2021. Glen Macnow is a longtime Philadelphia sports talk radio host at Sports Radio 94 WIP.

36. Hunter Felt, "The Growing Acceptance of Tanking Is Good for the NBA," *Guardian*, April 6, 2017, https://www.theguardian.com/sport/blog/2017/apr/06/tanking-nba-los-angeles-lakers-brooklyn-nets.

37. K. Damon Aiken, Ajay Sukhdial, Richard M. Campbell, Jr., and Aubrey Kent, "Investigating Sport Fan Attitudes toward Tanking: The Role of Values-Based Connections," *Sport Marketing Quarterly* 29, no. 4 (2020), http://doi.org/10.32731/SMQ.294.122020.02.

38. NBA.com staff, "NBA Draft Lottery: Schedule, Odds, and How It Works," NBA, August 20, 2020, https://www.nba.com/nba-draft-lottery-explainer.

39. Riley McAtee, "Somehow, Some Way, the Jets' Tank is Still Alive," *The Ringer*, December 6, 2020, https://www.theringer.com/nfl/2020/12/6/22157619/jets-tank-adam-gase-raiders-trevor-lawrence.

40. Nick Selbe, "Giants Players React to Eagles' Tank Job vs. Washington in Season Finale," *Sports Illustrated*, January 4, 2021, https://www.si.com/nfl/2021/01/04/new-york-giants-players-frustrated-philadelphia-eagles-tanking.

41. Matt Moore, "NBA Formally Announces New Flopping Rule," CBS Sports, October 3, 2012, https://www.cbssports.com/nba/news/nba-formally-announces-new-flopping-rule/.

42. Alejandro Chacoff, "The Fall: How Diving Became Football's Worst Crime," *Guardian*, April 6, 2016, https://www.theguardian.com/football/2016/apr/06/the-fall-how-diving-became-football-worst-crime. This is an adapted version of an essay from *n+1 magazine*; Alejandro Chacoff, "Falling Men," *n+1 Magazine*, Spring 2016, https://www.nplusonemag.com/issue-25/essays/falling-men/.

43. Eric Levenson, "Dissecting America's Hatred of the Flop Is a World Cup Tradition," *Atlantic* (From the archive of *The Wire*), June 16, 2014, https://www.theatlantic.com/culture/archive/2014/06/dissecting-american-soccers-hatred-of-the-flop-is-a-world-cup-tradition/372839/; Eric Levenson, "Dissecting American Soccer's Hatred of the Flop Is a World Cup Tradition," *The Wire*, June 16, 2014, https://www.thewire.com/culture/2014/06/dissecting-american-soccers-hatred-of-the-flop-is-a-world-cup-tradition/372839/. The Wire Link is no longer available.

44. ESPN.com News Services, "NBA to Crack Down on Flopping," ESPN, October 3, 2012, https://

www.espn.com/nba/story/_/id/8457259/nba-establishes-new-anti-flopping-penalties-fine-players.

45. Jack Maloney, "DeMarcus Cousins Says Flopping Is Hurting the 'Competitive Spirit of Basketball,'" CBS Sports, December 7, 2017, https://www.cbssports.com/nba/news/demarcus-cousins-says-flopping-is-hurting-the-competitive-spirit-of-basketball/.

46. Rob Dauster, "Flop Rule Flops: Missouri State Loses When Technical Is Given for Questionable Flop," NBC Sports, November 16, 2019, https://collegebasketball.nbcsports.com/2019/11/16/flop-rule-flops-missouri-state-loses-when-technical-is-given-for-questionable-flop/.

47. Jeff Zillgitt, "Are Intentional 'Hack-a-Player' Fouls Good For NBA?" *USA Today*, May 7, 2015, https://www.usatoday.com/story/sports/nba/2015/05/07/intentional-fouls-hack-a-shaq-deandre-jordan-dwight-howard-gregg-popovich/70956628/; Kevin McCormick, "Doc Rivers Talks Impact of 'Hack-A-Ben' in Game 5 Loss," *Sports Illustrated*, June 17, 2021, https://www.si.com/nba/76ers/news/sixers-doc-rivers-talks-impact-of-hack-a-ben-in-game-5-loss.

48. Shlomo Sprung, "Grayson Allen Discusses Why He Still Gets Booed despite Barely Playing in the NBA, No Longer at Duke," *Forbes*, November 29, 2018, https://www.forbes.com/sites/shlomosprung/2018/11/29/grayson-allen-discusses-why-he-still-gets-booed-despite-barely-playing-in-the-nba-no-longer-at-duke/?sh=71f6a8a67cb2; Dana O'Neil, "Is Grayson Allen the Next Hated White Duke Player," ESPN, February 9, 2016, https://www.espn.com/mens-college-basketball/story/_/id/14644805/grayson-allen-being-hated-white-player-duke-blue-devils; Alex Butler, "Duke's Grayson Allen Commits Cheap Shot Flagrant Foul Against USC," UPI, March 10, 2018, https://www.upi.com/Sports_News/College-Basketball/2018/03/10/Dukes-Grayson-Allen-commits-cheap-shot-flagrant-foul-against-UNC/7961520699113/.

49. Jerry Barca, "White House Communications Director Cites Paterno in Talking About Honor," *Forbes*, July 27, 2017, https://www.forbes.com/sites/jerrybarca/2017/07/27/white-house-communications-director-cites-paterno-in-talking-about-honor/?sh=213b75e971cd.

50. Dwayne McClary, "How Smokin' Joe Frazier Fought Unfair 'Uncle Tom' Slurs," *Grio*, November 11, 2008, https://thegrio.com/2011/11/08/smokin-joe-frazier-fought-uncle-tom-slur-his-whole-life/.

51. Michael Cohen, "Richard Sherman's Immature Gloating Shows He's Not Ready for Sport Stardom," *Guardian*, January 21, 2014, https://www.theguardian.com/commentisfree/2014/jan/21/richard-sherman-interview-horrible-sportsmanship.

52. SI.com staff, "Isiah Thomas Regrets Handshake Snub against Bulls in 1991 Playoffs," *Sports Illustrated*, October 4, 2013, https://www.si.com/nba/2013/10/04/isiah-thomas-michael-jordan-pistons-bulls-1991-playoffs; NBA TV, "NBA TV Open Court: Handshake," https://www.youtube.com/watch?v=lFK82GvfYyc.

53. William C. Rhoden, "A Handshake Is Not Too Much to Ask, Even from a King," *New York Times*, June 2, 2009, https://www.nytimes.com/2009/06/02/sports/basketball/02rhoden.html; Michael Wilbon, "Before LeBron James Is Truly a 'Winner,' He's Got to Be a Good Sport," *Washington Post*, June 2, 2009, https://www.washingtonpost.com/wp-dyn/content/article/2009/06/01/AR2009060102949.html.

54. Scott Davis, "Bombshell ESPN Report Says Patriots 'Spygate' Scandal Was Way Worse Than People Realized," *Business Insider*, September 8, 2015, https://www.businessinsider.com/espn-report-patriots-spygate-scandal-2015-9; Don Van Natta, Jr., and Seth Wickersham, "Spygate to Deflategate: Inside What Split the NFL and Patriots Apart," ESPN, September 7, 2015, https://www.espn.com/espn/otl/story/_/id/13533995/split-nfl-new-england-patriots-apart.

55. "Deflategate Timeline: After 544 Days, Tom Brady Gives In," ESPN, September 3, 2015, https://www.espn.com/blog/new-england-patriots/post/_/id/4782561/timeline-of-events-for-deflategate-tom-brady.

56. "Tape of 49ers' Practice Draws $50k Fines for Broncos, McDaniels," NFL.com, November 27, 2010, https://www.nfl.com/news/tape-of-49ers-practice-draws-50k-fines-for-broncos-mcdaniels-09000d5d81c7301a.

57. ESPN.com News Services, "NFL Hammers Saints for Bounties," ESPN, March 21, 2012, https://www.espn.com/nfl/story/_/id/7718136/sean-payton-new-orleans-saints-banned-one-year-bounties; "Saints Bounty Scandal," ESPN, February 26, 2013, http://www.espn.com/nfl/topics/_/page/new-orleans-saints-bounty-scandal.

58. Ryan Wilson, "Gregg Williams on Bountygate: It Was 'Nothing That Hadn't Been Done Before,'" CBS Sports, July 26, 2015, https://www.cbssports.com/nfl/news/gregg-williams-on-bountygate-it-was-nothing-that-hadnt-been-done-before/.

59. Dave Anderson, "Sports of the Times; The Backfire from Buddy Ryan's 'Bounties,'" *New York Times*, November 26, 1989, https://www.nytimes.com/1989/11/26/sports/sports-of-the-times-the-backfire-from-buddy-ryan-s-bounties.html.

60. Dave Birkett, "Ndamukong Suh's 5 Most Memorable Moments at Ford Field," *Detroit Free Press*, December 14, 2014, https://www.freep.com/story/sports/nfl/lions/2014/12/14/ndamukong-suh-stomp/20394297/.

61. Mark Feinsand, "Hinch, Luhnow Are Suspended For '20, Then Let Go," MLB.com, January 13, 2020, https://www.mlb.com/news/astros-sign-stealing-penalty.

62. Chris Bumbaca, "Little League Teams from California to Pennsylvania Ban 'Astros' Nickname After Cheating Scandal," *USA Today*, February 20, 2020, https://www.usatoday.com/story/

sports/mlb/astros/2020/02/20/astros-cheating-little-leagues-begin-banning-use-team-name-2020/4818324002/.

63. Aiden Gonzalez, "Angels Star Mike Trout Rips Astros, Calls for More Punishment," ESPN, February 17, 2020, https://www.espn.com/mlb/story/_/id/28723423/angels-star-mike-trout-rips-astros-calls-more-punishment.

64. Eric Chesterton, "The 'Pine Tar Incident' Remains One of the Craziest Stories Baseball Has Ever Told," MLB, July 24, 2018, https://www.mlb.com/cut4/what-is-the-pine-tar-game-c286938216.

65. "Yankees' Michael Pineda Suspended 10 Games For Using Pine Tar," CBS News, April 24, 2014, https://www.cbsnews.com/news/yankees-michael-pineda-suspended-10-games-for-using-pine-tar/.

66. Matthew Trueblood, "Pitchers Shouldn't Be Allowed to Use Foreign—Period," Fox Sports, May 28, 2015, https://www.foxsports.com/stories/other/pitchers-shouldnt-be-allowed-to-use-foreign-substances-period.

67. Bill Madden, "Baseball's Most Famous 'Foreign Substance' Abuser Gaylord Perry Says Pine Tar is Definitely a 'Performance Enhancing Substance'—Tony La Russa Agrees," *New York Daily News*, April 25, 2014, https://www.nydailynews.com/sports/baseball/madden-gaylord-perry-pine-tar-performance-enhancing-substance-article-1.1767845.

68. Matthew Trueblood, "Pitchers Shouldn't Be Allowed to Use Foreign Substances—Period," Fox Sports, May 28, 2015, https://www.foxsports.com/stories/other/pitchers-shouldnt-be-allowed-to-use-foreign-substances-period.

69. Bernie Pleskoff, "Enforcing New Sticky Substance Guidelines Is Shaking up MLB, but Is There a Solution?" *Forbes*, June 24, 2021, https://www.forbes.com/sites/berniepleskoff/2021/06/24/could-the-mlb-sticky-foreign-substance-controversy-be-a-diversionary-tactic/?sh=5f2fcef44d14.

70. Adam Felder, "Battering the Batter," *Atlantic*, May 5, 2015, https://www.theatlantic.com/entertainment/archive/2015/05/no-more-battering-the-batter/391991/.

71. Lenn Robbins, "A Real Biting Chance-Tyson-Golota Bout a Blueprint for Bedlam," *New York Post*, October 21, 2000, https://nypost.com/2000/10/21/a-real-biting-chance-tyson-golota-bout-a-blueprint-for-bedlam/.

72. "Skater Nancy Kerrigan Attacked," *History*, January 6, 1994, https://www.history.com/this-day-in-history/skater-nancy-kerrigan-attacked.

73. Christine Brennan, "Harding Stripped of Title; Banned for Life," *Washington Post*, July 1, 1994, https://www.washingtonpost.com/wp-srv/sports/longterm/olympics1998/history/timeline/articles/time_070194.htm; Chris Harris, "Tonya Harding Speaks Out About Nancy Kerrigan Attack: 'The Media Had Me Convicted,'" *People*, December 21, 2017, https://people.com/crime/tonya-harding-nancy-kerrigan-media-convicted/; Eudie Pak, "Tonya Harding and Nancy Kerrigan: A Complete Timeline of Kerrigan's Attack and Aftermath," *Biography*, January 4, 2021, https://www.biography.com/news/tonya-harding-nancy-kerrigan-attack-photos.

74. A.J. Perez, "Tonya Harding Admits During ABC Special She Heard Talk of Planned Attack," *USA Today*, January 11, 2018, https://www.usatoday.com/story/sports/olympics/2018/01/11/tonya-harding-admits-prior-knowledge-nancy-kerrigan-attack-during-abc-special/1023907001/; Lauren Effron and Alexa Valiente, "Tonya Harding Says She 'Knew Something Was up' before Infamous 1994 Baton Attack on Nancy Kerrigan," ABC News, January 2, 2018, https://abcnews.go.com/U.S./tonya-harding-knew-infamous-1994-baton-attack-nancy/story?id=52048510.

75. Vi-An Nguyen, "'She Was the Cry Baby': 7 Shocking Quotes from Tonya Harding's Price of Gold Interview," *Parade*, January 17, 2014, https://parade.com/254285/viannguyen/she-was-the-cry-baby-7-shocking-quotes-from-tonya-hardings-price-of-gold-interview/. Directed by Nanette Burstein, ESPN 30 for 30, "The Price of Gold," January 16, 2014, http://www.espn.com/30for30/film/_/page/thepriceofgold.

76. Dan Shaughnessy, "Nancy Kerrigan Has Very Little to Say about 'I Tonya,' *Boston Globe*, January 11, 2018, https://www.bostonglobe.com/sports/2018/01/11/nancy-kerrigan-has-very-little-say-about-tonya/YoRRIf1zA3OFa2SsU616zI/story.html.

77. David Edelstein, "*I, Tonya* Turns Tonya Harding into a Sympathetic Character," *Vulture*, December 8, 2017, https://www.vulture.com/2017/12/i-tonya-turns-tonya-harding-into-a-sympathetic-character.html.

78. Jennifer Latson, "How One Woman Won a Marathon and Barely Broke a Sweat," *Time*, April 21, 2015, https://time.com/3822577/rosie-ruiz-history/.

79. Ron Clements, "Female 'Winner' of St. Louis Marathon Sneaks onto Course Mid-Race; DQ'd from Boston," *Sporting News*, April 16, 2015, https://www.sportingnews.com/us/other-sports/news/female-winner-of-st-louis-marathon-cheater-fraud-kendall-schler-disaqualified-boston-marathon/19xjv6b9olzb610jfncrn22du2.

80. Rick Maese and Kelyn Soong, "I Messed Up; 61-Year-Old Runner Caught Cheating on Marathon Route," *Washington Post*, November 20, 2015, https://www.washingtonpost.com/sports/marine-corps-marathon-bans-runner-who-appears-to-have-cut-corners/2015/11/20/c05ef754-8f41-11e5-934c-a369c80822c2_story.html.

Chapter 3

1. *Murphy v. National Collegiate Athletic Association*, https://www.supremecourt.gov/opinions/17pdf/16-476_dbfi.pdf.

2. Matthew Dziok, "Sports Law—Sports Gambling In a Post-Murphy World: Ensuring Emerging Sports Gambling Laws Adequately Protect the Integrity of College Sports," *Western New England Law Review* 44, no. 2 (2022): 149, https://digitalcommons.law.wne.edu/lawreview/vol44/iss2/2/.

3. Email interview with Walter Cherepinsky, September 19, 2020. Walter Cherepinsky is the founder and operator of WalterFootball.com.

4. Doug Bukowski, "80 Years Ago, He Was Banished from Baseball," *Chicago Tribune*, October 20, 1999, https://www.chicagotribune.com/news/ct-xpm-1999-10-20-9910200163-story.html.

5. Graham Womack, "Will Shoeless Joe Jackson Ever Get in the Baseball Hall of Fame?" *Sporting News*, September 8, 2015, https://www.sportingnews.com/us/mlb/news/shoeless-joe-jackson-baseball-hall-of-fame-reinstatement-rob-manfred-black-sox/1oj4kwwym8irzlwbzstoha7w; Shirley Povich, "Say it Ain't So, Joe," *Washington Post via the Shoeless Joe Jackson Museum and Baseball Library*, April 11, 1941, https://www.shoelessjoejackson.org/media/1941-washington-post.

6. Womack, "Will Shoeless Joe Jackson Ever Get in the Baseball Hall of Fame?"

7. Thomas Sowell, "Protecting the Integrity of Baseball," Human Events, *Washington* 59, no. 10 (March 24, 2003): 24.

8. "MLB Won't Reinstate Shoeless Joe Jackson," ESPN, September 1, 2015, https://www.espn.com/mlb/story/_/id/13555698/mlb-commissioner-rob-manfred-reinstate-shoeless-joe-jackson.

9. "Rule 21. Misconduct," MLB, accessed September 28, 2020, http://content.mlb.com/documents/8/2/2/296982822/Major_League_Rule_21.pdf.

10. "Pete Rose," Britannica, accessed September 28, 2020, https://www.britannica.com/biography/Pete-Rose; James Pilcher, "MLB Commissioner Upholds Pete Rose's Ban from Baseball," *Cincinnati Enquirer*, December 14, 2015, https://www.cincinnati.com/story/sports/mlb/reds/2015/12/14/pete-rose-reinstatement-decision-main/26319063/.

11. Eric Macramalla, "Why Pete Rose Should Never Be Admitted to the Hall of Fame," *Forbes*, March 18, 2015, https://www.forbes.com/sites/ericmacramalla/2015/03/18/despite-being-one-of-the-greatest-of-all-time-pete-rose-should-never-be-admitted-to-hall-of-fame/#698ff9538771.

12. Stephen D. Mosher, "Fielding Our Dreams: Rounding Third in Dyersville," *Sociology of Sport Journal* 8, no. 3 (1991): 272–280, https://journals.humankinetics.com/view/journals/ssj/8/3/article-p272.xml; Mark Harris, "Rose's Fate Uproots Fan's Illusion," *The New York Times*, August 27, 1989.

13. "Leo Durocher," *National Baseball Hall of Fame*, accessed September 29, 2020, https://baseballhall.org/hall-of-famers/durocher-leo.

14. Peter King, "How the NFL First Addressed Players Gambling on Games," NBC Sports, December 2, 2019, https://sports.nbcsports.com/2019/12/02/how-the-nfl-first-addressed-players-gambling-on-games/.

15. John Breech, "Suspended NFL Player Who Got Caught Gambling on the Buccaneers Gets Reinstated After 21-Game Ban," CBS Sports, March 25, 2021, https://www.cbssports.com/nfl/news/suspended-nfl-player-who-got-caught-gambling-on-the-buccaneers-gets-reinstated-after-21-game-ban/; David Purdum, "Raiders, NFL Took Different Paths to Las Vegas," ESPN, September 22, 2020, https://www.espn.com/chalk/story/_/id/29933346/raiders-nfl-took-different-paths-las-vegas; Michael Rothstein, "NFL Suspends Atlanta Falcons WR Calvin Ridley for at Least 2022 Season for Betting on Games," ESPN, March 7, 2022, https://www.espn.com/nfl/story/_/id/33446869/nfl-suspends-atlanta-falcons-wr-calvin-ridley-least-2022-season-betting-games.

16. Philip Conneller, "MLB Signs Historic Sports Betting Deal With MGM Resorts," *Casino.org*, November 28, 2018, https://www.casino.org/news/mlb-signs-historic-sports-betting-deal-with-mgm-resorts/.

17. Jeff Legwold, "Broncos Agree to Multiyear Partnership with FanDuel," ESPN, June 15, 2020, https://www.espn.com/nfl/story/_/id/29314786/broncos-agree-multi-year-partnership-fanduel.

18. Joe Goldstein, "Explosion: 1951 Scandals Threaten College Hoops," ESPN, November 19, 2003, https://www.espn.com/classic/s/basketball_scandals_explosion.html.

19. Maury Allen quotation in Dave Zirin, "The NBA Has to Beat the Odds," *Los Angeles Times*, July 29, 2007, https://www.latimes.com/la-op-zirin29jul29-story.html.

20. Mark Story, "Mark Story: The First Kentucky Wildcats to Go 25–0 Were No Slouches, Either," *Herald-Leader*, February 14, 2015, https://www.kentucky.com/sports/college/kentucky-sports/uk-basketball-men/article44554212.html.

21. Eric Schmitt, "Rick Kuhn Recalls Point Shaving Case," *New York Times*, June 26, 1985, https://www.nytimes.com/1985/06/26/sports/rick-kuhn-recalls-point-shaving-case.html; David Purdum, "The Worst Fix Ever," ESPN, October 3, 2014, https://www.espn.com/espn/chalk/story/_/id/11633538/betting-chronicling-worst-fix-ever-1978-79-bc-point-shaving-scandal; Tom Van Riper, "ESPN Looks Back on Boston College Point Shaving Scandal-and a Player Speaks Out," *Forbes*, October 1, 2014, https://www.forbes.com/sites/tomvanriper/2014/10/01/espn-looks-back-on-boston-college-point-shaving-scandal-and-a-player-speaks-out/?sh=93aeccc26b8f.

22. Malcolm Moran, "Boston College Bans 13 Football Players Over Bets," *New York Times*, November 7, 1996, https://www.nytimes.com/1996/11/07/sports/boston-college-bans-13-football-players-over-bets.html; Associated Press, "Suspended BC Players to Miss Rest Of Season," Associated Press, November 11, 1996, https://apnews.com/article/9e4fe3f0b832bb7ee2e61adc0a7179d5.

23. Associated Press, "Ex-ASU Star Is Going to Prison," *Deseret News*, November 16, 1999, https://www.deseret.com/1999/11/16/19475859/ex-asu-star-is-going-to-prison.

24. Matt O'Connor, "4 Sentenced in Gambling Plot at NU," *Chicago Tribune*, November 25, 1998, https://www.chicagotribune.com/news/ct-xpm-1998-11-25-9811250093-story.html; Nicole Ziegler Dizon, "Ex-Northwestern Teammates Get Jail," Associated Press, November 24, 1998, https://apnews.com/article/65eff5ab88da9003e7f46b7a74d4f02b.

25. Sharon Robb, "Tulane's Return Painful," *South Florida Sun-Sentinel*, March 3, 1990, https://www.sun-sentinel.com/news/fl-xpm-1990-03-03-9001270552-story.html.

26. Jeff Barker, "Former Terps Star McMillan Predicts 'Major Gambling Scandal' Tied to College Sports Betting in the Future," *Baltimore Sun*, January 22, 2019, https://www.baltimoresun.com/politics/bs-md-tom-mcmillen-sports-betting-20190122-story.html.

27. Morgan Moriarty, "You Can't Bet on Rutgers in New Jersey, Which is Funny, but a lot of States Will Have Gambling Laws Like That," *SBNation*, June 14, 2018, https://www.sbnation.com/college-football/2018/6/14/17464124/rutgers-bets-new-jersey-sports-gambling.

28. Pat Milton, "Former NBA Referee Tim Donaghy Pleads Guilty to Felony Charges," *Seattle Times*, August 15, 2007, https://www.seattletimes.com/sports/nba/former-nba-referee-tim-donaghy-pleads-guilty-to-felony-charges/; "Disgraced NBA Ref Gets 15 Months in Betting Scam," CBC Sports, July 29, 2008, https://www.cbc.ca/sports/basketball/disgraced-nba-ref-gets-15-months-in-betting-scam-1.752955; Scott Eden, "From the Archives: How Former Ref Tim Donaghy Conspired to Fix NBA Games," ESPN, July 9, 2020, https://www.espn.com/nba/story/_/id/25980368/how-former-ref-tim-donaghy-conspired-fix-nba-games; Associated Press, "Donaghy Bet on Games He Worked In '06–07 Season, Feds Say," ESPN, May 17, 2008, https://www.espn.com/nba/news/story?id=3400551.

29. Ashley Branca, "Ex-NBA Ref Tim Donaghy: 'Organized Crime Will Always Have a Hand in Sports,'" *The Guardian*, May 22, 2015, https://www.theguardian.com/sport/2015/may/22/ex-nba-ref-tim-donaghy-organized-will-always-have-a-hand-in-sports.

30. Kate Snow, "Senators to Propose Ban on Gambling on Amateur Sports," CNN, January 26, 2000, https://www.cnn.com/2000/ALLPOLITICS/stories/01/26/college.gambling/index.html.

31. Jeffrey L. Derevensky and Tom Paskus, "Mind, Body, and Sport: Gambling among Student-Athletes," NCAA, accessed October 3, 2020, https://www.ncaa.org/sport-science-institute/mind-body-and-sport-gambling-among-student-athletes.

32. S. Johnson and C. McCaslin, *UO Student Gambling Survey* (Eugene, OR: Steve Johnson & Associates, June 2010), accessed October 5, 2020, https://preventionlane.org/college-student-gambling-survey (link no longer available).

33. "Risk Education for Athletes Program," National Council on Problem Gambling, accessed October 6, 2020, https://www.ncpgambling.org/programs-resources/programs/risk-education-for-athletes/.

34. "Gambling on College Campuses," National Center for Responsible Gaming, accessed October 6, 2020, https://www.icrg.org/sites/default/files/oec/pdfs/ncrg_fact_sheet_gambling_college_campuses.pdf.

35. Elijah McKown, "The New College Student Craze: Sports Gambling," *State News*, February 20, 2020, https://statenews.com/article/2020/02/sports-gambling-and-college-students?ct=content_open&cv=cbox_latest.

36. "Compulsive Gambling," Mayo Clinic, accessed October 7, 2020, https://www.mayoclinic.org/diseases-conditions/compulsive-gambling/symptoms-causes/syc-20355178.

37. Dana Hunsinger Benbow, "'It's Sad and It's Tragic': Ex-Colts QB Art Schlichter's life behind bars," *Indianapolis Star*, August 6, 2020, https://www.indystar.com/story/sports/nfl/colts/2020/08/06/art-schlichter-ex-colts-qb-remains-jail-after-ticket-scheme/2580251001/; Associated Press, "Art Schlichter Sentenced to 11 Years," ESPN, May 4, 2012, https://www.espn.com/college-football/story/_/id/7890630/ex-ohio-state-buckeyes-indianapolis-colts-qb-art-schlichter-gets-11-years-prison; Art Schlichter and Jeff Snook, *Busted: The Rise and Fall of Art Schlichter* (Wilmington, OH: Orange Frazer Press, 2009).

38. Mike Robinson, "Designed to Deceive: How Gambling Distorts Reality and Hooks Your Brain," *Conversation*, August 13, 2018, https://theconversation.com/designed-to-deceive-how-gambling-distorts-reality-and-hooks-your-brain-91052.

39. Email interview with Dr. Carolyn E. Hawley, June 15, 2021. Dr. Carolyn E. Hawley is an associate professor in the Department of Rehabilitation Counseling at Virginia Commonwealth University.

40. Josh Peter, "Sports Betting Ruling Will Lead To Costly Rise in Gambling Addiction, Experts Warn," *USA Today*, May 14, 2018, https://www.usatoday.com/story/sports/2018/05/14/sports-betting-rise-gambling-addiction/608989002/.

Chapter 4

1. Email interview with Chris Goldberg, October 11, 2020. Chris Goldberg is the founder and operator of PhillyLacrosse.com.

2. Michael Popke/AB Staff, "As Media Coverage Increases, So Can Scrutiny of Your Programs," *Athletic Business*, February 28, 2001, https://www.athleticbusiness.com/sports-media/as-media-coverage-increases-so-can-scrutiny-of-your-programs.html.

3. Email interview with Aaron Carter, April 30, 2021. Aaron Carter is a *Philadelphia Inquirer* sports reporter.

4. Dick Weiss, "Oklahoma State Coach Mike Gundy Berates Local Columnist," *New York Daily News*, September 24, 2007, https://www.nydailynews.com/sports/more-sports/oklahoma-state-coach-mike-gundy-berates-local-columnist-article-1.243255.

5. Thayer Evans, "Coach's Tirade a Boon for Oklahoma State," *New York Times*, October 19, 2007, https://www.nytimes.com/2007/10/19/sports/ncaafootball/19gundy.html.

6. Rick Brown, "Iowa Coach Fran McCaffery Angry with Dan Dakich," *Des Moines Register*, January 22, 2015, https://www.indystar.com/story/sports/college/2015/01/22/iowa-coach-fran-mccaffery-angry-dan-dakich/22173103/.

7. Goldberg, email interview.

8. Ahiza Garcia, "Meet the First Woman to Call an NFL Game in 30 Years," CNN Business, September 11, 2017, https://money.cnn.com/2017/09/11/media/beth-mowins-nfl-espn-gayle-sierens/index.html; "Historic All-Women Broadcast Team Calls Baltimore Orioles-Tampa Bay Rays for MLB Game of the Week On YouTube," ESPN, July 20, 2021, https://www.espn.com/mlb/story/_/id/31849568/historic-all-women-broadcast-team-call-baltimore-orioles-tampa-bay-rays-mlb-game-week-youtube.

9. Larry Atkins, "It's Time to Have Female Play-By-Play Announcers in the NFL," *Huffington Post*, September 4, 2012, https://www.huffpost.com/entry/its-time-to-have-female-p_b_1834186; Vinnie Iyer, "NFL Announcers 2022: A Complete Guide to New Broadcast Teams at ESPN, FOX, NBC, CBS, and Amazon," *Sporting News*, September 15, 2022, https://www.sportingnews.com/us/nfl/news/nfl-announcers-2022-espn-fox-nbc-cbs-amazon/zlhdymf2atxg7xhceckvjwb4.

10. "Cam: 'Funny to Hear a Female Talk About Routes,'" NFL.com, October 4, 2017, https://www.nfl.com/news/cam-funny-to-hear-a-female-talk-about-routes-0ap3000000856806; Daniel Rapaport, "Cam Newton: It's Funny to Hear a Female Talk About Routes," *Sports Illustrated*, October 4, 2017, https://www.si.com/nfl/2017/10/04/cam-newton-sexist-comment-female-reporter-routes-1.

11. David Newton, "Cam Newton Apologizes for Response to Female Reporter," ESPN, October 5, 2017, https://www.espn.com/nfl/story/_/id/20928510/cam-newton-carolina-panthers-apologizes-response-female-reporter; Ron Clements, "Cam Newton Apologizes for 'Degrading and Disrespectful' Word Choice," *Sporting News*, October 5, 2017, https://www.sportingnews.com/us/nfl/news/cam-newton-apologizes-degrading-and-disrespectful-word-choice-jourdan-rodrigue/l4dq12ecp9a1af3d6c5jxcxpff.

12. Email interview with Leslie Gudel, May 26, 2021. Leslie Gudel is a journalist, reporter, entrepreneur, and chief operating officer at Elevate Sports & Media.

13. Gudel, email interview.

14. "Joe Namath Fast Facts," CNN, May 29, 2013, https://www.cnn.com/2013/05/29/us/joe-namath-fast-facts/index.html.

15. Jane McManus, "Sainz Incident Helped Jets Grow Up," ESPN, September 10, 2013, https://www.espn.com/new-york/columns/nfl/story/_/id/9658974/new-york-jets-ines-sainz-incident-helped-spark-change-jets-locker-room; CBS Interactive Staff, "Ines Sainz, TV Reporter, Allegedly Harassed by Jets," CBS News, September 13, 2010, https://www.cbsnews.com/news/ines-sainz-tv-reporter-allegedly-harassed-by-jets/.

16. Meghan Keneally, "Erin Andrews Awarded $55 Million in Lawsuit," ABC News, March 7, 2016, https://abcnews.go.com/U.S./erin-andrews-jury-set-deliberate-75-million-lawsuit/story?id=37460110; Dylan Byers, "Erin Andrews Settles Stalker Lawsuit with Hotel," CNN Business, April 25, 2016, https://money.cnn.com/2016/04/25/media/erin-andrews-hotel-settlement/.

17. Emma Baccellieri, "The Everlasting Legacy of Melissa Ludtke, Who Dared to Join the Boys Club of the Baseball Press," *Sports Illustrated*, September 28, 2018, https://www.si.com/mlb/2018/09/28/melissa-ludtke-lawsuit-anniversary; Leigh Montville, "But Is She Serious?" *Boston Globe*, October 1, 1978; Melissa Ludtke, "The Fight for Women Sports Reporters' Access to Locker Rooms Is History—Or Is It?" ESPN.com, October 11, 2017, https://www.espn.com/espnw/voices/story/_/id/20988967/the-fight-women-sports-reporters-access-locker-rooms-history-it.

18. Gudel, email interview.

19. Gudel, email interview.

20. Gayle Jansen Brisbane, Patrick Ferrucci, and Edson Tandoc, "Side-By-Side Sports Reporters: A Between-Subjects Experiment of the Effect of Gender in Reporting on the NFL," *Communication & Sport* 11, no. 1 (2021), https://journals.sagepub.com/doi/abs/10.1177/2167479521995462; Laurence Etling and Raymond Young, "Sexism and the Authoritativeness of Female Sportscasters," *Communication Research Reports* 24, no. 2 (2007): 121–130, https://www.tandfonline.com/doi/abs/10.1080/08824090701304816; Hans C. Schmidt, "'Still a Boys club': Perspectives on Female Sports and Sports Reporters in University Student Newspapers," *Qualitative Research Reports in Communication* 16, no. 1 (2015): 65–74, https://www.tandfonline.com/doi/abs/10.1080/17459435.2015.1086422; Hans C. Schmidt, "Forgotten Athletes and Token Reporters: Analyzing the Gender Bias in Sports Journalism," *Atlantic Journal of Communication* 26, no. 1 (2018): 59–74, https://www.tandfonline.com/doi/abs/10.1080/15456870.2018.1398014.

21. Johnny Smith and Randy Roberts, "Why Are Sportswriters Whitewashing Baseball's Dark Secrets," *Daily Beast*, March 29, 2018, https://www.thedailybeast.com/why-are-sportswriters-whitewashing-baseballs-dark-secrets.

22. Ed Sherman, "Reporting on Rumors and

the Personal Lives of Athletes," *Poynter*, March 12, 2015, https://www.poynter.org/reporting-editing/2015/reporting-on-rumors-and-the-personal-lives-of-athletes/.

23. Susan Reimer, "Newspaper Defends Its Inquiry into Arthur Ashe's Health USA Today Sports Chief Says It's News When Public Figure Has Fatal Illness," *Baltimore Sun*, April 9, 1992, https://www.baltimoresun.com/news/bs-xpm-1992-04-09-1992100129-story.html; Richard Cohen, "Did We Have to Know?" *Washington Post*, April 10, 1992, https://www.washingtonpost.com/archive/opinions/1992/04/10/did-we-have-to-know/3ee54b5d-88b5-4c3a-b3dc-fc21832d0575/.

24. Mike Missanelli, email interview, January 3, 2021. Mike Missanelli is a podcaster, former *Philadelphia Inquirer* sports reporter and former sports talk radio host.

25. Carter, email interview.

26. John Kunda, "Silent Even in Farewell," *The Morning Call*, June 26, 1986, https://www.mcall.com/news/mc-xpm-1986-06-26-2519222-story.html.

27. Rob Maaddi, "Marshawn Lynch Talks about Why He Doesn't Talk to the Media," Associated Press/*USA Today*, January 29, 2015, https://www.usatoday.com/story/sports/nfl/2015/01/29/marshawn-lynch-talks-about-why-he-doesnt-talk-to-the-media/22533561/; Rana Cash, "Marshawn Lynch Finally Speaks, Expresses Frustration," *Sporting News*, June 2, 2015, https://www.sportingnews.com/au/nfl/news/marshawn-lynch-super-bowl-speaks-frustrated-interview-media-seahawks-patriots/77ny96j82o8z1usqttyvqj783; Polly Mosendz, "The Marshawn Chronicles: Lynch Speaks! Tells Media to Go Away," *Newsweek*, January 29, 2015, https://www.newsweek.com/marshawn-lynch-speaks-tells-media-go-away-303501.

28. Jacob Lauing, "Here's Why Fans Hate Fox Broadcaster Joe Buck So Much," *Mashable*, January 14, 2017, https://mashable.com/2017/01/14/joe-buck-packers-cowboys/; Andrew Dorff, "Get Troy Aikman and Joe Buck Banned From Announcing Green Bay Packer's Games," Change.org, https://www.change.org/p/nfl-get-troy-aikman-and-joe-buck-banned-from-announcing-green-bay-packer-s-games.

29. Al Seracevic, "Fox Announcer Buck Says He Isn't Biased," *San Francisco Chronicle/SFGate*, October 22, 2012, https://www.sfgate.com/giants/article/Fox-announcer-Buck-says-he-isn-t-biased-3972581.php.

30. Email interview with Ari Bluestein, Sportscaster and co-founder and CEO of the Sports Fan Base Network, September 15, 2020.

31. Associated Press, "List of Incidents Involving Bob Knight," *Houston Chronicle*, August 10, 2011, https://www.chron.com/sports/college-basketball-men/article/List-of-incidents-involving-Bob-Knight-1849372.php; "Bob Knight Incidents," Associated Press, March 11, 1998, https://apnews.com/article/84958f0dcacbe77ce73388ff4402441f.

32. Steve Gardner, "Sports Figures vs. Reporters: Top Confrontations, from Billy Martin To Russell Westbrook," *USA Today*, June 25, 2019, https://www.usatoday.com/story/sports/2019/06/25/athletes-vs-reporters-confrontations-mets-callaway-billy-martin-russell-westbrook/1560088001/.

33. Goldberg, email interview.

34. Bluestein, email interview.

35. Alex Ben Block, "Why Sports Radio Is Hitting It Out of the Park (Analysis)," *Hollywood Reporter*, April 12, 2013, https://www.hollywoodreporter.com/news/why-sports-radio-is-hitting-435666.

36. Macnow, email interview.

37. Macnow, email interview.

38. "Calgary Radio Host Suspended After Rider 'Death' Comment," CBC News, November 9, 2012, https://www.cbc.ca/news/canada/calgary/calgary-radio-host-suspended-after-rider-death-comment-1.1207160.

39. ESPN.com News Services, "Atlanta Radio Program Hosts Fired," ESPN, June 18, 2013, https://www.espn.com/nfl/story/_/id/9398057/atlanta-radio-hosts-fired-mocking-former-nfl-player-lou-gehrig-disease.

40. Ledger.com, "WDAE Fires Dan Sileo After He Calls NFL Players 'Monkeys,'" *Herald-Tribune*, March 14, 2012, https://www.heraldtribune.com/article/LK/20120314/News/605197758/SH; Scott Bordow, "Fox Sports 910 Hire Dan Sileo Has Repeatedly Been Fired for Racist and Sexist Comments," The Athletic, August 29, 2019, https://theathletic.com/1172066/2019/08/29/fox-sports-910-hire-dan-sileo-has-repeatedly-been-fired-for-racist-and-sexist-comments/.

41. Kendall Baker, "Dan Le Batard Denounces Trump, Rips ESPN's No-Politics Policy," *Axios*, July 19, 2019, https://www.axios.com/dan-le-batard-donald-trump-ilhan-omar-espn-161fdd6b-3147-410a-9c6a-8abad28b5053.html.

42. Tyler Lauletta, "ESPN's Dan Le Batard Rips into Racist 'Send Her Back' Chants during Trump Rally, Breaking from Company's Apolitical Stance," *Business Insider*, July 19, 2019, https://www.businessinsider.com/video-dan-le-batard-trump-rally-nick-wright-espn-2019-7.

43. James Andrew Miller, "James Andrew Miller: Jemele Hill Waves Goodbye to ESPN And Hello to 'Places Where Discomfort Is OK,'" *Hollywood Reporter*, October 1, 2018, https://www.hollywoodreporter.com/news/jemele-hill-interview-leaving-espn-joining-atlantic-1148171; Rob Tornoe, "Trump Goes after Suspended ESPN Host Jemele Hill and Threatens The NFL," *Philadelphia Inquirer*, October 10, 2017, https://www.inquirer.com/philly/news/politics/presidential/trump-jemele-hill-espn-nfl-suspended-20171010.html; Pat Eaton-Robb, "ESPN Suspends Anchor Jemele Hill for Breaking Social Media Rules," Associated Press (*Press Democrat*), October 10, 2017, https://www.pressdemocrat.com/article/sports/espn-suspends-anchor-jemele-hill-for-breaking-social-media-rules/.

44. Missanelli, email interview, January 3, 2021.

45. "Vince Carter Addresses the Negative Effects of Social Media on Athletes/OTL," ESPN, January 17, 2020, https://www.youtube.com/watch?v=1cX5_2YadU4.

46. Josh Planos, "Student Athletes Will Soon Be Social Media Influencers. And One College Program Is Helping Them Do It," *FiveThirty Eight*, June 8, 2020, https://fivethirtyeight.com/features/student-athletes-will-soon-be-social-media-influencers-and-one-college-program-is-helping-them-do-it/.

47. Carter, email interview.

Chapter 5

1. Emily Sullivan, "Laura Ingraham Told LeBron James to Shut Up and Dribble; He Went to the Hoop," NPR, February 19, 2018, https://www.npr.org/sections/thetwo-way/2018/02/19/587097707/laura-ingraham-told-lebron-james-to-shutup-and-dribble-he-went-to-the-hoop.

2. Yannick Kluch, "'My Story Is My Activism!':(Re-) Definitions of Social Justice Activism Among Collegiate Athlete Activists." *Communication & Sport* 8, no. 4–5 (2020): 566–590, https://doi.org/10.1177/2167479519897288.

3. Andrew Wolfson, "Muhammad Ali Lost Everything in Opposing the Vietnam War. But in 1968, He Triumphed," *Louisville [KY] Courier Journal (USA Today)*, February 19, 2018, https://www.usatoday.com/story/news/2018/02/19/1968-project-muhammad-ali-vietnam-war/334759002/.

4. Bill Chappell, "'A World Without Muhammad Ali': Reactions to a Champion's Death," NPR, June 4, 2016, https://www.npr.org/sections/thetwo-way/2016/06/04/480748285/a-world-without-muhammad-ali-reactions-to-a-champions-death; Arnie Seipel, "READ: President Obama's Remembrance of Muhammad Ali," NPR, June 4, 2016, https://www.npr.org/2016/06/04/480743833/read-president-obamas-remembrance-of-muhammad-ali.

5. Tim Layden, "Fists of Fury," *Sports Illustrated*, October 3, 2018, https://www.si.com/olympics/2018/10/03/john-carlos-tommie-smith-1968-olympics-black-power-salute.

6. Tribune Staff Report, "Track Legends John Carlos and Tommie Smith to Be Inducted into Olympic Hall of Fame," *Philadelphia Tribune*, October 2, 2019, https://www.phillytrib.com/track-legends-john-carlos-and-tommie-smith-to-be-inducted-into-olympic-hall-of-fame/article_772febc7-2a31-5bde-9f6e-dbc11210a0a3.html.

7. David Davis, "Olympic Athletes Who Took a Stand," *Smithsonian Magazine*, August 2008, https://www.smithsonianmag.com/articles/olympic-athletes-who-took-a-stand-593920/; Douglas Hartmann, *Race, Culture, and the Revolt of the Black Athlete: The 1968 Olympic Protests and Their Aftermath* (Chicago: University of Chicago Press, 2004).

8. Emma Thomasson, "No Regrets for Fist-Raising Olympic Champion Sprinter 50 Years On," Reuters, September 19, 2018, https://www.reuters.com/article/csports-us-athletics-activism-smith-idCAKCN1LZ1MW-OCASP; Frank Pingue, "On This Day: Born June 6, 1944: Tommie Smith, American Sprinter," Reuters, June 5, 2020, https://www.reuters.com/article/sport-anniversary-smith-idINKBN23C0P0.

9. Dr. Ketra Armstrong, University of Michigan sport management professor, email interview, August 17, 2021.

10. Jenna West, "USOPC Will Not Sanction Athletes for Peaceful Social Justice Protests at Olympics," *Sports Illustrated*, December 10, 2020, https://www.si.com/olympics/2020/12/10/olympics-peaceful-social-justice-protests-not-sanctioned-usopc; Graham Dunbar, "IOC Gives Athletes More Scope for Protest at Tokyo Olympics," Associated Press, July 2, 2021, https://apnews.com/article/tokyo-olympic-games-2020-tokyo-olympics-race-and-ethnicity-sports-3f8d420b7e94bbafa037d22327efb38b; Joshua Barajas, "'Sport is Political.' How Athletes Are Keeping Human Rights Center Stage at the Olympics," PBS, August 4, 2021, https://www.pbs.org/newshour/arts/sport-is-political-how-athletes-are-keeping-human-rights-center-stage-at-the-olympics; Sakura Murakami, "Fencing-U.S. Fencer Imboden Says × Mark on Hand Was Protest against Olympic Charter Rule," Reuters, August 4, 2021, https://www.reuters.com/lifestyle/sports/fencing-us-fencer-imboden-says-x-mark-hand-was-protest-against-olympic-charter-2021-08-04/; Ben Church, "'I'm Just Here to Represent,' Says U.S. Athlete Gwen Berry after Raising Her Fist at Tokyo 2020," CNN, August 3, 2021, https://www.cnn.com/2021/08/03/sport/gwen-berry-fist-social-justice-tokyo-spt-intl/index.html.

11. WNYC Newsroom, "When Black Athletes Took a Stand (Part 2)," WNYC, November 6, 2018, https://www.wnyc.org/story/when-black-athletes-took-stand-part-2/; Jelani Scott, "Jim Brown Praises Harmony Between Black, White Athletes in Fight Against Racism," NFL.com, June 26, 2020, https://www.nfl.com/news/jim-brown-praises-harmony-between-black-white-athletes-in-fight-against-racism; Raymond Arsenault, "Arthur Ashe's Real Legacy Was His Activism, Not His Tennis," *The Guardian*, September 9, 2018, https://www.theguardian.com/sport/2018/sep/09/arthur-ashe-legacy-activism-tennis; Sam Dodge, "Arthur Ashe Courage Recipient Is Celtics Legend Bill Russell," *Heavy*, July 10, 2019, https://heavy.com/sports/2019/07/arthur-ashe-courage-award-bill-russell/; Max Resetar, "BMH 2019: Bill Russell is a Basketball and Civil Rights Champion," *SLAM*, February 8, 2019, https://www.slamonline.com/bhm2019/bhm-bill-russell/.

12. Jamiles Lartey, "The 'Ali Summit': A Turning Point in Sports' Fight against Injustice," *The Guardian*, October 23, 2017, https://www.theguardian.com/sport/2017/oct/23/colin-

kaepernick-muhammad-ali-summit-sports-activism.

13. Bruce Schreiner, "Ali, Jim Brown Reunite Years After Ali's Legal Fight," Associated Press/*Detroit News*, September 27, 2014, https://www.detroitnews.com/story/sports/2014/09/27/ali-vietnam-reunion/16352069/.

14. Jack Holmes, "Stephen A. Smith Has Always Been Stephen A. Smith," *Esquire*, September 26, 2022, https://www.esquire.com/sports/a41356518/stephen-a-smith-know-mercy-podcast-interview/; Simone Carter, "Stephen A. Smith Says Colin Kaepernick Was 'Blackballed,' Violated No Laws," *Newsweek*, September 26, 2022, https://www.newsweek.com/espn-stephen-smith-colin-kaepernick-blackballed-comments-1746416.

15. Brian Stelter, "With 'Son of a Bitch' Comments, Trump Tried to Divide NFL and Its Players," CNN Business, September 23, 2017, https://money.cnn.com/2017/09/23/media/donald-trump-nfl-protest-backlash/index.html; USA Today Sports, Contributing: Nashville Tennessean, Alysha Tsuji, "NFL Players Union Vows Donald Trump Comments Will Not Deter Stand on Protests, Safety," *USA Today*, September 23, 2017, https://www.usatoday.com/story/sports/nfl/2017/09/23/donald-trump-nfl-players-union/696109001/.

16. My Northwest Staff, "Donald Trump on Colin Kaepernick: He Should Find Another Country," KIRO Radio (*Dori Monson Show*), August 29, 2016, https://mynorthwest.com/379820/donald-trump-on-colin-kaepernick-he-should-find-another-country/.

17. A.J. Perez, "Report: Colin Kaepernick, Eric Reid Got Less than $10 Million in NFL Collusion Settlement," *USA Today*, March 21, 2019, https://www.usatoday.com/story/sports/nfl/2019/03/21/colin-kaepernick-eric-reid-nfl-collusion-settlement/3237678002/.

18. Emmanuel Acho, "National Anthem Protests Pt. 1 ft. Roger Goodell/Uncomfortable Conversations with a Black Man Ep 8," August 23, 2020, https://www.youtube.com/watch?v=ljgkEcc4B1k; Aris Folley, "NFL's Goodell to Kaepernick on Protesting: 'I Wish We Had Listened Earlier," *The Hill*, August 23, 2020, https://thehill.com/blogs/in-the-know/in-the-know/513320-nfls-goodell-to-kaepernick-on-protesting-i-wish-we-had-listened; Jace Evans, "Saints QB Drew Brees Expounds on Protest Apology: 'I Am sorry. And I Will Do Better,'" *USA Today*, June 4, 2020, https://www.usatoday.com/story/sports/nfl/saints/2020/06/04/drew-brees-instagram-apology-national-anthem-protests/3150362001/.

19. *All Things Considered*, "The Veteran and NFL Player Who Advised Kaepernick to Take a Knee," NPR, September 9, 2018, https://www.npr.org/2018/09/09/646115651/the-veteran-and-nfl-player-who-advised-kaepernick-to-take-a-knee%C2%A0%C2%A0%C2%A0%C2%A0.

20. Eric Reid, "Eric Reid: Why Colin Kaepernick and I Decided to Take a Knee," *New York Times*, September 25, 2017, https://www.nytimes.com/2017/09/25/opinion/colin-kaepernick-football-protests.html?_r=0&referer=https://www.google.com/%C2%A0%C2%A0%C2%A0%C2%A0%C2%A0%C2%A0%C2%A0.

21. Steve Wyche, "Colin Kaepernick Explains Why He Sat during National Anthem," NFL.com, August 27, 2016, https://www.nfl.com/news/colin-kaepernick-explains-why-he-sat-during-national-anthem-0ap3000000691077.

22. Christopher C. Towler, Nyron N. Crawford, and Robert A. Bennett, "Shut up and Play: Black Athletes, Protest Politics, and Black Political Action," *Perspectives on Politics* 18, no. 1 (2020): 111–127, https://doi.org/10.1017/S1537592719002597.

23. Cork Gaines, "Championship Teams Visiting the White House Has Turned into a Mess—Here Is How Trump and the Teams Have Wrecked the Tradition," *Business Insider*, June 26, 2019, https://www.businessinsider.com/championship-teams-trump-white-house-2019-4.

24. Deena Zaru, "Why Athletes Are Getting More Political in the Age of Trump," CNN, August 14, 2017, https://www.cnn.com/2017/02/10/politics/donald-trump-colin-kaepernick-athletes-activism-sports/index.html.

25. Tim Bontemps, "Michael Jordan Stands Firm on 'Republicans Buy Sneakers, Too' Quote, Says It Was Made in Jest," ABC News (ESPN), May 3, 2020, https://abcnews.go.com/Sports/michael-jordan-stands-firm-republicans-buy-sneakers-quote/story?id=70483289; Directed by Jason Hehir, "The Last Dance," ESPN, April 19, 2020, https://www.espn.com/watch/catalog/2806434b-1deb-4c5c-aae0-04b1ab8eebf7/the-last-dance/_/bucketId/29894; https://www.espn.com/watch/catalog/2806434b-1deb-4c5c-aae0-04b1ab8eebf7/the-last-dance/_/bucketId/29894; AJ Neuharth-Keusch, "Michael Jordan Donating $2 Million to Help Address Police-Related Shootings," *USA Today*, July 25, 2016, https://www.usatoday.com/story/sports/nba/2016/07/25/michael-jordan-speaks-out-recent-shootings-police-violence/87527386/.

26. K.C. Johnson, "Hodges: Right Now, Playing Basketball Isn't Getting It Done," NBC Sports Chicago, August 26, 2020, https://www.nbcsports.com/chicago/bulls/why-former-bulls-guard-craig-hodges-proud-boycotts-across-american-sports.

27. Christopher Clarey, "In 2017, Many Athletes Found Their Voices," *New York Times*, December 20, 2017, https://www.nytimes.com/2017/12/20/sports/year-sports-protests.html.

28. ESPN.com News Services, "Heat Don Hoodies after Teen's Death," ESPN, March 23, 2012, https://www.espn.com/nba/truehoop/miamiheat/story/_/id/7728618/miami-heat-don-hoodies-response-death-teen-trayvon-martin; Greg Botelho and Holly Yan, "George Zimmerman Found Not Guilty of Murder in Trayvon Martin's Death," CNN, July 13, 2013, https://www.cnn.com/2013/07/13/justice/zimmerman-trial/index.html.

29. Associated Press, "Appeals Court Upholds $2 Billion Sale of Clippers," ESPN, November 16, 2015, https://www.espn.com/nba/story/_/id/14147968/donald-sterling-loses-appeal-reverse-2-billion-sale-los-angeles-clippers.

30. Ross Dellenger, "How 18 Words on Twitter Helped Change a Flag and Unlocked the Power of the College Athlete," *Sports Illustrated*, September 23, 2020, https://www.si.com/college/2020/09/23/kylin-hill-mississippi-state-flag-daily-cover; https://twitter.com/H_Kylin/status/1275128689638936581.

31. Dan Bernstein, "Chuba Hubbard Threatens Oklahoma State Holdout in Response To 'Insensitive' Mike Gundy Photo," *Sporting News*, June 15, 2020, https://www.sportingnews.com/us/ncaa-football/news/chuba-hubbard-mike-gundy-photo-oklahoma-state/197j6p7nf1zm718xbtmazfunqk.

32. Yannick Kluch, "'My Story Is My Activism!':(Re-) Definitions of Social Justice Activism Among Collegiate Athlete Activists," *Communication & Sport* 8, no. 4–5 (2020): 566–590, https://doi.org/10.1177/2167479519897288.

33. Anna North, "Why the President Is Feuding with Megan Rapinoe, Star of the U.S. Women's Soccer Team," *Vox*, July 3, 2019, https://www.vox.com/identities/2019/7/3/20680073/megan-rapinoe-trump-world-cup-soccer.

34. "Megan Rapinoe Refuses to Back Down over Donald Trump and White House," *The Guardian*, June 27, 2019, https://www.theguardian.com/football/2019/jun/27/megan-rapinoe-donald-trump-white-house.

35. Matt Lavietes, "Soccer Star Megan Rapinoe Receives Presidential Medal of Freedom," NBC News, July 7, 2022, https://www.nbcnews.com/nbc-out/nbc-out-proud/soccer-star-megan-rapinoe-receives-presidential-medal-freedom-rcna37141.

36. Thomas Schlarp, "Why Doesn't Megan Rapinoe Sing the National Anthem? A Timeline of the USWNT Star's Protests," *Sporting News*, July 7, 2019, https://www.sportingnews.com/us/soccer/news/megan-rapinoe-national-anthem-uswnt-protests-timeline/3e29b7c112yl1u1xts3b4mkgb.

37. Associated Press, "Members of U.S. Women Soccer National Team Appeal Court Decision Against Equal Pay," *Chicago Tribune*, April 14, 2021, https://chicago.suntimes.com/soccer/2021/4/14/22384417/us-women-soccer-national-team-appeal-court-decision-against-equal-pay.

38. Jeff Carlisle, "USWNT, U.S. Soccer Federation Settle Equal Pay Lawsuit for $24 million," ESPN, February 22, 2022, https://www.espn.com/soccer/united-states-usaw/story/4599482/uswntus-soccer-federation-settle-equal-pay-lawsuit-for-$24-million.

39. "Navratilova, Martina," Encyclopedia.com, May 29, 2018, accessed May 22, 2021, https://www.encyclopedia.com/people/sports-and-games/sports-biographies/martina-navratilova; Knight Ridder/Tribune, "Navratilova Serves up Gay Card," *Chicago Tribune*, October 15, 1995, https://www.chicagotribune.com/news/ct-xpm-1995-10-15-9510150142-story.html; "Battle of the Sexes Film Discussion Guide," Women's Sports Foundation, accessed May 22, 2021, https://www.womenssportsfoundation.org/wp-content/uploads/2018/01/bots-discussion-guide-final-web.pdf.

40. Chris Bumbaca, "Maya Moore Marries Jonathan Irons, Man She Helped Free from Prison This Year," *USA Today*, September 16, 2020, https://www.usatoday.com/story/sports/wnba/2020/09/16/maya-moore-marries-jonathan-irons/5815133002/.

41. Sean Hurd, "Maya Moore, the Game-Changer: 'This is the Epitome of Using Your Platform,'" *Undefeated*, July 2, 2020, https://theundefeated.com/features/maya-moore-game-changer-jonathan-irons-epitome-of-using-your-platform/.

42. Evan Andrews, "How Ping-Pong Diplomacy Thawed the Cold War," *History*, April 8, 2016, https://www.history.com/news/ping-pong-diplomacy.

43. Robert Hormats, "Fifty Years On, We Could Learn Still from U.S.-China 'Ping Pong Diplomacy,'" *The Hill*, January 12, 2021, https://thehill.com/opinion/national-security/533073-fifty-years-on-we-could-learn-still-from-us-china-ping-pong.

44. Matt Spetalnick, "U.S. Nixes Deal for Major League Baseball to Sign Cuban Players," Reuters, April 8, 2019, https://www.reuters.com/article/us-cuba-usa-baseball/u-s-nixes-deal-for-major-league-baseball-to-sign-cuban-players-idUSKCN1RK27U.

45. Cesar Brioso, "Opinion: Trump's Scuttling of MLB-Cuba Deal Means Defections, Human Trafficking Will Continue," *USA Today*, April 9, 2019, https://www.usatoday.com/story/sports/mlb/2019/04/09/mlb-cuba-defection-human-trafficking/3410593002/; Franco Ordoñez, "Trump Will Play Ball with MLB on Cuban Players If League Helps with Venezuela," NPR, June 12, 2019, https://www.npr.org/2019/06/12/731966442/trump-will-play-ball-with-mlb-on-cuban-players-if-league-helps-with-venezuela.

46. "List of Cuban Defectors," *Baseball-Reference*, accessed May 14, 2021, https://www.baseball-reference.com/bullpen/List_of_Cuban_Defectors; SI Staff, "Baseball's Notable Cuban Defectors," *Sports Illustrated*, January 11, 2010, https://www.si.com/mlb/2010/01/11/11notable-cuban-defectors-#gid=ci02558a7d00422781&pid=jos-fernndez.

47. Daniel Trotta and Sarah Marsh, "Cuban Deal With MLB Allows Players to Sign without Defecting," Reuters, December 19, 2018, https://www.reuters.com/article/csports-us-usa-cuba-baseball-idCAKCN1OI2L5-OCASP.

48. "MLB, MLBPA Reach Deal With Cuban Federation," MLB.com, December 19, 2018, https://www.mlb.com/news/mlb-announces-deal-with-cuban-federation-c302036110.

49. Steve Gardner, "Mets, Marlins Walk off the Field after 42-Second Moment of Silence Honoring Jackie Robinson," *USA Today*, August 27, 2020, https://www.usatoday.com/story/sports/mlb/2020/08/27/mets-marlins-protest-jackie-robinson-mlb/5651142002/.

50. Tim Bontemps, "NBA, NBPA Announce Playoffs to Resume Saturday, New Initiatives," ESPN, August 28, 2020, https://www.espn.com/nba/story/_/id/29759939/nba-announces-playoffs-resume-saturday.

51. Emma Steinberg, "These Stadiums Are Serving as Polling Sites for the 2020 General Election," *Sports Illustrated*, October 5, 2020, https://www.si.com/sports-illustrated/2020/10/05/sports-stadiums-arenas-polling-centers-election-list.

52. Michael Lee, "How Athletes Built a Voter-Turnout Machine for 2020 and Beyond," *Washington Post*, December 3, 2020, https://www.washingtonpost.com/sports/2020/12/03/nba-wnba-turnout-georgia-primary/; Sean Gregory, "'We Did That': Inside the WNBA's Strategy to Support Raphael Warnock—and Help Democrats Win the Senate," *Time*, January 7, 2021, https://time.com/5927075/atlanta-dream-warnock-loeffler/.

53. Caitlin McFall, "Trump Slams NBA as a 'Political Organization,'" Fox News, August 27, 2020, https://www.foxnews.com/politics/trump-nba-political-organization.

54. "Mike Ditka against Kneelers in New Football League, ... 'Get the Hell Outta the Country,'" *TMZ Sports*, July 26, 2020, https://www.tmz.com/2020/07/26/mike-ditka-x-league-national-anthem-protests-womens-football/.

55. Alex Reimer, "Charlie Kirk and Right-Wing Pundits Express Outrage at NBA Players' Anthem Protests—Again and Again," *Forbes*, July 31, 2020, https://www.forbes.com/sites/alexreimer/2020/07/31/charlie-kirk-and-right-wing-pundits-express-fake-outrage-at-nba-players-protesting-during-anthem/?sh=115e2b33434a https://twitter.com/charliekirk11/status/1288975274709671936.

56. Emily Sullivan, "Laura Ingraham Told LeBron James to Shut Up and Dribble; He Went to the Hoop," NPR, February 19, 2018, https://www.npr.org/sections/thetwo-way/2018/02/19/587097707/laura-ingraham-told-lebron-james-to-shutup-and-dribble-he-went-to-the-hoop.

57. Greg Beacham, "LeBron James Says He 'Will Definitely Not Shut Up and Dribble,'" Associated Press (*NBA.com*), February 17, 2018, https://www.nba.com/news/lebron-james-says-he-will-definitely-not-shut-and-dribble.

58. Kareem Copeland, "Athletes Using Sports Platforms to PushYe for Social Change," Associated Press, July 25, 2016, https://apnews.com/article/2dfa7ed280da4e9da7dc3440df896f48.

59. Dave Zirin, "Taking a Knee: It's Working," *The Progressive*, December 1, 2017, https://progressive.org/magazine/taking-a-knee-its-working/.

60. Larry Atkins, "The Time for Athletes to Speak Out Is Now," *Real Clear Politics*, August 22, 2020, https://www.realclearpolitics.com/2020/08/22/the_time_for_athletes_to_speak_out_is_now_521048.html.

Chapter 6

1. Eric Simons, "The Psychology of Why Sports Fans See Their Teams as Extensions of Themselves," *Washington Post*, January 30, 2015, https://www.washingtonpost.com/opinions/the-psychology-of-why-sports-fans-see-their-teams-as-extensions-of-themselves/2015/01/30/521e0464-a816-11e4-a06b-9df2002b86a0_story.html?utm_term=.a750cc16591b.

2. Dr. Susan Krauss Whitbourne, "The Psychology of Sports Fans," *Psychology Today*, December 30, 2011, https://www.psychologytoday.com/blog/fulfillment-any-age/201112/the-psychology-sports-fans; Robert B. Cialdini, Richard J. Borden, Avril Thorne, Marcus Randall Walker, Stephen Freeman, and Lloyd Reynolds Sloan, "Basking in Reflected Glory: Three (Football) Field Studies," *Journal of Personality and Social Psychology* 34, no. 3 (1976): 366, https://doi.org/10.1037/0022-3514.34.3.366.

3. Chris Jones, "What Do You Mean, 'We'?" *Grantland*, October 25, 2011, http://grantland.com/features/what-do-mean-we/.

4. "Sports Fandom and the NCAA Student-Athlete," NCAA.org, accessed May 20, 2020, http://www.ncaa.org/health-and-safety/sports-fandom-and-ncaa-student-athlete; Shelley E. Smith, Frederick G. Grieve, Ryan K. Zapalac, W. Pitt Derryberry, and Jacqueline Pope, "How Does Sport Team Identification Compare to Identification with Other Social Institutions?" *Journal of Contemporary Athletics* 6, no. 2 (2012): 69.

5. Larry Atkins, "Yo, Sixers, When is Our Parade?" *Philadelphia Inquirer*, June 9, 2015, http://www.philly.com/philly/sports/sixers/Yo-Sixers-when-is-our-parade.html; Larry Atkins, "Enough of the Tanking. Philadelphia 76ers Need to Aggressively Pursue Free Agents," *Huffington Post*, June 17, 2015, https://www.huffingtonpost.com/larry-atkins/enough-of-the-tanking-phi_b_7608008.html.

6. Scott Stump, "Meet the 5 Friends Who Have Attended Every Single Super Bowl," *Today*, February 5, 2016, https://www.today.com/news/meet-5-friends-who-have-attended-every-single-super-bowl-t70936.

7. Gary Buiso, "Meet Three Guys Who Have Been to Every Super Bowl," *New York Post*, February 2, 2014, https://nypost.com/2014/02/02/meet-three-guys-who-have-been-to-every-super-bowl/.

8. Anna Almendrala, "How Being a Sports Fan Makes You Happier and Healthier," *Huffington Post*, January 30, 2015, https://www.huffingtonpost.com/2015/01/30/sports-fan-mental-health-benefits_n_6565314.html; Daniel L. Wann, Merrill J. Melnick, Gordon W. Russell,

and Dale G. Pease, *Sport Fans: The Psychology and Social Impact of Spectators* (Abingdon: Routledge, 2001).

9. John Keilman and Genevieve Bookwalter, "Cubs Victory Gives Fans Psychological Boost," *Chicago Tribune*, November 4, 2016, http://www.chicagotribune.com/sports/baseball/cubs/ct-cubs-psychology-of-winning-met-20161104-story.html.

10. Steve Hartman, "Young Ohio State Fan Beats Cancer after Calling It 'Michigan,'" CBS News, November 29, 2013, https://www.cbsnews.com/news/young-ohio-state-fan-beats-cancer-after-calling-it-michigan/; Edward Sutelan, "Grant Reed/2000–2019: Ohio State Fan Battling Childhood Tumors Named Cancer 'Michigan,'" *Columbus Dispatch*, February 11, 2019, https://www.dispatch.com/news/20190211/grant-reed-2000-2019-ohio-state-fan-battling-childhood-tumors-named-cancer-michigan.

11. Peter King, "Ten Years Later: The Saints and Katrina," *Sports Illustrated*, August 26, 2015, https://www.si.com/mmqb/2015/08/26/new-orleans-saints-hurricane-katrina-anniversary-nfl-mailbag.

12. Jon Terbush, "How Sports Can Help Boston Cope with Tragedy," *The Week*, April 16, 2013, http://theweek.com/articles/465485/how-sports-help-boston-cope-tragedy.

13. Mike Morsch, "Outta Leftfield: McGwire's Admission Disappointing, but Doesn't Change the Real Story," *Montgomery Newspapers*, January 13, 2010, http://www.montgomerynews.com/perkasienewsherald/opinion/outta-leftfield-mcgwire-s-admission-disappointing-but-doesn-t-change/article_7ab6ec42-b4f1-50b2-a760-337ad5248309.html.

14. Seth Meyers, *Late Night With Seth Meyers*, September 27, 2017, https://ps-af.facebook.com/LateNightSeth/videos/954558731361473/ or https://www.youtube.com/watch?v=H-gg99q0_x0.

15. Darren Heitner, "Playing Ball in the Multi-Billion Dollar Sports Collectible Market," *Forbes*, April 11, 2016, https://www.forbes.com/sites/darrenheitner/2016/04/11/playing-ball-in-the-multi-billion-dollar-sports-collectible-market/#7766cbaa14e3.

16. Larry Atkins, "Game, Set, Eagles Camp!" *Philadelphia Daily News*, August 10, 2007, https://www.inquirer.com/philly/opinion/20070810_GAME__SET__EAGLES_CAMP_.html.

17. Tom Van Riper, "Are Sports Fans Crazy? No More Than Anyone Else," *Forbes*, February 20, 2016, https://www.forbes.com/sites/tomvanriper/2016/02/20/are-sports-fans-crazy-no-more-than-anyone-else/; L. Jon Wertheim and Sam Sommers, *This Is Your Brain on Sports: The Science of Underdogs, the Value of Rivalry, and What We Can Learn from the T-Shirt Cannon* (New York: Three Rivers Press, 2016).

18. Jerry Crasnick, "Red Sox Fans Still as Passionate as Ever," ESPN, September 15, 2009, http://www.espn.com/boston/mlb/columns/story?columnist=crasnick_jerry&id=4474049.

19. Email interview with Glen Macnow, May 25, 2021. Glen Macnow is a longtime Philadelphia sports talk radio host at Sports Radio 94 WIP.

20. Christopher J. Boudreaux, Shane D. Sanders, and Bhavneet Walia, "A Natural Experiment to Determine the Crowd Effect upon Home Court Advantage," *Journal of Sports Economics* 18, no. 7 (2017): 737–749.

21. Marc Tracy, "Storming the Court, a Cherished Rite, Can Be a Danger," *New York Times*, March 4, 2016, https://www.nytimes.com/2016/03/05/sports/ncaabasketball/storming-the-court-a-cherished-rite-can-be-a-danger.html; Joe Rodgers, "Pac-12 to Fine Schools up to $100,000 If Fans Storm Court, Field," *Sporting News*, May 24, 2016, https://www.sportingnews.com/us/ncaa-basketball/news/court-storm-field-college-football-pac-12-fine-teams-rules/1d9vmp0aiyreb1o5rm5qxndjeb.

22. J.P. Butler, "A 'Travesty' at the Reilly Center," *Olean Times Herald*, February 4, 2017, https://www.oleantimesherald.com/sports/area_college/a-travesty-at-the-reilly-center/article_225042ac-eb57-11e6-b830-a377b1fff96a.html.

23. Thomas O'Toole, "Security Workers Get Physical with Fans after Houston's Victory over Temple," *USA Today*, December 5, 2015, https://www.usatoday.com/story/sports/ncaaf/aac/2015/12/05/security-fans-rush-field-houston-temple-american-athletic-conference-title-game/76860474/.

24. Eben Novy-Williams, "Storming Court Creates 'Devastating Liability for NCAA Schools," *Bloomberg*, February 24, 2015, https://www.bloomberg.com/news/articles/2015-02-24/storming-court-creates-devastating-liability-for-ncaa-schools.

25. Jeff Eisenberg, "Sean Miller Wants Court Storming Banned before Player Punches Fan," *Yahoo Sports*, February 25, 2016, https://sports.yahoo.com/blogs/ncaab-the-dagger/sean-miller-wants-court-storming-banned-before-player-punches-fan-163047652.html.

26. Reid Forgrave, "To Those Now Screaming for a Court-Storming Ban: You're Wrong," Fox Sports, February 24, 2015, https://www.foxsports.com/stories/college-basketball/to-those-now-screaming-for-a-court-storming-ban-youre-wrong.

27. Joe Dejka, "Are Students Going Too Far in the Way They Boo? Administrators Try to Keep Them from Crossing the Line," *Omaha World-Herald*, March 8, 2016, http://www.omaha.com/news/education/are-students-going-too-far-in-the-way-they-boo/article_1c9bd474-7d09-52c4-a771-dde842f1f8f8.html. Ryan Harding, "Wisconsin Sportsmanship Guidelines Set Dangerous Precedent," *The Daily Illini*, January 19, 2016, https://dailyillini.com/opinions-stories/2016/01/19/wisconsin-sportsmanship-guidelines-set-dangerous-precedent/.

28. Emily Attwood, "Developing a Universal Code of Conduct for HS Sports Fans," *Athletic*

Business, December 2016, https://www.athleticbusiness.com/sportsmanship/developing-a-universal-code-of-conduct-for-hs-sports-fans.html; Maddie Koss, "Public-Address Announcers Can Have Positive Effect on Crowd Control," National Federation of State High School Associations, September 12, 2016, https://nfhs.org/articles/public-address-announcers-can-have-positive-effect-on-crowd-control/.

29. Email interview with Jack Kapenstein, December 29, 2017. Jack Kapenstein is a photographer, television commentator, coach, sports official.

30. Justin Zaremba, "EXCLUSIVE: Video Shows Fans' Racist Taunts at High School Basketball Game," *NJ.com*, February 2, 2017, https://www.nj.com/morris/2017/02/jefferson_crowd_hurls_racial_remarks_at_dover_play.html; Dave Carlin, "Jefferson High Fans Accused of Hurling Racial Taunts during Game against Dover," CBS New York, February 3, 2017, https://newyork.cbslocal.com/2017/02/03/jefferson-dover-basketball-taunts/.

31. Bob Cook, "The Taunting Trump Chants at High School Sporting Events Just Won't Stop," *Forbes*, March 6, 2017, https://www.forbes.com/sites/bobcook/2017/03/06/the-taunting-trump-chants-at-high-school-sporting-events-just-wont-stop/#560de68967e7.

32. Barbara Bruno, "A Refresher Course on the Etiquette of Booing, Part I: When Booing Is Wrong, *Huffington Post*, June 5, 2012, https://www.huffingtonpost.com/barbara-bruno/sports-booing_b_1571306.html.

33. Dave Solomon, "I Was Thinking: Is It OK to Boo College Athletes?" *The Register Citizen*, December 27, 2009, http://www.registercitizen.com/news/article/I-WAS-THINKING-Is-it-OK-to-boo-college-athletes-12105374.php.

34. Eamonn Brennan, "Cousins Receives Racist Messages," ESPN, February 16, 2010, http://www.espn.com/blog/collegebasketballnation/post/_/id/3993/cousins-receives-of-racist-messages.

35. Joe Christensen, "College Athletes Feeling the Love/Hate on Twitter," *Star Tribune*, May 28, 2015, http://www.startribune.com/college-athletes-feeling-the-love-and-hate-on-twitter/304836191/.

36. Jack Harris, "Social Media and College Football: How ASU Was Pushed to the Forefront of the National Discussion," *Cronkite Sports*, September 12, 2017, http://www.cronkitesports.com/social-media-and-college-football-how-asu-was-pushed-to-the-forefront-of-the-national-discussion/.

37. Nicole Sanderson, "The Good and Bad of Twitter and College Athletes," *USA Today*, January 10, 2013, https://www.usatoday.com/story/sports/college/other/2013/01/10/college-athletes-twitter-criticism-johnny-manziel-kentucky/1823959/.

38. Joe Christensen, "College Athletes Feeling the Love/Hate on Twitter," *Star Tribune*, May 28, 2015, http://www.startribune.com/college-athletes-feeling-the-love-and-hate-on-twitter/304836191/.

39. Gus Turner, "15 Signs You're a Bandwagon Sports Fan," *Complex*, July 30, 2013, http://www.complex.com/sports/2013/07/signs-youre-bandwagon-fan/.

40. Associated Press, "Domi Fined Maximum Amount Possible," ESPN, March 30, 2001, https://www.espn.com/nhl/news/2001/0330/1164795.html.

41. Jared Diamond, "The 10th Anniversary of the Malice at the Palace," *Wall Street Journal*, November 19, 2014, https://www.wsj.com/articles/BL-DFB-22170.

42. Dave Seminara, "Over the Glass and into Hockey Lore," *New York Times*, December 23, 2009, https://www.nytimes.com/2009/12/23/sports/hockey/23brawl.html.

43. Derek John, "July 12, 1979: 'The Night Disco Died—or Didn't," NPR, July 16, 2016, https://www.npr.org/2016/07/16/485873750/july-12-1979-the-night-disco-died-or-didnt.

44. Martin Rogers, "San Francisco Fan Bryan Stow and His Story of Hope, Resilience & Inspiration," Fox Sports, April 15, 2021, https://www.foxsports.com/stories/mlb/san-francisco-giants-fan-bryan-stow-hope-resilience-inspiration; Kerry Crowley, "How Giants Fan Bryan Stow Has Turned His Trauma into a Message for Thousands of Kids," *Mercury News*, February 12, 2021, https://www.mercurynews.com/2021/02/12/how-giants-fan-bryan-stow-has-turned-his-trauma-into-a-message-for-thousands-of-kids/; Michael Martinez, "Dad of Severely Beaten Giants Fan Calls Two Sentenced Men 'Cretins,'" CNN, February 20, 2014, https://www.cnn.com/2014/02/20/justice/california-dodgers-baseball-beating/index.html.

45. Kent Babb and Steven Rich, "A Quietly Escalating Issue for NFL: Fan Violence and How to Contain It," *Washington Post*, October 28, 2016, https://www.washingtonpost.com/sports/redskins/a-quietly-escalating-issue-for-nfl-fan-violence-and-how-to-contain-it/2016/10/28/4ec37964-9470-11e6-bb29-bf2701dbe0a3_story.html?utm_term=.7e6a41331df8; Bob Hille, "Dallas-Area Man Shot Outside Cowboys' Stadium Dies," *Sporting News*, October 15, 2015, https://www.sportingnews.com/us/nfl/news/cowboys-fan-shot-dies-att-stadium-arlington-shooting/15mfr45pha7o71q8be2x1ij52q; "Man Charged in Death of Fan," ESPN, February 21, 2014, https://www.espn.com/nfl/story/_/id/10496586/man-charged-death-fan-arrowhead-stadium.

46. Quint Forgey, "Steve Bartman, Infamous Cubs Fan, Gets World Series Ring," *Wall Street Journal*, July 31, 2017, https://www.wsj.com/articles/steve-bartman-infamous-cubs-fan-gets-world-series-ring-1501529140.

47. "Notable Sports Riots," Fox Sports, October 20, 2016, http://www.foxsports.com/mlb/gallery/notable-sports-riots-gallery-040212; Bay City News, "Vandals Cause over $140k in Damages to

Buses after Giants Win," ABC7 News, November 10, 2014, https://abc7news.com/world-series-san-francisco-giants-vandals-muni-buses/389621/.

48. Tiffanie Wen, "A Sociological History of Soccer Violence," *Atlantic*, July 14, 2014, https://www.theatlantic.com/health/archive/2014/07/a-sociological-history-of-soccer-violence/374396/; Nick Ames, "Why the Ugly Spectacle of Fan Violence Has Returned to Soccer," *Time*, June 16, 2016, https://time.com/4371606/euro-2016-fan-violence-hooligan-england/.

49. Soraya Nadia McDonald, "Brazilian Soccer Player Dani Alves Responds to Racist Taunt," *Washington Post*, April 28, 2014, https://www.washingtonpost.com/news/morning-mix/wp/2014/04/28/brazilian-soccer-player-dani-alves-responds-to-racist-taunt/.

50. Richard Lapchick, "Lapchick: The Year in Racism and Sports," ESPN, January 25, 2017, http://abcnews.go.com/Sports/lapchick-year-racism-sports/story?id=45041640.

51. Errin Haines Whack, "Boston Sports Struggle with Perception Built on Racist Past, Associated Press (*The Day*), May 3, 2017, http://www.theday.com/article/20170503/NWS12/170509812.

52. Reporting by Philip O'Connor, Shrivathsa Sridhar, Manasi Pathak and Kanishka Singh, editing by Ed Osmond, Peter Rutherford, Himani Sarkar and Christian Radnedge, "FA Condemns Racist Abuse of Players After England's Euro 2020 Final Loss," Reuters, July 12, 2021, https://www.reuters.com/lifestyle/sports/fa-condemns-racist-abuse-players-following-englands-final-loss-2021-07-12/.

53. Justin Tejada, "Sports Fans Need to Get a Grip," *GOOD*, April 11, 2017, https://www.good.is/sports/mike-greenberg-bad-sports-fans.

54. Jerry Barca, "Why Sports Fans Misbehave, and the Worst Group of All," *Forbes*, July 28, 2015, https://www.forbes.com/sites/jerrybarca/2015/07/28/why-sports-fans-misbehave-and-the-worst-group-of-all/#73593ea54f92; Justine Gubar, *Fanaticus: Mischief and Madness in the Modern Sports Fan* (Lanham, MD: Rowman & Littlefield, 2015).

55. Brian Handwerk, "Sports Riots: The Psychology of Fan Mayhem," *National Geographic News*, June 20, 2005, https://news.nationalgeographic.com/news/2005/06/0620_050620_.sportsriots.html (link no longer available); Mark Memmott, "Win or Lose, Some Fans Choose to Riot," NPR, June 16, 2011, https://www.npr.org/sections5thetwo-way/2011/06/16/137216984/win-or-lose-some-fans-choose-to-riot.

56. Matt Beardmore, "When Fans Turn Fanatical," *Psychology Today*, November 29, 2013, https://www.psychologytoday.com/blog/time-out/201311/when-fans-turn-fanatical.

57. Jerry Middleton Lewis, *Sports Fan Violence in North America* (Lanham, MD: Rowman & Littlefield, 2007).

58. Jeff Barker, "Fan Brawls Are a Persistent Game-Day Problem," *Baltimore Sun*, October 30, 2017, http://www.baltimoresun.com/sports/bs-md-nfl-fan-brawls-20161005-story.html.

59. Dennis Van Milligen, "How to Prevent Fan Violence at Sporting Events," *Athletic Business*, February 2015, reprinting the article "Leaders of the Packed," *Gameday Security*, Winter 2015, https://www.athleticbusiness.com/stadium-arena-security/how-to-prevent-fan-violence-at-sporting-events.html.

60. Bridget Fitzpatrick, "Broken Bats and Broken Bones: Holding Stadium Owners Accountable for Alcohol-Fueled Fan-on-Fan Violence." *Jeffrey S. Moorad Sports LJ* 22 (2015): 663, https://heinonline.org/HOL/LandingPage?handle=hein.journals/vse22&div=23&id=&page=.

Chapter 7

1. Bruce Anderson, "Just a Pipp of a Legend. The Man Who Was Benched in Favor of Iron Horse-To-Be Lou Gehrig Thereby Earned an Enduring Fame in His Own Right," *Sports Illustrated*, June 29, 1987, https://vault.si.com/vault/1987/06/29/just-a-pipp-of-a-legend.

2. Associated Press, "Bears' Jay Cutler Has Knee Sprain," ESPN Chicago, January 24, 2011, https://www.espn.com/chicago/nfl/news/story?id=6054047.

3. KNBR Staff, "Raheem Mostert Goes on Twitter Rant after Injury Criticism from Fantasy Players," KNBR, December 21, 2020, https://www.knbr.com/2020/12/21/raheem-mostert-goes-on-twitter-rant-after-injury-criticism-from-fantasy-players/; Mostert's tweets: https://twitter.com/RMos_8Ball/status/1341102186735034375?ref_src=twsrc%5Etfw, https://twitter.com/RMos_8Ball/status/1341102916619427840?ref_src=twsrc%5Etfw.

4. Paul Zeise, "Paul Zeise: If the Players and Coaches Don't Care About These Bowl Games, Why Should We?" *Pittsburgh Post-Gazette*, December 23, 2022, https://www.post-gazette.com/sports/paul-zeise/2022/12/23/paul-zeise-sports-column-college-football-pitt-penn-state-sun-bowl/stories/202212220109.

5. Criss Partee, "The NBA Has a Load Management Problem that Commissioner Adam Silver Has Done Nothing About," *Deadspin*, October 20, 2022, https://deadspin.com/the-nba-has-a-load-management-problem-that-commissioner-1849684269.

6. Johnny Miller, "Ronnie Lott Stunned by Loss of Fingertip, 1986," *San Francisco Chronicle*, July 31, 2011, https://www.sfgate.com/entertainment/article/Ronnie-Lott-stunned-by-loss-of-fingertip-1986-2352531.php.

7. "This Day in Sports: Willis Reed Limps Out of a Tunnel and into a Championship," ESPN, May 8, 2010, https://www.espn.com/blog/sportscenter/post/_/id/50116/this-day-in-sports-willis-reed-limps-out-of-a-tunnel-and-into-a-championship.

8. Zac Al-Khateeb, "Did Michael Jordan

Actually Have the Flu in the 'Flu Game'?" *Sporting News*, May 18, 2020, https://www.sportingnews.com/us/nba/news/did-michael-jordan-actually-have-the-flu-in-the-flu-game/1t6gp4l2rxbri1bv29ddmk19c1.

9. Gaby Del Valle, "Karolyi's 'You Can Do It' Made All the Difference," *Bustle*, August 11, 2016, https://www.bustle.com/articles/178073-who-did-bela-karolyi-say-you-can-do-it-to-the-moment-of-encouragement-went-down.

10. Sal Paolantonio, "Reid Questioned for Not Pulling McNabb," ESPN, November 18, 2002, https://www.espn.com/nfl/columns/paolantonio_sal/1462641.html.

11. Ian Browne, "Schilling's Bloody Sock the Bridge to history," MLB.com, October 19, 2014, https://www.mlb.com/news/curt-schillings-bloody-sock-the-bridge-to-history/c-98978666.

12. Andy Riga, "Montreal Olympics: Despite a Broken Knee, Japanese Gymnast Won Gold," *Montreal Gazette*, July 25, 2016, https://montrealgazette.com/sports/montreal-olympics-despite-a-broken-knee-japanese-gymnast-won-gold.

13. Ben Mathis-Lilley, "All the People, Entities, and Cultural Mythologies That Might Be to Blame for Kevin Durant's Apparent Achilles Tear," *Slate*, June 11, 2019, https://slate.com/culture/2019/06/kevin-durant-injury-blame-assignment.html.

14. ESPN, "Charles Barkley Blames the Warriors for Kevin Durant's Achilles Injury| Get Up," June 11, 2019, https://www.youtube.com/watch?v=PzKCh6T0OG0; Liz Roscher, "Charles Barkley: 'I Blame the Warriors for Kevin Durant's Achilles Injury,'" *Yahoo! Sports*, June 11, 2019, https://www.yahoo.com/now/charles-barkley-i-blame-the-warriors-for-kevin-durants-achilles-injury-161753620.htm.

15. Harvard Medical School, "Legal and Ethical Factors That Affect NFL Players' Health," *Science Daily*, November 17, 2016, https://www.sciencedaily.com/releases/2016/11/161117155506.htm.

16. Jochen Mayer, Stephanie Burgess, and Ansgar Thiel, "Return-to-Play Decision Making in Team Sports Athletes. A Quasi-Naturalistic Scenario Study," *Frontiers in Psychology* 11 (2020): 1020, https://doi.org/10.3389/fpsyg.2020.01020.

17. "Eating Disorders & Athletes," National Eating Disorders Association, accessed May 23, 2021, https://www.nationaleatingdisorders.org/eating-disorders-athletes.

18. Julie Deardorff, "It Feels Like There's a Beast inside Me," *Chicago Tribune*, July 28, 1994, https://www.chicagotribune.com/news/ct-xpm-1994-07-28-9407280155-story.html.

19. Steve Wilstein, "First Guilt, Shame; Finally Starvation," Associated Press (*News & Record*), August 11, 1994, https://greensboro.com/first-guilt-shame-finally-starvation/article_126629d4-1374-56e9-92e3-1aa30ee1db73.html; Deardorff, "It Feels Like There's a Beast Inside Me."

20. Athelia Knight, "Weight Loss Methods Probed after 3 College Wrestlers Die," *Washington Post*, December 18, 1997, https://www.washingtonpost.com/archive/sports/1997/12/18/weight-loss-methods-probed-after-3-college-wrestlers-die/3dcb7763-8491-4b8f-bac6-6991b2ef64b2/.

21. Bonnie Taub-Dix, "Wrestling with Their Weight ... Literally," *U.S. News & World Report*, September 28, 2012, https://health.usnews.com/health-news/blogs/eat-run/2012/09/28/wrestling-with-their-weight-literally.

22. Newsweek Staff, "The Pressure to Lose," *Newsweek*, May 1, 1994, https://www.newsweek.com/pressure-lose-188802.

23. Josh Moyer, "Former Penn State Kicker Joey Julius Shares Experience with Eating Disorder," *Centre Daily Times*, November 13, 2017, https://www.centredaily.com/sports/college/penn-state-university/psu-football/article184463803.html.

24. "Sports Psychology," American Psychological Association, 2008, https://www.apa.org/ed/graduate/specialize/sports.

25. Rob Demovsky, "Aaron Rodgers Applauds Packers' Hiring of Sports Psychologist," ESPN, April 2, 2020, https://www.espn.com/green-bay-packers/post/_/id/48818/aaron-rodgers-applauds-packers-hiring-of-sports-psychologist.

26. Talkspace, clinically reviewed by Jill E. Daino, LCSW-R, "The Weight of Gold with Michael Phelps," Talkspace, July 29, 2020, https://www.talkspace.com/blog/weight-of-gold-michael-phelps-documentary/.

27. Tim McManus, "Eagles' Brandon Brooks Brings Recognition of Battle with Anxiety," ESPN, November 25, 2019, https://www.espn.com/blog/philadelphia-eagles/post/_/id/24284/eagles-brandon-brooks-brings-winning-battle-against-anxiety.

28. Jon Wertheim, "Royce White Takes on MMA," *Sports Illustrated*, April 13, 2020, https://www.si.com/mma/2020/04/13/royce-white-takes-on-mma.

29. Scott Gleeson and Erik Brady, "When Athletes Share Their Battles with Mental Illness," *USA Today*, August 30, 2017, https://www.usatoday.com/story/sports/2017/08/30/michael-phelps-brandon-marshall-mental-health-battles-royce-white-jerry-west/596857001/.

30. Vritti Rashi Goel, "Naomi Osaka Withdraws from French Open, Citing Struggle with Depression and Anxiety," CBS News, May 31, 2021, https://www.cbsnews.com/news/naomi-osaka-withdraws-from-french-open-mental-health-depression-anxiety/; Rachel Axon, "Distraught Simone Biles Pulls Out of Olympics Team Final: 'I Was Still Struggling with Some Things,'" *USA Today*, July 27, 2021, https://www.usatoday.com/story/sports/olympics/2021/07/27/simone-biles-pulls-out-tokyo-olympics-gymnastics-team-final/5383286001/.

31. Justin Baragona, "Right-Wing Media Launches Unhinged Attack on Simone Biles," *The Daily Beast*, July 28, 2021, https://www.thedailybeast.com/right-wing-media-attacks-weak-simone-biles-selfish-sociopath; Brian Niemietz,

"Piers Morgan Asks if Mental Health is 'Now the Go-To Excuse' Following Simone Biles' Exit from Team Competition," *New York Daily News*, July 27, 2021, https://www.nydailynews.com/news/national/ny-piers-morgan-simone-biles-mental-health-20210727-5fwkhiipjzeibbxpctxw7maao4-story.html; https://twitter.com/piersmorgan/status/1420027274565390355?ref_src=twsrc%5Etfw.

32. Sarah Hearon, "Aly Raisman, Laurie Hernandez and More React to Simone Biles Withdrawing from Tokyo Olympics Gymnastics Final," *Us Weekly*, August 4, 2021, https://www.usmagazine.com/entertainment/pictures/simone-biles-withdraws-from-tokyo-olympics-gymnastics-final-reactions/.

33. D'Arcy Maine, "Simone Biles Returns to Gymnastics Competition at Tokyo Olympics, Wins Bronze Medal on Balance Beam," ESPN, August 3, 2021, https://www.espn.com/olympics/gymnastics/story/_/id/31947782/simone-biles-returns-competition-wins-bronze-medal-balance-beam.

34. David Cassilo, "Royce White, DeMar DeRozan and Media Framing of Mental Health in the NBA," *Communication & Sport* 10, no. 1 (2022): 97–123, https://journals.sagepub.com/doi/abs/10.1177/2167479520933548; Otto E. Wahl, Amy Wood, and Renee Richards, "Newspaper Coverage of Mental Illness: Is it Changing?" *Psychiatric Rehabilitation Skills* 6, no. 1 (2002): 9–31, https://www.tandfonline.com/doi/abs/10.1080/10973430208408417; Rob Whitley and Sarah Berry, "Trends in Newspaper Coverage of Mental Illness in Canada: 2005–2010," *The Canadian Journal of Psychiatry* 58, no. 2 (2013): 107–112, https://doi.org/10.1177/070674371305800208.

35. James Ellingworth, "UEFA Wants Concussion Rule Change to Protect Players," Associated Press, May 29, 2019, https://apnews.com/article/0268890030644b169d6d193d637694cb.

36. St. Michael's Hospital, "Concussions in Elite Soccer Not Assessed According to Expert Recommendations," *Science Daily*, May 30, 2019, https://www.sciencedaily.com/releases/2019/05/190530101211.htm.

37. Associated Press, "'You Had One Job': Tearful Simone Biles Attacks USAG over Nassar Scandal," *Guardian*, August 8, 2019, https://www.theguardian.com/sport/2019/aug/08/simone-biles-usa-gymnastics-larry-nassar-abuse.

38. Nick Crain, "NBA Season Suspended as Rudy Gobert Tests Positive for COVID-19 on a Wild Night in Oklahoma City," *Forbes*, March 11, 2020, https://www.forbes.com/sites/nicholascrain/2020/03/11/the-nba-season-is-suspended-until-further-notice-after-rudy-gobert-tests-positive-for-covid-19-in-oklahoma-city/?sh=6d9184b67f0e.

39. Larry Atkins, "Filling Stadiums with Fans Is Shortsighted and Dangerous," *Street & Smith's Sports Business Journal*, July 27, 2020, https://www.sportsbusinessjournal.com/SB-Blogs/COVID19-OpEds/2020/07/27.

40. Written by Jason Vermes with files from Ashley Fraser and Steve Howard, "Empty Seats at Tokyo Olympics Could Hinder Some Athletes—but Help Others," CBC Radio, July 25, 2021, https://www.cbc.ca/radio/checkup/how-do-you-feel-about-the-2020-tokyo-olympics-1.6115846/empty-seats-at-tokyo-olympics-could-hinder-some-athletes-but-help-others-1.6116033; Arthur Syin, Helen Regan and Brad Lendon, "Tokyo Reports More than 1,700 New Covid-19 Cases amid Olympic Games," CNN, July 25, 2021, https://www.cnn.com/world/live-news/tokyo-2020-olympics-07-25-21-spt/h_5fdd9f5474d3c5910a50477a414ac083; Andrew Beaton, "Jon Rahm, Bryson DeChambeau Test Positive for COVID-19 Before Olympic Golf," *Wall Street Journal*, July 25, 2021, https://www.wsj.com/articles/jon-rahm-covid-reinfection-bryson-dechambeau-test-positive-olympic-golf-11627182738.

41. Patrick Finley, "NFL Teams with COVID-19 Outbreaks Could Forfeit Games," *Chicago Sun-Times*, July 22, 2021, https://chicago.suntimes.com/2021/7/22/22589123/nfl-teams-covid-19-outbreak-forfeit-bears-matt-nagy-deandre-hopkins-cardinals-competitive-advantage.

42. Bill Francis, "1918 Flu Pandemic Did Not Spare Baseball," National Baseball Hall of Fame, accessed April 12, 2021, https://baseballhall.org/discover/1918-flu-pandemic-didnt-spare-baseball.

43. Cassandra Negley, "Here's What Sports Looked Like during the 1918 Spanish Flu Pandemic," *Yahoo! Sports*, May 15, 2020, https://news.yahoo.com/coronavirus-heres-what-sports-looked-like-during-the-1918-spanish-flu-pandemic-184042838.html.

44. Callum Rice-Coates, "How the Great Spanish Flu Pandemic Sheds Light on Sport's Careful Response to Coronavirus," *Independent*, April 24, 2020, https://www.independent.co.uk/sport/coronavirus-pandemic-spanish-flu-influenza-babe-ruth-a9481476.html.

45. Jason Owens, "Remembering Hank Gathers 30 Years after His Tragic Death during Tournament Game," *Yahoo! Sports*, March 4, 2020, https://sports.yahoo.com/remembering-hank-gathers-30-years-after-his-tragic-death-072917409.html; Myron Medcalf, "Hank Gathers, 25 Years Later," ABC News (ESPN), March 4, 2015, https://abcnews.go.com/Sports/hank-gathers-25-years/story?id=29382399.

46. Jack McCallum, "The Cruelest Thing Ever," *Sports Illustrated*, June 30, 1986, https://vault.si.com/vault/1986/06/30/the-cruelest-thing-ever; Jeff Zillgitt, "Opinion: The Len Bias Story Remains One of the Saddest 'What-Ifs' in Sports History," *USA Today*, June 26, 2020, https://www.usatoday.com/story/sports/nba/columnist/jeff-zillgitt/2020/06/26/len-bias-1986-nba-draft-death-cruel-story-sports-history/3260046001/.

47. Mallika Kallingal, "University of Maryland Reaches $3.5 Million Settlement with Football Player Jordan McNair's Family," CNN, January 16, 2021, https://www.cnn.com/2021/01/16/

us/jordan-mcnair-settlement/index.html; Michael McCann, "How Do the Findings of Jordan McNair Investigation Impact Lawsuit, Durkin's Future," *Sports Illustrated*, September 22, 2018, https://www.si.com/college/2018/09/22/jordan-mcnair-death-investigation-findings-maryland-dj-durkin-lawsuit.

48. Owen Gibson, "Lance Armstrong 'Comes Clean' in Oprah Winfrey Interview to Doping Past," *Guardian*, January 15, 2013, https://www.theguardian.com/sport/2013/jan/15/lance-armstrong-admits-doping-winfrey; "The Life and Times of Lance Armstrong," CBC News, August 24, 2012, https://www.cbc.ca/news/world/the-life-and-times-of-lance-armstrong-1.1192077.

49. SI staff, "The Loser," *Sports Illustrated*, October 3, 1988, https://vault.si.com/vault/1988/10/03/the-loser.

50. ESPN.com news services, "McGwire Apologizes to La Russa, Selig," ESPN, January 11, 2010, https://www.espn.com/mlb/news/story?id=4816607.

51. Kevin Cowherd, "Steroid Users Strike Out with Fans of Honest Home Runs," *Baltimore Sun*, March 9, 2006, https://www.baltimoresun.com/news/bs-xpm-2006-03-09-0603090185-story.html.

52. Nicholas L. Parsons, and Michael J. Stern, "There's No Dying in Baseball: Cultural Valorization, Collective Memory, and Induction into the Baseball Hall of Fame," *Sociology of Sport Journal* 29, no. 1 (2012), https://doi.org/10.1123/ssj.29.1.62.

53. Ryan Fagan, "Joe Morgan Asks Hall of Fame Voters Not to Elect Steroid Users," *Sporting News*, November 21, 2017, https://www.sportingnews.com/us/mlb/news/joe-morgan-letter-to-hall-of-fame-voters-about-steroid-users/113hnc7c78rx1gzw9op25nfd9.

54. Tom Joyce, "Stop Pretending Steroid Users Shouldn't Be in the Baseball Hall of Fame," *Washington Examiner*, January 21, 2019, https://www.washingtonexaminer.com/opinion/stop-pretending-steroid-users-shouldnt-be-in-the-baseball-hall-of.

55. ESPN.com news services, "Mitchell report: Baseball Slow to React to Players' Steroid Use," ESPN, December 13, 2007, https://www.espn.com/mlb/news/story?id=3153509; CNN's Steve Robinson and Alanne Orjoux contributed to this report. "Clemens, Pettite Named in Baseball Steroid Report," CNN, December 13, 2007, https://www.cnn.com/2007/U.S./12/13/steroid.report/; Reuters Staff, Compiled by Gary Crosse, editing by Patricia Zengerle, "FACTBOX: Baseball Players Named in Mitchell Report," Reuters, December 13, 2007, https://www.reuters.com/article/us-baseball-steroids-players/factbox-baseball-players-named-in-mitchell-report-idUSN1325006720071213; "Notable Players Linked to PEDs," ESPN, July 30, 2009, https://www.espn.com/mlb/news/story?id=4366683.

56. Chris Smith, "Why It's Time to Legalize Steroids in Professional Sports," *Forbes*, August 24, 2012, https://www.forbes.com/sites/chrissmith/2012/08/24/why-its-time-to-legalize-steroids-in-professional-sports/?sh=18f332ac65d2.

57. Ian Steadman, "How Sports Would Be Better with Doping," *Wired*, September 18, 2012, https://www.wired.com/2012/09/sports-and-doping/.

58. Joe Valerio, Zoom interview October 2, 2020, confirmed and revised by email, June 21, 2021. Joe Valerio is a former NFL player with the Kansas City Chiefs and St. Louis Rams and an adjunct professor at Arcadia University's School of Global Business.

59. Marie Overbye, "An (Un) Desirable Trade of Harms? How Elite Athletes Might React to Medically Supervised 'Doping' and Their Considerations of Side-Effects in This Situation," *International Journal of Drug Policy* 55 (2018): 14–30.

60. Mark Starr, "Starr: Now for the Doping Confessions," *Newsweek*, May 30, 2007, https://www.newsweek.com/starr-now-doping-confessions-100867.

61. Valerio, Zoom interview, confirmed and revised by email, June 21, 2021.

62. *Vernonia Sch. Dist. 47J v. Acton* (94–590), 515 U.S. 646 (1995), https://www.law.cornell.edu/supct/html/94-590.ZO.html.

63. Samantha Myers, "Proposed Bill Would Require High Schools to Create Random Drug Testing Policies," Fox59, January 25, 2019, https://fox59.com/news/proposed-bill-would-require-high-schools-to-create-random-drug-testing-policies/.

64. Staff Report, "Steroid Testing of NJSIAA Athletes during 2016–17 Yields One Positive Result," MyCentralJersey.com, December 11, 2017, https://www.mycentraljersey.com/story/sports/high-school/2017/12/11/steroid-testing-njsiaa-athletes-during-2016-17-yields-one-positive-result/940275001/.

65. Sharon Levy and Miriam Schizer, "Adolescent Drug Testing Policies in Schools," *Pediatrics* 135, no. 4 (2015): e1107–12, https://doi.org/10.1542/peds.2015-0055.

66. Bob Cook, "Parents' Rebellion against Drug Testing High School Athletes Evidence of Policy's Failure," *Forbes*, October 7, 2017, https://www.forbes.com/sites/bobcook/2017/10/07/parents-rebellion-against-drug-testing-high-school-athletes-evidence-of-policys-failure/?sh=5c20ac2c434d.

67. *Hill v. National Collegiate Athletic Assn.* (1994) 7 Cal. 4th 1, 26 Cal. Rptr. 2d 834; 865 P.2d 633, https://scocal.stanford.edu/opinion/hill-v-national-collegiate-athletic-assn-31368.

68. Craig Neff, "Bosworth Faces the Music," *Sports Illustrated*, January 5, 1987, https://vault.si.com/vault/1987/01/05/bosworth-faces-the-music-brian-bosworth-was-a-conspicuous-casualty-of-the-ncaas-steroid-crackdown; George Volsky, "Bosworth Tells Of Steroid Use," *New York Times*, December 27, 1986, https://www.nytimes.com/1986/12/27/sports/bosworth-tells-of-steroid-use.html.

69. Associated Press, "NFL Bust Mandarich

Says He Used Steroids at Michigan State," ESPN, September 30, 2008, https://www.espn.com/nfl/news/story?id=3618195.

70. "Frequently Asked Questions about Drug Testing," NCAA (Sport Science Institute), https://www.ncaa.org/sport-science-institute/topics/frequently-asked-questions-about-drug-testing.

71. Matt Connolly, "Drug Test Appeal Denied. Now 2 Clemson Players Will Miss All of 2019 Season," *The State*, May 24, 2019, https://www.thestate.com/sports/college/acc/clemson-university/article230787064.html.

72. Bob Nightengale, "MLB Toughens Drug Agreement Provisions," *USA Today*, March 28, 2014, https://www.usatoday.com/story/sports/mlb/2014/03/28/mlb-toughens-drug-agreement-provisions/7023401/.

73. USA Today Sports, "MLB and Players Union Release Its Annual Drug Test Report," *USA Today*, December 1, 2017, https://www.usatoday.com/story/sports/mlb/2017/12/01/mlb-and-players-union-release-its-annual-drug-test-report/914346001/.

74. CNN Newsource, "Performance Enhancing Drugs in Sports Fast Facts," May 26, 2021, KTVZ, https://ktvz.com/news/national-world/2021/05/26/performance-enhancing-drugs-in-sports-fast-facts/.

75. Mark Maske, "NFL, Players' Union Order Report on Eric Reid's Claim of Drug-Testing Targeting," *Washington Post*, December 23, 2018, https://www.washingtonpost.com/sports/2018/12/23/nfl-players-union-order-report-drug-program-administrator-eric-reids-allegations/.

76. Jonathan Jones, "The Bizarre and Statistically Improbable Case of Eric Reid's Random Drug Testing," *Sports Illustrated*, December 20, 2018, https://www.si.com/nfl/2018/12/20/eric-reid-panthers-nfl-random-drug-testing; Marcel Louis-Jacques, "Panthers S Eric Reid: Random Drug Tests Don't Feel So Random after 5 in 8 Weeks," *Charlotte Observer*, November 28, 2018, https://www.charlotteobserver.com/sports/nfl/carolina-panthers/article222249375.html.

77. Jeff Zillgitt, "NBA Will Test for HGH in 2015–16," *USA Today*, April 16, 2015, https://www.usatoday.com/story/sports/nba/2015/04/16/nba-nbpa-announce-hgh-testing-penalties-starting-in-2015-16-season/25898759/.

78. Staff Report, "Former Memphis Tigers Star Tyreke Evans Banned from the NBA," *Commercial Appeal*, May 17, 2019, https://www.commercialappeal.com/story/sports/college/memphis-tigers/basketball/2019/05/17/tyreke-evans-suspension-nba-drug-policy-violation/3711442002/.

79. Nick Butler, "Coaches Can Influence Whether Athletes Decide to Dope, Claims Scottish Study," March 6, 2014, *Inside the Games*, https://www.insidethegames.biz/articles/1018731/coaches-can-influence-whether-athletes-decide-to-dope-claims-scottish-study; Justine Allen, Paul Dimeo, Rhiannon Morris, Sarah Dixon, and Leigh Robinson, "Precipitating or prohibiting factor? Examining coaches' perspectives of their role in doping and anti-doping," 2013, https://www.wada-ama.org/en/resources/social-science-research/precipitating-or-prohibiting-factor-examining-coaches.

80. Jade Scipioni, "Fmr NBA Player Jay Williams: 80% Of Players Use Marijuana," Fox Business, March 16, 2016, https://www.foxbusiness.com/features/fmr-nba-player-jay-williams-80-of-players-use-marijuana.

81. Kierra Frazier, "USADA Says Marijuana Rules Can't Be Changed Unilaterally," *Axios*, July 9, 2021, https://www.axios.com/usada-addresses-marijuana-olympics-shcarri-6f67d90e-b181-45c9-87da-eb1ad1349981.html; German Lopez, "The Olympics Are Stuck in the 1980s on Marijuana," *Vox*, July 7, 2021, https://www.vox.com/22565419/shacarri-richardson-olympics-marijuana-ban-war-on-drugs.

82. Jessica Reaves, "The Casey Martin Case: The Supreme Court Takes up Golf," *Time*, May 29, 2001, http://content.time.com/time/nation/article/0,8599,128306,00.html; *PGA TOUR, INC. V. MARTIN* (00–24) 532 U.S. 661 (2001); Cornell Law School, Legal Information Institute, https://www.law.cornell.edu/supct/html/00-24.ZO.html; Associated Press, "Supreme Court Upholds Earlier Martin Ruling," ESPN, May 29, 2001, https://www.espn.com/golf/story?id=1206060.

83. Larry Atkins, "Sorry, Golf Is Not a Sport," *Chicago Tribune*, April 19, 2002, https://www.chicagotribune.com/news/ct-xpm-2002-04-19-0204190149-story.html.

84. Brett Cyrgalls, "Tiger Woods Burns John Daly with Surprising Cart Complaint," *New York Post*, May 14, 2019, https://nypost.com/2019/05/14/tiger-woods-burns-john-daly-with-surprising-cart-complaint/.

85. Melissa Ann Resslar, "PGA Tour, Inc. v. Martin: A Hole in One for Casey Martin and the ADA." *Loyola University of Chicago Law Journal* 33 (2001): 631, https://heinonline.org/HOL/LandingPage?handle=hein.journals/luclj33&div=27&id=&page=.

86. Biography.com Editors, "Oscar Pistorius Biography," Biography.com, November 24, 2017, https://www.biography.com/athlete/oscar-pistorius.

87. Gregg Doyel, CBS Sports (article no longer available online), https://www.cbssports.com/olympics/story/19560712/pistorius-story-great-but-fallout-from-his-running-could-ruin-the-olympics; Travis Waldron, "No Oscar Pistorius Will Not 'Ruin the Olympics,'" *Think Progress*, July 13, 2012, https://archive.thinkprogress.org/no-oscar-pistorius-will-not-ruin-the-olympics-575042e48d59/.

88. "Techno-Doping," *PCMag Encyclopedia*, accessed June 6, 2021, https://www.pcmag.com/encyclopedia/term/techno-doping.

89. Brendan Burkett, Mike McNamee, and Wolfgang Potthast, "Shifting Boundaries in Sports

Technology and Disability: Equal Rights or Unfair Advantage in the Case of Oscar Pistorius?" in *Moving Beyond Boundaries in Disability Studies*, ed. Michele Moore (London: Routledge, 2013), 143–154.

90. Giuseppe Lippi and Camilla Mattiuzzi, "Pistorius Ineligible for the Olympic Games: The Right Decision," *British Journal of Sports Medicine* 42, no. 3 (2008): 160–161, https://bjsm.bmj.com/content/42/3/160.short.

91. S.D. Edwards, "Should Oscar Pistorius be Excluded from the 2008 Olympic Games?" *Sport, Ethics and Philosophy* 2, no. 2 (2008): 112–125, 10.1080/17511320802221802. Steven D. Edwards, "Should Oscar Pistorius Be Excluded from the 2008 Olympic Games?" in *Ethics, Disability and Sports*, ed. Ejgil Jespersen and Mike NcNamee (London: Routledge, 2013), 26–39.

92. Ryan McDonald, "History Making Utah Runner Hunter Woodhall Found Silver Linings in Cancellation of NCAA Championships, Postponement of Paralympics," *Deseret News*, May 23, 2020, https://www.deseret.com/sports/2020/5/23/21251952/runner-hunter-woodhall-silver-linings-ncaa-championships-postponement-paralympics.

93. ESPN.com news services, "Four Visually Impaired Paralympians Beat Olympic Gold Time in 1,500," ESPN, September 13, 2016, https://www.espn.com/olympics/story/_/id/17535217/four-visually-impaired-paralympians-beat-olympic-gold-medal-1500m.

94. Will Heilpern, "Why the Olympics and Paralympics Are Still Separate Events," *Business Insider*, August 17, 2016, https://www.businessinsider.com/why-the-olympics-and-paralympics-are-separate-events-2016-8.

95. Giles Tremlett, "The Cheats," *Guardian*, September 15, 2004, https://www.theguardian.com/sport/2004/sep/16/gilestremlett.features11; Rodolphe Desseauve, "Olympic Scandals: The Revolving Spanish Sham at the 2000 Sydney Paralympic Games," *Yahoo! Sports*, July 15, 2021, https://www.yahoo.com/now/olympics-2021-scandals-spain-paralympics-2000-sydney-games-051520629.html.

96. BBC, "Paralympian Natalie Du Toit Aims to Make Impact in New Role," BBC, February 9, 2013, https://www.bbc.com/sport/disability-sport/21394927.

97. Matt Trowbridge, "One Legged NCAA Wrestling Champ Did Not Have an Advantage," *Rockford Register Star*, March 23, 2011, https://www.rrstar.com/article/20110323/BLOGS/303239849.

98. Mark Palmer, "InterMat Rewind: Opportunity for All," Intermatwrestle.com, August 23, 2011, https://intermatwrestle.com/articles/8826; Seth Staskey, "Evans Eyes HOF Induction," *Times Leader*, October 3, 2010, https://www.timesleaderonline.com/sports-columns/2010/10/evans-eyes-hof-induction/.

99. Sam Marsdale, "Report: 'Multiple Teams' Have Expressed Interest in Former Seahawks Linebacker Shaquem Griffin," *247Sports*, May 10, 2021, https://247sports.com/Article/Seattle-Seahawks-Shaquem-Griffin-multiple-teams-expressed-interest-NFL-free-agents--165238214/; "One-Handed LB Shaquem Griffin Drafted by Seahawks, Reunited with Twin Brother Shaquill," ESPN, April 28, 2018, https://www.espn.com/nfl/draft2018/story/_/id/23347129/one-handed-lb-shaquem-griffin-drafted-seattle-seahawks-reunited-twin-brother-shaquill.

100. Sheldon Spencer, "Living with 63 Yards—and Beyond," ESPN, October 28, 2010, https://www.espn.com/nfl/news/story?id=5739850; Brett Martel, "Ex-NFL Kicker, Saints Hero Tom Dempsey Dies at 73," Associated Press (*Worcester Telegram*), April 5, 2020, https://www.telegram.com/news/20200405/ex-nfl-kicker-saints-hero-tom-dempsey-dies-at-73.

101. Sam Gardner, "Rocky Bleier Recalls Vietnam War, 40 Years after It Ended," Fox Sports, January 9, 2017, https://www.foxsports.com/stories/nfl/rocky-bleier-recalls-vietnam-war-40-years-after-it-ended.

102. Len Pasquarelli, "Rolle Says Epilepsy under Control; 'I'm Not Scared,'" ESPN, November 21, 2007, https://www.espn.com/nfl/news/story?id=3122595.

103. Peter J. Wallner, "How Jim Abbott Settled His Insecurity over Deformed Hand to Become a Successful Big League Pitcher," *MLive.com*, May 2, 2012, https://www.mlive.com/sports/grand-rapids/2012/05/how_jim_abbott_settled_his_ins.html.

104. Mel Marmer, "Pete Gray," Society for American Baseball Research (SABR), accessed May 23, 2021, https://sabr.org/bioproj/person/pete-gray/; Justin Mears, "'One-Armed Wonder': 75 Years Ago, Pete Gray Inspired MLB Fans,"*Yardbarker*, June 29, 2020, https://www.yardbarker.com/mlb/articles/one_armed_wonder_75_years_ago_pete_gray_inspired_mlb_fans/s1_13132_32277692.

105. Dan Tylicki, "30 MLB Players Who Overcame Physical/Mental Obstacles to Achieve Their Dreams," *Bleacher Report*, May 16, 2012, https://bleacherreport.com/articles/1182893-30-mlb-players-who-overcame-physicalmental-obstacles-to-achieve-their-dreams.

106. Jessica Marie, "12 Incredible Athletes with Disabilities," *Bleacher Report*, August 21, 2013, https://bleacherreport.com/articles/1743213-12-incredible-athletes-with-disabilities.

107. "Student-Athletes with Disabilities," NCAA.org, accessed May 24, 2021, https://www.ncaa.org/about/resources/inclusion/student-athletes-disabilities.

108. "History," SpecialOlympics.org, accessed May 24, 2021, https://www.specialolympics.org/about/history.

109. "Paralympic Games," *Encyclopedia Britannica*, accessed May 24, 2021, https://www.britannica.com/sports/Paralympic-Games; "Paralympics History," International Paralympic

Committee, accessed May 24, 2021, https://www.paralympic.org/ipc/history.

110. "The Invictus Games," Invictus Games Foundation, accessed May 25, 2021, https://invictusgamesfoundation.org/games/.

111. Joseph Shapiro, "Paralympian's Pursuit Enables Aspiring Athletes," NPR, August 31, 2012, https://www.npr.org/2012/09/02/160382788/paralympians-pursuit-enables-aspiring-athletes.

112. "How Many Students Are Hazed?" Alfred University, accessed May 27, 2021, https://www.alfred.edu/about/news/studies/high-school-hazing/how-many-students.cfm.

113. StopHazing Research Lab, "Hazing: The Issue," StopHazing Consulting, December 2020, https://stophazing.org/issue/.

114. "What Is Bullying," StopBullying.gov, accessed May 27, 2021, https://www.stopbullying.gov/bullying/what-is-bullying.

115. "Research Shows Youth Sports Hazing Victims Often in Denial," Vanderbilt University Medical Center, *VUMC Reporter*, May 5, 2016, https://news.vumc.org/2016/05/05/research-shows-youth-sports-hazing-victims-often-in-denial/; Alex B. Diamond, S. Todd Callahan, Kelly F. Chain, and Gary S. Solomon, "Qualitative Review of Hazing in Collegiate and School Sports: Consequences from a Lack of Culture, Knowledge and Responsiveness," *British Journal of Sports Medicine* 50, no. 3 (2016): 149–153, https://bjsm.bmj.com/content/50/3/149.short.

116. Tom Schad, "Richie Incognito Joins Anti-Bullying Campaign Five Years After Jonathan Martin Incident," *USA Today*, July 23, 2018, https://www.usatoday.com/story/sports/nfl/bills/2018/07/23/richie-incognito-nfl-anti-bullying-campaign-jonathan-martin/817988002/; Tom Pelissero, "Wells Report: Incognito, Two Teammates Had Pattern of Harassment," *USA Today*, February 14, 2014, https://www.usatoday.com/story/sports/nfl/dolphins/2014/02/14/richie-incognito-jonathan-martin-ted-wells-report-miami-bullying-mike-pouncey-john-jerry/5482571/.

117. USA Today High School Sports, *USA Today*, accessed May 20, 2021, https://usatodayhss.com/?s=hazing.

118. Matt Wixon and Greg Riddle, "SportsDayHS Best Of: 2017 Special Report: How Culture of Hazing, Bullying in High School Sports Is Only Getting Worse," *Dallas Morning News*, May 25, 2018, https://www.dallasnews.com/high-school-sports/2018/05/25/sportsdayhs-best-of-2017-special-report-how-culture-of-hazing-bullying-in-high-school-sports-is-only-getting-worse/.

119. Keith Schweigert, "3 'Ringleaders' of 2022 Middletown Football Hazing Incident Have Been Convicted in Juvenile Court, Prosecutors Say," FOX43, September 28, 2023, https://www.fox43.com/article/news/local/dauphin-county/middletown-football-hazing-incident-3-ringleaders-convicted-juvenile-court/521-2ea7896b-21d7-4fe2-86be-fa20165e4967.

120. Logan Newman, "Report: Bixby HS Football Players Accused of Raping Teammate with Pool Cue Agree to Lesser Charge," *USA Today*, February 20, 2019, https://usatodayhss.com/2019/bixby-high-school-pool-cue-rape-accusations-agree-lesser-charge; Samantha Vicent, "Former Bixby Players Accused of Raping Teammate Ordered to Pay $300 in Restitution on Amended Assault Charge, Court Records Show," *Tulsa World*, February 20, 2019, https://tulsaworld.com/news/local/crime-and-courts/former-bixby-players-accused-of-raping-teammate-ordered-to-pay/article_7ea7c7f2-5518-5cc4-a218-d6a32881c832.html; Associated Press, "Oklahoma Teens Accused of Rape Accept Lesser Charge," FOX Sports, February 19, 2019, https://www.foxsports.com/stories/other/oklahoma-teens-accused-of-rape-accept-lesser-charge.

121. Tim Whelan, Jr., "Lawsuit Filed in Ill. Over Football Team Hazing That Led to Sexual Assault," *USA Today*, November 28, 2018, https://usatodayhss.com/2018/lawsuit-filed-in-ill-over-football-team-hazing-that-led-to-sexual-assault; Robin Levinson-King, "The Brutal Secret of School Sport Initiations," BBC, January 9, 2019, https://www.bbc.com/news/world-us-canada-46282988; https://casetext.com/case/brookman-ex-rel-ab-v-reed-custer-cmty-unit.

122. Brynn Gingras, "Cancellation of Sayreville High School Football Season Approved amid Hazing Probe," NBC New York, October 8, 2014, https://www.nbcnewyork.com/news/local/sayreville-high-school-season-canceled-new-jersey-bombers-investigation-nj-hazing-bullying/878537/.

123. Report compiled by Mary Wilfert, Education Services, "Positively Challenging. Building New Traditions. Hazing Prevention in College Athletics," NCAA.org, 2007, https://ncaaorg.s3.amazonaws.com/ssi/other/SSI_hazingpreventionhandbook.pdf.

124. Jeff Jonas, "Hazing in High School Athletics," National Federation of State High School Associations, NFHS.org, September 6, 2017, https://www.nfhs.org/articles/hazing-in-high-school-athletics/.

125. Bill Doyle, "Hazing Is Rare, but a Concern for Area High Schools," *Telegram & Gazette*, November 18, 2018, https://www.telegram.com/news/20181118/hazing-is-rare-but-concern-for-area-high-schools.

126. Jay Johnson and Jessica W. Chin, "Seeking New Glory (d)Haze: A Qualitative Examination of Adventure-Based, Team Orientation Rituals as an Alternative to Traditional Sport Hazing for Athletes and Coaches," *International Journal of Sports Science & Coaching* 11, no. 3 (2016): 327–341, https://journals.sagepub.com/doi/abs/10.1177/1747954116643648.

Chapter 8

1. "ESPN Survey: MLB Fans Back More Safety Netting," ESPN, June 24, 2019, https://www.

espn.com/mlb/story/_/id/27046280/mlb-fans-back-more-safety-netting; James C. Kozlowski, "MAJORITY "BASEBALL RULE" LIMITS SPECTATOR LIABILITY," 2013, https://mason.gmu.edu/~jkozlows/lawarts/05MAY13.pdf, Reprinted as James C. Kozlowski, J.D., Ph.D., "Majority 'Baseball Rule' Limits Spectator Liability," *Parks and Recreation Magazine*, May 1, 2013, https://www.nrpa.org/parks-recreation-magazine/2013/may/majority-baseball-rule-limits-spectator-liability/.

2. Wallace Matthews, "Baseball Improved Fan Safety, but in Court, It's Teams That Are Protected," *New York Times*, March 28, 2018, https://www.nytimes.com/2018/03/28/sports/baseball/extended-netting-fan-safety.html; Benjamin Trachman, "Going to Bat for the Baseball Rule: Atlanta National League Baseball Club, Inc. v. FF et al," *Harvard Journal of Sports & Entertainment Law* 7 (2016): 209, https://heinonline.org/HOL/LandingPage?handle=hein.journals/harvsel7&div=10&id=&page=.

3. Stefan A. Mallen, "Touchdown—A Victory for Injured Fans at Sporting Events," *Missouri Law Review* 66 (2001): 487, https://heinonline.org/HOL/LandingPage?handle=hein.journals/molr66&div=25&id=&page=; Paul M. Anderson, "Sports Law in the State of Wisconsin," *Marquette Sports Law Review* 425, no. (2005), https://scholarship.law.marquette.edu/facpub/190/?utm_source=scholarship.law.marquette.edu%2Ffacpub%2F190&utm_medium=PDF&utm_campaign=PDFCoverPages.

4. Michael McCann, "Yankees Incident Revives an Old Question: How Responsible Are Teams for Foul Ball Injuries?" *Sports Illustrated*, September 21, 2017, https://www.si.com/mlb/2017/09/21/new-york-yankees-netting-ballpark-injury; Kelsey McKinney, "What a Foul Ball Can Do," *Deadspin*, June 27, 2019, https://deadspin.com/what-a-foul-ball-can-do-1835706809.

5. David Glovin, "Baseball Caught Looking as Fouls Injure 1,750 Fans a Year," *Bloomberg News*, September 9, 2014, https://www.bloomberg.com/news/articles/2014-09-09/baseball-caught-looking-as-fouls-injure-1-750-fans-a-year.

6. Paul Hagen, "MLB Recommends Netting between Dugouts," MLB.com, December 9, 2015, https://www.mlb.com/news/mlb-issues-recommendations-on-netting/c-159233076.

7. Tom Schad and Scott Gleeson, "Here's a Look at the 30 MLB Ballparks and Their Safety Netting for Dangerous Foul Balls," *USA Today*, May 30, 2019, https://www.usatoday.com/story/sports/mlb/2019/05/30/mlb-safety-nets-stadium/1284310001/.

8. Samuel Chamberlain, "Fan Struck in Head by Foul Ball at Dodger Stadium, Rushed to Hospital," Fox News, June 23, 2019, https://www.foxnews.com/sports/fan-hit-by-foul-ball-at-dodger-stadium-hospitalized.

9. "Girl Struck by Foul Ball at Astros-Cubs Game Has Permanent Brain Injury, Lawyer Says," CBS News, January 8, 2020, https://www.cbsnews.com/news/girl-struck-by-foul-ball-astros-cubs-game-permanent-brain-injury-2020-01-08/.

10. Chris Bumbaca, "Two U.S. Senators Ask MLB Commissioner Rob Manfred for Data on Fan Injuries from Foul Balls," *USA Today*, August 7, 2019, https://www.usatoday.com/story/sports/mlb/2019/08/07/mlb-netting-tammy-duckworth-richard-durbin-ask-rob-manfred-data/1941347001/.

11. Ben Bergman, "After Numerous Foul Ball Fan Injuries, Baseball Reconsiders Protective Netting," NPR, July 13, 2019, https://www.npr.org/2019/07/13/739967250/after-numerous-foul-ball-fan-injuries-baseball-reconsiders-protective-netting; Scott King, "White Sox Host 1st MLB Game with Foul Pole-To-Pole Netting," Associated Press, July 22, 2019, https://apnews.com/article/4cda494a0c29463dbbb9b777586aae32; Mark Anderson, "Fan-Safety Advocate Urges Baseball to Increase Measures," *Las Vegas Review-Journal*, March 8, 2021, https://www.reviewjournal.com/sports/baseball/fan-safety-advocate-urges-baseball-to-increase-measures-2297508/.

12. Matt Martell, "Crying Foul over Ballpark Injuries," *Sports Illustrated*, August 10, 2021, https://www.si.com/mlb/2021/08/10/crying-foul-mlb-netting-daily-cover.

13. David Barron, "Astros Sued over T-shirt Fired into Stands," *Houston Chronicle*, April 9, 2019, https://www.houstonchronicle.com/sports/astros/article/Astros-sued-over-T-shirt-fired-into-stands-13753474.php; Michael P. Schmidt, "Misbehaving Mascots," Villanova University, Jeffrey S. Moorad Center for the Study of Sports Law, November 12, 2020, https://www1.villanova.edu/villanova/law/academics/sportslaw/commentary/mslj_blog/2020/misbehaving-mascots.html.

14. CBC News, "13-Year-Old Fan Killed after Hit by Puck at NHL Game," CBC.ca, March 20, 2002, https://www.cbc.ca/news/world/13-year-old-fan-killed-after-hit-by-puck-at-nhl-game-1.338919.

15. Grady Trimble, "Lightning Fan Struck by Flying Hockey Puck during Playoff Game," WGRZ, April 16, 2018, https://www.wgrz.com/article/sports/nhl/lightning/lightning-fan-struck-by-flying-hockey-puck-during-playoff-game/67-540083756.

16. Sarah Farrell, "Sports Leagues Taking Steps to Further Protect Fans from Balls, Bats, and Pucks," *Cronkite News*, August 26, 2019, https://cronkitenews.azpbs.org/2019/08/26/sports-fan-safety-protective-nets/.

17. Stefan A. Mallen, "Touchdown—A Victory for Injured Fans at Sporting Events," *Missouri Law Review* 66 (2001): 487, https://heinonline.org/HOL/LandingPage?handle=hein.journals/molr66&div=25&id=&page=.

18. Michael McCann, "Yankees Incident Revives an Old Question: How Responsible Are Teams for Foul Ball Injuries?" *Sports Illustrated*, September 21, 2017, https://www.si.com/mlb/2017/09/21/new-york-yankees-netting-ballpark-injury.

19. Nathaniel Grow and Zachary Flagel, "The Faulty Law and Economics of the Baseball Rule," *William & Mary Law Review* 60 (2018): 59, https://heinonline.org/HOL/LandingPage?handle=hein.journals/wmlr60&div=6&id=&page= https://scholarship.law.wm.edu/wmlr/vol60/iss1/3/.

20. Peter Carfagna, Zoom interview, June 16, 2021, confirmed and revised by email June 21, 2021. Peter Carfagna teaches sports law at Harvard University Law School and the University of Miami, is faculty supervisor of Harvard Law School's Sports Law Clinical Program, is chairman/CEO of Magis, LLC, a privately owned sports marketing, management and investment company, and was chief legal officer and general counsel of International Management Group (IMG).

21. Aaron Caputo, Zoom interview, June 16, 2021, confirmed and revised by email June 21, 2021. Aaron Caputo is the executive director of legal and client services at the Superlative Group, Inc., a sports marketing and advertising company, and he teaches sports law at Case Western Reserve University School of Law.

22. Bree Fowler, "NBA Players Sentenced in Brawl," Associated Press (CBS News), September 23, 2005, https://www.cbsnews.com/news/nba-players-sentenced-in-brawl/.

23. ABC News via GMA, "How One Punch Changed Professional Sports," ABC News, January 6, 2006, https://abcnews.go.com/GMA/story?id=125540&page=1; UPI, "Tomjanovich and Lakers Reach Agreement on Suit," *New York Times*, April 21, 1981, https://www.nytimes.com/1981/04/21/sports/tomjanovich-and-lakers-reach-agreement-on-suit.html.

24. CBC Sports, "Steve Moore Confirms Settlement in Bertuzzi Case," CBC, September 4, 2014, https://www.cbc.ca/sports/hockey/nhl/steve-moore-confirms-settlement-in-bertuzzi-case-1.2756008.

25. Thomas Heath and DeNeen L. Brown, "McSorley Gets Probation for Slash," *Washington Post*, October 7, 2000, https://www.washingtonpost.com/archive/sports/2000/10/07/mcsorley-gets-probation-for-slash/3c81aaa4-3a71-48e8-bd28-37ee7b1d8e34/; Associated Press, "McSorley Found Guilty of Assault," October 6, 2000, https://apnews.com/article/9be8d5e820687c581c5502be26d736fe.

26. Associated Press, "Castillo Gets Jail, Probation," ESPN, August 6, 2009, https://www.espn.com/minorlbb/news/story?id=4381593.

27. Diana P. Cortes, "Same Injury; Different Coverage: How Privatized Insurance Policies Affect Injured Elite and Non-Elite Professional Athletes." *Villanova Sports & Entertainment Law Journal* 13 (2006): 133, https://heinonline.org/HOL/LandingPage?handle=hein.journals/vse13&div=15&id=&page=; Benjamin A. Kling, "Should Athletes Be Subject to Civil Liability for Their Extra-Athletic Actions?" *Northern Kentucky Law Review*, February 15, 2020, https://northernkentuckylawreview.com/blog/should-athletes-be-subject-to-civil-liability-for-their-extra-athletic-actions; Michael K. Zitelli, "Unnecessary Roughness: When On-field Conduct Leads to Civil Liability in Professional Sports," *Willamette Sports Law Journal* 8 (2010): 1, https://heinonline.org/HOL/LandingPage?handle=hein.journals/wlmsplj8&div=3&id=&page=.

28. Janine DeFao, "Romanowski Settles Ex-Teammate's Lawsuit for $415,000," *San Francisco Chronicle*, May 27, 2005, https://www.sfgate.com/sports/article/Romanowski-settles-ex-teammate-s-lawsuit-for-2631758.php; Alan Grant, "Cracked Code," ESPN, August 15, 2005, https://www.espn.com/espnmag/story?id=3736899.

29. Carfagna, Zoom interview. Confirmed and revised by email.

30. Aaron Caputo, Zoom interview. Confirmed and revised by email.

31. Associated Press, "Ex-NFL Agent Terry Watson Pleads Guilty to Giving Cash to 3 Former UNC Players," ESPN, April 17, 2017, https://www.espn.com/college-football/story/_/id/19180813/ex-nfl-agent-pleads-guilty-multi-year-north-carolina-tar-heels-sports-agent-probe; Aaron Beard, "Violation of Sports Agent Laws Tough for States to Prosecute," Associated Press, November 1, 2017, https://apnews.com/article/e0fcaf946a464b2999964e67c10712bd.

32. Jeff Donn, "UMass Stripped of '96 Final Four Finish," Associated Press, May 8, 1997, https://apnews.com/article/135e6f8e2301a0cd16f2252e8874f123; Andrew Wolfson, "What Led to Vacated Final Fours in the Past?" *Courier-Journal*, October 19, 2016, https://www.courier-journal.com/story/sports/college/louisville/2016/10/19/what-led-vacated-final-fours-past/92372758/.

33. The Week Staff, "Top 5 'Pay to Play' Scandals Rocking College Football," *The Week*, January 6, 2011, https://theweek.com/articles/488252/5-pay-play-scandals-rocking-college-football; John DeShazier, "Reggie Bush Gives before the Heisman Trust Can Take, and Has New Orleans Saints Fans to Embrace Him," *The Times-Picayune*, September 15, 2010, https://www.nola.com/sports/saints/article_46a36bb9-94eb-58b6-9d5e-080a18a18326.html; Nick Bromberg, "Heisman Trust Won't Give Reggie Bush Back the 2005 Heisman Unless the NCAA Reinstates Him," *Yahoo! Sports*, July 2, 2021, https://www.yahoo.com/news/heisman-trust-wont-give-reggie-bush-back-his-heisman-until-the-ncaa-takes-action-213440089.html; SI Staff, "Confessions of an Agent," *Sports Illustrated*, October 12, 2010, https://www.si.com/more-sports/2010/10/12/agent; ESPN.com News Services, "Josh Luchs Says He Paid Players," ESPN, October 12, 2010 (Information from the Associated Press was used in this report), https://www.espn.com/college-football/news/story?id=5678493.

34. Aaron Moody, "Here's a Master Guide to the College Basketball Corruption Scandal and FBI Investigation," *The News & Observer*, October 26, 2018, https://www.newsobserver.com/sports/article208880939.html; Mark Schlabach, "Your

Guide to College Basketball's Ongoing NCAA Investigations," ESPN, November 6, 2020, https://www.espn.com/mens-college-basketball/story/_/id/30262819/your-guide-college-basketball-ongoing-ncaa-investigations; Dennis Dodd, "NCAA Head of Enforcement Is 'Frustrated and Disappointed' Most Bribery and Corruption Cases Are Still Ongoing," CBS Sports, January 15, 2021, https://www.cbssports.com/college-basketball/news/ncaa-head-of-enforcement-is-frustrated-and-disappointed-most-bribery-and-corruption-cases-are-still-ongoing/.

35. Carfagna, Zoom interview. Confirmed and revised by email.

36. Joshua Lens, "Application of the UAAA, RUAAA, and State Athlete-Agent Laws to Corruption in Men's College Basketball and Revisions Necessitated by NCAA Rule Changes." *Marquette Sports Law Review* 30 (2019): 47, https://heinonline.org/HOL/LandingPage?handle=hein.journals/mqslr30&div=7&id=&page=. Seth Myers, "An Intentional Foul: Corruption in NCAA Basketball & the Aftermath of the 2017 Scandal," *DePaul Journal of Sports Law* 15 (2019): 65, https://heinonline.org/HOL/LandingPage?handle=hein.journals/jspocpd15&div=7&id=&page=.

37. Carfagna, Zoom interview. Confirmed and revised by email.

38. Caputo, Zoom interview. Confirmed and revised by email.

39. "Title IX Frequently Asked Questions," NCAA.org, accessed December 20, 2020, https://www.ncaa.org/about/resources/inclusion/title-ix-frequently-asked-questions.

40. Juan A. Lozano, "Zaharias Changed the Perception of the Female Athlete," Associated Press (*The Ledger*), May 19, 2003, https://www.theledger.com/article/LK/20030519/News/608138045/LL.

41. Jim Sargent, "Dorothy Schroeder," All-American Girls Professional Baseball League, 1997, https://www.aagpbl.org/profiles/dorothy-schroeder-dottie/559.

42. Larry Atkins, "King V. Riggs 'Battle of the Sexes' Led to Significant Changes in Sports and Society," *Huffington Post*, September 4, 2017, https://www.huffpost.com/entry/king-vs-riggs-battle-of-the-sexes-led-to-significant_b_59ad5b58e4b0c50640cd60c3; Larry Atkins, "The Day She Was a Better Man: Billie Jean King vs. Bobby Riggs," *Philadelphia Inquirer*, 1999 (link no longer available).

43. Wayne Cavadi, "7 Schools with the Most Women's D1 Basketball National Championships," NCAA.org, April 5, 2021, https://www.ncaa.com/news/basketball-women/article/2021-04-05/7-schools-most-womens-basketball-national-championships; Alexa Philippou, "UConn's Women's Basketball Team Boasts 21 Final Four Appearances to Arizona's One, but Friday Night Anything Can Happen," *Hartford Courant*, April 1, 2021, https://www.courant.com/sports/uconn-womens-basketball/hc-sp-uconn-women-arizona-advance-20210402-20210402-r4iavqlsubc73ndg2oj4jq7fgu-story.html; Stephen Hawkins, "1st Timer Arizona Joins Mainstays in Women's NCAA Final Four," Associated Press/ABC News, March 30, 2021, https://abcnews.go.com/Sports/wireStory/1st-timer-arizona-joins-mainstays-womens-ncaa-final-76782261; Doug Bonjour, "UConn Women Looking to Start New Winning Streak," *Connecticut Post* (*CT Post*), January 5, 2019, https://www.ctpost.com/uconn/article/UConn-women-looking-to-start-new-winning-streak-13511312.php; Staff Report, "South Carolina Again Leads Nation in Women's Basketball Attendance," *Post and Courier*, June 21, 2018, https://www.postandcourier.com/sports/south-carolina-again-leads-nation-in-womens-basketball-attendance/article_46e4c5b2-7584-11e8-b192-971656c9db3f.html; Kelli Stacy, "A Look at UConn's Top Teams' Attendance, Revenue, and Expenses," *Hartford Courant*, July 10, 2018, https://www.courant.com/sports/uconn-womens-basketball/hc-sp-uconn-attendance-revenue-and-expenses20180703-story.html; Brian Windhorst, "Team USA Women's Hoops Wins Seventh Straight Gold Medal at Tokyo Olympics," ESPN, August 7, 2021, https://www.espn.com/olympics/story/_/id/31984277/team-usa-women-hoops-wins-seventh-straight-gold-medal-tokyo-olympics.

44. Beth A. Brooke-Marciniak and Donna de Varona, "Amazing Things Happen When You Give Female Athletes the Same Funding as Men," *World Economic Forum*, August 25, 2016, https://www.weforum.org/agenda/2016/08/sustaining-the-olympic-legacy-women-sports-and-public-policy/.

45. Morgan Turner, "Past Women's World Cup Champions," *Sports Illustrated*, June 7, 2019, https://www.si.com/soccer/2019/06/07/womens-world-cup-winners-list-past-champions-finals.

46. Aaron Beard, "Title IX Major Factor for Colleges Looking at Sports Cuts," Associated Press, May 27, 2020, https://apnews.com/article/mens-sports-womens-sports-financial-markets-sc-state-wire-virus-outbreak-460bb54fbe5cec7ce1f8321bf69dc164; Bill Whitaker, "Some Colleges Axing 'Secondary Sports' Like Gymnastics and Tennis as Pandemic Continues," CBS News, December 6, 2020, https://www.cbsnews.com/news/college-sports-cuts-gymnastics-swimming-pandemic-60-minutes-2020-12-06/.

47. Gabriel Fernandez, "Stanford Reverses Decision to Cut 11 of Its Varsity Sports Programs," CBS Sports, May 18, 2021, https://www.cbssports.com/general/news/stanford-reverses-decision-to-cut-11-of-its-varsity-sports-programs-per-report/; Joshua Needelman, "Clemson to Reinstate Men's Track and Field, Cross Country Programs," *Post and Courier*, April 22, 2021, https://www.postandcourier.com/sports/clemson/clemson-to-reinstate-mens-track-and-field-cross-country-programs/article_5a9724a6-a39e-11eb-865a-7f6eadc4bbc6.html.

48. Molly Hensley-Clancy, "Colleges Cut Sports to Save Money amid the Pandemic. Then Came the Title IX Lawsuits," *Washington Post*, March 25,

2021, https://www.washingtonpost.com/sports/2021/03/25/college-sports-cuts-title-ix/.

49. Ross Dellenger and Pat Forde, "A Collegiate Model in Crisis: The Crippling Impact of Schools Cutting Sports," *Sports Illustrated*, June 11, 2020, https://www.si.com/college/2020/06/11/college-sports-program-cuts-ncaa-olympics.

50. "Title IX's Impact on Men's Sports," WBUR, Only a Game, June 23, 2012, https://www.wbur.org/onlyagame/2012/06/23/title-ix-men.

51. Dr. Ketra Armstrong, University of Michigan sport management professor, email interview, August 17, 2021.

52. Dr. Andrea Caporale Seiss, email interview, August 19, 2021. Dr. Andrea Caporale Seiss is the Title IX coordinator at Temple University.

53. "U.S. Women Soccer Players Appeal Decision against Equal Pay," Associated Press, April 14, 2021, https://apnews.com/article/international-soccer-soccer-womens-soccer-lawsuits-court-decisions-d1af156f3a00671287079416c200b779.

54. Anne M. Peterson, "U.S. Men's and Women's Soccer Teams Formally Sign Equal Pay Agreements," Associated Press/PBS.org, September 6, 2022, https://www.pbs.org/newshour/economy/us-mens-and-womens-soccer-teams-formally-sign-equal-pay-agreements.

55. Bill Rankin, "The Bizarre Times of Michael Vick: From All-Pro to Prison," *Atlanta Journal-Constitution*, April 17, 2020, https://www.ajc.com/sports/football/the-bizarre-times-michael-vick-from-all-pro-prison/VpWQZeRcIBMJDpV4NYtBPN/; Thomas Gerbasi, "From Prison to the Prize Ring, Bernard Hopkins Keeps up the Good Fight," *The Daily Beast*, March 9, 2013, updated July 11, 2017, https://www.thedailybeast.com/from-prison-to-the-prize-ring-bernard-hopkins-keeps-up-the-good-fight.

56. Peter Schmuck, "Ray Rice Situation Didn't Help Adrian Peterson," *Baltimore Sun*, November 11, 2014, https://www.baltimoresun.com/sports/bs-sp-schmuck-column-1119-20141118-column.html; Ian Rapoport, "Ray Rice Speaks on Kareem Hunt, Reflects on Own Actions," NFL.com, December 1, 2018, https://www.nfl.com/news/ray-rice-speaks-on-kareem-hunt-reflects-on-own-actions-0ap3000000994218; Bill Chappell, "Domestic Violence Charges Dropped against the NFL's Ray Rice," May 21, 2015, NPR, https://www.npr.org/sections/thetwo-way/2015/05/21/408460234/domestic-violence-charges-dropped-against-the-nfl-s-ray-rice.

57. Ben Estes, SI Wire, "Vikings Adrian Peterson Pleads No Contest to Misdemeanor," *Sports Illustrated*, November 4, 2014, https://www.si.com/nfl/2014/11/04/adrian-peterson-minnesota-vikings-trial-plea.

58. CNN Wire Staff/Tom Faust, "Boxer Floyd Mayweather Sentenced to 3 Months for Domestic Violence," CNN, December 21, 2011, https://www.cnn.com/2011/12/21/justice/nevada-mayweather-sentence; Associated Press, "Floyd Mayweather Released from Jail," ESPN, August 3, 2012, https://www.espn.com/boxing/story/_/id/8228834/floyd-mayweather-jr-released-vegas-jail-serving-2-months.

59. Associated Press, "PLUS: BASEBALL; Canseco Sentenced," *New York Times*, January 8, 1998, https://www.nytimes.com/1998/01/08/sports/plus-baseball-canseco-sentenced.html; Associated Press, "Canseco Pleads No Contest," January 7, 1998, https://apnews.com/article/8b8cf45f763529b844a63f7c41dc7cf0.

60. Associated Press, "Chad Johnson Gets Probation," ESPN, September 21, 2012, https://www.espn.com/nfl/story/_/id/8406775/chad-johnson-gets-probation-domestic-battery-case.

61. Richard Winton, "Rodman Pleads No Contest," *Los Angeles Times*, June 25, 2008, https://www.latimes.com/archives/la-xpm-2008-jun-25-me-rodman25-story.html; Associated Press, "Dennis Rodman Pleads No Contest to Spousal Battery," Fox News, June 24, 2008, https://www.foxnews.com/story/dennis-rodman-pleads-no-contest-to-spousal-battery.

62. Kyle Goon, "Lakers Granted Jason Kidd Permission to Interview for Knicks' Coaching Job," *Orange County Register*, June 22, 2020, https://www.ocregister.com/2020/06/22/lakers-granted-jason-kidd-permission-to-interview-for-knicks-coaching-job/; Mike Mazzeo, "History of Jason Kidd's past Incidents," ESPN, June 30, 2014, https://www.espn.com/blog/newyork/brooklyn-nets/post/_/id/19596/history-of-jason-kidds-past-incidents.

63. History.com Editors, "Star Boxer Mike Tyson Convicted of Rape," *History.com*, accessed December 21, 2020, https://www.history.com/this-day-in-history/boxing-legend-convicted-of-raping-beauty-queen.

64. Eric Levenson and Holly Yan, "Aaron Hernandez's Murder Conviction Cleared after Suicide," CNN, May 9, 2017, https://www.cnn.com/2017/05/09/us/aaron-hernandez-murder-conviction-abated.

65. Brent Schrotenboer, "Slayings Not Forgotten, Ray Lewis Not Forgiven," *USA Today*, January 10, 2013, https://www.usatoday.com/story/sports/nfl/2013/01/10/ray-lewis-baltimore-ravens-atlanta-murder-2000/1566198/.

66. Michael Middlehurst-Schwartz, "Browns Sign Ex-Chief RB Kareem Hunt as NFL Investigation Remains Ongoing," *USA Today*, February 11, 2019, https://www.usatoday.com/story/sports/nfl/browns/2019/02/11/kareem-hunt-cleveland-browns-sign-kansas-city-chiefs/2839394002/.

67. Khadrice Rollins, "Why Is O.J. Simpson In Prison?" *Sports Illustrated*, July 20, 2017, https://www.si.com/nfl/2017/07/20/why-oj-simpson-prison.

68. Sarah Spain, "O.J. Simpson: The Patient Zero of Athlete Privilege," ESPNW, June 9, 2016, https://www.espn.com/espnw/voices/story/_/id/16085823/oj-made-america-original-story-athlete-entitlement.

69. Jeffrey Kluger, "Why On-Field Violence Continues Off-Field," *Time*, September 18, 2014, https://time.com/3398946/nfl-violence-psychology/; https://www.arrestnation.com/.

70. Rachael Rettner, "Are Pro Athletes Prone to Violence?" *Live Science*, September 23, 2014, https://www.livescience.com/47949-pro-athletes-domestic-violence.html; Benjamin Morris, "The Rate of Domestic Violence Arrests among NFL Players," fivethirtyeight.com, July 31, 2014, https://fivethirtyeight.com/features/the-rate-of-domestic-violence-arrests-among-nfl-players/; "NFL Player Arrests Database: Records since 2000," *USA Today*, accessed October 14, 2022, https://databases.usatoday.com/nfl-arrests/.

71. "Sexual Assault and Interpersonal Violence," NCAA.org, accessed December 22, 2020, https://www.ncaa.org/sport-science-institute/sexual-assault-and-interpersonal-violence; "Sexual Violence Prevention," NCAA.org, accessed December 20, 2020, https://ncaaorg.s3.amazonaws.com/ssi/violence/SSI_SexualViolencePreventionToolkit.pdf; "NCAA Releases New Handbook Addressing Sexual Assault," NCAA.org, September 3, 2014, https://www.ncaa.org/about/resources/media-center/news/ncaa-releases-new-handbook-addressing-sexual-assault.

72. Zach Osterman, "New IU Policy Bans Athletes with History of Sexual or Domestic Violence," *Indianapolis Star*, April 19, 2017, https://www.indystar.com/story/sports/college/indiana/2017/04/19/indiana-hoosiers-sexual-violence-athlete-ban-fred-glass/100660758/.

73. David Ching, "SEC: Schools Can't Take Transfers with Serious Misconduct Past," ESPN, May 29, 2015, https://www.espn.com/college-football/story/_/id/12977228/sec-adopts-proposal-prevents-transfer-students-histories-domestic-violence-sexual-assault.

74. Paula Lavigne, "Lawyers, Status, Public Backlash Aid College Athletes Accused of Crimes," ESPN, June 12, 2015, https://www.espn.com/espn/otl/story/_/id/13065247/college-athletes-major-programs-benefit-confluence-factors-somes-avoid-criminal-charges.

75. Bethany P. Withers, "Athletes Get off Easy When They Are Violent," *New York Times*, July 1, 2013, https://www.nytimes.com/roomfordebate/2013/07/01/should-character-matter-in-pro-sports/athletes-get-off-easy-when-they-are-violent.

76. Jane McManus, "When It Comes to Law Enforcement, Do Athletes Get Preferential Treatment? ESPN, October 8, 2014, https://www.espn.com/espnw/news-commentary/story/_/id/11666671/when-comes-law-enforcement-do-athletes-get-preferential-treatment.

77. Lindsay H. Jones, "49ers Ray McDonald Won't Be Charged in Domestic Violence Case," *USA Today*, November 10, 2014, https://www.usatoday.com/story/sports/nfl/49ers/2014/11/10/ray-mcdonald-not-charged-felony-domestic-violence-assault/18801223/.

78. Jones, "49ers Ray McDonald Won't Be Charged in Domestic Violence Case."

79. SI Wire, "Dennis Wideman's Suspension Reduced to 10 Games," *SI.com*, March 11, 2016, https://www.si.com/nhl/2016/03/11/dennis-wideman-calgary-flames-suspension-reduced-10-games.

80. Chris Bahr, "Flashback: Roberto Alomar Spits on Umpire John Hirschbeck," FOX Sports, September 27, 2015, https://www.foxsports.com/stories/mlb/flashback-roberto-alomar-spits-on-umpire-john-hirschbeck.

81. ESPN.com news service, "Young Suspended 50 Games for Bat Toss," ESPN, May 9, 2006, https://www.espn.com/mlb/news/story?id=2438919.

82. Bryan Swanson, "Pierluigi Collina Warns of a Global Shortage of Referees If Abuse Is Not Acted Upon," *Sky Sports*, March 16, 2018, https://www.skysports.com/football/news/11095/10810551/pierluigi-collina-warns-of-a-global-shortage-of-referees-if-abuse-is-not-acted-upon; Reuters staff, reporting by Hardik Vyas in Bengaluru, editing by Sudipto Ganguly, "Collina Calls for Steps against Abuse Towards Referees," Reuters, March 23, 2017, https://www.reuters.com/article/us-soccer-fifa-collina-idUSKBN16U0SM.

83. DJ Sixsmith, "How Athletes Are Stepping up Their Security with Guns and Bodyguards," *Complex*, January 17, 2017, https://www.complex.com/sports/2017/01/how-athletes-stepping-up-security-with-guns-bodyguards.

84. Wilborn P. Nobles III, "Ex-Saint Will Smith Shot to Death in New Orleans, Coroner Confirms," *Times-Picayune*, April 10, 2016, https://www.nola.com/sports/saints/article_a6f26207-a45b-5b42-8a97-1c7e7ddec931.html.

85. Wayne Drehs, "The Professional Athlete as Target: 'Am I Next?'" ESPN, November 29, 2007, https://www.espn.com/espn/news/story?id=3133995.

86. David Leon Moore, "NFL Players: Three Out of Four Own Guns," *USA Today*, December 6, 2012, https://www.usatoday.com/story/sports/nfl/2012/12/06/jovan-belcher-kansas-city-chief-nfl-guns/1752195/.

87. "Factbox: Professional Athletes and High-Profile Crime," Reuters (*Chicago Tribune*), March 6, 2014, https://www.chicagotribune.com/news/ct-xpm-2014-03-06-sns-rt-us-usa-patriots-hernandezbre95k16c-20130621-story.html; SI Wire, "Jayson Williams: I was a 'Coward' for Covering up Limo Driver Shooting," *Sports Illustrated*, December 5, 2016, https://www.si.com/nba/2016/12/05/jayson-williams-gus-christofi-killing-alcohol-rehab-interview; "Plaxico Burress Released from Prison," UPI, June 6, 2011, https://www.upi.com/Sports_News/2011/06/06/Plaxico-Burress-released-from-prison/41491307367844/.

88. DJ Sixsmith, "How Athletes Are Stepping up Their Security with Guns and Bodyguards," *Complex*, January 17, 2017, https://www.complex.com/sports/2017/01/how-athletes-stepping-up-security-with-guns-bodyguards; Jeff Legwold,

"Report: Broncos' Aqib Talib Shot Himself in Leg in June," ESPN, October 4, 2016, https://www.espn.com/nfl/story/_/id/17716226/police-conclude-denver-broncos-aqib-talib-shot-leg; "Gilbert Arenas Says Beef with Jarvis Crittenton from Trash Talk," ESPN, August 7, 2018, https://www.espn.com/nba/story/_/id/24312447/gilbert-arenas-says-gun-incident-trash-talking-not-money.

89. Dan Treadway, "Bob Costas Defends Gun Control and Other Political Stances on Late Night with Seth Meyers," *Sports Illustrated*, April 3, 2014, https://www.si.com/extra-mustard/2014/04/03/bob-costas-defends-gun-control-and-other-political-stances-late-night-seth-meyers.

90. ABC News via GMA, "How One Punch Changed Professional Sports," ABC News, January 6, 2006, https://abcnews.go.com/GMA/story?id=125540&page=1.

91. Gwen Knapp, "40 Years Later, the Fight Resonates in a Positive Way," *SFGate.com*, August 21, 2005, https://www.sfgate.com/sports/knapp/article/40-years-later-The-Fight-resonates-in-a-positive-2646178.php.

92. Dave Anderson, "Harrelson Remembers, with Respect, Rose's Help as a Rookie," *New York Times*, October 9, 1973, https://www.nytimes.com/1973/10/09/archives/harrelson-remembers-with-respect-roses-help-as-a-rookie-a-mayoral.html.

93. "What Are the Biggest Brawls in Red Sox History? Ranking the Top 10," NBC Sports Boston, accessed June 2, 2020, https://www.nbcsports.com/boston/red-sox/what-are-biggest-brawls-red-sox-history-ranking-top-10; "Zimmer Makes Emotional Apology for Role in Fight," ESPN, October 13, 2003, http://www.espn.com.sg/espn/wire/_/id/1636947.

94. Jason Foster, "Aug. 12, 1984: When the Braves and Padres Had the Greatest Brawl Ever," *Sporting News*, August 12, 2015, https://www.sportingnews.com/us/mlb/news/braves-padres-fight-brawl-august-12-1984-pascual-perez-alan-wiggins/17ozuqr13fhut1v9j1fsnj47vz.

95. Charlie Nobles, "THE N.B.A. PLAYOFFS; Seething Riley Says Van Gundy Lost His Cool," *New York Times*, May 3, 1998, https://www.nytimes.com/1998/05/03/sports/the-nba-playoffs-seething-riley-says-van-gundy-lost-his-cool.html.

96. "Pens, Isles Meet Again 2 Months after Fight Night," Fox Sports, April 7, 2011, https://www.foxsports.com/stories/nhl/pens-isles-meet-again-2-months-after-fight-night.

97. *Reid v. Kenowa Hills Public Schools*, 261 Mich. App. 17, 680 N.W.2d 62 (2004), https://casetext.com/case/reid-v-kenowa-hills-public-schools.

98. Cynthia M. Allen, "With 'Tim Tebow' Bill, Texas Can Level Field for Home-Schoolers in Sports, Activities," *Fort Worth Star-Telegram*, May 14, 2021, https://www.star-telegram.com/opinion/cynthia-m-allen/article251391438.html.

99. "UIL Equal Access Bill," Texas Homeschool Coalition, accessed June 22, 2021, https://thsc.org/political-action/tim-tebow-bill/.

100. Michael Atkinson, "Let them play: Why Kentucky Should Enact a Tebow Bill Allowing Homeschoolers to Participate in Public School Sports," *Journal of Law and Education* 43 (2014): 433, https://heinonline.org/HOL/LandingPage?handle=hein.journals/jle43&div=28&id=&page=.

101. *Santa Fe Independent School District v. Doe*, 530 U.S. 290 (2000), https://www.law.cornell.edu/supct/html/99-62.ZS.html; Douglas C. Dow, "Santa Fe Independent School District v. Doe," First Amendment Encyclopedia, accessed June 4, 2021, https://www.mtsu.edu/first-amendment/article/672/santa-fe-independent-school-district-v-doe.

102. Jonathan Stempel, "High School Football Coach Who Prayed after Games Loses Appeal-U.S. Appeals Court," Reuters (*U.S. News & World Report*), March 18, 2021, https://www.usnews.com/news/top-news/articles/2021-03-18/high-school-football-coach-who-prayed-after-games-loses-appeal-us-appeals-court; Richard Wolf, "Supreme Court Refuses to Consider Appeal from High School Football Coach Fired for Praying after Games," *USA Today*, January 22, 2019, https://www.usatoday.com/story/news/politics/2019/01/22/supreme-court-wont-hear-praying-football-coach-case/1943694002/; Ariane de Vogue, "Washington High School Football Coach to Take Appeal over Prayer to Supreme Court," CNN, July 19, 2021, https://www.cnn.com/2021/07/19/politics/joe-kennedy-football-coach-prayer-supreme-court/index.html.

103. *Kennedy v. Bremerton School District*, https://www.supremecourt.gov/opinions/21pdf/21-418_i425.pdf; Pete Williams, "Supreme Court Rules for Former Coach in Public School Prayer Case," NBC News, June 27, 2022, https://www.nbcnews.com/politics/supreme-court/supreme-court-rules-coach-public-school-prayer-case-rcna31662.

104. Phoebe Suy, "Court Upholds Texas High Schools' Right to Add Bible Verses to Cheer Signs," Associated Press, August 31, 2018, https://apnews.com/article/fd6808bb985b47f59a69a4b336c6c718.

Chapter 9

1. Ben Nuckols, "Put Me In, Coach: Youth Baseball Participation on the Rise," Associated Press/*USA Today*, August 23, 2019, https://www.usatoday.com/story/sports/mlb/2019/08/23/put-me-in-coach-youth-baseball-participation-on-the-rise/40002827/; "State of Play," Aspen Institute, October 2019, https://www.aspeninstitute.org/wp-content/uploads/2019/10/2019_SOP_National_Final.pdf.

2. Molly C. Easterlin, Paul J. Chung, Mei Leng, and Rebecca Dudovitz, "Association of Team Sports Participation with Long-Term Mental Health Outcomes among Individuals Exposed to Adverse Childhood Experiences," *JAMA Pediatrics* 173, no. 7 (2019): 681–688, doi:10.1001/jamapediatrics.2019.1212.

3. "Benched (Full Segment)," *HBO Real Sports with Bryant Gumbel* (00:11:54), April 22, 2021, https://www.youtube.com/watch?v=7azd8_hitIE.

4. Jeremy Fowler, "Steelers' James Harrison Strips Kids of Non-Winning Participation Trophies," ESPN, August 15, 2015, https://www.espn.com/nfl/story/_/id/13447657/james-harrison-pittsburgh-steelers-takes-away-kids-participation-trophies-says-awards-earned.

5. Nancy Ann Jeffrey, "Trophy Overload," *Wall Street Journal*, March 11, 2005, https://www.wsj.com/articles/SB111050718773276858.

6. Vivian Diller, Ph.D, "Do We All Deserve Gold? Setting Kids up to Fail," *Psychology Today*, November 19, 2011, https://www.psychologytoday.com/us/blog/face-it/201111/do-we-all-deserve-gold-setting-kids-fail.

7. Lisa Heffernan, "In Defense of Participation Trophies: Why They Really Do Teach the Right Values," *Today*, August 31, 2015, https://www.today.com/parents/defense-participation-trophies-kids-t40931.

8. Gabriel Andrade, "A Rawlsian Defense of Participation Trophies," *Philosophia* (2022): 1–14, https://doi.org/10.1007/s11406-022-00515-x; Joseph Heath, "Rawls on Global Distributive Justice: A Defence," *Canadian Journal of Philosophy Supplementary Volume* 31 (2005): 193–226, https://www.cambridge.org/core/journals/canadian-journal-of-philosophy-supplementary-volume/article/abs/rawls-on-global-distributive-justice-a-defence/5BA53702BA25986AE31D6EF2586C6C93.

9. Britni de la Cretaz, "More Girls Are Playing Football. Is That Progress?" *New York Times*, February 2, 2018, https://www.nytimes.com/2018/02/02/well/family/football-girls-concussions.html.

10. Mark Stewart, "Girls Wrestling Gaining Hold at Milwaukee High School as Sport of Its Own," *Milwaukee Journal Sentinel* (*USA Today*), March 15, 2018, https://usatodayhss.com/2018/girls-wrestling-wisconsin-numbers-increasing.

11. USA Wrestling High School Development Committee Co-Chairs Joan Fulp and Andrea Yamamoto, accessed May 12, 2021, https://nwhof.org/wp-content/uploads/2018/06/Hall-of-Fame-Chapter-Directors-meeting-5_31_18.pdf.

12. Gary Abbott, "Women's Wrestling Week: Alaska's Michaela Hutchinson Was First Girl to Win State Title against Boys," USA Wrestling, March 13, 2016, https://www.teamusa.org/USA-Wrestling/Features/2016/March/13/Michaela-Hutchison-becomes-first-to-win-boys-state-meet; Sean Keeler, "Two Girl Wrestlers Made History Becoming the First Girls to Place at the State Tournament. 'She's Strong. She's Quick. She's Really Good,'" *Denver Post*, February 23, 2019, https://www.denverpost.com/2019/02/23/two-colorado-wrestlers-made-state-tournament-history/.

13. Luke Meredith, "Iowa Wrestling Star Refuses to Face Girl," *Salon*, February 17, 2011, https://www.salon.com/2011/02/17/iowa_wrestler_refuses_girl/.

14. Associated Press, "High School Sports: PIAA Overhauls Rules to Essentially Ban Boys on Girls Teams," *The Sentinel*, June 20, 2014, https://cumberlink.com/sports/high-school-sports-piaa-overhauls-rules-to-essentially-ban-boys-on-girls-teams/article_9780bb18-f8b8-11e3-aa23-001a4bcf887a.html.

15. William Romba, "There's No Such Thing as a Girl's Sport or a Boy's Sport," *The Outlook* (Monmouth University), June 25, 2014, https://outlook.monmouth.edu/opinion/33-volume-85-fall-2013-spring-2014/625-there-s-no-such-thing-as-a-girl-s-sport-or-a-boy-s-sport; NBC New York, "Panel Allows Boy to Play Girls' Field Hockey on Long Island," May 15, 2012, https://www.nbcnewyork.com/news/local/field-hockey-boy-long-island-smithtown-girls-team/1978858/; Stephen Haynes, "Southampton Field Hockey Player Keeling Pilaro Will Attend School in Virginia," *Newsday*, July 6, 2013, https://www.newsday.com/sports/high-school/field-hockey/southampton-field-hockey-player-keeling-pilaro-will-attend-school-in-virginia-1.5634239.

16. Erin E. Buzuvis, "Attorney General v. MIAA at Forty Years: A Critical Examination of Gender Segregation in High School Athletics in Massachusetts," *Texas Journal on Civil Liberties & Civil Rights* 25 (2019): 1, https://heinonline.org/HOL/LandingPage?handle=hein.journals/tfcl25&div=6&id=&page=.

17. Maggie Mertens, "Separating Sports by Sex Doesn't Make Sense," *The Atlantic*, September 17, 2022, https://www.theatlantic.com/culture/archive/2022/09/sports-gender-sex-segregation-coed/671460/.

18. Peter Dawson, "Transgender Wrestler Mack Beggs Is Booed After Second Straight Title Win," *Fort Worth Star-Telegram*, February 24, 2018, https://www.star-telegram.com/sports/article202001904.html; "Judge Tosses Suit That Sought to Block Transgender Athletes," Associated Press, April 25, 2021, https://apnews.com/article/sports-e881f5a74c82b931650142dee0e59fd3; Associated Press, "Judge Dismisses Lawsuit That Sought to Block Transgender Athletes from Girls High School Sports in Connecticut," ESPN, April 25, 2021, https://www.espn.com/espn/story/_/id/31334446/judge-dismisses-lawsuit-sought-block-transgender-athletes-girls-high-school-sports-connecticut; Christina Maxouris, "3 Connecticut High School Girls Are Suing over a Policy That Allows Trans Athletes to Compete in Girls' Sports," CNN, February 14, 2020, https://www.cnn.com/2020/02/14/us/transgender-athletes-connecticut-lawsuit/index.html.

19. Nolan D. McCaskill and Steven Overly, "Laws Banning Transgender Student Athletes Splinter GOP," *Politico*, May 6, 2021, https://www.politico.com/news/2021/05/06/transgender-athlete-laws-gop-484799.

20. Tal Axelrod, "Mississippi Governor Signs Year's First Ban on Transgender Athletes in Women's Sports," *The Hill*, March 11, 2021, https://

thehill.com/homenews/state-watch/542747-mississippi-governor-signs-years-first-ban-on-transgender-athletes-in.

21. Joanna Hoffman, "Billie Jean King, Megan Rapinoe, and Candace Parker Join Nearly 200 Athletes Supporting Trans Youth Participation in Sports," *Athlete Ally*, December 21, 2020, https://www.athleteally.org/amicus-trans-athletes/; "Statement of Women's Rights and Gender Justice Organizations in Support of Full and Equal Access to Participation in Athletics For Transgender People," accessed July 12, 2021, ACLU, https://www.aclu.org/sites/default/files/field_document/womens-groups-sign-on-letter-trans-sports-4.1.19.pdf; "The Coordinated Attack on Trans Student Athletes," ACLU, February 26, 2021, https://www.aclu.org/news/lgbtq-rights/the-coordinated-attack-on-trans-student-athletes/.

22. Elizabeth A. Sharrow, "Sports, Transgender Rights and the Bodily Politics of Cisgender Supremacy," *Laws* 10, no. 3 (2021): 63, https://doi.org/10.3390/laws10030063; Ashland Johnson, Liam Miranda, and Mark Lee, "Play to Win: Improving the Lives of LGBTQ Youth in Sports," Washington: Human Rights Campaign Foundation, *https://assets2.hrc.org/files/assets/resources/PlayToWin-FINAL.pdf* (2018); Molly C. Easterlin, Paul J. Chung, Mei Leng, and Rebecca Dudovitz, "Association of Team Sports Participation with Long-Term Mental Health Outcomes among Individuals Exposed to Adverse Childhood Experiences," *JAMA Pediatrics* 173, no. 7 (2019): 681–688, doi:10.1001/jamapediatrics.2019.1212; Elizabeth Levy Paluck and Chelsey S. Clark, "Can Playing Together Help Us Live Together?" *Science* 369, no. 6505 (2020): 769–770, https://www.science.org/doi/abs/10.1126/science.abb9990; Ellen J. Staurowsky, Mary Jane De Souza, Kathleen E. Miller, Don Sabo, Sohaila Shakib, Nancy Theberge, Philip Veliz, A. Weaver, and Nancy I. Williams, "Her Life Depends on It III: Sport, Physical Activity, and the Health and Well-Being of American Girls and Women," *Women's Sports Foundation* (2015), https://eric.ed.gov/?id=ED570479; GLSEN, Separation and Stigma: Transgender Youth and School Facilities, 2017; Shoshana K. Goldberg and Theo Santos, "The Importance of Sports Participation for Transgender Youth," Center for American Progress, 2021, https://www.americanprogress.org/article/fact-sheet-importance-sports-participation-transgender-youth/.

23. Kenneth R. Ginsburg, "The Committee on Communications and the.... Healthy Child Development and Maintaining Strong Parent-Child Bonds," *Pediatrics* 119.1 (January 2007): 182–191, https://doi.org/10.1542/peds.2006-2697; "The Loss of Children's Play: A Public Health Issue," *Alliance for Childhood Policy Brief*, https://web.mit.edu/writing/2016/FEE/July2016/Readings/Health_brief.pdf. www.allianceforchildhood.org.

24. Esther Entin, "All Work and No Play: Why Your Kids Are More Anxious, Depressed," *Atlantic*, October 12, 2011, https://www.theatlantic.com/health/archive/2011/10/all-work-and-no-play-why-your-kids-are-more-anxious-depressed/246422/. This article originally appeared on The DoctorWillSeeYouNow.com.

25. Amber Smith, "'Sandlot Day' Would Be Youth Baseball without Adult Interference," *Syracuse.com*, March 30, 2010, https://www.syracuse.com/cny/2010/03/sandlot_day_would_be_youth_baseball_without_adult_interference.html.

26. Jane E. Brody, "How to Avoid Burnout in Youth Sports," *New York Times*, May 7, 2018, https://www.nytimes.com/2018/05/07/well/how-to-avoid-burnout-in-youth-sports.html.

27. "Parents Speak Out about the Skyrocketing Cost of Youth Sports," ABC News, September 1, 2017, https://abcnews.go.com/Lifestyle/parents-speak-skyrocketing-cost-youth-sports/story?id=49549146.

28. Zoom interview with Dr. Avery Faigenbaum, October 16, 2020, confirmed and revised by email, June 11, 2021. Dr. Avery Faigenbaum is a full professor in the Department of Health and Exercise Science at the College of New Jersey. He teaches several courses, including health promotion, exercise prescription, and clinical exercise physiology.

29. Ryan Jaslow, "Study: Kids Hurt during Sports Once Every 25 Seconds," CBS News, August 6, 2013, https://www.cbsnews.com/news/study-kids-hurt-during-sports-once-every-25-seconds/.

30. Faigenbaum, Zoom interview.
31. Faigenbaum, Zoom interview.
32. Faigenbaum, Zoom interview.
33. Faigenbaum, Zoom interview.

34. Kelly Wallace, "How to Make Your Kid Hate Sports without Really Trying," CNN, January 21, 2016, https://www.cnn.com/2016/01/21/health/kids-youth-sports-parents/index.html.

35. John O'Sullivan, "Changing the Game in Youth Sports. John O'Sullivan@TEDx Bend," June 20, 2014, https://www.youtube.com/watch?v=VXw0XGOVQvw.

36. Faigenbaum, Zoom interview.
37. Faigenbaum, Zoom interview.
38. Faigenbaum, Zoom interview.

39. Stephanie Chen, "Going to Extreme Measures for Child Athletes," CNN, January 20, 2011, http://edition.cnn.com/2011/LIVING/01/20/making.of.sports.superstar/index.html; Sherman Hollar, "Gabby Douglas," Encyclopaedia Brittanica, accessed May 22, 2021, https://www.britannica.com/biography/Gabby-Douglas.

40. Ramona Shelburne, "Sills, 13, Commits to USC," ESPN, February 4, 2010, https://www.espn.com/los-angeles/ncf/news/story?id=4888515; Langston Wertz, Jr., "A 9 Year Old Youth Football Player Gets a Scholarship Offer? Yep, You Bet," *Charlotte Observer*, June 24, 2017, https://www.charlotteobserver.com/sports/article158025389.html; Photography by Melissa Lyttle, Intro by Kyle Bonagura, "Too Young for Division 1?" ESPN, October 23, 2017, https://www.espn.com/espn/feature/story/_/id/20924695/

10-year-old-maxwell-bunchie-young-touted-next-big-thing-football-coaches-bought-in.

41. Jim Taylor, Ph.D., "Sports Parents, We Have a Problem," *Psychology Today*, December 3, 2018, https://www.psychologytoday.com/us/blog/the-power-prime/201812/sports-parents-we-have-problem.

42. Brett Bodner, "Out of Bounds: Parents Who Crossed the Line at Their Children's Sporting Events," *New York Daily News*, August 3, 2017, https://www.nydailynews.com/news/crime/parents-crossed-line-children-sports-games-article-1.3403707; "Man Released from Mass. Prison after Serving Time for Beating Death of Fellow Hockey Dad," Fox News, August 27, 2010, https://www.foxnews.com/us/man-released-from-mass-prison-after-serving-time-for-beating-death-of-fellow-hockey-dad; ESPN.com news services, "Hockey Coach Gets Jail Time for Trip," ESPN, February 26, 2013, https://www.espn.com/espn/story/_/id/8993128/pee-wee-hockey-coach-martin-tremblay-gets-15-days-jail-tripping-player.

43. Sophie Sherry and Christina Zdanowicz, "Parents Brawl over a 13-Year-Old Umpire's Call at Youth Baseball Game. Police Say They're 'Disgusted,'" CNN, June 19, 2019, https://www.cnn.com/2019/06/19/us/parents-brawl-little-league-baseball-trnd/index.html.

44. Taylor Seely, "This Youth Sports Referee Shames Who Yell, Fight by Posting Videos of Them Online," *USA Today*, July 19, 2018, https://www.usatoday.com/story/life/allthemoms/2018/07/19/kids-referee-scolds-parents-who-misbehave-posting-them-facebook/801873002/.

45. Scott Stump, "Youth Sports Referees across the U.S. Are Quitting Because of Abusive Parents," *Today*, March 29, 2018, https://www.today.com/parents/youth-sports-referees-across-us-are-quitting-because-abusive-parents-t126087.

46. "Parent Code of Conduct," Little League Baseball, accessed May 20, 2021, https://www.littleleague.org/downloads/parent-code-conduct/.

47. Email interview with Brian Schiff, May 28, 2021.

48. Ahmad Austin, "Wrestling Official Suspended for Buena Dreadlocks Incident Has Lawsuit Dismissed," *The Press of Atlantic City*, May 7, 2021 (the *Philadelphia Inquirer* contributed to this report), https://pressofatlanticcity.com/news/local/wrestling-official-suspended-for-buena-dreadlocks-incident-has-lawsuit-dismissed/article_4cb7ddd3-55a6-5a29-9f7f-05691cf5e474.html; Justin Carissimo, "High School Wrestler Forced to Cut Dreadlocks or Forfeit Match," CBS News, December 23, 2018, https://www.cbsnews.com/news/alan-maloney-high-school-wrestler-forced-to-cut-dreadlocks-or-forfeit-match-by-new-jersey-referee/; Melanie Burney, "Judge Dismisses Lawsuit by Wrestling Official in Controversial South Jersey Dreadlocks Case," *Philadelphia Inquirer*, May 6, 2021, https://www.inquirer.com/education/nj-education-wrestling-dreadlocks-buena-andrew-johnson-referee-alan-maloney-20210506.html.

49. Leah Asmelash, "A Black Softball Player Says She Was Forced to Cut Off Her Hair Beads at a Game. Her Family Wants to Change the Rule They Say Is Discriminatory," CNN, May 14, 2021, https://www.cnn.com/2021/05/14/us/hair-discrimination-softball-durham-trnd/index.html.

50. Justin L. Mack, "Federal Appeals Court Says School Can't Make Basketball Player Cut His Hair," *Indy Star*, February 25, 2014, https://www.indystar.com/story/news/crime/2014/02/25/federal-appeals-court-says-school-cant-make-basketball-player-cut-his-hair/5810037/.

51. "Mandatory Play: What Parents Need to Know," Little League, accessed May 23, 2021. https://www.littleleague.org/university/articles/mandatory-play-what-parents-need-to-know/#:~:text=Tournament%20Play,-For%20all%20levels&text=If%20a%20tournament%20team%20has%2012%20or%20fewer%20eligible%20players,bat%20at%20least%20one%20time; Jon Solomon, "Why Project Play Recommends Equal Playing Time for Kids," Aspen Institute, accessed May 24, 2021, https://www.aspenprojectplay.org/equal-playing-time-story#:~:text=USA%20Hockey%20recommends%20equal%20playing,or%20disregarding%20the%20coaches'%20instructions.; "Harrisonburg Youth Football League (HYFL) Program Handbook 2019," City of Harrisonburg Parks & Rec, accessed May 26, 2021, https://www.harrisonburgva.gov/sites/default/files/Parks/files/2019%20HYFL%20Football%20Handbook.pd.

52. Scott Kretchmar, "Bench Players: Do Coaches Have a Moral Obligation to Play Benchwarmers?" in *The Ethics of Coaching Sports: Moral, Social and Legal Issues*, ed. Robert L. Simon (Boulder: Routledge, 2018), 121–136.

53. Schiff, email interview May 28, 2021.

54. Email interview with Aaron Carter, April 30, 2021.

Chapter 10

1. Steve Berkowitz, "Southeastern Conference Generated $721 Million in Revenue for 2019 Fiscal Year," *USA Today*, January 30, 2020, https://www.usatoday.com/story/sports/ncaaf/sec/2020/01/30/sec-generated-721-million-revenue-still-trails-big-ten/2856234001/.

2. Adam Rittenberg, "Big Ten Completes 7-Year, $7 Billion Media Rights Agreement with Fox, CBS, NBC," ESPN, August 18, 2022, https://www.espn.com/college-football/story/_/id/34417911/big-ten-completes-7-year-7-billion-media-rights-agreement-fox-cbs-nbc.

3. David M. Hale and Dave Wilson, "Pac-12 Revenue up 7 Percent, ACC Down Slightly In 2018–2019 Fiscal Year," ESPN, July 10, 2020, https://www.espn.com/college-sports/story/_/

id/29441623/pac-12-revenue-7-acc-slightly-2018-19-fiscal-year.

4. Stephen Hawkins, "Big 12 Distribution Down Only Slightly amid Pandemic," Associated Press, May 29, 2020, https://www.usnews.com/news/sports/articles/2020-05-29/big-12-revenue-distribution-down-only-slightly-amid-pandemic.

5. "NCAA Salaries," *USA Today*, accessed April 2, 2021, https://sports.usatoday.com/ncaa/salaries/.

6. Gregory Raucoules, "Tennessee Makes Danny White the 2nd-Highest Paid Athletic Director in the Country," WATE, January 22, 2021, https://www.wate.com/sports/orange-and-white-nation/tennessee-makes-danny-white-the-2nd-highest-paid-athletic-director-in-the-country/; "2019–2020 Athletic Directors," FBS Athletic Director Database, accessed June 10, 2021, http://www.sportsinfo.pro/AthleticDirector2020.html; Mike Wilson, "Danny White to Receive Five-Year Contract as Tennessee Athletics Director," *Knoxville News Sentinel*, January 22, 2021, https://www.knoxnews.com/story/sports/college/university-of-tennessee/football/2021/01/22/danny-white-tennessee-athletics-director-contract-salary-buyout/6675563002/.

7. Steve Berkowitz, "Power Five Conferences Had over $2.9 Billion in Revenue in Fiscal 2019, New Tax Records Show," *USA Today/Austin American-Statesman*, July 12, 2020, https://www.statesman.com/story/sports/college/2020/07/12/power-five-conferences-had-over-29-billion-in-revenue-in-fiscal-2019-new-tax-records-show/113870976/.

8. "Do All Universities Offer Athletic Scholarships?" *AthleticScholarships.net*, accessed June 5, 2021, https://www.athleticscholarships.net/question/do-all-universities-offer-athletic-scholarships; "Prospective Athlete Information," The Ivy League, July 28, 2017, https://ivyleague.com/sports/2017/7/28/information-psa-index.aspx.

9. Horace Mitchell, "Students Are Not Professional Athletes," *U.S. News & World Report*, January 6, 2014, https://www.usnews.com/opinion/articles/2014/01/06/ncaa-athletes-should-not-be-paid.

10. Kevin Allen, "Here are Some Benefits NCAA Athletes Already Are Eligible for That You Might Not Know About," *USA Today*, October 1, 2019, https://www.usatoday.com/story/sports/college/2019/10/01/ncaa-football-basketball-benefits-college-athletes-now-can-receive/2439120001/.

11. Michael Cunningham, "UGA Stipend Ranks Ninth in SEC," *Atlanta Journal Constitution*, September 23, 2016, https://www.ajc.com/sports/uga-stipend-ranks-ninth-sec/pNgiItpmBTTz6E35EogR6L/.

12. Will Hobson, "Cost of Attendance Stipends Show Which Sports Colleges Want to Spend On," *Washington Post*, May 22, 2015, https://www.washingtonpost.com/news/sports/wp/2015/05/22/cost-of-attendance-stipends-show-which-sports-colleges-want-to-spend-on/.

13. Hank Kurz, Jr., "ACC Players: Cost of Attendance Stipend Helps in Many Ways," Associated Press, October 31, 2018, https://apnews.com/article/d5bc51a726754b3489151613f6ba3fac.

14. Phone interview with Fran Dunphy, March 18, 2021, confirmed and revised by email, June 28, 2021. Fran Dunphy is the men's head basketball coach at La Salle University, the former men's head basketball coach at Temple University and the University of Pennsylvania, and the former interim athletic director at Temple University.

15. Ben Pickman, "Colorado Governor Signs Bills Allowing NCAA Athletes to Profit Off Name, Likeness," *Sports Illustrated*, March 20, 2020, https://www.si.com/college/2020/03/20/colorado-gov-signs-ncaa-bill-likeness; Media Center, "NCAA Responds to California Senate Bill 206," NCAA, September 11, 2019, https://www.ncaa.org/news/2019/9/11/ncaa-responds-to-california-senate-bill-206.aspx.

16. "Board of Governors Moves toward Allowing Student-Athlete Compensation for Endorsements and Promotions," NCAA, April 29, 2020, https://www.ncaa.org/news/2020/4/29/board-of-governors-moves-toward-allowing-student-athlete-compensation-for-endorsements-and-promotions.aspx.

17. Steve Berkowitz, "Florida Governor Signs Bill on College Athletes' Name, Image and Likeness," *USA Today*, June 12, 2020, https://www.usatoday.com/story/sports/college/2020/06/12/florida-bill-college-athletes-name-image-likeness/5347470002/.

18. Dan Murphy, "Federal Bill Pushes for Unrestricted NIL Endorsements for NCAA Athletes," ESPN, February 4, 2021, https://www.espn.com/college-sports/story/_/id/30833820/federal-bill-pushes-unrestricted-nil-endorsements-ncaa-athletes%C2%A0%C2%A0%C2%A0.

19. Dan Murphy, "Congressional Bill Introduced Would Allow College Athletes to Form Unions, Become Employees," ESPN, May 27, 2021, https://www.espn.com/college-sports/story/_/id/31521100/congressional-bill-introduced-allow-college-athletes-form-unions-become-employees.

20. Dunphy, phone interview, confirmed and revised by email, June 28, 2021.

21. Jay Bilas, "College Athletes Should Be Compensated," *New York Times*, March 14, 2012, https://www.nytimes.com/roomfordebate/2012/03/13/ncaa-and-the-interests-of-student-athletes/college-athletes-should-be-compensated.

22. Joe Valerio, Zoom interview, October 2, 2020, confirmed and revised by email, June 21, 2021.

23. Dunphy, phone interview, confirmed and revised by email, June 28, 2021.

24. "Northwestern Football Union Timeline," ESPN, August 17, 2015, https://www.espn.com/college-football/story/_/id/13456482/northwestern-football-union-line.

25. Jake New, "NLRB Punts on Northwestern Union," *Inside Higher Education*, August 18, 2015,

https://www.insidehighered.com/news/2015/08/18/national-labor-relations-board-declines-assert-role-northwestern-football-union.

26. Ian Millhiser, "The Supreme Court's Unanimous Decision on Paying NCAA Student-Athletes, Explained," *Vox*, June 21, 2021, https://www.vox.com/2021/6/21/22543598/supreme-court-ncaa-alston-student-athletes-football-basketball-sports-antitrust.

27. Dan Murphy, "Dan Lambert Plans $500-A-Month Endorsement Deal for Every Miami Hurricanes Football Player on Scholarship," ESPN, July 6, 2021, https://www.espn.com/college-football/story/_/id/31771563/dan-lambert-plans-500-month-endorsement-deal-every-miami-hurricanes-football-player-scholarship; Douglas S. Wood and David Close, "Here Are Some of the Ways NCAA Athletes Are Embracing the New World of the 'NIL' Deal," CNN, July 4, 2021, https://www.cnn.com/2021/07/04/us/ncaa-athletes-nil-deals/index.html; Alex Scarborough, "Sources: Alabama Crimson Tide QB Bryce Young Has Already Signed More than $800K in NIL Deals," ESPN, July 29, 2021, https://www.espn.com/college-football/story/_/id/31911674/sources-alabama-crimson-tide-qb-bryce-young-already-signed-800k-nil-deals; Dan Murphy, "Let's Make a Deal: NCAA Athletes Cashing In on Name, Image, and Likeness," ESPN, July 1, 2021, https://www.espn.com/college-sports/story/_/id/31738893/ncaa-athletes-cashing-name-image-likeness%C2%A0%C2%A0%C2%A0; John L. Pitts, "Mississippi State's Tanner Allen Makes History, Sells Autographed Cards," *Daily Journal*, July 7, 2021, https://www.djournal.com/sports/college/mississippi-state/mississippi-states-tanner-allen-makes-history-sells-autographed-cards/artigcle_3284474f-31dd-5116-9f65-36f755d3abc2.html.

28. Thilo Kunkel, Bradley J. Baker, Thomas A. Baker III, and Jason P. Doyle, "There is No Nil in NIL: Examining the Social Media Value of Student-Athletes' Names, Images, and Likeness," *Sport Management Review* 24, no. 5 (2021): 839–861, https://www.tandfonline.com/doi/abs/10.1080/14413523.2021.1880154; Andrea N. Geurin, "Elite Female Athletes' Perceptions of New Media Use Relating to Their Careers: A Qualitative Analysis," *Journal of Sport Management* 31, no. 4 (2017): 345–359, https://journals.humankinetics.com/view/journals/jsm/31/4/article-p345.xml.; A.N. Geurin-Eagleman and G. Clavio, "Utilizing Social Media as a Marketing Communication Tool: An Examination of Mainstream and Niche Sport Athletes' Facebook Pages," *International Journal of Sport Management* 16, no. 2 (2015): 488–497; Sangwon Na, Thilo Kunkel, and Jason Doyle, "Exploring Athlete Brand Image Development on Social Media: The Role of Signalling Through Source Credibility," *European Sport Management Quarterly* 20, no. 1 (2020): 88–108, https://www.tandfonline.com/doi/abs/10.1080/16184742.2019.1662465; J.P. Doyle, Y. Su, and T. Kunkel, "Athlete Branding Via Social Media: An Examination of the Content That Drives Fan Engagement on Instagram," *European Sport Management Quarterly* (2020), 1–21, https://doi.org/10.1080/16184742.2020.1806897; Thilo Kunkel and Rui Biscaia, "Sport Brands: Brand Relationships and Consumer Behavior," *Sport Marketing Quarterly* 29, no. 1 (2020): 3–17, http://doi.org/10.32731/SMQ.291.032020.01, https://fitpublishing.com/articles/sport-brands-brand-relationships-and-consumer-behavior; Thilo Kunkel, Rui Biscaia, Akiko Arai, and Kwame Agyemang, "The Role of Self-Brand Connection on the Relationship between Athlete Brand Image and Fan Outcomes," *Journal of Sport Management* 34, no. 3 (2019): 201–216, https://journals.humankinetics.com/view/journals/jsm/34/3/article-p201.xml.

29. Bethany Bradsher, "Compensating College Athletes," *CQ Researcher*, April 24, 2020, pp. 1–21, library.cqpress.com/cqresearcher/cqresrre2020042400; Julie Wurth, "Experts: It's 'a Whole Different Ballgame' Once Athletes Get Paid," *The News-Gazette*, October 13, 2019, https://www.news-gazette.com/news/local/special-reports/experts-it-s-a-whole-different-ballgame-once-athletes-get/article_c0b4447d-7859-5493-954c-dd07e5fbf166.html.

30. Christopher Palmieri, "The Billion Dollar Industry That Has Never Paid Its Money-Makers: The NCAA's Attempt at Compensation through Names, Images and Likeness," *Touro Law Review* 37 (2021): 1605, https://heinonline.org/HOL/LandingPage?handle=hein.journals/touro37&div=56&id=&page=.

31. Milan Simonich, "Young Pros Owed Spencer Haywood Large Vote of Thanks," *Pittsburgh Post-Gazette*, November 27, 2003, https://www.post-gazette.com/sports/other-sports/2003/11/28/Young-pros-owe-Spencer-Haywood-large-vote-of-thanks/stories/200311280087; ESPN.com, "Players Who Made the Most Successful Jumps from High School to the NBA," ESPN, April 2, 2020, https://www.espn.com/nba/story/_/id/28971664/players-made-most-successful-jumps-high-school-nba.

32. Coleman Collins, "The One-And-Done Conundrum," ESPN, June 15, 2016, https://www.espn.com/nba/story/_/id/16237629/ten-years-nba-one-done-rule-no-less-controversial.

33. Josh Slagter, "While Blasting NCAA, Stan Van Gundy Calls One-And-Done Rule Racist," *MLive*, February 26, 2018, https://www.mlive.com/pistons/2018/02/while_blasting_ncaa_stan_van_g.html; Vince Ellis, "Detroit Pistons' Stan Van Gundy: NCAA 'One of Worst Organizations,'" *Detroit Free Press*, February 25, 2018, https://www.freep.com/story/sports/nba/pistons/2018/02/25/detroit-pistons-stan-van-gundy-ncaa/371252002/.

34. Tim Reynolds, "AP Source: NBA, Union Forward Talks on Ending 'One and Done,'" Associated Press, February 21, 2019, https://apnews.com/article/f96ea437b5004e7a94660a87696bd0c0?utm_campaign=socialflow&utm_source=twitter&utm_medium=ap_sports&utm_

medium=ap_sports&utm_source=twitter&utm_campaign=socialflow; David Cobb, "Would the Lowering of the NBA Draft Age and Ending the One-And-Done Era Help or Hurt College Basketball?" CBS Sports, September 20, 2022, https://www.cbssports.com/college-basketball/news/would-the-lowering-of-the-nba-draft-age-and-ending-the-one-and-done-era-help-or-hurt-college-basketball/; Kurt Helin, "New Overtime Elite League Chips Away at Traditional College Path to NBA," NBC Sports, March 9, 2021, https://nba.nbcsports.com/2021/03/09/new-overtime-elite-league-chips-away-at-traditional-college-path-to-nba/.

35. Dunphy, phone interview, confirmed and revised by email, June 28, 2021.

36. Mike Decourcy, "R.J Hampton Didn't Make History By Passing On College—He Merely Skipped It," *Sporting News*, May 28, 2019, https://www.sportingnews.com/us/ncaa-basketball/news/rj-hampton-passing-on-college-history/b2cb1j1ws6bg1xqe0ws0qt4wp; Sam Perley, "Australian Rules Basketball: How the LaMelo Ball Effect Captivated the Land Down Under," NBA.com, May 12, 2021, https://www.nba.com/hornets/australian-rules-basketball-how-lamelo-ball-effect-captivated-land-down-under.

37. Garrett Stepien, "Isaiah Todd Explains NBA G League Signing, Michigan Decommitment," *247Sports.com*, April 17, 2020, https://247sports.com/Article/Isaiah-Todd-NBA-G-League-decision-explained-Michigan-Wolverines-basketball-recruiting-146171315/; Dave McMenamin, "Sources: G League Pushing Forward; Eyeing Reduced Bubble, Shortened Season," ESPN, December 17, 2020, https://www.espn.in/nba/story/_/id/30540803/sources-g-league-pushing-forward-eyeing-reduced-bubble-shortened-season; Adam Zagoria, "After Choosing NBA G League Path over College, Jalen Green Wishes He Were Playing Games Now but He Doesn't Regret His Decision," *Forbes*, December 3, 2020, https://www.forbes.com/sites/adamzagoria/2020/12/03/after-choosing-nba-g-league-path-over-college-jalen-green-wishes-he-were-playing-games-now-but-doesnt-regret-his-decision/?sh=77d63e25f490.

38. Adam Zagoria, "Shaka Smart Can See '10 or 12' High School Players Going the G-League Route Each Year," *Forbes*, April 27, 2020, https://www.forbes.com/sites/adamzagoria/2020/04/27/shaka-smart-can-see-10-or-12-high-school-players-going-the-nba-g-league-route-each-year/?sh=1fce266a3977.

39. Dan Wolken, "These Two New Leagues Aim to Challenge College Basketball for Top High School Players," *USA Today*, May 19, 2021, https://www.usatoday.com/story/sports/2021/05/19/college-basketball-two-new-leagues-coming-top-high-school-players/5154042001/; Martenzie Johnson, "Overtime Elite Pro Basketball League, Launching in September, Will Compensate High School-Aged Players," ESPN (*The Undefeated*), March 24, 2021, https://www.espn.com/nba/story/_/id/31002105/over-elite-pro-basketball-league-launching-september-compensate-high-school-aged-players.

40. Tom Luicci, "Should College Football Players Be Allowed to Leave for the NFL Any Time They Want," *Sports Illustrated*, May 8, 2020, https://www.si.com/college/tmg/tmg-maven/jim-harbaugh-proposal-for-leaving-college-early.

41. Michael A. McCann and Joseph S. Rosen, "Legality of Age Restrictions in the NBA and the NFL," *Case Westers Reserve Law Review* 56 (2005): 731, https://heinonline.org/HOL/LandingPage?handle=hein.journals/cwrlrv56&div=38&id=&page=.

42. Daniel Kaplan, "Debate Reopens on NFL's Age Restrictions," *Sports Business Daily*, January 14, 2019, https://www.sportsbusinessdaily.com/Journal/Issues/2019/01/14/Leagues-and-Governing-Bodies/NFL-age.aspx.

43. Valerio, Zoom interview, confirmed and revised by email, June 21, 2021.

44. Cherepinsky, email interview, September 19, 2020.

45. Bob Kravitz, "The Rat That Roared, Scored, and Prospered," *Sports Illustrated*, November 25, 1985, https://vault.si.com/vault/1985/11/25/the-rat-that-roared-scored-and-prospered; Ken Campbell, "Will NHL Raise the Draft Age to 19?" *Sports Illustrated*, October 27, 2017, https://www.si.com/hockey/news/will-nhl-raise-the-draft-age-to-19.

46. "First-Year Player Draft," MLB.com, accessed May 21, 2021, http://mlb.mlb.com/mlb/draftday/rules.jsp.

47. Will Dunham, "With a Fling of His Trademark Towel onto the...," UPI, January 14, 1989, https://www.upi.com/Archives/1989/01/14/With-a-fling-of-his-trademark-towel-onto-the/4167600757200/; Will Dunham, "Newspage Sports Georgetown Coach Walks Out of Basketball Game," UPI.com, January 14, 1989, https://www.upi.com/Archives/1989/01/14/Newspage-sports-Georgetown-coach-walks-out-of-basketball-game/8672600757200/.

48. Gary McCann, "Proposition 48/Nearly Five Years After Its Inception, Debate Still Surrounds Ruling," *News & Record*, May 25, 1991, https://greensboro.com/proposition-48-nearly-five-years-after-its-inception-debate-still-surrounds-ruling/article_58bb5f85-637e-58e1-b273-55ddd2817550.html.

49. Michelle Brutlag Hosick, "Divisions I and II Extend COVID-19 Initial-Eligibility Policies," NCAA.org, April 14, 2021, https://www.ncaa.org/about/resources/media-center/news/divisions-i-and-ii-extend-covid-19-initial-eligibility-policies.

50. Jeff Borzello, "NCAA: 15 Division 1 Programs Face Postseason Bans over APR Results," ESPN, May 19, 2020, https://www.espn.com/college-sports/story/_/id/29194905/ncaa-hits-15-division-programs-postseason-bans-apr-results; "Academic Progress Rate Explained," NCAA.org, accessed October 23, 2020, http://www.ncaa.org/

about/resources/research/academic-progress-rate-explained#:~:text=Teams%20must%20earn%20a%20four,under%2Dperform%20academically%20over%20time.

51. Tom Goldman, "Challenging the NCAA: HBCUs Say No More Discrimination in Academic Rules," NPR, December 10, 2020, https://www.npr.org/2020/12/10/944982415/challenging-the-ncaa-hbcus-say-no-more-discrimination-in-academic-rules.

52. Marc Tracy, "N.C.A.A.: North Carolina Will Not Be Punished For Academic Scandal," *New York Times*, October 13, 2017, https://www.nytimes.com/2017/10/13/sports/unc-north-carolina-ncaa.html; Dan Kane, "UNC Scandal Is Part of Senator's Report, Panel on Academic Fraud in College Sports," *News & Observer*, July 25, 2019, https://www.newsobserver.com/sports/article233059037.html.

53. Dunphy, phone interview, revised and confirmed by email, June 28, 2021.

54. Pat Forde, "Louisville Basketball's Infractions Case Will Be a Fascinating One for the NCAA," *Sports Illustrated*, May 4, 2020, https://www.si.com/college/2020/05/04/louisville-basketball-scandal-ncaa-rick-pitino; Colin Dwyer, "Rick Pitino Fired as Louisville Basketball Coach Amid Massive Bribery Probe," NPR, October 16, 2017, https://www.npr.org/sections/thetwo-way/2017/10/16/558129077/rick-pitino-fired-as-louisville-basketball-coach-amid-massive-bribery-probe; Chris Kenning, "Louisville Basketball Coach Rick Pitino Fired Amid Corruption Probe," Reuters, October 16, 2017, https://www.reuters.com/article/us-usa-crime-basketball-louisville/louisville-basketball-coach-rick-pitino-fired-amid-corruption-probe-idUSKBN1CL2WO.

55. Matt Norlander, "College Basketball Bribery Trial: Ex-Arizona Assistant Coach Sentenced to Three Months in Prison," CBS Sports, June 6, 2019, https://www.cbssports.com/college-basketball/news/college-basketball-bribery-trial-ex-arizona-assistant-coach-sentenced-to-three-months-in-prison/; Adam Zagoria, "Arizona Coach Book Richardson Making Comeback after Doing Jail Time in College Bribery Scheme," *Forbes*, August 17, 2020, https://www.forbes.com/sites/adamzagoria/2020/08/17/ex-arizona-coach-book-richardson-making-comeback-after-doing-jail-time-in-college-bribery-scheme/?sh=1d4dec9f4de1; Larry Neumeister, "Ex-Arizona Assistant Coach Pleads Guilty to Bribery Charge," Associated Press, January 22, 2019, https://apnews.com/article/e56c3336ba4a4e798b82d7422745a433; Matt Norlander, "FBI Recordings Catch Former Arizona Assistant Claiming Sean Miller Paid Deandre Ayton," CBS Sports, May 1, 2019, https://www.cbssports.com/college-basketball/news/fbi-recordings-catch-former-arizona-assistant-claiming-sean-miller-paid-deandre-ayton/; Anne Ryman and Craig Harris, "Newly Released NCAA Allegations: Bribes, Fake Transcripts Under UA Head Basketball Coach Sean Miller," *AZCentral.com*, March 5, 2021, https://www.azcentral.com/story/news/local/arizona-investigations/2021/03/05/university-arizona-basketball-sean-miller-ncaa-notice-allegations-bribery/4592889001/; Jeff Borzello, "Arizona Wildcats Fire Men's Basketball Coach Sean Miller," ESPN, April 7, 2021, https://www.espn.com/mens-college-basketball/story/_/id/31209814/sources-arizona-wildcats-fire-coach-sean-miller; Mark Schlabach, "Arizona Wildcats Men's Basketball Faces Allegations of Five Level 1 Rules Violations," ESPN, March 5, 2021, https://www.espn.com/mens-college-basketball/story/_/id/31013131/arizona-wildcats-men-basketball-faces-allegations-five-level-rules-violations; Mark Schlabach, "Your Guide to College Basketball's Ongoing NCAA Investigations," ESPN, November 6, 2020, https://www.espn.com/mens-college-basketball/story/_/id/30262819/your-guide-college-basketball-ongoing-ncaa-investigations.

56. Martin J. Greenberg and Lindsay Ruch, "Tattoogate," *Marquette National Sports Law Institute*, January 10, 2012, https://law.marquette.edu/national-sports-law-institute/tattoogate-january-10-2012; Joshua Lens, "Voiding the NCAA Show-Cause Penalty: Analysis and Ramifications of a California Court Decision, and Where College Athletics and Show-Cause Penalties Go From Here," *University of New Hampshire Law Review* 19 (2020): 21, https://heinonline.org/HOL/LandingPage?handle=hein.journals/plr19&div=6&id=&page=; Nicole Auerbach (contributing Dan Wolken), "The Perception and Reality of NCAA Show-Cause Penalties," *USA Today*, May 27, 2014, https://www.usatoday.com/story/sports/college/2014/05/27/ncaa-show-cause-penalty-bruce-pearl-kelvin-sampson/9632273/; Associated Press, "Minnesota Put On 4 Year Probation," CBS News, October 4, 2000, https://www.cbsnews.com/news/minnesota-put-on-4-year-probation/; Kyle Boone, "NCAA Appeals Committee Upholds Violations and Show-Cause Order for Ex-UConn Coach Kevin Ollie," CBS Sports, May 6, 2020, https://www.cbssports.com/college-basketball/news/ncaa-appeals-committee-upholds-violations-and-show-cause-order-for-ex-uconn-coach-kevin-ollie/; ESPN.com News Services, "Bozeman Returns from Eight-Year Ban," ESPN, April 28, 2006, https://www.espn.com/mens-college-basketball/news/story?id=2425197.

57. Nicole Auerbach, "The Perception and Reality of NCAA Show-Cause Penalties," *USA Today*, May 27, 2014, https://www.usatoday.com/story/sports/college/2014/05/27/ncaa-show-cause-penalty-bruce-pearl-kelvin-sampson/9632273/.

58. Dunphy phone interview confirmed and revised by email, June 28, 2021.

59. Edith Honan, "NCAA Sanctions Penn State for Sandusky Scandal," Reuters, July 23, 2012, https://www.reuters.com/article/us-usa-

pennstate/ncaa-sanctions-penn-state-for-sandusky-scandal-idUSBRE86L07F20120724; CNN Editorial Staff, "Penn State Scandal Fast Facts," CNN, October 28, 2013, https://www.cnn.com/2013/10/28/us/penn-state-scandal-fast-facts/index.html; NPR Staff and Wires (Tim Lambert of member station WITF in Harrisburg, Pennsylvania, contributed to this report, which contains material from The Associated Press), "2 Penn State Officials Step Down amid Abuse Scandal," NPR, November 7, 2011, https://www.npr.org/2011/11/07/142085416/curley-schultz-step-down-amid-penn-state-scandal; Kris Maher and John W. Miller, "Penn State Concealed Sex Abuse, Report Says," *Wall Street Journal*, July 13, 2012, https://www.wsj.com/articles/SB10001424052702303740704577522603440183734; Tony Manfred, "Why They Should Burn the Penn State Football Program to the Ground," *Business Insider*, July 12, 2012, https://www.businessinsider.com/penn-state-football-death-penalty-2012-7; George Stephanopoulos, "James Carville: Suspending Penn State Football Is a 'Really Dumb Idea,'" ABC News, July 15, 2012, https://abcnews.go.com/blogs/politics/2012/07/james-carville-suspending-penn-state-football-is-a-really-dumb-idea; Jake New, "Penn State Postseason Restored," *Inside Higher Education*, September 9, 2014, https://www.insidehighered.com/news/2014/09/09/ncaa-lifts-penn-states-postseason-ban-two-years-early.

60. Kris Maher and John W. Miller, "Penn State Concealed Sex Abuse, Report Says," *Wall Street Journal*, July 13, 2012, https://www.wsj.com/articles/SB10001424052702303740704577522603440183734.

61. Eric Dodds, "The 'Death Penalty' and How the College Sports Conversation Has Changed," *Time*, February 25, 2015, https://time.com/3720498/ncaa-smu-death-penalty/; Dennis Dodd, "30 Years Later: The Legacy of SMU's Death Penalty and Six Teams Nearly Hit With One," CBS Sports, February 22, 2017, https://www.cbssports.com/college-football/news/30-years-later-the-legacy-of-smus-death-penalty-and-six-teams-nearly-hit-with-one/; Mike Drago, "Nearly a Decade Later, 'Death Penalty' Still Stings SMU," Associated Press, August 7, 1996, https://apnews.com/article/55d7931c35f507d07bf72ad01d4493d4; Craig Thomas, "SMU's Miracle on Mockingbird," NCAA.org, September 5, 2014, https://www.ncaa.com/news/football/flashback-friday/2014-09-03/smu-returns-death-penalty-miracle-mockingbird.

62. Mike DeCourcy, "It's Time to Kill Talk of Louisville Getting NCAA Death Penalty," *Sporting News*, October 12, 2018, https://www.sportingnews.com/us/ncaa-basketball/news/louisville-basketball-death-penalty-infractions-rick-pitino-kenny-johnson-brian-bowen-adidas-fbi/33jol07hmv7r1oc9bxqvv8nza.

63. NCAA.org.

64. Glenn Guilbeau, "LSU Self-Imposes Bowl Ban for This Football Season as Part of Penance for NCAA Violations," *Lafayette Daily Advertiser* (*USA Today*), December 9, 2020, https://www.usatoday.com/story/sports/ncaaf/sec/2020/12/09/lsu-self-imposes-bowl-ban-ncaa-violations-college-football/3873898001/.

65. Pat Forde, "The Self-Imposed Ban Strategy Is Spreading, but It's Still Not Fooling Anyone," *Sports Illustrated*, December 29, 2020, https://www.si.com/college/2020/12/29/arizona-lsu-auburn-self-imposed-postseason-bans.

66. "The Undefeated Years," *Centre Daily Times*, November 4, 2010, https://www.centredaily.com/news/special-reports/joe-paterno/article42802191.html.

67. Heather Dinich, "College Football Playoff Will Consider Proposal for Expanding to 12-Team Format," ESPN, June 10, 2021, https://www.espn.com/college-football/story/_/id/31604970/college-football-playoff-consider-expanding-12-team-format.

68. Heather Dinich and Pete Thamel, "College Football Playoff to Expand to 12-Team Format," ESPN, September 2, 2022, https://www.espn.com/college-football/story/_/id/34509443/board-managers-decide-12-team-college-football-playoff-sources-say.

69. Heather Dinich, "Spring 16-Team Playoff Bracket Approved for FCS football," ESPN, September 22, 2020, https://www.espn.com/college-football/story/_/id/29947215/spring-16-team-playoff-bracket-approved-fcs-football.

70. Matthew A. Starcke and Rebecca E. Crandall, "The Academic Impact of Participating in College Football Playoff Games," *Journal for the Study of Sports and Athletes in Education* 12, no. 3 (2018): 258–279, https://www.tandfonline.com/doi/abs/10.1080/19357397.2018.1525151.

71. Christopher Walsh, "Oklahoma and Texas Officially Join the Southeastern Conference," *Sports Illustrated*, July 30, 2021, https://www.si.com/college/alabama/bamacentral/oklahoma-and-texas-officially-join-southeastern-conference-july-30-2021.

72. Kevin Skiver, "USC, UCLA to Join Big Ten: Latest News, Updates on College Football's Next Reported Conference Shakeup," *Sporting News*, July 1, 2022, https://www.sportingnews.com/us/ncaa-football/news/usc-ucla-big-ten-news-updates-college-football/pktssarszndixtcdlcmgtpam.

Chapter 11

1. Milton Jamail, "Charles Comiskey," Encyclopaedia Britannica, accessed November 12, 2020, https://www.britannica.com/biography/Charles-Comiskey.

2. Joel D. Treese, "President Herbert Hoover and Baseball," WhiteHouseHistory.org, accessed November 12, 2020, https://www.whitehousehistory.org/president-herbert-hoover-and-baseball.

3. Ray Sanchez, "His Rebellious Act Led to Free

Agency in Sports. Now Curt Flood's Children Want Him in the Hall of Fame," CNN, December 29, 2019, https://www.cnn.com/2019/12/29/us/curt-flood-mlb-free-agency-trnd.

4. Nick Acocella, "Flood of Free Agency," ESPN, accessed November 13, 2020, https://www.espn.com/classic/biography/s/Flood_Curt.html.

5. Ray Sanchez, "His Rebellious Act Led to Free Agency in Sports. Now Curt Flood's Children Want Him in the Hall of Fame," CNN, December 29, 2019, https://www.cnn.com/2019/12/29/us/curt-flood-mlb-free-agency-trnd.

6. Associated Press, "Lawmakers Push for Curt Flood's Enshrinement in Hall of Fame," *USA Today*, February 27, 2020, https://www.usatoday.com/story/sports/mlb/2020/02/27/lawmakers-push-for-curt-floods-enshrinement-in-hall-of-fame/111376166/.

7. Email interview with Jun Kim, Associate Professor and Program Director of Sport Management in the School of Global Business at Arcadia University, March 5, 2021.

8. Ben Pickman, "The First NBA Free Agent to Sign Never Expected This Kind of Movement," *Sports Illustrated*, July 5, 2019, https://www.si.com/nba/2019/07/05/basketball-free-agency-tom-chambers.

9. Jace Evans, "Biggest NBA Free Agency Moves of the Past 25 Years, from Shaq to LeBron to Kevin Durant," *USA Today*, June 25, 2019, https://www.usatoday.com/story/sports/nba/2019/06/25/nba-free-agency-biggest-moves-past-25-years/1495469001/.

10. Sean Deveney, "Paying Anthony: Where $33 million Isn't Really $33 Million," *Sporting News*, March 10 2014, https://www.sportingnews.com/us/other-sports/news/carmelo-anthony-33-million-contract-cba-new-york-knicks-chicago-bulls-lakers-nba-free-agency-2014-phil-jackson/j7fiqe841thh1ore6c9na4ozr.

11. Clark Judge, "How Did NFL Free Agency Begin? With Reggie White and the Sound of a Gavel," *Sports Illustrated*, March 20, 2021, https://www.si.com/nfl/talkoffame/nfl/nfl-free-agency-in-1993.

12. Peter Carfagna, Zoom interview, June 16, 2021, confirmed and revised by email, June 21, 2021.

13. Aaron Caputo, Zoom interview, June 16, 2021, confirmed and revised by email, June 21, 2021.

14. SI Staff, "Wit and Wisdom of Hockey," *Sports Illustrated*, October 1, 2013, https://www.si.com/nhl/2013/10/01/nhl-hockey-wit-and-wisdom#gid=ci0255c71cd0032781&pid=doug-larson.

15. Associated Press, "Boogaard Had Brain Ailment Caused by Blows to Head: Report," Associated Press/CBC, December 5, 2011, https://www.cbc.ca/sports/hockey/nhl/boogaard-had-brain-ailment-caused-by-blows-to-head-report-1.976515.

16. Ken Dryden, "Dryden: Case for Fighting in Hockey Continues to Get Weaker and Weaker," *Globe and Mail*, November 2, 2013, https://www.theglobeandmail.com/sports/hockey/dryden-case-for-fighting-in-hockey-continues-to-get-weaker-and-weaker/article15232138/; Ken Dryden, *Game Change: The Life and Death of Steve Montador and the Future of Hockey* (Oxford: Signal, 2017).

17. Grace C. Plassche, Thomas A. Fortney, Cole Morrissette, John F. Korzelius, and Charles A. Popkin, "Fighting in Professional Ice Hockey: It's Time for a Change," *The Physician and Sportsmedicine* 51, no. 5(2022): 1–9, https://www.tandfonline.com/doi/full/10.1080/00913847.2022.2078170.

18. Kelvin Tiemstra, "Eddie Shack," The Canadian Encyclopedia, November 26, 2015, https://www.thecanadianencyclopedia.ca/en/article/eddie-shack.

19. Adam Proteau, "An Oral History of the Broad Street Bully-Era Philadelphia Flyers," *Sports Illustrated*, The Hockey News, November 10, 2014, https://www.si.com/hockey/news/an-oral-history-of-the-broad-street-bully-era-philadelphia-flyers.

20. Scott Altman, "The 10 Dirtiest Teams in Sports History," *Bleacher Report*, November 11, 2010, https://bleacherreport.com/articles/512472-the-top-10-dirtiest-teams-in-sports-history.

21. Phil Mushnick, "Documentary on '74–75 Flyers Hits Mark," *New York Post*, May 2, 2010, https://nypost.com/2010/05/02/documentary-on-74-75-flyers-hits-mark/.

22. Stephen Whyno, "Fighting Down, Hatred Still High in NHL Playoff Rivalries," Associated Press, April 11, 2018, https://apnews.com/article/baefbcca7bcc4eb58a419bd5c639a034.

23. Chris Kuc, "Why Is Fighting Vanishing from the NHL?" *Chicago Tribune*, February 6, 2016, https://www.chicagotribune.com/sports/blackhawks/ct-hockey-fighting-fading-spt-0207-20160206-story.html.

24. Lewis H. Margolis, Greg Canty, Mark Halstead, and John D. Lantos, "Should School Boards Discontinue Support for High School Football?" *Pediatrics* 139, no. 1 (2017), https://publications.aap.org/pediatrics/article-abstract/139/1/e20162604/51997/Should-School-Boards-Discontinue-Support-for-High; "Faculty Member Says High School Football Is Not Worth Health Risk to Young Players," UNC.edu, December 5, 2016, https://sph.unc.edu/sph-news/maternal-and-child-health-professor-argues-that-high-school-football-is-not-worth-health-risk-to-players/.

25. Bob Cook, "Why High School Football Is Dying a Slow Death (It's Not Just Concussion)," *Forbes*, August 31, 2018, https://www.forbes.com/sites/bobcook/2018/08/31/why-high-school-football-is-dying-a-slow-death-its-not-just-concussions/?sh=79f337077540.

26. Ryan Wilson, "Brett Favre Reiterates He Wouldn't Want Son to Play Football," CBS Sports, July 16, 2014, https://www.cbssports.com/nfl/news/brett-favre-reiterates-he-wouldnt-want-son-to-play-football/; "A Warning from the Future/Favre 4 Flag," Concussion Legacy Foundation, August 17, 2021, https://www.youtube.com/watch?

v=LCeEP8QPV_I; "Brett Favre Featured in Powerful New PSA Begging Parents to Keep Children Out of Tackle Football until Age 14 to Lower CTE Risk," Concussion Legacy Foundation, August 17, 2021, https://concussionfoundation.org/news/press-release/brett-favre-featured-powerful-PSA-lower-CTE-risk; Jason Duaine Hahn, "Brett Favre Warns Parents against Letting Kids Play Tackle Football Too Young: 'Not Worth the Risk,'" *People*, August 17, 2021, https://people.com/sports/brett-favre-asks-parents-not-to-let-children-under-14-play-football/; "Brett Favre's Urgent Message for Football Parents," Concussion Legacy Foundation, https://concussionfoundation.org/Favre4Flag.

27. Jacob Feldman, "Four States Considering Youth Tackle Football Bans," *Sports Illustrated* April 4, 2018, https://www.si.com/nfl/2018/04/04/four-states-consider-banning-youth-football-themmqb-newsletter.

28. Los Angeles Times Editorial Board, "Editorial: Banning Tackle Football for Kids? There's Nothing 'Nanny State' about It If the Science Is Sound," *Los Angeles Times*, February 2, 2018, https://www.latimes.com/opinion/editorials/la-ed-football-concussions-youths-20180202-story.html.

29. Andy Staples, "With Rugby and Robots, College Football's Top Teams are Battling for the Perfect Tackle," *Sports Illustrated*, August 15, 2017, https://www.si.com/college/2017/08/15/college-football-tackling-methods-robots-targeting-rule; Kip Hill and Chad Sokol, "Washington Companies Develop New Technologies to Make Football Safer," *The Spokesman-Review*, July 1, 2018, https://www.spokesman.com/stories/2018/jul/01/washington-companies-develop-new-technologies-to-m/.

30. NFL Football Operations, "Health & Safety Rules Changes," accessed June 4, 2021, https://operations.nfl.com/the-rules/rules-changes/health-safety-rules-changes/.

31. "Medical Examination Tents to Improve Injury Evaluations on NFL Sidelines," NFL.com, August 1, 2017, https://www.nfl.com/player healthandsafety/health-and-wellness/player-care/medical-examination-tents-to-improve-injury-evaluations-on-nfl-sidelines.

32. Zoom interview with Joe Valerio, October 2, 2020, confirmed and revised by email, June 21, 2021.

33. Valerio, Zoom interview, confirmed and revised by email, June 21, 2021.

34. Hallie Grossman, "Virtual Reality and Robotic Tackling Dummies—How Dartmouth is Shaping the Future of Football," ESPN, August 14, 2019, https://www.espn.com/college-football/story/_/id/27347621/virtual-reality-robotic-tackling-dummies-how-dartmouth-shaping-future-football.

35. Frank Schwab, "'Make Football Violent Again': Players Express More Frustration with Helmet Rule," *Yahoo! Sports*, August 3, 2018, https://www.yahoo.com/lifestyle/make-football-violent-players-express-frustration-helmet-rule-184321034.html.

36. Jamiles Lartey, "Concussion: Doctor Who Fought NFL Says 'No Equipment Can Prevent' Such Injuries," *Guardian*, December 28, 2015, https://www.theguardian.com/us-news/2015/dec/28/concussion-prevention-football-safety-brain-injury-bennet-omalu-nfl-will-smith.

37. Steve Almasy and Jill Martin, "Judge Approves NFL Concussion Lawsuit Settlement," CNN, April 22, 2015, https://www.cnn.com/2015/04/22/us/nfl-concussion-lawsuit-settlement/index.html.

38. Zac Al-Khateeb, "NFL, Players Association Reportedly Nearing Agreement to Keep Concussed Players from Returning to Games," *Sporting News*, October 1, 2022, https://www.sportingnews.com/us/nfl/news/nfl-players-association-concussed-players-returning-games/fcbsgqzrepj4jz8agmvohuem; Eric Levenson, Kevin Dotson, and Zoe Sottile, "NFL and Players Union Agree to Updated Concussion Protocol," CNN.com, October 8, 2022. https://www.cnn.com/2022/10/08/football/nfl-concussion-protocol-change-spt/index.html.

39. Jacques Berlinerblau, "Damar Hamlin's Collapse Should Have All Football Fans Feeling Complicit," MSNBC.com, January 3, 2023, https://www.msnbc.com/opinion/msnbc-opinion/damar-hamlins-cardiac-arrest-make-nfl-fans-feel-complicit-rcna64045.

40. Mike Jones, "Opinion: Luke Kuechly Retirement Continues NFL Trend. Good for Him, and for Fellow Players," *USA Today*, January 15, 2020, https://www.usatoday.com/story/sports/nfl/columnist/mike-jones/2020/01/14/luke-kuechly-rob-gronkowski-andrew-luck-early-nfl-retirement/4475069002/.

41. Valerio, Zoom interview, confirmed and revised by email.

42. Peter McCabe, "How Many More Young People Must Die before Mixed Martial Arts Is Banned?" *Guardian*, April 15, 2016, https://www.theguardian.com/commentisfree/2016/apr/15/mixed-martial-arts-mma-banned-joao-carvalho-fighter.

43. CBC News, "City Places Temporary Ban on Combative Sports in Edmonton," CBC, December 8, 2017, https://www.cbc.ca/news/canada/edmonton/moratorium-combative-sports-edmonton-tim-hague-1.4440597.

44. Matthew Doarnberger, "Why Is Mixed Martial Arts Only Banned in New York," *Newsweek*, July 28, 2015, https://www.newsweek.com/why-mixed-martial-arts-banned-only-new-york-357899; Matthew Doarnberger, "Why Unions Want to Ban MMA," Foundation for Economic Education, July 27, 2015, https://fee.org/articles/why-unions-want-to-ban-mma/. Matthew Doarnberger operates the website Libertarian Sports Fan, where the original version of this article first appeared. This iteration appeared on the Anything Peaceful blog of the Foundation for Economic Education.

45. Aaron Smith, "MMA Wins Long Fight to Be Legal in New York State," CNN, March 23, 2016, https://money.cnn.com/2016/03/23/news/mma-ufc-fight-in-new-york/index.html.

46. Daniel Neyra, "Fight Kids: The Future of Mixed Martial Arts or a Detriment to America's Youth? A Call to Regulate Children's MMA," *Family Court Review* 51, no. 4 (2013): 727–741.

47. Chris Mannix, "Don't Count on Oscar De La Hoya and Other Legends' Comebacks to Save Boxing," *Sports Illustrated*, March 31, 2021, https://www.si.com/boxing/2021/03/31/de-la-hoya-old-boxers-out-of-retirement.

48. Ralph Wiley, "Then All the Joy Turned to Sorrow," *Sports Illustrated*, November 22, 1982, https://vault.si.com/vault/1982/11/22/then-all-the-joy-turned-to-sorrow.

49. Lem Satterfield, "Revisiting a Fight with No Winners," *Baltimore Sun*, April 20, 2005, https://www.baltimoresun.com/news/bs-xpm-2005-04-20-0504200221-story.html.

50. "Biography: Hayes Edward Sanders," Olympics.com, accessed June 11, 2021, https://olympics.com/en/athletes/hayes-edward-sanders.

51. Dan Rafael, "Johnson Dies from Brain Injury Sustained in Title Fight," ESPN, September 22, 2005, https://www.espn.com/sports/boxing/news/story?id=2169415.

52. "50 Years after Death, Ohio Town Honors Boxer Davey Moore," WBUR, September 28, 2013, https://www.wbur.org/onlyagame/2013/09/28/davey-moore-statue.

53. "Cinema: The New Pictures, May 21, 1956," *Time*, May 21, 1956, http://content.time.com/time/subscriber/article/0,33009,808541,00.html.

54. Ben Morse, "Each Year, 13 Boxers on Average Die in the Ring," *CNN*, October 17, 2019, https://www.cnn.com/2019/10/17/sport/boxing-deaths-patrick-day-spt-intl-trnd/index.html; Joseph R. Svinth, "Death under the Spotlight: The Manuel Velazquez Collection," 2011, https://ejmas.com/jcs/velazquez/Death_Under_the_Spotlight_2011_Final.pdf.

55. Declan Warrington, "Brain Injury Charity Headway Calls for Boxing to be Banned after Scott Westgarth death," *Evening Standard*, February 27, 2018, https://www.standard.co.uk/sport/brain-injury-charity-headway-calls-for-boxing-to-be-banned-after-scott-westgarth-death-a3777336.html; "Death of Boxer 'Shocking and Unacceptable Waste' Says Brain Injury Charity," Headway.org.uk, February 27, 2018, https://www.headway.org.uk/news-and-campaigns/news/2018/death-of-boxer-shocking-and-unacceptable-waste-says-brain-injury-charity/.

56. George Vecsey, "Sports of the Times; Cosell Says 'I've Had It,'" *New York Times*, December 6, 1982, https://www.nytimes.com/1982/12/06/sports/sports-of-the-times-cosell-says-i-ve-had-it.html.

57. Victoria Stagg Elliott, "AMA Pulls No Punches, Reiterates Boxing Ban: Ringside Physicians Were Denied Endorsement for Their Efforts to Make the Sport Safer (AMA Annual Meeting News)," *American Medical News*, July 8 2002, pp. 23+.

58. Tony Sheldon, "Boxing Should Be Banned Unless Rules are Tightened," *BMJ* 327, no. 1186 (2003), https://web.archive.org/web/20041223110345id_/http://bmj.bmjjournals.com:80/cgi/reprint_abr/327/7425/1186-b.pdf.

59. D.K. Sokol, "The Not-So-Sweet Science: The Role of the Medical Profession in Boxing," *Journal of Medical Ethics* 30, no. 5 (2004): 513–514, http://dx.doi.org/10.1136/jme.2003.004952.

60. Nigel Collins, "Does Boxing Need to Be Saved?" ESPN, April 20, 2017, https://www.espn.com/boxing/story/_/id/19204063/does-boxing-need-saved.

61. D.K. Sokol, "The Not-So-Sweet Science: The Role of the Medical Profession in Boxing." *Journal of Medical Ethics* 30, no. 5 (2004): 513–514, http://dx.doi.org/10.1136/jme.2003.004952; Angus Phillips, "WBC Limits Title Fights to 12 Rounds," *Washington Post*, December 10, 1982, https://www.washingtonpost.com/archive/sports/1982/12/10/wbc-limits-title-fights-to-12-rounds/370e0dff-01bb-446a-a9e9-c98a1e9bcb27/.

62. Erik Brady, "50 Senators Sign Letter Urging Redskins to Change Team Name," *USA Today*, May 22, 2014, https://www.usatoday.com/story/sports/nfl/redskins/2014/05/22/washington-redskins-senate-nickname-american-indians-daniel-snyder/9439613/.

63. Austin Knoblauch, "Roger Goodell Doesn't See Redskins Name Change," NFL.com, January 30, 2018, https://www.nfl.com/news/roger-goodell-doesn-t-see-redskins-name-change-0ap3000000912193.

64. SI Wire, "Poll: 9 in 10 Native Americans Not Offended by Redskins Name," *Sports Illustrated*, May 19, 2016, https://www.si.com/nfl/2016/05/19/washington-redskins-nickname-native-american-poll-not-offended.

65. Fred Bowen, "Is the Redskins Name a Big Deal? Poll Results Say It's Not," *Washington Post*, May 23, 2016, https://www.washingtonpost.com/lifestyle/kidspost/is-the-redskins-name-a-big-deal-poll-results-say-its-not/2016/05/23/df217bba-1dd7-11e6-9c81-4be1c14fb8c8_story.html.

66. Naomi Schaefer Riley, "Redskins Need to Ignore PC Culture and Keep Their Name," *New York Post*, September 4, 2016, https://nypost.com/2016/09/04/redskins-need-to-ignore-pc-culture-and-keep-their-name/.

67. Dan Barry, "A Heated Linguistic Debate: What Makes 'Redskins' a Slur?" *New York Times*, May 22, 2016, https://www.nytimes.com/2016/05/22/sports/football/redskins-poll-prompts-a-linguistic-debate.html.

68. John Keim, "How the Events of 2020 Have Changed the Washington Football Team," ESPN, August 20, 2020, https://www.espn.com/nfl/story/_/id/29460299/how-events-2020-changed-washington-football-team.

69. Cory Collins, "Sports Teams That Retired

Native American Mascots, Nicknames," *Sporting News*, October 12, 2015, https://www.sportingnews.com/us/nfl/list/washington-redskins-native-american-mascot-controversies-history/1wmax2elthrth1kvstmdeyre65.

70. Mark Meltzer, "Braves Stay Out of Indians' Mascot Controversy," *Atlanta Business Chronicle*, January 30, 2018, https://www.bizjournals.com/atlanta/news/2018/01/30/braves-stay-out-of-indians-mascot-controversy.html; Michael Shapiro, "Here's Why Cleveland Chose 'Guardians' for New Team Name," *Sports Illustrated*, July 23, 2021, https://www.si.com/mlb/2021/07/23/cleveland-guardians-name-change-decision-explained.

71. Gabriel Burns, "Braves Use 'Tomahawk Chop' during Home Opener," *Atlanta Journal-Constitution*, April 9, 2021, https://www.ajc.com/sports/atlanta-braves/braves-use-tomahawk-chop-during-home-opener-against-phillies/Z2LLQXRGXNHWDDQQZ5Y4QAKPJE/.

72. Sid Hartman, "Hartman: Globetrotters Bring Back Important Memories," *Star Tribune* (*Winona Daily News*), March 24, 2016, https://www.winonadailynews.com/sports/hartman-globetrotters-bring-back-important-memories/article_22df991d-b317-5cc9-87ca-09a2cf5c4d60.html; Scott Rafferty, "Harlem Globetrotters: The Team That Changed Basketball Forever," Ca.nba.com, February 25, 2021, https://ca.nba.com/news/harlem-globetrotters-the-team-that-changed-basketball-forever/rhgkudku82qe1f85ze49hy3g6; HarlemGlobetrotters.com, "Our Story," Harlem Globetrotters, accessed June 4, 2021, https://www.harlemglobetrotters.com/About.

73. Robert W. Peterson, "The Negro Leagues Gain Prominence," Encyclopaedia Britannica, accessed June 4, 2021, https://www.britannica.com/sports/Negro-league/The-Negro-leagues-gain-prominence.

74. Riley Neubauer, "Basketball Legend Earl Lloyd and Other Sports Pioneers Left a Lasting Legacy," *Sports Illustrated Kids*, March 5, 2015, https://www.sikids.com/kid-reporter/lasting-legacyhttps://www.nydailynews.com/sports/basketball/legends-rebound-espn-documentary-black-college-stars-article-1.286035-earl-lloyd.

75. The Undefeated, "Basketball's Battle for Racial Equality," *Undefeated*, September 18, 2018, https://theundefeated.com/features/excerpt-basketball-a-love-story-battle-for-racial-equality/ https://andscape.com/features/excerpt-basketball-a-love-story-battle-for-racial-equality/; Jackie MacMullan, Rafe Bartholomew, and Dan Klores, *Basketball: A Love Story* (New York: Crown Archetype, 2018); Kyle Hightower, "NBA Laid Key Foundation during 1960s amid Off-Court Chaos," Associated Press, November 22, 2021, https://apnews.com/article/ahmaud-arbery-nba-sports-boxing-race-and-ethnicity-316cc3269afbcaf80a42c31ef6661ebe; Steve Aschburner, "How a Trio of Pioneers Gave Rise to Racial Integration in the NBA," NBA.com, March 31, 2022, https://www.nba.com/news/how-chuck-cooper-nat-clifton-earl-lloyd-changed-nba-racial-integration.

76. Ian Begley, "Legends Rebound in ESPN Documentary about Black College Stars," *New York Daily News*, March 11, 2008, https://www.nydailynews.com/sports/basketball/legends-rebound-espn-documentary-black-college-stars-article-1.286035; Fred Jeter, "Cleo Hill to Be Inducted into Collegiate Hall of Fame," *Richmond Free Press*, September 29, 2017, http://richmondfreepress.com/news/2017/sep/29/cleo-hill-be-inducted-collegiate-hall-fame/.

77. Deron Snyder, "The Root: Football as a Measure of Progress," WBUR, September 30, 2010, https://www.wbur.org/npr/130235701/story.php; Patrick Hruby, "'We've Come So Far': How Black Quarterbacks Defied a Racist Past to Become the NFL's Future," *Guardian*, September 20, 2019, https://www.theguardian.com/sport/2019/sep/20/black-quarterbacks-history-stereotypes.

78. Associated Press, "Limbaugh Quits Job on Pregame Show," *New York Times*, October 1, 2003, https://www.nytimes.com/2003/10/01/sports/football/limbaugh-quits-job-on-pregame-show.html; ESPN.com News Services, "Limbaugh Resigns from NFL Show," ESPN, October 2, 2003 (information from the Associated Press was used in this report), https://www.espn.com/gen/news/2003/1001/1628537.html.

79. Mike Sando, "Rooney Rule in Reverse: Minority Coaching Hires Have Stalled," ESPN, July 19, 2016, https://www.espn.com/nfl/story/_/id/17101097/staggering-numbers-show-nfl-minority-coaching-failure-rooney-rule-tony-dungy.

80. Jemele Hill, "Some Team Has to Want Me," *Atlantic*, February 5, 2021, https://www.theatlantic.com/i https://www.nytimes.com/2022/04/01/sports/football/nfl-bruce-arians-todd-bowles-tampa-bay.htmldeas/archive/2021/02/black-coaches-see-the-limits-of-the-nfls-racial-reckoning/617943/.

81. Kurt Streeter, "Bruce Arians Gave the N.F.L. a Diversity Blueprint it Shouldn't Ignore," *New York Times*, April 1, 2022, https://www.nytimes.com/2022/04/01/sports/football/nfl-bruce-arians-todd-bowles-tampa-bay.html.

82. Carfagna, Zoom interview. confirmed and revised by email.

83. Caputo, Zoom interview, confirmed and revised by email.

84. Dr. Ketra Armstrong, University of Michigan sport management professor, email interview, August 17, 2021.

85. Marcus Hayes, email interview, August 11, 2021. Marcus Hayes is a *Philadelphia Inquirer* sports columnist.

86. Jarrett Bell, "With Monumental NFL Lawsuit, Brian Flores Boldly Stepped Where Others Desired/Opinion," *USA Today*, October 2, 2022, https://www.usatoday.com/story/sports/nfl/columnist/bell/2022/10/02/brian-flores-lawsuit-change-anything-black-nfl-coaches/8152808001/;

Joe Rivera, "What Happened to Brian Flores? Revisiting the Dolphins Scandal, Firing That Led to Lawsuit against NFL," *Sporting News*, September 29, 2022, https://www.sportingnews.com/us/nfl/news/brian-flores-dolphins-scandal-firing-nfl-lawsuit/vxcywrbhznx066mowbjkunbp.

87. Bob Nightengale, "Orioles' Adam Jones Berated by Racist Taunts at Fenway Park," *USA Today*, May 1, 2017, https://www.usatoday.com/story/sports/mlb/2017/05/01/orioles-adam-jones-berated-racist-taunts-fenway-park-peanuts/101187172/.

88. ESPN.com news services, "Banana Thrown at Wayne Simmonds," ESPN, September 22, 2011, https://www.espn.com/nhl/story/_/id/7007219/fan-throws-banana-philadelphia-flyers-winger-wayne-simmonds.

89. Euan McKirdy, "Racial Slur Sprayed on LeBron's House: 'It's Tough Being Black in America,'" CNN, May 31, 2017, https://www.cnn.com/2017/05/31/sport/lebron-james-racist-graffiti-incident/index.html.

90. Richard Lapchick, "Racist Acts in Sports Were on the Rise in 2017," ESPN, January 11, 2018 (Blair Neelands contributed significantly to this column), https://www.espn.com/espn/story/_/id/22041345/racism-continued-rear-ugly-head-sports-2017.

91. Richard Lapchick, "Once Again, Racist Acts in Sports Are on the Rise," ESPN, January 3, 2019 (Meaghan Coleman made significant contributions to this column), https://www.espn.com/espn/story/_/id/25675586/racism-sports-continued-rear-ugly-head-2018.

92. Laura Gozzi, "Moise Kean: Italian Media Reaction to Racist Chanting," BBC, April 3, 2019, https://www.bbc.com/sport/football/47808611.

93. Tom McGowan and Paul Gittings, "Villarreal Give Life Ban to Rogue Fan Who Threw Banana at Dani Alves," CNN, April 29, 2014, http://edition.cnn.com/2014/04/28/sport/football/dani-alves-banana-racism-football/index.html.

94. "England Work Placements for BAME Coaches," BBC, August 14, 2018, https://www.bbc.com/sport/football/45180368.

95. "England FA Condemn Racist Abuse Aimed at Marcus Rashford, Bukayo Saka, Jadon Sancho after Euro 2020 Shootout Loss," ESPN, July 11, 2021, https://www.espn.com/soccer/england-eng/story/4431389/england-fa-condemn-racist-abuse-aimed-at-rashfordsakasancho-after-euro-shootout-loss.

96. Ernie Suggs, "Willie O'Ree: First African-American to Play in NHL Skates into the Hall of Fame," *Atlanta Journal-Constitution*, June 26, 2018, https://www.ajc.com/news/willie-ree-breaking-the-color-line-ice/w4U4mnVONZQn4TgkkRrYWP/; Blake Edwards, "List of Black Hockey Players," *Ranker*, July 13, 2020, https://www.ranker.com/list/black-hockey-players/sportsyeah; "List of Black NHL Players," Wikipedia, accessed June 16, 2021, https://en.wikipedia.org/wiki/List_of_black_NHL_players.

97. Camila Domonoske, "Legendary Boxer Jack Johnson Gets Pardon, 105 Years after Baseless Conviction," NPR, May 24, 2018, https://www.npr.org/sections/thetwo-way/2018/05/24/614114966/legendary-boxer-jack-johnson-gets-pardon-105-years-after-baseless-conviction; ESPN.com news services, "Jack Johnson Pardoned for Violation of Mann Act in 1913," ABC News, May 24, 2018, https://abcnews.go.com/Sports/jack-johnson-pardoned-violation-mann-act-1913/story?id=55412992.

98. "Owens, Jesse 1913–1980," Encyclopedia.com, accessed June 19, 2021, https://www.encyclopedia.com/people/sports-and-games/sports-biographies/jesse-owens.

99. Nigel Collins, "Louis-Schmeling: More than a Fight," ESPN, June 19, 2013, https://www.espn.com/boxing/story/_/id/9404398/more-just-fight.

100. "Remembering Jackie," Baseball Hall of Fame," accessed June 20, 2021, https://baseballhall.org/discover-more/stories/baseball-history/remembering-jackie.

101. Associated Press, "List of Major Sports League's Franchise Relocations," *USA Today*, January 27, 2017, https://www.usatoday.com/story/sports/nfl/2017/01/27/list-of-major-sports-leagues-franchise-relocations/97125258/.

102. Richard Florida, "The Never-Ending Stadium Boondoggle," *Bloomberg*, September 10, 2015, https://www.bloomberg.com/news/articles/2015-09-10/u-s-sports-stadiums-continue-to-be-funded-with-taxpayer-money.

103. Berkeley Economic Review Staff, "The Economics of Sports Stadiums: Does Public Financing of Sports Stadiums Create Local Economic Growth, or Just Help Billionaires Improve Their Profit Margin," *Berkeley Economic Review*, April 4, 2019, https://econreview.berkeley.edu/the-economics-of-sports-stadiums-does-public-financing-of-sports-stadiums-create-local-economic-growth-or-just-help-billionaires-improve-their-profit-margin/; Andrew Zimbalist and Roger G. Noll, "Sports, Jobs & Taxes: Are New Stadiums Worth the Cost," Brookings, June 1, 1997, https://www.brookings.edu/articles/sports-jobs-taxes-are-new-stadiums-worth-the-cost/.

104. Kim, email interview.

Chapter 12

1. International Olympic Committee, "Welcome to the Ancient Olympic Games," Olympics.com, accessed October 21, 2022, https://olympics.com/ioc/ancient-olympic-games.

2. "The Games," Penn Museum, accessed October 11, 2020, https://www.penn.museum/sites/olympics/olympicorigins.shtml.

3. "The Olympics: A Guide to Reference Sources," Library of Congress, accessed October 11, 2020, https://www.loc.gov/rr/main/olympics/dates.html.

4. Morgan Jerkins, "Usain Bolt: What the

World's Fastest Man Means to Jamaica," *Rolling Stone*, July 28, 2016, https://www.rollingstone.com/culture/culture-sports/usain-bolt-what-the-worlds-fastest-man-means-to-jamaica-99518/.

5. Jerkins, "Usain Bolt: What the World's Fastest Man Means to Jamaica."

6. Brennan K. Berg, Seth A. Kessler, and Thomas M. Hunt, "A Realist Perspective of Sport and International Relations: U.S. Governmental Perceptions of Olympic Boycott Movements, 1936–2008," in *The 'Olympic and Paralympic' Effect on Public Policy*, ed. Daniel Bloyce and Andy Smith (London: Routledge, 2015), 7–20.

7. "Sport's Not Immune to Politics," *Economic Times*, January 18, 2007.https://economictimes.indiatimes.com/sports-not-immune-to-politics/articleshow/1259213.cms?from=mdr; Reuters Staff, "FACTBOX: Olympics-Past Boycotts and Cancellations," Reuters, March 23, 2020, https://www.reuters.com/article/health-coronavirus-olympics/factbox-olympics-past-boycotts-and-cancellations-idUSL8N2BG3M2.

8. History.com Editors, "President Carter Announces Olympic Boycott," History, March 19, 2020, https://www.history.com/this-day-in-history/carter-announces-olympic-boycott.

9. U.S. Department of State Archive, "The Olympic Boycott, 1980," accessed October 14, 2021, https://2001-2009.state.gov/r/pa/ho/time/qfp/104481.htm.

10. Christine Brennan, "Opinion: For 1980 Athletes, Olympic Postponement Brings Bittersweet Memories of Boycott," *USA Today*, April 8, 2020, https://www.usatoday.com/story/sports/columnist/brennan/2020/04/08/olympic-boycott-40-years-later-us-athletes/2964840001/.

11. Brennan, "Opinion: For 1980 Athletes, Olympic Postponement Brings Bittersweet Memories of Boycott."

12. Gerhard Peters and John T. Woolley, "Jimmy Carter, Remarks to Representatives of U.S. Teams to the 1980 Summer Olympics," American Presidency Project, accessed October 15, 2020, https://www.presidency.ucsb.edu/node/250176.

13. Lynn Zinser, "Phone Call from China Transformed '84 Games," *New York Times*, July 14, 2008, https://www.nytimes.com/2008/07/14/sports/olympics/14olympics.html.

14. Jim Reineking, "Nikki Haley, U.S. Ambassador to U.N., Says It's An 'Open Question' If U.S. Athletes Will Compete In 2018 Games," *USA Today*, December 7, 2017, https://www.usatoday.com/story/sports/2017/12/07/nikki-haley-us-ambassador-un-2018-winter-olympics/929800001/.

15. Nikki Haley, "Amb. Nikki Haley: Biden Should Boycott China's Winter Olympics Next Year," Fox News, February 25, 2021, https://www.foxnews.com/opinion/biden-boycott-china-winter-olympics-2022-nikki-haley.

16. Raisa Patel, "MPs Call to Relocate 2022 Beijing Games over China's Reported Abuses of Uighur Minority," CBC, February 6, 2021, https://www.cbc.ca/news/politics/mps-call-for-relocation-of-2022-beijing-olympics-1.5904286.

17. MacIntosh Ross, Zumretay Arkin, Frances Hui, Chemi Lhamo, Teng Biao, Michael Heine, Ann Peel, et al, "Critical Commentary: A Call to Boycott the 2022 Beijing Olympic Games and Establish Minimum Human Rights Standards for Olympic Hosts," *Journal of Emerging Sport Studies* 6 (2021), https://doi.org/10.26522/jess.v6i.3589.

18. Gerry Shih, "India Joins Diplomatic Boycott of Beijing Olympics over Role of Chinese Soldier from Border Clash," *Washington Post*, February 3, 2022, https://www.washingtonpost.com/sports/olympics/2022/02/03/olympics-india-china-torch-boycott/.

19. Anne Applebaum, "Boycott Beijing. The Olympics Are a Perfect Place for a Protest," *Slate*, March 24, 2008, https://slate.com/news-and-politics/2008/03/the-olympics-are-the-perfect-place-for-a-protest.html.

20. Dr. Ketra Armstrong, University of Michigan sport management professor, email interview, August 17, 2021.

21. Nicholas Sarantakes, "An Olympic Boycott Is Never the Answer," *New York Times*, February 6, 2014, https://www.nytimes.com/roomfordebate/2014/02/06/when-should-countries-boycott-the-olympics/an-olympic-boycott-is-never-the-answer.

22. David Shoemaker and Karen O'Neill, "Beijing 2022: A Boycott Is Not the Answer," *Globe and Mail*, February 4, 2021, https://www.theglobeandmail.com/sports/olympics/article-beijing-2022-a-boycott-is-not-the-answer/.

23. Marc Stein, "Chapter 1: The Three Endings," ESPN, August 9, 2012, https://www.espn.com/olympics/summer/2012/basketball/story/_/id/8245769/remembering-1972-us-olympic-squad-40-years-later-three-endings.

24. Stein, "Chapter 1: The Three Endings"; Sean Ingle, "50 Stunning Olympic Moments. No. 1: USA v. USSR, Basketball Final, 1972," *Guardian*, November 16, 2011, https://www.theguardian.com/sport/blog/2011/nov/16/usa-ussr-olympic-basketball-1972.

25. Ingle, "50 Stunning Olympic Moments. No.1: USA v. USSR, Basketball Final, 1972."

26. Marc Stein, "Chapter 1: The Three Endings," ESPN, August 9, 2012, https://www.espn.com/olympics/summer/2012/basketball/story/_/id/8245769/remembering-1972-us-olympic-squad-40-years-later-three-endings.

27. National Public Radio (heard on *All Things Considered*), "Add a Judge and Things Get Tricky: The Quandary of Subjective Sports," NPR, February 21, 2014, https://www.npr.org/2014/02/21/280759146/add-a-judge-and-things-get-tricky-the-quandary-of-subjective-sports.

28. Staff Writer, "More Olympic Sports Rely on Judges to Determine Winner," *The Columbus Dispatch*, February 8, 2014, https://www.dispatch.com/story/news/2014/02/08/more-olympic-sports-rely-on/24170808007/.

29. Amy Shipley, "2 French Skating Officials Banned," *Washington Post*, May 1, 2002, https://www.washingtonpost.com/archive/politics/2002/05/01/2-french-skating-officials-banned/e0169ea6-0e5a-4109-9294-a48160e6fcfa/; Associated Press, "Sale, Pelletier Share Gold with Russian Pair," ESPN, February 15, 2002, https://www.espn.com/olympics/winter02/figure/news?id=1333280; Christopher Clarey, "FIGURE SKATING; 2 French Officials Suspended 3 Years in Skating Scandal," *New York Times*, May 1, 2002, https://www.nytimes.com/2002/05/01/sports/figure-skating-2-french-officials-suspended-3-years-in-skating-scandal.html.

30. John Branch, "Who Needs Stopwatches? From the Shadows Judges Take Starring Roles," *New York Times*, February 6, 2014, https://www.nytimes.com/2014/02/06/sports/olympics/who-needs-stopwatches-from-shadows-judges-are-co-stars.html.

31. John Ashdown, "50 Stunning Olympic Moments No. 14: Roy Jones, Jr. Cheated Out Of Gold," *Guardian*, February 15, 2012, https://www.theguardian.com/sport/blog/2012/feb/15/olympic-moments-roy-jones-jr.

32. Pat Putnam, "Travesty. The U.S. Placed Six Boxers In the Final Rounds—Then They Had To Take On the Judges," *Sports Illustrated*, October 10, 1988, https://vault.si.com/vault/1988/10/10/boxing-travesty-the-us-placed-six-boxers-in-the-final-rounds-then-they-had-to-take-on-the-judges; Ashdown, "50 Stunning Olympic Moments No. 14: Roy Jones, Jr. Cheated Out Of Gold."

33. Marshall B. Jones, "The Home Advantage in Individual Sports: An Augmented Review," *Psychology of Sport and Exercise* 14, no. 3 (2013): 397–404, https://doi.org/10.1016/j.psychsport.2013.01.002; Charles J. Ansorge, and John K. Scheer, "International Bias Detected in Judging Gymnastic Competition at the 1984 Olympic Games," *Research Quarterly for Exercise and Sport* 59, no. 2 (1988): 103–107, https://doi.org/10.1080/02701367.1988.10605486; Nigel J. Balmer, Allan M. Nevill and Andrew M. Lane, "Do judges enhance home advantage in European championship boxing?" *Journal of Sports Sciences* 23, no. 4 (2005): 409–416, https://doi.org/10.1080/02640410400021583; Nigel J. Balmer, Alan M. Nevill, and A. Mark Williams, "Home Advantage in the Winter Olympics (1908–1998)," *Journal of Sports Sciences* 19, no. 2 (2001), 129–139, https://doi.org/10.1080/026404101300036334; Nigel J. Balmer, Alan M. Nevill, and A. Mark Williams, "Modelling home advantage in the Summer Olympic Games," *Journal of Sports Sciences* 21, no. 6 (2003): 469–478, https://doi.org/10.1080/0264041031000101890; R. Park and P. Werthner. "Analysis of Politicized Bias in Judging at the Olympic Diving Competitions, Montreal, 1976," *Canadian Journal of Applied Sports Sciences* 2 (1977): 225; Richard Seltzer and Wayne Glass, "International Politics and Judging in Olympic Skating Events: 1968–1988," *Journal of Sport Behavior* 14, no. 3 (1991): 189, https://www.proquest.com/openview/ce6503fbb33c7e92be9a6951db06f812/1?pq-origsite=gscholar&cbl=1819738.

34. Alex Abad-Santos, "Winter Olympics 2018: Figure Skating Scoring Explained for People Who Don't Follow Figure Skating," *Vox*, February 14, 2018, https://www.vox.com/culture/2018/2/14/17004314/figure-skating-scoring-winter-olympics-2018.

35. "Subjectively Judged Sports Stress Athletes," University of Tennessee Knoxville News, February 13, 2002, https://news.utk.edu/2002/02/13/subjectively-judged-sports-stress-athletes/.

36. Philip Hersh, "New Math: Figure Skating's Latest Recalculations Change Skaters' Formula for Success," NBC Sports, May 20, 2020, https://olympics.nbcsports.com/2020/05/20/figure-skating-judging-changes-nathan-chen/.

37. Emma Daly and David Fickling, "Barcelona and Sydney: The Hosts Who Got the Most," *Guardian*, December 8, 2002, https://www.theguardian.com/politics/2002/dec/08/athletics.olympics2012.

38. Justin Clark, "Opinion: What L.A. Can Learn From the 1992 Barcelona Olympics," *Los Angeles Times*, October 6, 2015, https://www.latimes.com/opinion/livable-city/la-ol-1006-2024-olympics-burbank-barcelona-olympics-20151005-story.html.

39. Allen Barra, "From Soccer to Tennis to Cycling, Spain Is Suddenly Dominating Sports," *Atlantic*, June 22, 2012, https://www.theatlantic.com/entertainment/archive/2012/06/from-soccer-to-tennis-to-cycling-spain-is-suddenly-dominating-sports/258837/.

40. Jack Todd, "Montreal Olympics: Our Love-Hate Relationship with the Big Owe," *Montreal Gazette*, July 29, 2016, https://montrealgazette.com/sports/montreal-olympics-our-love-hate-relationship-with-the-big-owe; The Canadian Press, "Forty Years On, Montreal's Olympic Stadium Remembered as More than Just a Money Pit," *National Post*, July 12, 2016, https://nationalpost.com/sports/olympics/forty-years-on-montreals-olympic-stadium-remembered-as-more-than-just-a-money-pit.

41. Email interview with Dr. Jun Kim, March 5, 2021. Dr. Jun Kim is an associate professor and program director of Sport Management in the School of Global Business at Arcadia University.

42. Associated Press, "Tokyo Governor Won't Speculate on Olympic Bribery Scandal," Fox Sports, February 18, 2019, https://www.foxsports.com/stories/olympics/tokyo-governor-wont-speculate-on-olympic-bribery-scandal; Sean Ingle, "Tokyo Olympic Games Corruption Claims Bring Scandal Back to the IOC," *Guardian*, May 11, 2016, https://www.theguardian.com/sport/2016/may/11/tokyo-olympic-games-2020-ioc-international-olympic-committee-corruption-bid-scandal; Antoni Slodkowski, Nathan Layne, Mari Saito, and Ami Miyazaki, "Exclusive: Japan Businessman Paid $8.2 Million by Tokyo Olympics Bid Lobbied Figure at Center of French Corruption Probe,"

Reuters, March 30, 2020, https://www.reuters.com/article/us-olympics-2020-lobbying-exclusive/exclusive-japan-businessman-paid-8-2-million-by-tokyo-olympics-bid-lobbied-figure-at-center-of-french-corruption-probe-idUSKBN21I0CX; Graham Dunbar, Associated Press Sportswriter, "Brisbane Picked to Host 2032 Olympics without a Rival Bid," ABC News, July 21, 2021, https://abcnews.go.com/Sports/wireStory/brisbane-picked-host-2032-olympics-rival-bid-78963209; Rachel Axon, "Arrest Raises More Questions about IOC's Response to Rio Scandal," *USA Today*, October 5, 2017, https://www.usatoday.com/story/sports/olympics/2017/10/05/arrest-raises-questions-ioc-response-rio-scandal/737180001/.

43. Associated Press, "Despite 2002 Bribery Scandal, Salt Lake City Aims to Host 2030 Olympics," CBC, December 18, 2020, https://www.cbc.ca/sports/olympics/salt-lake-city-2030-winter-olympics-1.4951389.

44. William Drozdiak and Amy Shipley, "IOC Votes to Expel 6 Members," *Washington Post*, January 25, 1999, https://www.washingtonpost.com/archive/politics/1999/01/25/ioc-votes-to-expel-6-members/11be6509-1cc8-43aa-a545-86837a63cff9/; Associated Press, "Despite 2002 Bribery Scandal, Salt Lake City Aims to Host 2030 Olympics," CBC, December 18, 2020, https://www.cbc.ca/sports/olympics/salt-lake-city-2030-winter-olympics-1.4951389.

45. James McBride, "The Economics of Hosting the Olympic Games," Council on Foreign Relations, January 19, 2018, https://www.cfr.org/backgrounder/economics-hosting-olympic-games.

46. Steve Almasy, "Olympic Luger Dies on Track Where Speed Caused Concern," CNN, February 13, 2010, https://www.cnn.com/2010/SPORT/02/12/olympic.luge.crash/index.html; Lisa Marie Segarra, "These Athletes Have Died While Competing in the Olympics over the Years," *Time*, February 14, 2018, https://time.com/5155540/athletes-who-have-died-competing-in-the-olympics/.

47. History.com editors, "Arab Terrorists Take Israeli Hostages at the Munich Olympics," History.com, November 13, 2009, https://www.history.com/this-day-in-history/arab-terrorists-take-israeli-hostages-at-the-olympics.

48. Mark Niesse, "Olympic Park Bombing Brought Terror Close to Home," *Atlanta Journal Constitution*, November 26, 2019, https://www.ajc.com/news/local-govt--politics/olympic-park-bombing-brought-terror-close-home/nY5aRea9uxPKr4vOo1dy5K/; CNN Editorial Research, "Eric Robert Rudolph Fast Facts," CNN, December 6, 2012, https://www.cnn.com/2012/12/06/us/eric-robert-rudolph---fast-facts/index.html.

49. Eric Adams, "The Security Savants Protecting the Winter Olympics," *Wired*, January 30, 2018, https://www.wired.com/story/winter-olympics-security/.

50. Jeff Daniels, "Around 60,000 Security Forces, Interceptor Drones Deployed to Protect Pyeongchang Olympics," CNBC, February 5, 2018, https://www.cnbc.com/2018/02/05/pyeongchang-olympics-deploy-60000-security-forces-anti-drone-tech.html.

51. Jack Tarrant, "Tokyo 2020 to up Security with Facial Recognition System," Reuters, August 6, 2018, https://www.reuters.com/article/us-olympics-2020-facial-recognition/olympics-tokyo-2020-to-up-security-with-facial-recognition-system-idUSKBN1KS0B5.

52. Tatiana Kanunnikova, "How to Tackle Tokyo 2020 Olympics Security Risks," *Asia Times*, April 23, 2019, https://asiatimes.com/2019/04/how-to-tackle-tokyo-2020-olympics-security-risks/.

53. Reuters Staff, writing by Candida Ng, Singapore Editorial Reference Unit, editing by David Fogarty, "TIMELINE: Olympic Torch Protests Around the World," Reuters, April 28, 2008, https://www.reuters.com/article/us-olympics-torch-disruptions/timeline-olympic-torch-protests-around-the-world-idUSSP17070920080428.

54. Rob Hodgetts, "Does Switching Nations Make You Less of an Olympian?" CNN, February 14, 2018, https://www.cnn.com/2018/02/08/sport/winter-olympics-athletes-switching-nations-pyeongchang/index.html.

55. Dan Wetzel, "30 Years after 'Cool Runnings' Debut, Jamaica Has Its First Women's Bobsled Team," *Yahoo! Sports*, February 10, 2018, https://sports.yahoo.com/30-years-cool-runnings-debut-jamaica-first-womens-bobsled-team-073152490.html; Justin Kirkland, "The Jamaican Women's Bobsleigh Team is in 18th Place. Start Casting *Cool Runnings 2*," *Esquire*, February 21, 2018, https://www.esquire.com/sports/a16637788/jamaican-womens-bobsleigh-team-cool-runnings-2/.

56. Peter Spiro, "It's Time for Olympic Free Agency," *Slate*, February 6, 2014, https://slate.com/culture/2014/02/sochi-olympics-citizenship-rules-you-shouldnt-have-to-be-an-american-to-compete-for-team-usa.html.

57. Olivia Blair, "Rio 2016 Refugee Team: Meet the Athletes Whose Stories Have Inspired the World," *Independent*, August 10, 2016, https://www.independent.co.uk/news/people/rio-2016-olympics-refugee-team-yusra-mardini-rami-anis-syria-yonas-kinde-anjelina-nadai-lohalith-a7181241.html.

58. James Ellingworth, "EXPLAINER: How Team of Refugee Athletes Made It to the Olympics," Associated Press, July 25, 2021, https://apnews.com/article/2020-tokyo-olympics-swimming-sports-iran-olympic-team-migration-fdf0cba94e5c254138962f50cd5e34a9.

Bibliography

Books

Berg, Brennan K., Seth A. Kessler, and Thomas M. Hunt. "A Realist Perspective of Sport and International Relations: US Governmental Perceptions of Olympic Boycott Movements, 1936–2008" in *The 'Olympic and Paralympic' Effect on Public Policy*, edited by Daniel Bloyce and Andy Smith. London: Routledge, 2015, 7–20.

Bowman, Nicholas David, and Gregory A. Cranmer. "Can Video Games Be a Sport?" in *Understanding eSports: An Introduction to a Global Phenomenon*, edited by Ryan Rogers. Lanham, MD: Lexington, 2019, 15–30.

Burkett, Brendan, Mike McNamee, and Wolfgang Potthast. "Shifting Boundaries in Sports Technology and Disability: Equal Rights or Unfair Advantage in the Case of Oscar Pistorius?" in *Moving Beyond Boundaries in Disability Studies*, edited by Michele Moore. London: Routledge, 2013, 143–154.

Congalton, K. Jeanine. "Competitive Eating as Sport" in *Sporting Rhetoric: Performance, Games, and Politics*. New York: Peter Lang, 2009, 175.

Dryden, Ken. *Game Change: The Life and Death of Steve Montador and the Future of Hockey*. Oxford: Signal, 2017.

Edwards, Steven D. "Should Oscar Pistorius Be Excluded from the 2008 Olympic Games?" in *Ethics, Disability and Sports*, edited by Ejgil Jespersen and Mike NcNameeLondon: Routledge, 2013, 26–39.

Gubar, Justine. *Fanaticus: Mischief and Madness in the Modern Sports Fan*. Lanham, MD: Rowman & Littlefield, 2015.

Hartmann, Douglas. *Race, Culture, and the Revolt of the Black Athlete: The 1968 Olympic Protests and Their Aftermath*. Chicago: University of Chicago Press, 2004.

Kretchmar, Scott. "Bench Players: Do Coaches Have a Moral Obligation to Play Benchwarmers?" in *The Ethics of Coaching Sports: Moral, Social and Legal Issues*, edited by Robert L. Simon. Boulder: Routledge, 2018, 121–136.

Lewis, Jerry Middleton. *Sports Fan Violence in North America*. Lanham, MD: Rowman & Littlefield, 2007.

MacMullan, Jackie, Rafe Bartholomew, and Dan Klores. *Basketball: A Love Story*. New York: Crown Archetype, 2018.

Schlichter, Art, and Jeff Snook. *Busted: The Rise and Fall of Art Schlichter*. Wilmington, OH: Orange Frazer Press, 2009.

Suits, Bernard. "The Elements of Sport" in *Ethics in Sport*, edited by William John Morgan. Champaign, IL: Human Kinetics, 2007, 9–19.

Wann, Daniel L., Merrill J. Melnick, Gordon W. Russell, and Dale G. Pease. *Sport Fans: The Psychology and Social Impact of Spectators*. Abingdon: Routledge, 2001.

Wertheim, L. Jon, and Sam Sommers. *This Is Your Brain on Sports: The Science of Underdogs, the Value of Rivalry, and What We Can Learn from the T-Shirt Cannon*. New York: Three Rivers Press, 2016.

Woods, Ronald B. *Social Issues in Sport*, 2d ed. Champaign, IL: Human Kinetics, 2011.

Email, Phone, and Zoom Interviews

Armstrong, Dr. Ketra. University of Michigan sport management professor. Email, August 17, 2021.

Bluestein, Ari. Sportscaster and co-founder and CEO of the Sports Fan Base Network. Email, September 15, 2020.

Caputo, Aaron. Zoom, June 16, 2021, confirmed and revised by email June 21, 2021. Aaron Caputo is the executive director of legal and client services at the Superlative Group, Inc., a sports marketing and advertising company, and he teaches sports law at Case Western Reserve University School of Law.

Carfagna, Peter. Zoom, June 16, 2021, confirmed and revised by email June 21, 2021. Peter Carfagna teaches sports law at Harvard University Law School and the University of Miami; is faculty supervisor of Harvard Law School's Sports Law Clinical Program; is chairman/CEO of Magis, LLC, a privately owned sports marketing, management, and investment company; and was chief legal officer and general counsel of International Management Group (IMG).

Carter, Aaron. Email, April 30, 2021. Aaron Carter is a *Philadelphia Inquirer* sports reporter.

Cherepinsky, Walter. Email, September 19, 2020. Walter Cherepinsky is the founder and operator of WalterFootball.com.

Dunphy, Fran. Phone, March 18, 2021, confirmed and revised by email, June 28, 2021. Fran Dunphy is the men's head basketball coach at La Salle University, the former men's head basketball coach at Temple University and the University of Pennsylvania, and the former interim athletic director at Temple University.

Faigenbaum, Dr. Avery. Zoom, October 16, 2020, confirmed and revised by email June 11, 2021. Dr. Avery Faigenbaum is a full professor in the Department of Health and Exercise Science at the College of New Jersey. He teaches several courses, including health promotion, exercise prescription, and clinical exercise physiology.

Goldberg, Chris. Email, October 11, 2020. Chris Goldberg is the founder and operator of PhillyLacrosse.com.

Gudel, Leslie. Email, May 26, 2021. Leslie Gudel is a journalist, reporter, entrepreneur, and chief operating officer at Elevate Sports & Media.

Hawley, Dr. Carolyn E. Email, June 15, 2021. Dr. Carolyn E. Hawley is an associate professor in the Department of Rehabilitation Counseling at Virginia Commonwealth University.

Hayes, Marcus. Email, August 11, 2021. Marcus Hayes is a *Philadelphia Inquirer* sports columnist.

Kapenstein, Jack. Email, December 29, 2017. Jack Kapenstein is a photographer, television commentator, coach, sports official.

Kim, Dr. Jun. Email, March 5, 2021. Dr. Jun Kim is an associate professor and program director of Sport Management in the School of Global Business at Arcadia University.

Kimball, Mary. Email, October 19, 2020. Mary Kimball is the executive director of U.S. Quidditch (Quadball).

Macnow, Glen. Email, May 25, 2021. Glen Macnow is a longtime Philadelphia sports talk radio host at Sports Radio 94 WIP.

Missanelli, Mike. Email, January 3, 2021. Mike Missanelli is a podcaster, former *Philadelphia Inquirer* sports reporter, and former sports talk radio host.

Schiff, Brian. Email, May 28, 2021. Brian Schiff was the head coach for eight gold medal United States Maccabiah 16 & Under Boys basketball teams, a former assistant coach at Abington Friends School and middle school head coach at AFS, and a member of the Philadelphia Jewish Sports Hall of Fame.

Seiss, Dr. Andrea Caporale. Email, August 19, 2021. Dr. Andrea Caporale Seiss is the Title IX coordinator at Temple University.

Valerio, Joe. Zoom, October 2, 2020, confirmed and revised by email, June 21, 2021. Joe Valerio is a former NFL player with the Kansas City Chiefs and St. Louis Rams and an adjunct professor at Arcadia University's School of Global Business.

Index

Abbott, Jim 120, 217
Abdul-Jabbar, Kareem 74, 84, 217
Academic Progress Rates (APR) 174–175
academics in college sports 163, 173–175, 179–180, 218
aerobic pole dancing 15
agents 104, 127, 132–133, 146, 175, 181, 217
Ali, Muhammad 35, 70–73, 84, 191, 217
Ali Summit 74
Americans with Disabilities Act 117, 122
Andrade, Gabriel 150
Andrews, Erin 35, 59
Armstrong, Ketra 72, 138, 196–197, 207
Armstrong, Lance 96, 111
Ashe, Arthur 64, 74, 84
athlete protests 70–79, 83
athletes and crime 127, 140–143, 146, 217
athletes and guns 143–144
auto racing 7, 16

bandwagon sports fans 95, 217
banning youth tackle football 156, 187
Barkley, Charles 36, 104
Bartman, Steve 96
baseball 1, 8, 10, 13, 15, 16, 17, 21, 23, 26, 30, 38–39, 42, 44–47, 52, 57, 59, 60, 65, 66, 70, 72, 81, 82, 89, 90, 93, 106, 109–112, 114, 115, 117, 120, 121, 123, 127–131, 134, 137, 140, 146, 147, 148, 154, 155, 159–162, 168, 170, 172, 173, 181, 182–185, 194, 199, 200, 202, 209, 216, 217
Baseball Rule 127, 129, 130, 146, 217
benchwarmers 161–162
benefits of playing sports 22–24
Bertuzzi, Todd 130–131
Bias, Len 110–111
Biden, Joe 78
Bilas, Jay 167, 169
Biles, Simone 107, 108
Black Sox scandal 44–46, 52
Bluestein, Ari 63–65
Bolt, Usain 87, 204–205
Bonds, Barry 111–112
booing college athletes 94
bounties in football 21, 26, 37, 40
boycotts of OLYMPICS 74, 203, 205–208, 215, 219
boys playing on girls teams 147, 150, 152, 153, 162, 218
Brady, Tom 11, 37

Broad Street Bullies 185–186
Brown, Jim 74, 84, 217
Bryant, Kobe 95, 169, 170
building new stadiums 200–202
bullfighting 20
Burke, Doris 56–57
burnout in youth sports 23, 147, 157, 158, 162, 218
Bush, Reggie 132
Buzuvis, Erin E. 152–153

Camby, Marcus 132
Caputo, Aaron 130, 132, 133, 184, 196
Carfagna, Peter 130, 131, 133, 183, 196
Carlos, John 70, 71, 73, 84, 217
Carlton, Steve 45, 63
Carter, Aaron 54, 62, 69, 162
Carter, Jimmy 205
cheating 21, 32, 40, 41, 111, 112
cheerleading 7–10, 156
Cherepinsky, Walter 43, 173
Chestnut, Joey 11
chronic traumatic encephalopathy (cte) 184, 187
civil liability and athletes 130–132, 146
Clark, Charles "Booby" 131
coaching 23, 54, 55, 66, 155, 160, 161
college athletes and academics see academics in college sports
College Football Playoffs 178–180
competitive dancing 17–19
competitive eating 10–11
concussions 3, 9, 13, 101, 108, 126, 131, 151, 156, 157, 180, 184, 185, 187–190, 192, 202, 218
conference realignment, NCAA 180
Congalton, K. Jeanine 11
Cornhole 10, 109
Coronavirus (COVID) 40, 108, 109, 124, 149, 157, 174, 179, 185, 204, 214
Cosell, Howard 1, 182, 191
cost of attendance stipends 48, 163, 165, 166, 218
court storming 85, 92
criminal liability and athletes 130–132
Cuban refugee baseball players 70, 81
cutting college sports programs 127, 134, 137–139, 146, 217–218

DeflateGate 21, 26, 36–37
Dempsey, Tom 120, 121
disabled athletes 3, 101, 117–122, 217

Dixon, Nicholas 27–28
Donaghy, Tim 42, 48–49
doping *see* steroids
Doty, Joseph 23–24
drug testing 114–116
Dunphy, Fran 165–167, 171, 175, 176
Durant, Kevin 103–104, 182
Dziok, Matthew 42

eating competitions *see* competitive eating
eating disorders 105–106
eSports 7, 11–13, 216

Faigenbaum, Avery 155–158
fair play *see* sportsmanship
fan behavior 92–100
fan criticism of athletes 94–95
fan violence 96–100, 217
fans and alcohol 99–100
fantasy sports 43, 47, 49, 50, 87, 95, 102
Favre, Brett 187
female athletes *see* women's and girls sports
female reporters and sportscasters 56–61
fighting in hockey 184–187
figure skating 39–40, 65, 203, 209–211
Fitzpatrick, Bridget 99
Flood, Curt 181–183
flopping 33–34, 216
Flores, Brian 198
Frazier, Joe 35, 71
free agency 77, 127, 181–184, 202, 214, 219

Gathers, Hank 110
Gehrig, Lou 101, 102
girls playing on boys teams 151–153, 162
Goldberg, Chris 54, 56, 65
golf 7, 16–18, 20, 21, 25, 109, 110, 116–117, 134, 137, 138, 152, 156, 217, 218
group of five NCAA conferences 28, 163, 165, 178–179, 218
Gudel, Leslie 58, 60
Gundy, Mike 55, 78
gymnastics 10, 13, 65, 101, 103, 105, 108, 135, 137, 138, 155, 156, 158, 159, 203, 208, 209, 211

Hackbart, Dale 131
Hall of Fame 10, 25, 38, 39, 40, 44–46, 57, 63, 71, 101, 110, 112, 120, 121, 134, 170, 171, 182, 196, 199
Hamlin, Damar 189
Harding, Tonya 39–40
Harlem Globetrotters 193–195
Hawley, Carolyn 50–51
Hayes, Marcus 197–198
Haywood, Spencer 169–170
hazing 3, 4, 101, 122–126, 217
high school sports 1, 4, 5, 9, 23, 24, 26, 27, 29–31, 53–56, 63, 65, 68, 69, 85, 92–94, 105, 108, 114, 115, 118, 119, 122–126, 127, 129, 133, 136, 144–146, 147, 150–158, 160–162, 169–173, 184, 187, 190, 192, 195, 201, 216, 218, 219
Hill, Cleo 194–195
Hill, Jemele 67
homeschooling and sports 144–146

horse racing 19–20
Houston Astros sign stealing scandal 26, 38

Incognito, Richie 123–124
Ingraham, Laura 70, 82–83
injuries *see* playing hurt
intentional fouls 34
International Olympic Committee (IOC) 8, 9, 17, 18, 20, 73, 74, 111, 117, 208, 212, 214

Jackson, Shoeless Joe 42, 44–46
James, LeBron 36, 70, 77, 82–84, 169, 170, 182, 198, 217
Johnson, Ben 111
Johnson, Jack 70, 192, 199
Johnson, Magic 36, 62, 77
Jones, Marshall B. 210–211
Jones, Roy, Jr. 210
Jordan, Michael 11, 36, 77, 103

Kaepernick, Colin 70, 75, 76, 84, 116, 217
Kapenstein, Jack 93–94, 137
Kerrigan, Nancy 39–40
Kim, Jun 182, 201, 212
Kimball, Mary 14–15
King, Billie Jean 80, 135, 153, 182
Kluch, Yannick 70, 78
Kunkel, Thilo 168

lacrosse 53, 54, 64, 65, 137, 218
Lapchick, Richard 98, 199
Lebed, Felix 8
legalization of steroids debate 101, 112–114, 126, 217
Little League 1, 4, 22, 23, 30, 35, 38, 90, 135, 147, 148, 159, 160
load management 102–103
Lombardi, Vince 25, 35
Louis, Joe 192 199–200
Ludtke, Melissa 59–60

Macnow, Glen 32, 66, 91
Malice at the Palace 96, 130
Malone, Moses 170, 171
Maradona, Diego 27, 88
Martin, Casey 116–117, 217
Martin, Jonathan 123–124
McFadden, Tatyana 122
McGwire, Mark 89, 111
McManus, Joseph 31
media bias and objectivity 53, 63–64, 69
media coverage of women's sports and nonrevenue sports 64–65
media criticism of athletes 53–56, 66, 69, 216
media relationship with coaches and players 64
media reporters giving political opinions 67–68
media reporting on athletes' private lives 53, 61–62, 69, 217
mental health of athletes 101, 105–108, 126, 217
mercy rule 30–31
Missanelli, Mike 62, 67–68
Mitchell Report 112
mixed martial arts (MMA) 108, 190, 202

Moore, Maya 80
Morgan, Joe 112
Mosher, Stephen D. 45
Mowins, Beth 56, 58
Murphy v. NCAA 42, 216

name, image, and likeness payments for NCAA athletes 3, 48, 55, 68, 94, 132, 163, 166–168, 218
NASCAR *see* auto racing
National Basketball Association (NBA) 1, 5, 31–36, 42, 47, 48, 56–58, 62, 65, 67, 68, 74, 75, 77, 78, 81–83, 87, 102–104, 107–111, 116, 130, 136, 140, 169–174, 182–184, 194, 195, 198, 218
National Football League (NFL) 26, 33, 35–38, 43, 46, 47, 56–59, 63, 67, 74, 75, 89, 91, 96, 99, 102, 104, 109, 110, 113, 114, 116, 120, 121, 124, 129, 132, 140, 141, 143, 144, 157, 167, 172, 173, 181, 183, 184, 187, 188, 189, 192, 194–198, 200–202, 218
National Hockey League (NHL) 17, 36, 47, 109, 129, 130, 173, 184–187, 194, 199, 200, 202, 218
Native American/Indigenous People's team nicknames 192–193, 202, 218
NCAA conference realignment 180
NCAA death penalty 176–177
NCAA self-imposed penalties 178
Newton, Cam 58
Northwestern football and unionization 163, 167

Obama, Barack 50, 71, 74, 81, 82
Olympics: and athlete safety 213; and athletes competing for other countries 214–215; bids by host cities 203, 211–213, 215, 219; boycotts 71, 74, 202, 205–208, 215, 219; and national pride 204–205, 215; 1972 U.S. v. U.S.S.R. basketball game 208–209; protests 71–74; and subjective judging 203, 209–211, 215, 219; and terrorism 203, 213–214, 219
One and Done Rule 163, 169–172, 218
Osaka, Naomi 107
O'Sullivan, John 157–158
Overbye, Marie 113–114
overscheduling in youth sports 158
Owens, Jesse 24, 192, 194, 199, 208

Palmieri, Christopher 169
paralympics 116, 119, 122
parenting in sports 147, 159–160
participation trophies 147–150, 162, 218
Paterno, Joe 176, 178
pay equity in women's sports 79
paying college athletes 163–169, 180, 218
Phelps, Michael 106, 107
pine tar in baseball 21, 26, 38–39
ping pong diplomacy 70, 80–81
Pipp, Wally 101, 102
Pistorius, Oscar 116–119, 217
playing hurt 101–104, 126, 217
playing time in youth sports 147, 160–162, 218
point shaving 4, 28, 42, 44, 47–48, 52, 216
poker 7, 10, 17, 43, 49, 216
Power Five NCAA Conferences 55, 65, 94, 163, 165, 169, 178, 179
prayer in public school sports 127, 144–146, 218

professional teams moving to new cities 181, 200–202, 219
Proposition 42 and 48 173
protective netting in stadiums 128–129
psychological benefits of being a sports fan 85, 88–89, 217

Quidditch (Quadball) 13–15, 216
Quinnipiac University cheerleading lawsuit 10

race and ethnicity in sports 70–79, 81–85, 94–95, 97–98, 192–200, 202, 218–219
racism *see* race and ethnicity in sports
Rapinoe, Megan 78–79, 137, 217
recruiting and recruiting violations in college 3, 4, 5, 147, 163, 166, 169, 175, 178, 180, 218
referees and officials 26, 42, 48–49, 93, 143, 159, 160, 209, 210
refugee team, Olympics 214–215
refusing to shake hands 36
Reid, Eric 75, 76, 116
religion in sports 22, 87, 144–146
Resslar, Melissa Ann 117
Revised Uniform Athlete Agents Act (RUAAA) 133
Rice, Ray 140
Riggs, Bobby 135
Robinson, Jackie 70, 192, 194, 200
Robles, Anthony 116, 119, 217
Rooney Rule 181, 192, 196–198, 202, 219
Rose, Pete 42, 44–45, 96, 144
Ruiz, Rosie 40
Runager, Max 90
running up the score 21, 26–31, 41, 216
Russell, Bill 74, 84, 194, 217
Ruth, Babe 88, 110, 181

salaries of pro athletes 181–184, 202, 219
Sandusky, Jerry 163, 176–177
Saunders, Raven 73–74
Schiff, Brian 25, 29, 30, 160, 161
Schmidt, Mike 1, 45, 72, 90
Seiss, Andrea Caporale 139
Sharrow, Elizabeth A. 153–154
show cause violations 176
Simpson, O.J. 19, 141
Smith, Tommie 70, 71, 73, 84, 217
soccer 1, 4, 10, 21, 25–28, 33, 34, 65, 73, 76, 78, 79, 81, 97, 106, 108, 109, 137, 138–140, 143, 147, 155, 156–158, 169, 187, 192, 199, 201, 209, 212, 216
social media 3, 11, 36, 48, 53, 56, 61, 62, 68, 69, 70, 77, 78, 82, 83, 87, 90, 94, 95, 98, 129, 132, 143, 148, 166, 168, 169, 199, 217
Sosa, Sammy 111
Special Olympics 116, 122
Sports Agent Responsibility and Trust Act (SPARTA) 133
sports announcers and objectivity 63–64
sports psychology 88, 106
sports talk radio 3, 4, 11, 32, 53, 56, 62, 64–69, 87, 91, 95
SpyGate 21, 26, 36–37
stealing signs in baseball *see* Houston Astros sign stealing scandal

steroids 45, 89, 101, 111–116, 126, 217
subjective Olympic judging *see* Olympics: subjective judging
Suits, Bernard 7

Tagovailoa, Tua 189
tanking 3, 21, 31–33, 41, 216
teamwork 21, 22, 147, 162
Tebow, Tim 144–145
tennis 1, 4, 26, 28, 61, 64, 65, 74, 79, 80, 90, 106, 107, 109, 110, 123, 135, 137, 147, 153, 156, 158
terrorism *see* Olympics: terrorism
Title IX 3, 7–10, 127, 134, 136–139, 146, 153, 216, 217
Tomjanovich, Rudy 130, 144
transgender athletes 150, 153–154
trash talking 35–36, 41, 71, 94, 216
Trump, Donald 67, 68, 75, 76, 78, 81, 82, 161, 199
Tyson, Mike 26, 39, 140

UFC 105, 108, 109, 190

Valerio, Joe 113, 114, 167, 172, 188, 189
Vick, Michael 96, 127, 140, 195, 217
violence in sports 3, 85, 96–100, 144, 181, 184–192

Washington, Kermit 130, 144
Washington Redskins name controversy *see* Native American/Indigenous People's team nicknames
women's and girls sports 133–140, 151–153, 217
Woodhall, Hunter 118–119
Woods, Ronald B. 7–8
wrestling 1, 4, 10, 21, 34, 101, 105, 116, 119, 120, 137, 147, 150–153, 160, 162, 204, 218

youth sports: burnout *see* burnout in youth sports; costs 159; injuries 155–157; organization of 154, 158; overscheduling *see* overscheduling of youth sports; parents *see* parenting in youth sports; playing time 30, 31, 146, 147, 150, 160–162; specialization 154, 155, 162, 218; travel teams 23, 147, 154, 161, 162

www.ingramcontent.com/pod-product-compliance
Lightning Source LLC
Chambersburg PA
CBHW060338010526
44117CB00017B/2870